'Dutifulness and Endurance'

Bearsted and Thurnham in two world wars
1914 - 1918, 1939 - 1945

Best Wishes
Kate Kersey, 2014

Other local books

Bearsted and Thurnham Remembered (edited by Kathryn Kersey)

Robert Fludd of Bearsted
(edited by Kathryn Kersey on behalf of Bearsted & District Local History Society)

A Brief History of the White Horse, Bearsted
(edited by Kathryn Kersey on behalf of Rosemary Pearce)

Bearsted and Thurnham At Play (edited by Kathryn Kersey)

Further Memories of Bearsted and Thurnham (edited by Kathryn Kersey)

Also by Kathryn Kersey

A School at Bearsted

'Dutifulness and Endurance' Bearsted and Thurnham 1914 - 1918, 1939 - 1945
(First edition)

The Lost Manor of Ware

Bearsted Scout Group, the first hundred years 1912 - 2012

An Introduction to the Flowers, Plants and Trees of Kent Before Written Records

'Dutifulness and Endurance'

Bearsted and Thurnham in two world wars
1914 - 1918, 1939 - 1945

Kathryn Kersey

with contributions from
John Franklin, James Kersey
Michael Perring and Roger Vidler

First published in 2005 by Kathryn Kersey
Re-printed June 2005

Second Edition with extensive revisions and further information 2014

Kathryn Kersey
5 Greensand Road, Bearsted, Maidstone, Kent ME15 8NY

All rights reserved © Kathryn Kersey, John Franklin,
James Kersey, Michael Perring and Roger Vidler, 2014

The rights of Kathryn Kersey, John Franklin, James Kersey, Michael Perring and Roger Vidler to be identified as the author and contributors, respectively, and Kathryn Kersey as editor of this work have been asserted by them in accordance with Section 77 of the Copyright, Designs and Patent Act 1988

This book is sold subject to the condition that it shall not, by way of trade or otherwise, be lent, resold, hired out or otherwise circulated without the publisher's prior consent in any form of binding or cover other than that in which it is published and without a similar condition being imposed upon the subsequent purchaser.

British Library In Cataloguing Publication Data

ISBN 9780954583187

Front and back covers:
A watercolour study of poppies by the late Richard Odell, November 2004

Digitally set in 11 pt, 14pt and 18pt Garamond, 8 pt and 10 pt Times New Roman
Printed and bound in Great Britain by Parchment (Oxford) Limited

Acknowledgments

A book like this does not happen by itself and in the course of its original compilation and later revisions; I have accrued many debts of thanks. At the forefront of these must be Evelyn Pearce and Margery Gibson for lending the original small booklet which recorded Bearsted's contribution to the First World War along with several photographs; also the family of the late Alan and Joy Ferrell for generous permission to use Joy's work on the Second World War casualties in Bearsted and Thurnham.

Thanks must be extended to Paul Johnson of the National Archives and Sally Richards of the Imperial War Museum; all the staff at the Kent History and Library Centre (and its predecessors, the Centre for Kentish Studies and Maidstone Reference Library) in fulfilling countless requests for information and generous permission to use it; and all the staff at Bearsted and Madginford branches of the Kent Library Service. All of these very helpful parties have unearthed many obscure documents and addressed a multitude of esoteric requests whilst giving wonderful assistance during research. I have been able to include many photographs and illustrations through the courtesy and generosity of the Downs Mail and the Kent Messenger newspaper group.

I thank Jean and John Franklin for generously sharing information, painstakingly compiled over many years, about George Lawrence and Pamela Thorpe. Further thanks must be offered to Beryl Doig and Margaret Tomalin for generously sharing both time and information about the Baker family and Mary Baker Milne for providing the extended military service details for her father, William Henry Baker, and granting permission for its use. My most grateful thanks too, to Eileen Crapp (née Burgess), together with her son Richard and his wife Angela, and our hostess Sonia Ashdown. An evening during October 2009 turned out to be quite a meeting during which I was introduced to a Civil Defence War Diary. Thank you all so much for allowing me to see it and then for sending me further information!

I remember with deep gratitude and appreciation, the late Richard Odell, for his exquisite painting of poppies and for his most generous permission to use it.

I would also like to acknowledge the kind assistance, together with permission to quote and use as a source of information and illustrations, the following people and organisations:

John Allison; Robin Ambrose; Sonia and Steve Ashdown; Mary Baker; Stanley Baker; Sylvia and Roy Barham; Bearsted and District Local History Society; Bearsted Parish Council; Bearsted Scout Group; Jenny Boniface; Irene Bourne; Joyce Bourne; Doris Britcher; Robin J Brooks; the late John Blamire Brown; William Buck; the late Mary Busbridge; George Cannon; the late Ella Cardwell; Allen Carr; Anthony Chadwick; Terry Clarke; the late Edith Coales; Lynda Copsey; Rev John Corbyn; Eileen, Richard and Angela Crapp; Alan Croucher; Roy Datson; the late Gladys Delves; Bill Drake; Terry Dunk; Theresa and the late David Elliott; Martin Elms; Janet and the late Rowland Fairbrass; Audrey and the late Eddie Fermor; Sheila and the late Tony Foster; Denis Fowle; Evelyn Fridd; Ron Gamage; Peter Gentry; John Gilbert; the late Norah Giles; Pat Grimes (née Robbins); Peggy Hammond and family; the late Joan Harden; John Hardy; Winifred Harris; the late Mary Hirst; Vivienne Hodges; Jacqueline Holt; Keith Holtum; Holy Cross church; Sally Hook and family; Jenni Hudson; Christine Hughes; Chris and Sue Hunt; Richard Hunt; Brenda Iacovides; Susan Imgrund and family; Oliver and Gloria Jessel; Trudy Johnson; Jean Jones; Kent Archaeological Society; Kent Messenger Newspaper Group; David King; Richard Kresja; Ian and Mary Lambert; Ann Lampard; Mark and Amanda Lane; the late Lucy Lang; Mark Lawrence and family; Eva and Leslie Lawson; Deidre Leadbetter; Ken Legood; Mark Litchfield and family; Maidstone Museum; Denis and Vic Matthews; Bryan McArthy; Betty and the late John Mills; Mirror Group newspapers; the late James Moore; the late John F Naylor; the late Jessie Page; Evelyn Palmer; Rosemary Pearce; Margaret Peat (née Lang); the late Lucienne Pennells; Margaret Plowright; Lesley Reynolds; Robin Rogers; Roseacre School; Peter Rosevear; Sir John and Lady Severne; Betty and David Smith; Colin Smith; the late Louie Smith and family; Rosemary Smith; Miriam Stevens (née Gardener); St Mary's church; Joan Thorne; Thurnham Parish Council; and Marjorie Wicks (née Avery).

David Barnes has generously allowed me to use information from his website about the Royal Flying Corps and the Royal Air Force, then available at http://www.rfc-rnas-raf-register.org.uk. Marion Hebblethwaite has also given permission to use information from her excellent website about the George Cross http://www.marionhebblethwaite.co.uk/gcindex.htm.

I am indebted to Trevor Hunt for permission to include an image concerning pig-keeping and can recommend his excellent website: http://wartimegardening.co.uk. Likewise, I also offer thanks to Peter Sauer for information about Maconochie stew and can recommend his well-researched articles about food during military operations available at http://joyoffieldrations.blogspot.co.uk.

I especially thank Anne and James Clinch, John Franklin, Michael Perring and Roger Vidler for their powers of general knowledge, observation and detection. I hugely appreciate their quite infectious enthusiasm and companionship during the hours spent undertaking additional research. I also offer deep thanks to Simon Kavanagh for his expertise which enabled me to complete this book.

I have continued to make reasonable efforts to contact the copyright holders for Mr C E Cornford and Miss L Grace Dibble but I have been wholly unsuccessful. Likewise, I have been unable to locate the copyright holder of a series of photographs of WAAF personnel at the former parish room at Thurnham taken during the 1940s and which were on display during August 2010 at Detling parish church. I have also been unable to trace the origins of an advertisement for Maconochie stew which appears on Peter Sauer's blog. I would welcome the opportunity to contact the correct people in all of these instances in order that formal permission may be obtained for using information from these sources, and I will be pleased to insert the appropriate acknowledgement in any subsequent re-printing of this book.

I acknowledge the generous financial support of the following organisations towards the costs of producing and publishing this book: Bearsted and District Local History Society; The Bearsted and Thurnham Fayre Committee, The Bearsted and Thurnham Society, Bearsted Parish Council; The Parochial Church Council of Holy Cross, Bearsted; The Parochial Church Council of St Mary's, Thurnham, and Thurnham Parish Council.

I thank Malcolm, James and George for their immense sensibility and observations. George's attention to detail is greatly appreciated whilst James' expertise and enthusiasm for his subject led to engrossing stints in the National Archives and the inclusion of much original research in this book. Gratitude, virtually beyond word or measure, is owed to Malcolm for also possessing unplumbed depths of patience and positive encouragement.

Abbreviations, Symbols and Other Conventions in the Text

IWM   Imperial War Museum, London
KHLC   Kent History and Library Centre, (previously the Centre for Kentish Studies), Maidstone, Kent
NA   The National Archives (formerly The Public Record Office), Kew, Surrey

<u>Latin</u>
ibid.   In the same place and refers to the previously named publication.
op.cit.   In the publication already named.
passim.   Wording used that is dispersed through the text rather than a direct quote.

An asterisk (*) indicates commemorated on the Bearsted war memorial which is situated in the churchyard of Holy Cross church, Church Lane, Bearsted.

A dagger (†) indicates commemorated on the Thurnham war memorial or framed Roll of Honour at St Mary's church, Thurnham Lane, Thurnham.

A cross (+) indicates commemorated on the school war memorial which is a sundial. It was originally located at Bearsted School but was transferred to the current school for Bearsted and Thurnham - Roseacre School, The Landway. An appointment should be made via the school office before seeking to visit this memorial.

Addresses given are all in Bearsted or Thurnham and place names in Kent unless otherwise stated.

For the First World War details, the first date given in each entry is usually the date of volunteering, enlisting or conscription, unless otherwise stated. Wherever possible, abbreviations relating to military units have been eliminated from personal details for clarity. However, they have been retained where information has been included from sources such as newspaper reports, to preserve the historical accuracy of that source.

Contents

Introduction ix

First World War: 1914 to 1918 1

Memories of the First World War 105

Keeping In Touch 118

Armistice, Peace and Aftermath 122

Second World War: 1939 to 1945 133

Pamela and George: two lives interrupted by war 227

They Also Served 235

Accommodation, Rest and Relaxation 254

RAF Station Detling 259

Memories of the Second World War 270

Peace Regained and Welcome Home 294

War memorials and records in Bearsted and Thurnham 300

    Appendix 1   Further entries for both World Wars 310

    Appendix 2   Battle of Britain casualties 314

    Appendix 3   Sources used for Pamela and George:
                             two lives interrupted by war 316

    Appendix 4   The Commonwealth War Graves Commission 317

Notes to the text 319

Select Bibliography 324

Introduction

When I wrote the Introduction to the first edition of this book, (reproduced overleaf) it was my intention that the contents should become a database for all the community and those who have an interest in Bearsted and Thurnham. But, I was more than aware that the record was incomplete and there were many gaps.

Since publishing the first edition, I am absolutely delighted to say that a further First World War Roll of Service for Thurnham has been unearthed and many people have contacted me with more details of their family, or offered further information about events or wartime arrangements in and around Bearsted and Thurnham. As a result of all of this extra information, it became apparent that another edition, showing all the revisions to date was required. Here, then, is that revised edition.

Readers should be aware that some of the detail consists only of a name and address or the area of service. Likewise, some of the Second World War memories have already appeared elsewhere in print. These have been included as they provide valuable information and contribute towards a bigger picture.

As before, I will be pleased to receive corrections and further details. It would be good to be in the fortunate position of requiring another revised account in the future.

As a community historian and researcher, born many years after the Second World War, I have found that research into wartime experience frequently includes powerful stories about humanity. Amongst the most moving of these accounts is one I came across a few years ago. It concerned an extended Dutch family who were staying with a colleague for a few days. On the first evening they talked about their visit: London, it seemed, was firmly on the agenda. This was not unexpected, but what was surprising was their <u>absolute</u> insistence that above all, what they really wanted to do was to hear the striking of Big Ben. As the request was fulfilled, the family burst into tears as they stood in Parliament Square listening to the bell strike the hour. The great grandmother regained her composure and then explained the significance of the sound: during the war, she and the rest of the family had listened in great secrecy, and often in immense danger, to the radio broadcasts from the BBC. To them, the sound of Big Ben came to symbolise a tiny corner of the world which was standing up to overwhelming aggression. Quite simply to this family, and undoubtedly countless others, the sound of Big Ben had come to represent the hope of a free world. What a sharp lesson in paying rather more attention to what, for some people, can be just a feature or background noise in everyday life!

At the time of writing this, yet another wartime anniversary looms upon us: the centenary of the outbreak of the First World War in August 1914. I hope that this account shows that when the need arose, the communities of Bearsted and Thurnham were more than equal to meeting hostile aggression, the demands and challenges of wartime, and of defending precious freedom.

Kathryn Kersey

Introduction to the First Edition

This book draws upon many records. The First World War section is largely based upon a Roll of Honour prepared by the vicar of Bearsted, Frederick Blamire Brown, in 1919. To this primary source has been added details from the 1918 Absent Voters Roll, and from the war memorials located in St Mary's church, Thurnham, and Holy Cross church, Bearsted.

For the Second World War, the primary source was a list prepared by the Welcome Home committee formed by Bearsted and Thurnham parish councils during 1945. A separate booklet about those named on the Bearsted war memorial compiled by the late Joy Ferrell was also consulted.

Other valuable information has been included - newspaper accounts, parish magazine extracts, oral history contributions, and treasured photographs of family members; some of whom 'went to serve their king and country' and never returned.

As Frederick Blamire Brown once wrote, this book is intended to record the names of all who gave wartime service; those who rendered 'Dutifulness and Endurance'. As the First World War begins to pass from living memory and the sixtieth anniversary of the end of World War Two is commemorated, it is important that the services of the local inhabitants in wartime are both recorded and recognised.

Although it is acknowledged that the record is incomplete, and gaps remain in the information for Thurnham, every effort has been made to obtain full details. However, Bearsted and District Local History Society will be pleased to receive corrections. The more information received, the more accurate and detailed will be the inevitable, future revised account.

It should be noted that the quality of the photographs that accompany some of the newspaper transcripts is variable. The original photographs were produced and printed on poor quality paper that was commonly available for newsprint in wartime. The original paper and corresponding picture quality had begun to deteriorate when it was microfilmed. The microfilm has now been used many times and become worn, further affecting the picture quality. Every effort has been made to achieve a good photographic reproduction.

I have now realised why Professor Richard Holmes, an immense authority on military matters, occasionally gazes upon his garden in a haze of tears. Compiling this book has been an honour and a tremendous privilege.

Kathryn Kersey

First World War: 1914 to 1918

Kent, lying in the south east corner of Britain, and facing a continent which is barely thirty miles from Dover, was one of the English counties most affected by the First World War. After the outbreak of hostilities, despite it being harvest-time, parts of the county were effectively turned into a huge transit camp as mobilisation took place and troops passed through, on their way to, and from, the Western Front. The inhabitants of Bearsted and Thurnham witnessed this change and more, as soldiers marched around parts of both parishes, practised digging trenches, and were either billeted locally or set up temporary camps.

Although Britain had a professional army, after entry to the war was declared on 4 August 1914, men immediately volunteered to join the armed forces. Maidstone, the nearest major town to Bearsted and Thurnham, had been a garrison town since the late eighteenth century and so became the headquarters of the recruiting area for the Royal West Kent Regiment. Such was the response to the declaration of war that the Kent Messenger newspaper announced on 15 August that 5,000 soldiers were now quartered in the barracks and town, largely comprising of men of good class and conduct who had volunteered to serve. The same edition of the newspaper carried the advertisement shown below; another example is shown on the next page and appeared in the Kent Messenger, 22 August 1914. Advertisements of this nature featured in the local press throughout the war.

YOUR KING & COUNTRY NEED YOU.

A CALL TO ARMS.

An addition of 100,000 men to His Majesty's Regular Army is immediately necessary in the present grave National Emergency.

TERMS OF SERVICE.

General Service for a period of 3 years or until the war is concluded.

Age of Enlistment between 19 and 30.

HOW TO JOIN.

Full Information can be obtained at any Post Office in the Kingdom, or at any Military Depot and Recruiting Offices.

GOD SAVE THE KING.

Reproduced courtesy of Kent Messenger newspaper group

First World War: 1914 to 1918

As a result of the increased numbers in the armed forces, the local regiments rapidly added new battalions. Eventually, the numbers of volunteers threatened to overwhelm the recruiting and training centres, so the details of men were noted. They returned home to await a summons. During the war, the Royal West Kent Regiment alone comprised twenty two battalions and half of these served overseas.

The Royal West Kent Regiment

A NEW BATTALION BEING RAISED.

SPECIAL RECRUITING CENTRES.

It has been arranged with Major Martyn, the Secretary Kent Territorial Force Association, that all Sub-Committees and Organisations, etc., who are assisting in Recruiting for the Army, should send men desirous of enlisting to the following Centres, where all the necessary Documents and Papers will be prepared and the men fully dealt with, medically examined, etc., and passed to their Units.

1. **MAIDSTONE.** Office in the Barracks.
   Recruiting Officer: CAPTAIN BEECHING.
2. **TONBRIDGE.** Office in Territorial Headquarters.
   Recruiting Officer: COLONEL RATTRAY.
3. **BROMLEY.** Office next to Drill Hall.
   Recruiting Officer: CAPTAIN TOWER.
4. **GRAVESEND.** Office in Barracks.
   Recruiting Officer: CAPTAIN BAILEY.
5. **CHATHAM.** Army Recruiting Office, Dock Road.
   Recruiting Officer: MAJOR ANDERSON.
6. **SHEERNESS.** Office in Trinity Road.
   Recruiting Officer: COLONEL STALLON, V.D.

It should be impressed on everyone that Recruits are urgently needed for the New Battalion of the Royal West Kent Regiment now being raised at Maidstone.

G. W. MAUNSELL, Colonel,
Commanding Depot Royal West Kent Regiment.

MAIDSTONE, 15th August, 1914.

Reproduced courtesy of Kent Messenger newspaper group

This undated photograph was taken in Whitstable, but gives a good indication of the nature of national army recruitment campaigns. Most local campaigns were a series of 'Patriotic Meetings' and the poster shown on the left hand side of the picture gives details of one such meeting. Note also the small boy on the right, cheekily saluting behind the soldier.

Reproduced courtesy of Roger Vidler

By early 1915 it was apparent that voluntary recruitment was not able to provide the numbers of men that it was envisaged would be required. The government's response to the projected shortfall was the National Registration Act which was passed on 15 July 1915 which recorded the numbers of men aged between 15 and 65.

First World War: 1914 to 1918

This is the front and back of the buff-coloured identification certificates which were issued under the National Registration Scheme:

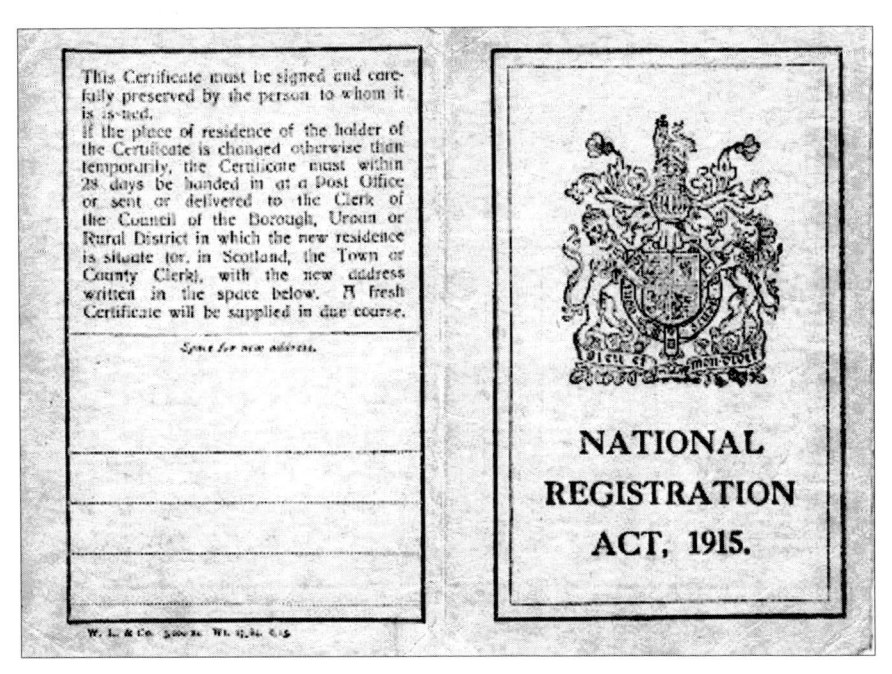

Reproduced courtesy of Malcolm Kersey

In January 1916, after the results of the registration became known and analysed, the government then had an indication of the numbers of the population which could serve the country. Compulsory service in the army, known as conscription, was introduced and applied to all single men between the ages of eighteen and forty one. The scheme was extended and service in the armed forces became universal to all men under the age of forty one, including those who were married, in May 1916. There were exemptions permitted for men in reserved occupations and Appeals Tribunals were held to consider cases for men claiming exemptions for other reasons, such as Conscientious Objection.

Many men that joined the army from Bearsted and Thurnham belonged to either the Royal West Kent Regiment or the East Kent Regiment. These postcards show the regimental insignia and their full titles.

Both reproduced courtesy of Roger Vidler

3

First World War: 1914 to 1918

ALLCORN, Harold
1 Acacia Villas, Willington Road
Parents Thomas and Harriet Allcorn
Single
2 October 1917
Posted overseas 1 April 1918
France April to October 1918
Loos
Demobilised 21 May 1919

ALLCORN, Reginald *
1 Acacia Villas, Willington Road
Parents Thomas and Harriet Allcorn
Single
29 October 1915 10th (Service) (Kent County) Battalion, The Queen's Own (Royal West Kent Regiment)
Service Number G/10495 Private
Posted overseas 5 May 1916
France May 1916 to March 1918
Wounded
Missing, presumed killed, 23 March 1918, aged 21
Commemorated Bay 7, Arras Memorial, Pas de Calais, France

A transcript of the report from the Kent Messenger, 22 February 1919:

**Pte. R. Allcorn (Maidstone)
10th R. W. K. R.**

MISSING MARCH 23rd, 1918

Could any of the 10th Battalion, 13th Platoon Royal West Kents give any information regarding No.10495 Pte. R. Allcorn, who was reported missing on the 23rd March 1918. Any information would be gratefully received by his parents and relatives at No.1 Acacia Villas, Willington Road, Maidstone, Kent.

Reproduced courtesy of Kent Messenger newspaper group

First World War: 1914 to 1918

ALLCORN, Thomas Louis *
1 Acacia Villas, Willington Road
Parents Thomas and Harriet Allcorn
Single
15 December 1914 1st Battalion, The Queen's Own (Royal West Kent Regiment)
Service Number G/5010 Private
Posted overseas 21 April 1915
France April 1915 to July 1916
Killed in action 30 July 1916, aged 23
Commemorated Pier and Face 11c, Thiepval Memorial, Pas de Calais, Somme, France

ALLEN, Alfred James Whitacre
Upper Barty
Married
12 January 1876 The Buffs (East Kent Regiment)
Zulu War 1879, Nile Expedition 1884 to 1885, Tirah 1897 to 1898
Ceylon 1909 to 1913
Companion of the Order of the Bath 1908
Rejoined 16 September 1914
Brigadier-General commanding 74th Infantry Brigade, 25th Division
England November 1914 to September 1915
Posted overseas 25 September 1915
France and Belgium September 1915 to February 1916
Commanding Halton Camp February 1916 to October 1916
Line R Lys-Ploegsteert
Mentioned in Secretary of State's Despatches 1917

ALLEN, Eric Hudson
Upper Barty
Single
22 January 1914 The Buffs (East Kent Regiment) from Royal Military College, Sandhurst
Captain
Posted overseas 22 October 1914
France October 1914 to December 1917
Egypt October 1918
First, Second Battle of Ypres, Somme, Lens, Hill 70, First, Second Battle of Cambrai
Twice wounded
Mentioned in Secretary of State's Despatches

ALLEN, John Frederick Whitacre
Upper Barty
Single
18 September 1909 The Buffs (East Kent Regiment) from Royal Military College, Sandhurst
Lieutenant 16 September 1911
Captain 29 May 1915
Attached Nigeria Regiment February 1914 to June 1916, February 1917 to June 1918
Cameroons September 1914 to March 1916
Nigeria March 1914 to July 1917
German East Africa September to December 1917
South Africa (Hospital) December 1917 to May 1918
England and Ireland 1918 to 1919
Twice wounded
Military Cross 1916 (London Gazette, June 1916)

John married Helen Florence Bell at Holy Cross on 7 August 1919

First World War: 1914 to 1918

APPS, Ernest John
Parents Edward and Elizabeth Apps of Thurnham
Single
7th (1st British Columbia Regiment) Battalion, Canadian Infantry
Service Number 227722
Killed 6 April 1917, aged 29
Buried in grave VI B 22, Ecoivres Military Cemetery, Mont-St, Eloi, Pas de Calais, France

APPS, George
West View, Roseacre
Married
8 June 1916 5th (Cinque Ports) Battalion, Royal Sussex Regiment
Posted overseas 13 September 1916
transferred to 242nd Labour Company attached to Royal Ordnance Corps
and to 48th Division, Army Service Corps
Service Number 420923
France September 1916 to November 1917
Italy November 1917 to April 1919
Somme 1916
Demobilised 28 April 1919

This photograph of George was taken in 1935:

Reproduced courtesy of Chris and Sue Hunt

ASHMAN, Percy Albert
Ware Street
Private Agricultural Company, Army Service Corps

ATTWOOD, Frank Thomas
Parents Robert and Frances Attwood of Church Cottages, Ware Street
Married
Wife Blanch (née Shepherd) of Toronto
Western Front

Frank was one of several members of the Attwood family to emigrate to Canada. He left Ware Street on 17 November 1904 from Liverpool to St John, Canada on board *The Bavarian*, Allan Shipping Line. He married Blanch Shepherd, 10 February 1908. He returned to Britain to serve with the Canadian Expeditionary Force.

First World War: 1914 to 1918

ATTWOOD, Frederick
Parents Robert and Frances Attwood of Church Cottages, Ware Street
Married
Wife Kate (née Waite) of 32 Allan Street, Maidstone
Children Robert, Albert, Frederick and Doris Ivy
7 June 1916
Service Number M2/227756, Driver
Posted overseas 18 October 1916
GH2 Troop, Motorised Transport, Royal Army Service Corps
Discharged Woolwich Dockyard 26 August 1920

Frederick was 39 years old when he was called up for service. He was working as a carpenter, builder and lorry driver with Mr King of Upper Fant Road, Maidstone who was fulfilling government contracts. Upon receiving his call-up papers, he applied to a military tribunal for exemption from service on the grounds that his employment meant that he was contributing to the national war effort and all of his brothers were already serving. Further, his parents were elderly, his father was 75 and his mother, 69, and although his father received an old age pension and did occasional carpentry work, there was no other source of income. Frederick stated that he was needed to assist his employer and with all his brothers absent, he was required to help his father in his free time. The appeal was dismissed 19 September 1916. During his service on the Western Front, Frederick was wounded, sustaining a badly lacerated hand.

ATTWOOD, Herbert Frederick
Parents Robert and Frances Attwood of Church Cottages, Ware Street
Married
Wife Mary Ann of 103 Gannet Avenue, Toronto, Canada
Service Number 452537
24 July 1915 Canadian Expeditionary Force, Western Front

Herbert was usually known as Bert. He left Ware Street to emigrate on 20 June 1912 from London, bound for Montreal on board *The Tonian*, Allan Shipping Line. Barely three years later, he returned to Britain to serve with the Canadian Expeditionary Force.

ATTWOOD, Leonard W
Parents Robert and Frances Attwood of Church Cottages, Ware Street
Single
Royal Field Artillery, Western Front

ATTWOOD, Sidney
Parents Robert and Frances Attwood of Church Cottages, Ware Street
Married
Wife Annie of 283 Christie Street, Toronto, Canada
Service Number 518375 Sergeant
22 November 1915 Canadian Expeditionary Force, Western Front
Military Medal

Sidney left Ware Street to emigrate on 9 April 1907 from Liverpool to St John, Canada, on board *The Mongolian*, Allan Shipping Line. He later returned to Britain to serve with the Canadian Expeditionary Force.

AVIS, Thomas
Tollgate
Married
24 May 1916 Royal Garrison Artillery including 307 S Brigade
Service Number 86139 Signaller also Gunner
Posted overseas 13 April 1917
Italy April 1917 to January 1919
November 1917 Retreat, Piave, Asiago
Demobilised 10 February 1919

BAKER, Albert Edward Cyril
Cross Keys Cottages, The Street
Born 20 April 1896
Parents Richard and Lucy Baker (née Mannering)
Single
March 1915 281st Company, Army Service Corps later 122nd Heavy Battery, Royal Garrison Artillery
Service Number 059362 Driver
Posted overseas April 1915 France

This photograph of Albert is undated but it is a good studio portrait.

Reproduced courtesy of Beryl Doig

Albert recorded some of his wartime experiences, together with those of his siblings. These are included in the *Memories of the First World War* chapter.

BAKER, George
Milgate
Married
1918 3rd Battalion, Norfolk Regiment

BAKER, George
Royal Navy

BAKER, Herbert
Gore Meadows
Single
September 1911 M (VIII) Battery, Royal Horse Artillery
Service Number 67317 Bombardier
Risalpur, India
Demobilised 17 May 1919

First World War: 1914 to 1918

BAKER, Jesse Walter Thomas
Cross Keys Cottages, The Street
Born 26 July 1898
Parents Richard and Lucy Baker (née Mannering)
Single
27 April 1917, 17th Battalion Essex Regiment
23 September 1917 Suffolk Regiment, 2nd Battalion
17 June 1918 Northamptonshire Regiment, Learner Heavy Driver 3 Reserve Motorised Transport Depot Base, Winchester
Essex Regimental Number 401257
Suffolk Regimental Number 41655
Northamptonshire Regimental Number 41712
Motorised Transport Regimental Number M/426307
Driver
12 December 1919, demobilised at Woolwich Dockyards

This photograph of Jesse is undated, but shows him as young man:

Reproduced courtesy of Beryl Doig

BAKER, John William
Cross Keys Cottages, The Street
Born 18 January 1892
Parents Richard and Lucy Baker (née Mannering)
Single
25 October 1915 enlisted at Maidstone
Army Service Corps No 3 Kent Brigade, later 136th Labour Company attached to 67th Divisional Train
Service Number 82856 Driver, Regimental Number 211177
Salonika 1916, Taranto, Italy 1918
11 February 1919, demobilised at Woolwich Dockyards

BAKER, Mark
Gore Meadow, Roundwell
Married
8 April 1916 2/4th Battalion, Norfolk Regiment, Territorial Force
later 1/7th Battalion, Royal Warwickshire Regiment, Territorial Force
Service Number 300003 Private
Posted overseas June 1917, France and Italy

First World War: 1914 to 1918

BAKER, Richard
Gore Meadows
Single
9 November 1915 West Kent Yeomanry (Queen's Own)
later 20th (Northern) Battalion, Rifle Brigade (The Prince Consort's Own)
Service Number 212226 Private

BAKER, Richard Frederick
Cross Keys Cottages, The Street
Parents Richard and Lucy Baker (née Mannering)
Born 5 June 1888
Married
Wife Mabel Edith (née Powell)
Royal Army Service Corps

This photograph is undated but shows Fred with his wife Mabel during the war:

Reproduced courtesy of Margaret Tomalin

BAKER, Walter Edward
Ware Street
3rd Machine Gun Squadron, Machine Gun Corps
Service Number 41447 Private

BAKER, William Henry
Cross Keys Cottage, The Street
Parents Richard and Lucy Baker (née Mannering)
Born 3 March 1894
Single
14 November 1914 Territorial Force
28 November 1914 No 1 Field Bakery, 95th Army Service Corps
Posted overseas 21-22 December 1914 Le Havre, France, via *SS Trafford Hall* from Southampton
27th Divisional Train and 20th Divisional Train
Service Number 038585
France December 1914 to February 1919
Corporal 1916, Acting Sergeant, 1918
Demobilised 26 March 1919, 160th Company at Woolwich Dockyard, transferred to Reserve

William was usually known as Bill. This photograph, taken in 1918, shows him as an Acting Sergeant:

Reproduced courtesy of Stanley Baker
and Mary Baker Milne

BAKER, William Richards
Barty Farm
Captain in Army

First World War: 1914 to 1918

BALL, Reginald Walter *
South View Cottages, The Street
Parents Walter and Ada Jane Ball, later at Mid Kent Golf Club, Gravesend
Single
13 August 1915 Royal Navy
Service Number J/43059 Boy First Class Rating
Lost at battle of Jutland 31 May 1916, aged 16, on *HMS Indefatigable*
Commemorated Panel 13 Column 2, Plymouth Naval Memorial, Plymouth Hoe, Devon

HMS Indefatigable was a battlecruiser built in Devonport Dockyard and launched in 1909. It was sunk after an attack by the German battlecruiser *SMS Von der Tann*. There were only two survivors from a crew of more than one thousand.

BALL, Walter
South View Cottages, The Street
Married
8 November 1915 23rd Labour Company, Army Service Corps later Transport Branch, Royal Engineers
Service Number 507533 Sapper
Posted overseas 6 December 1915 France

BARSTOW, John Montagu Orczy
Snowfield
Parents Montague Barstow and Baroness Emmuska Orczy
Single
3 May 1917 Royal Military College, Sandhurst
18 April 1918 17th (Duke of Cambridge's Own) Lancers
Second Lieutenant
The Curragh April 1918 to November 1918
Belgium November 1918 to January 1919
Passed into Reserve of Officers 23 April 1919
Lieutenant May 1919

BARTHOLOMEW, Arthur George

BARTHOLOMEW, Frederick William George
Royal Engineers

BARTON, Alan Henry
Parsonage Farm
Married
10 October 1902 Royal Field Artillery
Rejoined 9 November 1914 Army Veterinary Corps
Service Number T390105 Sergeant
Posted overseas 24 November 1914
France, Egypt, Palestine
Demobilised 10 July 1919

BATES, Stanley
4 Mote Hall Villas
Father Mr T Bates
Single
16 March 1917 Training Reserve Battalion France
Second Lieutenant later Lieutenant Royal Sussex Regiment

11

First World War: 1914 to 1918

BATES, Thomas Henry
Mote Villas
Married
Volunteer Training Corps later 2nd Volunteer Brigade, Royal West Kent

BAXTER, Percy William †
Weavering Street but also at Southfields, Surrey
Parents John and Edith Baxter of 2 Golf View Cottages, Ware Street
Married
Wife Annie (née Relf)
Depot, 12th (Service) (Bermondsey) Battalion, East Surrey Regiment
Service Number 22582 Private
Died 12 December 1918, aged 34, of wounds sustained in action
Buried in grave K 438, Wandsworth (Putney Vale) Cemetery

BEDOW, Stanley G C
217 Winifred Road
Royal Army Medical Corps
Captain

BEER, Edward Arthur
London Regiment, Western Front

BEER, Harry
The Den, Chapel Lane
Sherwood Foresters (Nottinghamshire & Derbyshire Regiment)
Service Number 92017 Private

BEESTON, Henry
Bearsted Court Lodge
Married
5 July 1918 Royal Navy Sick Berth Rating
Royal Naval Barracks, Chatham
Demobilised 5 May 1919

BELLINGHAM, Arthur

BENNETT, Alfred Charles
West View, Roseacre
Single
Royal Army Medical Corps
Service Number 49334 Private
Demobilised 7 April 1919

BENNETT, William
Roseacre
Single
9 July 1917 Royal Navy
Service Number J73503 Ordinary Seaman
HMS Chester
North Sea Convoys September 1917 to July 1918
Egyptian Convoy November to December 1918
Demobilised 28 June 1919

First World War: 1914 to 1918

BENTON, William Manstead *
Kulm Lodge
Married
14 August 1914 Chaplain
Second Lieutenant 1915 12th (Service) Battalion, Manchester Regiment
France September 1914 to August 1916
Captain June 1915
Acting Major 1916
Four times wounded
Died of wounds at No 36 Casualty Clearing Station 17 August 1916
Buried in grave II F 12, Heilly Station Cemetery, Mericourt-L'Abbe, Somme, France

A partial transcript of the report from The South Eastern Gazette, 29 August 1916:

THE LATE CAPTAIN BENTON

Captain William Benton, whose death we recorded last week, had a remarkable career of adventure. He started life with some fortune and went into the Royal Artillery. He ran through his fortune and had to leave the Army. He emigrated to Australia, and was getting his living there, when the South African war broke out. He enlisted in one of the Australian regiments and served with credit throughout the war, receiving the King's and the Queen's medals.

When peace came Mr Benton began to take a serious view of life, and took holy orders in the Church of England. He was curate of St Peter's, Walsall, for three years, and then went out to South Africa again, but this time as a man of peace and not a man of war. He was priest-in-charge of All Saints, Springbokfontein, in Namaqualand, not far from the border of German South West Africa, and then from 1910 to 1912 assistant curate at St Barnabas, Cape Town. He returned to England two years before the war, and took charge of the parish of Bearsted during the incumbency of the Rev T G L Lushington.

When the present war broke out, Mr Benton found the struggle between war and peace raging strong in his blood. He attempted to compromise it by going to the Front as an Army chaplain. But he could not be content with a mere 'cushy' job, and resigned his chaplaincy to take a commission in the Manchester Regiment. As a combatant officer he did excellent work, his strength of character, resourcefulness and energy making him a born leader of men. He was soon given charge of the snipers in his section of the front line and organised them most admirably. On being wounded and invalided to England in 1915 he was appointed to organise and supervise an important scheme of scouting and sniping here. In this work, Captain Benton was most successful, his energy bearing ample fruit.

Returning to the Front in February 1916, he was again appointed brigade sniping officer, and fulfilled the duties ably. He was wounded while gallantly attempting the rescue of a wounded man, who was crawling back from the German trenches. He had to lie there for three days. When, at length, brought in. it was found necessary to amputate his leg, but this unfortunately, did not save his life. His loss will be deeply felt by all who knew him.

Our Bearsted correspondent writes:-
   Captain Benton was a man who had played many parts, and the story of his life which he delivered at Bearsted from the pulpit some time ago, left a lasting impression on the people who heard it. And his experiences made him a splendid helpmate to men, to whom he made himself most popular by his urbanity of manner and among whom he has been much missed. The deepest sympathy is extended to his wife and young children in their irreparable loss.

MEMORIAL SERVICE AT BEARSTED

For the repose of the soul of Captain Benton, a requiem service was held at Bearsted Parish Church at 8 o'clock on Sunday morning, when many parishioners who formerly worshipped with the late officer as their curate attended. Later in the day a special service of memorial of the fallen also took place at the Church.

Reproduced courtesy of Kent Messenger newspaper group

First World War: 1914 to 1918

BETTS, Albert
Bell Cottage, Ware Street
Single
Parents Albert and Mary Betts
Royal Defence Corps

The Royal Defence Corps was formed in August 1917 from garrison battalions of infantry regiments. Garrison battalions usually comprised soldiers who could not serve overseas for a variety of reasons. Duties involved guarding prisoner of war camps or strategic locations such as ports or bridges.

BETTS, Charles David
Bell Cottage, Ware Street
Single
Parents Albert and Mary Betts
Service Number 22079 Sergeant
40th (Fortress) Company, Royal Engineers

BETTS, Ernest
Bell Cottage, Ware Street
Single
Parents Albert and Mary Betts
Sergeant
Royal Engineers, Western Front and Mesopotamia

BETTS, Ernest Edward
Bell Lane
Royal Air Force
Service Number 406789 Sergeant, Aircraft Mechanic 2nd Class

BILLS, Arthur
The Buffs, (Royal East Kent Regiment), Western Front

BILLS, Frank Albert
Ware Street
Service Number 373966 Corporal
752nd Area E Company, Royal West Kent Regiment

BODIAM, Albert
Milgate Lodge
Single
19 March 1917 4th (Extra Reserve) Battalion, Bedfordshire Regiment
France
Demobilised 3 December 1919

BODIAM, Edward John
Oak Cottages
Service Number 43757 Lance Corporal
1st Battalion, Princess Charlotte of Wales's (Royal Berkshire Regiment)

First World War: 1914 to 1918

BODIAM, Frank Henry
Lodge Gate, Milgate
Single
1 November 1915 2nd Battalion, Duke of Cambridge's Own (Middlesex Regiment)
later 16th (Service) (Public Schools) Battalion, Duke of Cambridge's Own (Middlesex Regiment)
Service Number 43139 Private
Posted overseas 7 August 1916
France

BODIAM, William Thomas
Lodge Gate, Milgate
Single
December 1914 2nd Battalion, Dorsetshire Regiment
Service Number 204506 Private
Egypt
Demobilised 7 April 1919

BOLTON, Thomas Henry
Aldington
Service Number M/225366 Private
Mechanical Transport, Army Service Corps

BOND, Albert Edward
Royal Army Service Corps later Royal Air Force
Home Service

BONNER, James Alfred
Parents George and Laura Bonner of The Bell public house, Ware Street
Single
The Queens Own (Royal West Kent Regiment)
Western Front

BOTTEN, Edward John
Oak Cottages
Married
4 October 1915 Suffolk Regiment Sergeant
later 52nd Graduated Battalion, Royal Warwickshire Regiment
Posted overseas 1 April 1917, France 1917 to 1918, Germany 1919
Wounded at Arras

BROMLEY, Alfred
Orchard Cottage, Roseacre
Married
30 October 1914 4th Battalion, The Buffs (East Kent Regiment), Territorial Force
later 698th Agricultural Company, Army Service Corps
Service Number 242024 Private
Demobilised 27 March 1919

BROMLEY, George
Roseacre
Single
10 August 1914 81st Field Ambulance, Royal Army Medical Corps attached 27th Division
Service Number 493249 Private
Posted overseas 20 December 1914, France, Serbia and Russia
Demobilised 8 August 1919

First World War: 1914 to 1918

BROWN, Arthur Stokes
Holly Villas, The Street
Single
2 December 1915 2nd Battalion, Coldstream Guards
Service Number 17615 Private
Posted overseas October 1916 France
Sailly, Fregicourt, Somme, Boesinghe
Wounded 1917, Invalided 1918

A transcript of the report from the Kent Messenger, 1 September 1917:

Private Arthur S. Brown (Bearsted)
Coldstream Guards

Private Arthur S. Brown, Coldstream Guards, is the youngest son of Mr and Mrs C. Brown, Holly Villas, Bearsted. He joined up December 1915, trained several months at Caterham and Windsor, proceeded to France 10th October 1916 and was wounded 30th July 1917. Both legs were badly hit and the right one has been amputated above the knee. He is now in Belton Park Military Hospital, Grantham, progressing favourably.

Reproduced courtesy of Kent Messenger newspaper group

BROWN, Charles Herbert
The Street
Single
3 February 1916 Royal Naval Air Service later Royal Air Force
Demobilised 14 September 1919

BROWN, Leonard Edwin
Parents John and Emma Brown
Court Farm
Single
20 April 1914 1/1st Kent Cyclist Battalion
29 June 1915 260th Company, Machine Gun Corps
India including Bangalore, Lahore and Bombay
Service Number 944 then 94519 Private, Lance Corporal from 26 September 1918
Demobilised 15 July 1919

BURBRIDGE, Hugh George
Fancy Row Cottages, Thurnham Lane
Devonshire Yeomanry

BUSH, John
Danedale
Married
September 1898 Royal Marine Light Infantry
Major
Recalled 30 July 1914 Antwerp, Egypt, Gallipoli, Anzac and Cape Helles
St Helena commanding Prisoners Camp 1916 to 1917, Pacific Coast 1917 to 1918, Turkey 1919
Wounded 21 June 1915 Mentioned in Secretary of State's Despatches

First World War: 1914 to 1918

BUSS, Arthur Herbert
Roseacre Terrace
Widowed then remarried
Wife Ethel Catherine (née Rolfe)
1 June 1917 Inland Waterways and Docks, Royal Engineers
Lieutenant then Captain 16 June 1918
Service in England
Resigned 4 February 1919

Ethel and Arthur were married on 1 June 1918 at Holy Cross church

BUTLER, James Edward
The Street
Married
July 1917 Royal Naval Air Service later Royal Air Force
Service Number 235857 Aircraft Mechanic 2nd Class

CABLE, Bert
Binbury Cottage
Service Number 3341 Private
697th Agricultural Company, Army Service Corps

CANSON, Edward John
Ware Street
The Buffs (East Kent Regiment)
Service Number 4931 Quartermaster Sergeant

CAPON, Frank
The Lodge, Aldington
Royal Fusiliers (City of London Regiment)
Service Number 58400 Private

CARR, Albert Thomas
Roseacre Terrace
Married
6 November 1916 Royal Naval Air Service Air Mechanic 1st class
Service Number F23271
Tanks 1917
HMS President
Demobilised 16 January 1919

CARR, Allan Gus
Kentish Yeoman public house
Married
17 February 1915
282nd Mechanical Transport, Army Service Corps attached 18th Brigade, Royal Garrison Artillery
Service Number 049563 Private
Posted overseas 17 April 1915
Demobilised 9 June 1919

CATHCART, David Andrew *†
The White Lodge, Ware Street
Married
Wife Emma Mahala
Children Ewart Aliwal Andrew and Hazel May
7 August 1900 2nd Dragoons (Royal Scots Greys)
Posted overseas August 1914
Second Lieutenant 7th (Service) Battalion, The Queen's Own (Royal West Kent Regiment)
France August 1914 to July 1916
Acting Captain
Mons, Marne, Ypres, Somme
Killed in action 13 July 1916, aged 33
Buried in grave I D 17, Peronne Road Cemetery, Maricourt, Somme, France

David was born in Ballymena, County Antrim. He had two siblings: James who was in the Scots Guards and John who was in the Royal Marines. Before the war, David was employed by Robert Boal of Co. Antrim. He was sent to a riding school at Canterbury as he was an excellent horseman. David married Emma Weeks at St Paul's church, Canterbury, 2 December 1909. They shared White Lodge in Bearsted with Emma's sisters.

David became a casualty on 13 July 1916, having being pierced by shrapnel, and died without gaining consciousness. Emma Cathcart died on 19 March 1917, aged 35. She had never recovered from the shock of her husband's death.

A transcript of the report from the Kent Messenger, 29 July 1916:

KENT'S TOLL IN THE GREAT ADVANCE

'For King and Country'

LIEUT. CATHCART

A fine young officer has been lost to the service and to the West Kents in particular, by the death of Second-Lieut. Cathcart, who was killed in action on July 14th Lieut. Cathcart who was a native of Glasgow, received his commission in December 1915 as a reward for excellent service in the field. He joined the Scots Greys in Edinburgh in 1901, was soon after made Corporal and sent to Canterbury to the Riding Establishment. In the following August, 1902, he left Canterbury to rejoin at Aldershot, before proceeding to South Africa.

After he had been with his regiment for a year and nine months, the Royal Scots Greys returned to England. He was quartered at various places until October 1910 when his regiment was ordered to York, where it remained until the outbreak of the war, but between 1910-1914, Second-Lieut. Cathcart passed through the Cavalry School at Netheravon (1911) and the Hythe School of

Musketry (1913). He was deservedly considered one of the finest horsemen in the British Army, was a prominent figure at the Annual Military Tournament in London during the past ten years and was the proud possessor of championship medals for heads and posts, driving, thrusting and lemon cutting. He was also the winner of the Sword, Lance and Revolver (combined) Competition (1914) both in the Northern Command and at the London Tournament of that year.

At his own request, on obtaining his commission, Second Lieutenant Cathcart joined the Royal West Kent Regiment in the trenches. He spent his last leave in April at White Lodge, Bearsted. A widow and two children mourn the loss of an exemplary husband and father, whose memory is held in much respect. His Major writes: "Although he had only been with is a comparatively short time, he had won the heart of all, and he is a real loss to the Battalion in every way." A private (his servant) writes: "He died doing his duty, leading his transport to the last. A braver man there could not have been; even when he was so badly wounded, he gave orders for the transport to get out of the danger. He died within an hour of being hit. I could not have lost a greater friend."

Reproduced courtesy of Kent Messenger newspaper group

CAUSON, Francis
41 Mill Street, Ayr
Parents Edward and Williamina Causon of 38 Broad Street, Canterbury
Married
Wife Jemima Crombie
2nd Battalion, Royal Scots Fusiliers
Service Number 9820 Sergeant
Missing, presumed killed, 24 October 1914, aged 24
Commemorated Panel 19 and 33, Menin Gate, Ypres, West Vlaanderen, Belgium

A transcript of the report from the Kent Messenger, 19 June 1915:

Sergt. F. Causon, Bearsted

MISSING

9820 Sergt Francis Causon of the 2nd Battalion Royal Scotch Fusiliers, has been missing since October 24th. He used to live at Ware Street, Bearsted, and before joining the Army seven years ago worked for Mr Montagu Ballard of East Farleigh. He was in South Africa with his regiment during the last rising. His wife is living at Ayr, Scotland while his father, who was a Quartermaster-Sergeant of the Army Pay Corps, is stationed at Canterbury with the Buffs.

Reproduced courtesy of Kent Messenger newspaper group

CHAMBERS, Arthur Edwin
Willington Court
Horse Transport Company, Army Service Corps attached to 1st Cavalry Division

First World War: 1914 to 1918

CHAMBERS, Thomas William
Army, Royal Defence Corps
Home Service

CHAPMAN, Horace †
Roundwell
Parents Mr and Mrs H Chapman of Roundwell
Single
8th (Service) Battalion, King's Own (Royal Lancaster Regiment)
Service Number 23191 Private
Posted as Missing, presumed killed, 13 November 1916, aged 23
Buried in Luke Copse Cemetery, Pas de Calais, France

A transcript of the report from the Kent Messenger, 10 March 1917:

Information Wanted

Pte. H. Chapman (Bearsted) K.O.R.L.R.

MISSING

Private H Chapman, 23191, 8th K.O.R.L Regiment has been missing since November 13th, 1916. Any news concerning him from any of his comrades would be very gratefully received by his father and mother, Mr and Mrs H. Chapman, Round Well, Bearsted, near Maidstone, Kent.

Reproduced courtesy of Kent Messenger newspaper group

CHAPMAN, James Thomas
Acacia Villas, Willington Road
Married
1901 Royal Navy
Leading Stoker
HMS Bat

CHAPMAN, William Henry
Roundwell
Single
Service Number 156107 Gunner
A Battery, 282nd A Brigade, Royal Horse Artillery
Demobilised 17 April 1919

First World War: 1914 to 1918

CHARMAN, Allan
Ware Street
Mechanical Transport, Army Service Corps
Service Number M2/176677 Sergeant
Military Medal 1918 (London Gazette, March 1919)

A transcript of the report from the Kent Messenger, 1 February 1919:

Sergt. A. Charman (Thurnham) A.S.C. (M.T.)

AWARDED THE MILITARY MEDAL

Sergt. Charman has been awarded the Military Medal for devotion to duty - saving the guns during the retreat at Mory on the night of March 22nd 1918, and getting ammunition to the battery under shell fire during the great advance.

Reproduced courtesy of Kent Messenger newspaper group

CHAWNER, Edward William
Ware Street
Service Number 505947 Private
572nd Agricultural Company
Army Service Corps and Royal West Kent Regiment

CHEESEMAN, Howard George
Thurnham
Parents Mr and Mrs Cheeseman of 38 Gordon Road, Gillingham
Single
2nd Battalion, South Wales Borderers
Service Number 10441 Sergeant
Killed 28 June 1915, aged 25
Commemorated Panel 80-84 or 219-220, Helles Memorial, Turkey

CLARKE, George James †
Maple Bar Gate
1st Battalion, Queen's (Royal West Surrey Regiment)
Service Number 3693 Private
Killed 25 September 1915
Buried in grave III A 1, Guards Cemetery, Windy Corner, Cuinchy, Pas de Calais, France

CLEGGETT, Ernest Alfred
Coldharbour
Service Number 2907896 Gunner
Royal Field Artillery

First World War: 1914 to 1918

CLISBY, John Charles
Bearsted
Parents Jane Ann Clisby of Ramsgate and the late Samuel Clisby
Married
Wife Phoebe Lydia
6th (Service) Battalion, Queen's (Royal West Surrey Regiment)
Service Number G/2829 Private
Killed 4 April 1916, aged 26
Commemorated Panel 13-15, Loos Memorial, Pas de Calais, France

COLEGATE, George
The Green
Married
16 March 1916 3rd (Reserve) Battalion, The Queen's Own (Royal West Kent Regiment)
Service Number 12619 Private
Posted overseas 16 June 1916
France June 1916 to November 1917, April 1918 to August 1919
Italy November 1917 to March 1918
Messines, Trones Wood, Hollebeke, Tower Hamlets
Twice wounded Thiepval, October 1916, 27 April 1918
Demobilised 8 September 1919

COOPER, Albert Edward
The Street
Single
27 September 1912 2nd Battalion, The Buffs (East Kent Regiment)
India 1914 Telegraphist
France November 1914
Ypres, Hooge, Hill 60
Corporal
Injured Ypres-Commines Canal, France
Invalided out 10 February 1916

COOPER, Alfred Charles
The Street
Single
21 May 1908 2nd Battalion, The Buffs (East Kent Regiment)
Service Number 8874 Sergeant
India and China
France 16 January 1915
Wounded 13 October 1915

COOPER, Frank
The Queens Own (Royal West Kent Regiment)
Western Front

COOPER, George Henry †
Ware Street
Parents George Henry and E Cooper of Ware Street
Single
7th (Service) Battalion, The Buffs (East Kent Regiment)
Service Number 15574 Private
Killed 18 November 1916
Buried in grave A 31, Stump Road Cemetery, Grandcourt, Somme, France

22

First World War: 1914 to 1918

COOPER, George Henry
West View Cottages
Married
The Buffs (East Kent Regiment) 1901 to 1913
South African War
2 January 1917 Royal Navy
Service Number K39354 Stoker 2nd Class
At sea June 1917 to July 1919
HMS Europa I   Aegean Sea, Salonika and Mudros
Demobilised 24 July 1919

COOPER, Walter
Milgate
Single
Royal Engineers

CORSCADEN, William
Bearsted
Service Number 98508 Private
324th Field Ambulance, Royal Army Medical Corps

COTTERELL, Alfred †
Thurnham
Parents Mr and Mrs Thomas Henry Cottrell of 37 Park Road, Ashford
Service Number 6622
1st/20th (County of London) Battalion (Blackheath and Woolwich)
Served in France and Flanders
Killed in action 30 October 1916, aged 21
Commemorated Panels 12 and 14, Ypres (Menin Gate) Memorial

Previous Service Number 3894 The Queen's Own (Royal West Kent Regiment). Alfred was born in Ashford, Kent and he enlisted in Maidstone.

COX, Albert
Parents William and Eliza Cox of Ware Street
Single
Army
Salonika, Western Front

CRADDOCK, Charles
Bearsted Spot
Married
Salonika

CRAMPTON, Robert Walter
Bearsted
Married
Wife Kate Ladysmith (née Bromley)
Private
Motorised Transport, Army Service Corps

First World War: 1914 to 1918

CRICK, Frederick
Woodcut
Single
October 1915 Royal Navy
Boy rating
HMS Erin and *HMS Inflexible* 1917

CRICK, Leslie
Woodcut
Single
1918 Royal Navy
Boy rating
HMS Impregnable

CROFT, Albert
Single
Army, Labour Corps
Home Service

CROFT, Frederick
Bell Lane
Parents Frederick and Sarah Ann Croft of Oak Cottage, Ware Street
Service Number 179403 Gunner
533rd Siege Battery, Royal Garrison Artillery
Salonika

CROFT, James Stanley †
Thurnham Lane
Parents Frederick and Sarah Ann Croft of Oak Cottage, Ware Street
2nd Battalion, The Buffs (East Kent Regiment)
Service Number G/4677
Served in France and Flanders
Killed in action 3 May 1915, aged 20
Commemorated Panels 12 and 14, Ypres (Menin Gate) Memorial

CROFT, Philip
Parents Frederick and Sarah Ann Croft of Oak Cottage, Ware Street
Single
Army, Western Front
Prisoner of War

CROSS, H D

CROUCHER, Albert Edward *
Bradley's Lane, Roseacre
Single
January 1916 King's Royal Rifle Corps
transferred to 1st Battalion, Oxfordshire and Buckinghamshire Light Infantry
Service Number 23485 Private
Posted overseas May 1916
Mesopotamia May 1916 to March 1918
Died in hospital 18 February 1918
Buried in grave II B 6, Baghdad (North Gate) War Cemetery, Iraq

First World War: 1914 to 1918

CROUCHER, Ambrose Alfred
Roseacre
Married
Wife Lily Naomi (née Swift)
14 April 1915 Army Service Corps Driver
transferred to 4th (Extra Reserve) Battalion, South Staffordshire Regiment 1917
France January 1918 to February 1919
Lewis Gunner
Somme, Arras
Gassed, Demobilised 9 March 1919

Ambrose married Lily on 1 January 1916 at Holy Cross church

CROUCHER, Charles †
Parents William and Esther Ellen Croucher (stepmother) of 1 Leather Bottle Cottages, Little Belmont,
    Ospringe, Faversham
Single
D Company 1st Battalion, The Buffs (East Kent Regiment)
Service Number L/10663 Private
Died 9 April 1917, aged 18
Buried in grave I N 35, Philosophe British Cemetery, Maxingarbe, Pas de Calais, France

CROUCHER, Frank
Bradley's Lane, Roseacre
Army

CROUCHER, Frederick John
Single
Roseacre
April 1915 Army Service Corps
transferred to 3rd (Reserve) Battalion, Prince of Wales's (North Staffordshire Regiment) 1917
Service Number 48779 Private
In hospital January 1917 to December 1918
Demobilised 14 April 1919

CUTLER, Albert
Royal Army Service Corps

CUTLER, Ernest
Rifle Brigade

CUTLER, George
Rifle Brigade

DANIELL, Oswald James
Orchards
Married
Wife May
11 May 1878 50th Regiment of Foot, Egypt, Cyprus (Medals Egypt 1882, Khedive's Star)
Captain 1885 The Queen's Own (Royal West Kent Regiment), Major 1893, Retired 1902
Rejoined 30 September 1914 T/Lieutenant-Colonel
Commanding 9th (Reserve) Battalion, The Queen's Own (Royal West Kent Regiment) 1915 to 1916
Lieutenant-Colonel 1916, Recruiting Duties 1917
Order of St Stanislaus 2nd class, Mentioned in Secretary of State's Despatches, 1917
Demobilised 1918

First World War: 1914 to 1918

DATSON, Charles Edward
The Street
Single
1 November 1915 18th Section Field Bakery
Service Number S4 14495 Corporal
Base Supply, Army Service Corps
Mesopotamia

DATSON, Harry William Arthur
The Street
Single
25 October 1915 Royal Naval Volunteer Reserve Ordinary Seaman
Service Number 3546 Able Seaman 2nd Class
HMS Europa II, HMS Vengeance

DATSON, Leonard Sidney
The Street
Single
13 November 1914 Army Service Corps attached to 202nd Infantry Brigade and Base Supply
Service Number S4 238855 Private

DATSON, Lionel Percy
The Street
Single
16 April 1915 Mechanical Transport, Army Service Corps
attached to 18th Field Ambulance, 6th Division, Royal Army Medical Corps
Service Number 077302
Posted overseas 24 April 1915
Corporal December 1915
France, Belgium April 1915 to November 1918
Germany November 1918 to June 1919
Sergeant September 1918
First, Second Battle of Ypres, Hooge, Hill 60, Somme 1916, Cambrai 1917, 1918 Retreat and Final Advance
Wounded
Military Medal 1917
Demobilised 25 June 1919

A transcript of the report from the Kent Messenger, 2 February 1918

Corpl. Datson (Bearsted) A.S.C. (M.T.)

AWARDED THE MILITARY MEDAL

Corporal Datson (A.S.C., M.T., attached R.A.M.C.) of Bearsted, has been awarded the Military Medal and Card of Honour for distinguishing himself at Marcoing on the 30th November 1917, when the village was being heavily shelled, by driving his ambulance to and from the advanced dressing station three times, thereby enabling it to be kept clear.

Reproduced courtesy of Kent Messenger newspaper group

First World War: 1914 to 1918

DATSON, Victor John
The Street
Single
19 May 1916 Royal Fusiliers (City of London Regiment) later Royal Engineers
Service Number 311401 Private
Posted overseas July 1916
Demobilised 19 November 1919

DEAR, Arthur James
Milgate Park
Married
19 October 1916 Mechanical Transport, Army Service Corps
later 7th Battalion, Gloucestershire Regiment
Service Number 38768 Lance Corporal then Sergeant Instructor
India

DENNY, Thomas David William *
Hill View, Tower Lane, Roseacre
Father Thomas Denny
Married
Wife Elsie May (née Holdsworth)
Second Lieutenant
3rd Battalion, Gloucestershire Regiment
Salonika
Died 6 March 1919 aged 28
Military Medal
Buried in north west corner of Holy Cross churchyard

Thomas rose through the ranks and received a Military Medal for leading an attack at Salonika in 1916. He was wounded twice. Elsie was born in London and lived with her aunt at Hill View. She married Thomas 12 January 1918 at Holy Cross church. She later remarried, becoming Elsie Gregory.

Regimental Cap Badges

During the war, many regiments became instantly recognisable from the insignia worn on their caps as badges. These are the insignia for the East Kent Regiment (left), the Royal West Kent Regiment (right):

Both reproduced courtesy of Malcolm Kersey

First World War: 1914 to 1918

DIBBLE, George
The Poplars, Roseacre
Volunteer Training Corps later 2nd Volunteer Brigade, Royal West Kent
Sergeant

George was Chairman of Thurnham parish council 1943-1948.

DICKENSON, Charles Edward
The Street
Married
1 October 1915 West Kent Yeomanry (Queen's Own)
1916 10th (Service) (Kent County) Battalion, The Queen's Own (Royal West Kent Regiment)
Posted overseas 5 December 1916
France December 1916 to November 1917
Italy March to November 1918
Germany November 1917 to February 1918, December 1918 to April 1919
Messines, Battle Wood, Hollebeke, Tower Hamlets, 1918 Retreat
Demobilised 5 April 1919

DINES, Thomas Edward
Willington
Parents William and Mrs Dines of Lower Shepway Court, Willington,
        later Kingsley Road, Maidstone
Single
Service Number 1115
Private
Enlisted 29 September 1914, Blackboy Hill, Western Australia
11th Infantry Battalion, Australian Infantry Force
Died 5 May 1915 aged 25 years
Buried in grave C 175, Alexandria (Chatby) Military and War Memorial Cemetery, Egypt

Thomas was born at Boughton Malherbe. He became a mechanic before emigrating on 8 December 1911 from London, bound for Fremantle on board *Omrah*, Orient Shipping Line. Initially reported as wounded through action in the Dardenelles, Thomas did not survive his injuries.

A transcript of the report from the Kent Messenger, 12 June 1915:

Pte. T. Dines, Willington

WOUNDED IN THE DARDENELLES

As already reported in the Kent Messenger, Mrs W Dines of Kingsley Road, Maidstone, late of Willington, has received official confirmation that her son, Pte T E Dines, 11th Battalion, Australian Contingent, has been wounded in action in the Dardenelles.

Reproduced courtesy of Kent Messenger newspaper group

First World War: 1914 to 1918

DINWIDDY, Malcolm James
Bell House
Married
14 August 1901 2nd Battalion, The Queen's Own (Royal West Kent Regiment)
South African War
India March 1914 to January 1915
Mesopotamia January 1915 to April 1916
Prisoner in Turkey 29 April 1916 to November 1918
Egypt 1919
Nasriya Battle 24 July 1915, Siege of Kut December 1915 to April 1916
Major 1918

DOE, Ernest Walter
Acacia Villas, Willington Road
Single
September 1917 Royal Navy Stoker
HMS Chester

DUNN, Henry Charles
Danefield Cottage, Church Lane
Married
10 January 1917 Royal Army Veterinary Corps later 2nd Reserve Section, Army Service Corps
Service Number S E 24928 Private
Posted overseas 29 January 1917
France January to November 1917
Demobilised 11 June 1919

DUREY, Mark
Roseacre
Married
22 February 1916 Duke of Cambridge's Own (Middlesex Regiment)
England February 1916 to May 1917
transferred to The Queen's Own (Royal West Kent Regiment) 13 May 1917
Private
France May 1917 to October 1917
Italy October 1917 to March 1918
Prisoner of War in France March 1918 to November 1918
Messines Ridge, Battle Wood, Hollebeke, Tower Hamlets
Wounded
Discharged 4 April 1919

EARL, James Walter William
Married
Wife Wilhelmina (née Causon) of Thurnham
Ware Street
Service Number 57328 Private
The Queen's Own (Royal West Kent Regiment)

James married Wilhelmina on 7 August 1915 at Mary's church.

First World War: 1914 to 1918

Everyday Comforts for the Front Line

During the war it was widely known that living conditions for the troops in the trenches were frequently extremely unsanitary, becoming perfect places for diseases to spread. Advertisements for Chemists and medical products, along with items promoted as gifts for men on active service and prisoners of war frequently featured in the popular press together with recommendations for being suitable for life serving for King and Country.

These advertisements appeared in The War Budget, published by the Daily Chronicle, in 1915:

MEDICAL SUPPLIES AND COMFORTS FOR THE TRENCHES

Boots The Chemists

VERMIN POWDER

War brings many horrors, not the least of which is the plague of parasites to which our soldiers are liable.
On field service the plague of vermin is prevalent.
Nothing is more disagreeable or so likely to impair the efficiency of the men.
Boots The Chemists special preparation against vermin in the trenches is thoroughly efficient, is in powder form, and is a most powerful and efficient antiparasitic.
Convenient, cleanly, and absolutely harmless.

Price 9d. Per Box.

Special Quotations for Quantities.

Boots The Chemists

WATER STERILIZERS

One of the most dreaded of all campaign dangers is impure water. Boots The Chemists manufacture and supply Tablets for Sterilizing and Purifying water for drinking purposes.

A shilling bottle contains 50 tablets, sufficient for the complete sterilization of 50 pints of water.

The tablets impart an agreeable lemon flavour to water, and render it a pleasant, safe thirst quenching drink.

Price 1/- Per Bottle of 50 Tablets.

11/- Per Dozen Bottles.

FOOD FOR PRISONERS OF WAR

If your soldier friend or relative is a Prisoner of War in Germany, he will appreciate
A PARCEL OF FOOD FROM HOME
more than anything else. Therefore write to us To-Day for a copy of our COMPLETE LIST OF PROVISION PARCELS, each article is in a separate air-tight tin, and GUARANTEED OF THE BEST QUALITY. The prices of these parcels are:— 5s., 7s. 6d., 10s. 15s., and 20s.

SEND US A POSTAL ORDER FOR 5s.

With the full address of the one to whom you require a parcel sent, we will forward him at once securely packed and properly declared for Customs purposes, a parcel containing the following:—

1lb. TIN BISCUITS (Plain).	½lb. TIN BUTTER.
1lb. TIN CHEESE.	½lb. TIN MARMALADE.
½lb. TIN CAFE AU LAIT.	1 GLASS MEAT PASTE.
1 TIN SARDINES.	1 TIN OPENER.

We will at the same time advise him that it has been sent, by means of a special post card, printed in both English and German; on which is included the address of the sender, so that he can acknowledge its receipt direct.

Post your order to-day to—
HUDSON BROS., LTD. (MILITARY HOME SUPPLIES DEPT.)
34, FARRINGDON ROAD, LONDON, E.C.
Branches throughout London and Provinces.

Make HIM Happy

Nothing could be more acceptable to your Soldier or Sailor friend — whether a Prisoner of War or with the Fighting Forces — than a generous supply of Wrigley's **SPEARMINT** Chewing Gum.

Allays thirst, renders the mouth cool and sweet, prevents fatigue, soothes the nerves and aids digestion. A very welcome change from Chocolate or Cigarettes.

WRIGLEY'S SPEARMINT CHEWING GUM

Send him some to-day. **It MUST be Wrigley's.**
He needs it badly.

MAMMOTH BOX Containing 40 Bars **1/6**

Larger quantities are supplied as follows:— Box containing 20 packets of 5 bars each, 4s.; 10 boxes (enough for 1,000 men), 35s. Wrigley's enjoys the largest sale of any chewing gum in the World (guaranteed pure and harmless), obtainable from all Chemists and Confectioners. Should any difficulty be experienced, write direct to—
WRIGLEY'S Ltd., Lambeth Palace Road, S.E.

All reproduced courtesy of Roger Vidler

First World War: 1914 to 1918

As the wartime became established, many manufacturers contributed to the propaganda effort. Their advertisements took on a patriotic bias, suggesting to customers that purchasing their products would assist the armed forces. The first two advertisements are taken from The War Budget, 1915, published by the Daily Chronicle whilst those for Caffyn & Co and Sunlight Soap appeared in the Kent Messenger, September 1914 and 1916.

SEND YOUR FRIENDS
BRAND'S
MEAT
LOZENGES
(PURE BEEF)

WORLD - RENOWNED for their sustaining properties.

"A Meal in the Vest Pocket"
No more acceptable gift can be made to officers and men

IN BOXES 1/-, 1/6 & 2/9, of Chemists and Stores or direct of—

BRAND & CO., LTD.,
Mayfair Works, Vauxhall, London, S.W.

They MUST Eat—
They Enjoy Washing—
and *DON'T* they Enjoy
Good Reading!

Our boys in Germany want good reading even more than the boys in training, or at the front — and *they* clamour for it, as you know.

Here are just the rattling good stories to keep them cheery :—

"Battle," by W. Douglas Newton
"For England," by Morice Gerard
"This Man and This Woman," by L. Clarke
"Love Tides," by Captain Frank H. Shaw
(Price 3d. each volume).

SPECIAL OFFER

All four will be sent post free to any man on Active service or British prisoner in Germany, upon receipt of his name and address and One Shilling, by "Lloyd's News" Home Novels, 12, Salisbury Square, London, E.C.

128 pages each.   In Three-Coloured Covers

Both reproduced courtesy of Roger Vidler

BUYING HINTS
FOR WARTIME.

BLANKETS. Lord Kitchener has appealed for gifts of Blankets for our Soldiers, as it is impossible to obtain sufficient quantities at once from the Manufacturers. The entire available stock of Brown Army Blankets is exhausted; it is suggested that many private people may have suitable Blankets by them.

Gifts of these will be greatly appreciated and should be sent to The Chief Ordnance Officer, Chatham, or Canterbury.

T. P. CAFFYN & CO. can supply REAL WITNEY BLANKETS at old prices to fill gaps made in household stores by such gifts.

These Blankets are the finest in the world, both as regards excellence of manufacture and quality of wool.

They are priced at 10/11, 13/11, 16/6, 17/11, 21/9 for single beds and 12/11, 17/11, 21/9, 24/6, 27/11, 32/6, 37/6 for double beds.

KNITTED SOCKS. Her Majesty the Queen has appealed for 300,000 pairs of Knitted Socks, and a similar quantity of Knitted Waist Belts, which are required for our Soldiers at the front early in November.

The most suitable Wools for these articles are :—
T. P. Caffyn & Co.'s Special Fingering Wool at 3/4 per lb.
T. P. Caffyn & Co.'s Khaki Fingering at 3/6 per lb. and
T. P. Caffyn & Co.'s well-known Sports Wool at 4/- per lb.
The most suitable colors are Khaki, Greys and Heather Mixtures.

Samples will be sent post free, but as there is a great demand for these Wools it is advisable to order at once.

T. P. CAFFYN & CO.,
45, 47, 54 & 56, Week Street,
. . . . . Maidstone . . . . .

SUNLIGHT SOAP

CLEANLINESS, LIKE MUSIC, HATH CHARMS!

WHILST Tommy has no "Hymn of Hate," he hates to be dirty and loves to be clean. Sunlight Soap is a boon to clean fighters.

The clean, chivalrous fighting instincts of our gallant soldiers reflect the ideals of our business life. The same characteristics which stamp the British Tommy as the cleanest fighter in the world have won equal repute for British goods.

Sunlight Soap is typically British. It is acknowledged by experts to represent the highest standard of Soap Quality and Efficiency. Tommy welcomes it in the trenches just as you welcome it at home.

£1,000 GUARANTEE OF PURITY ON EVERY BAR.

Include a Tablet in your next parcel to the Front.

The name Lever on Soap is a Guarantee of Purity and Excellence.
LEVER BROTHERS LIMITED, PORT SUNLIGHT.

Both reproduced courtesy of Kent Messenger newspaper group

First World War: 1914 to 1918

EARLL, Bertie
Church Lane
Single
18 January 1915 Royal Engineers Signals, 13th Division and 13th Siege Company
Service Number 60575 Sapper
Posted overseas June 1915
Gallipoli, Egypt, Mesopotamia, Kut, Baghdad, Samarea, Kirkuk
Demobilised 8 May 1919

EDWARDS, Charles Friend
Parsonage Cottage
Service Number 209049 Gunner
6th Reserve Brigade, Royal Field Artillery

EDWARDS, Percy Harold
Roundwell
Single
November 1915 116th (Ontario County Infantry) Battalion, Canadian Infantry
Posted overseas February 1917

EDWARDS, William Temple
Roundwell
Single
July 1915 Royal Naval Air Service

ELLIOTT, ------
Royal Army Medical Corps, Somerset Light Infantry
India

ELLIOTT, James Edwin
Roseacre Terrace
Single
4 May 1916 82nd Field Ambulance, Royal Army Medical Corps
1918 2nd Battalion, The Buffs (East Kent Regiment)
Service Number 204488 Private
Salonika August 1916 to November 1918
Struma, Dorian
Turkey 1918 to 1919
Demobilised 5 September 1919

This undated photograph shows James wearing his medals

Reproduced courtesy of
David and Theresa Elliott

First World War: 1914 to 1918

ELLIS, Bernard George
Home Cottage, Roundwell
Parents May Bennett Ellis and the late Henry Charles Ellis
Single
September 1914 19th (Service) Battalion (2nd Public Schools), Royal Fusiliers (City of London Regiment)
Posted overseas 8 November 1915
France, Festubert Line
Second Lieutenant 9th (Reserve) Battalion, The Buffs (East Kent Regiment) 1916
later 3/5th Battalion, The Buffs (East Kent Regiment), Territorial Force
Lieutenant January 1918
India October 1916 to May 1918, 1919
Mesopotamia 1918
Wounded
Albert Medal 1918 (London Gazette, July 1919)

A transcript of the reports from the Kent Messenger, 26 July 1919 and 2 August 1919:

Lieut. Bernard George Ellis
3-5th Buffs

A MAIDSTONE HERO
The Albert Medal Awarded

Lieut. Bernard George Ellis, the 3-5 Batt. 'The Buffs', East Kent Regiment of Maidstone, has been awarded the Albert Medal for a very gallant deed, which is thus described in the 'London Gazette': 'On the 21st August, 1918, Lieutenant Ellis was with a party at Shahraban under instruction in the firing of rifle grenades. A volley was fired, but one of the grenades, owing to a defective cartridge, did not leave the rifle, but fell back into the barrel with the fuse burning. The firer lost his head and dropped the rifle and grenade in the trench, but Lieutenant Ellis, who was separated from the man by four other men in a narrow trench, at once forced his way past them and seized the rifle. Failing to extract the grenade, he dropped the rifle and placed his steel helmet over the grenade, which at once exploded, severely injuring him. There can be no doubt that his prompt and courageous action greatly minimised the force of the explosion and saved several men from death or severe injury'.

Lieut. Ellis, who will be remembered as a keen sportsman, is a son of the late Mr Henry Charles Ellis and of Mrs May Bennett Ellis, of Home Cottage, Roundwell, Bearsted. He is the younger brother of Mr Charles Harold Ellis, and nephew to Mr A J Ellis, partner in the firm of Messrs Ellis and Ellis, solicitors, Earl Street, Maidstone. He thus belongs to an old Maidstone family. His great grandfather, Mr Charles Ellis, was Mayor of Maidstone, first assuming office in 1854. Born on November 21st, 1890, Lieut. B G Ellis was educated at Cathedral School, Salisbury and Montpellier, Paignton, South Devon.

At the outbreak of the war he was on the staff of the Union of London and Smith's Bank, Maidstone. He joined up with the Public Schools Corps in September, 1914, as a private, trained with them at various stations, including Epsom, and went in November 1915, to France, where he served for six months in the trenches opposite the Hohenzollern Redoubt, and during that period the Germans blew the biggest mine that had gone up on the Western Front at that date. Pte. Ellis returned to England, trained at Oxford, and was given his commission, being gazetted to the Buffs. After being stationed for a time at Dover he went with his battalion to India, and subsequently to Mesopotamia, where he fought in the advanced trenches in charge of his company, and directed bombing operations, in which he had always specialised as bomb instructor to a brigade. It was then that the incident occurred as above recorded.

After his gallant adventure Lieut. Ellis was invalided back to India, where he is still serving as captain of the guard to Lord Willingdon, stationed in the hills. Although Lieut. Ellis still carries 350 pieces of the exploded grenade, 77 of which are lodged in his right arm, he is keeping fit and in good health.

Reproduced courtesy of Kent Messenger newspaper group

The Albert Medal was introduced in 1866. It was devised to be Britain's highest award for bravery in saving lives by a civilian or a military person in acts of great heroism, other than in battle. The George Cross was introduced on 24 September 1940. The Albert Medal continued to be awarded until 1949. By 1970, it was felt that there was little recognition of the Albert Medal and so surviving holders of the medal were invited to exchange it for a George Cross. In 1971, Bernard was one of sixty five people that applied to exchange his medal. Bernard moved away from Kent and he died on 1 July 1979 in Letchworth, Hertfordshire. An obituary was printed in The Daily Telegraph, 10 July 1979.

ELLIS, William
Egypt Cottages
Married
18 May 1915 14th later 725th Labour Company, Army Service Corps
Service Number 304527 Private
Posted overseas 6 June 1915

FAREWELL, Charles Ernest
Oliver's Row
Married
28 December 1902 1st Battalion, The Buffs (East Kent Regiment)
Recalled August 1914
Service Number 24669 Private
Posted overseas 8 September 1914
France September 1914 to 28 December 1915
Aisne, Flanders 1914 to 1915
Time expired; Discharged
Recalled July 1917 8th (Service) Battalion, The Buffs (East Kent Regiment)
France July 1917 to April 1919
Demobilised 4 April 1919

FEAKINS, Albert Amos Edward
Woodcut
Single
28 June 1918 252nd Divisional Employment Company, Labour Corps
Posted overseas 1 November 1918 Germany
Demobilised 25 September 1919

First World War: 1914 to 1918

FEAKINS, John
Barty Farm Cottages, Barty Farm
Single
8 December 1915, Maidstone
Service Number 202534 Private Bomber
3rd Battalion, Suffolk Regiment
Salonika
Medically discharged 22 February 1919

Before joining the Army, John worked as a gamekeeper on the Fremlin estate, Milgate Park. John sailed on a troop ship from Southampton on 21 March and arrived at Salonika, 30 May 1917. Shortly after arrival, he contracted malaria and as a severe case, was returned to Marseilles in a hospital isolation wagon on 11 June. Further bouts of malaria involved admittance to 49th, 63rd, 64th and 82nd military field and base depot hospitals in Salonika between 17 March and 14 August 1918. He was posted home on 23 August to Felixstowe, Suffolk.

On 15 October 1918, a medical Examination and Board agreed he was suffering from severe malaria and recommended that he should not be sent to a theatre of war where the disease was prevalent! After a further stay in a military hospital in Maidstone, the Board agreed he should be discharged as medically unfit and should be regarded as disabled in 1919.

FERRIS, John
Maple Bar Gate
Service Number 159682 Private
338th (Home Service) Works Company, Labour Corps

FLOOD, Bertie William
Royal Navy

FLOOD, John William
Ware Street
The Queen's Own (Royal West Kent Regiment)
Service Number 265279 Private

FLOOD, William Thomas
Ware Street
2nd Battalion, Queen's (Royal West Surrey Regiment)
Service Number 5318 Private

William was a Prisoner of War at Stendal, Germany, from 1915 to the end of the war. This photograph of him was taken around 1920.

Reproduced courtesy of Jean Jones

First World War: 1914 to 1918

FOREMAN, Frederick
Ware Street
Single
10 December 1915, Maidstone, Army Reserve 11 December 1915
23 March 1916, Maidstone
Service Numbers 1549, G26050, 25703 Lance Corporal and 15670 Corporal then 93760
Royal Fusiliers, Devonshire Regiment, Duke of Cornwall's Light Infantry,
157 Company Labour Corps, Company AC I 611/17 Agricultural Company, 572 Agricultural Company
11 December 1915 to 5 May 1916 Britain, 7 May 1916, Expeditionary Force to France
Demobilised 20 February 1919, Crystal Palace

Frederick was born in Cranbrook and lodged with Miss Tilby in Ware Street. Before the war he worked as a labourer.

FOREMAN, Thomas Henry
Roseacre
Married
1904 Royal Navy
1915 Invalided
1915 Royal Fleet Auxiliary

FOSTER, George
Church Lane
Single
Volunteer Training Corps later 2nd Volunteer Brigade, Royal West Kent

FOSTER, William
Church Lane
Single
1st Canadian Labour Battalion
Wounded August 1917

This photograph of William was taken in 1935:

Reproduced courtesy of Chris and Sue Hunt

FOSTER, William
Rosherville, The Green
Married
26 November 1915 The Queen's Own (Royal West Kent Regiment)
transferred to East Surrey Regiment and attached to 89th Labour Corps
Posted overseas 27 February 1917
France February 1917 to February 1919
Demobilised 27 February 1919

First World War: 1914 to 1918

FRAZIER, Alfred
The Green
Royal Army Medical Corps

FRAZIER, George
The Green
Married
16 November 1914 Army Service Corps

FRAZIER, James
Smarts Cottages, The Green
Single
1910 2nd Battalion, Leicestershire Regiment
Ranikhet, India
Service Number 8933 Private
France October 1914
Egypt 1915, Persian Gulf 1916
Indian Expeditionary Force
9 March 1916 Wounded
Distinguished Conduct Medal, 7 January 1916

A transcript of the report from the Kent Messenger, 13 May 1916

Pte. J. Frazier (Bearsted)
2nd Leicestershire Regiment

AWARDED THE D.C.M.

Pte. J. Frazier of the 2nd Leicestershire Regiment, with the I.E.F., whose home is Bearsted Green, has earned the D.C.M. He had been several years in India when war broke out, and went from that country to the Western Front, in October 1914. He was home on leave in October last and was subsequently ordered to proceed to the Persian Gulf, where he was wounded on March 9th, having meanwhile (on January 7th) won the coveted distinction by saving the life of his commanding officer from destruction by a Turk. He has two brothers in France, George in the A.S.C. and Alfred in the R.A.M.C.

Reproduced courtesy of Kent Messenger newspaper group

FRIDD, Thomas Alfred
Roseacre
Service Number 14293S Private
Royal Marines, Deal

First World War: 1914 to 1918

FULLER, George
The Green
Married
Volunteer Training Corps later 2nd Volunteer Brigade, Royal West Kent

FULLER, George Betsworth
The Green
Single
24 November 1915 Royal Navy Boy rating later Wireless Telegraphist
HMS Conqueror, Torpedo Boat Division
Vimeria
Germany and Russia 1919

GAIN, Herbert Lionel
The Den
Service Number 111176 Gunner
231st Siege Battery, Royal Garrison Artillery

GATLAND, Frank Stanley
Milgate Park
Married
27 April 1906 14th (King's) Hussars
India
Reserve 1913
Recalled 4 August 1914 Royal Horseguards
Service Number 47601 Trooper
Posted overseas 5 October 1914
Belgium October 1914
transferred to Machine Gun Guards October 1918
First, Second Battle of Ypres, Arras 1917, Somme
Demobilised 1 March 1919

This photograph of Frank was taken in 1935:

Reproduced courtesy of Chris and Sue Hunt

GILBERT, William Alfred
Ware Street
Royal Dublin Fusiliers
Service Number 27531 Private

William's son, Thomas (usually called Tom) recorded some of his family's wartime experiences. These are included in the *Memories of the First World War* chapter.

GILES, Montague William
Ware Street
Labour Corps

GILHAM, Herbert George
5 Acacia Villas, Willington Road
3rd (Reserve) Battalion, The Queen's Own (Royal West Kent Regiment)
Lieutenant

GIRLING, William Sidney
5 Acacia Villas, Willington Road
Mechanical Transport, Army Service Corps

First World War: 1914 to 1918

GOLDING, Thomas Ashdown *
Roseacre
Parents John Ashdown and Annie Maria Golding
Single
20 December 1914 2nd Battalion, The Buffs (East Kent Regiment)
Service Number G/5230 Private
Posted overseas 28 February 1915 France
Thomas sustained a head injury on 1 May 1915. Upon recovery, he resumed military operations but was subsequently posted as Missing, presumed killed, 28 September 1915 aged 32
Commemorated Panel 15 to 19, Loos Memorial Pas de Calais, France

A transcript of the report from the Kent Messenger, 19 June 1915 about Thomas being wounded:

Pte. T. Golding, Bearsted

WOUNDED

5230. Pte. T Golding, only son of Mr and Mrs Golding, of Rose Acre, Bearsted, was wounded in the head whilst on sentry on May 1st, near Ypres. He served four years in the West Kent Territorials and joined the 2nd Buffs in December, leaving England for France early in March. He is now in hospital at Rouen.

Reproduced courtesy of Kent Messenger newspaper group

GOODHEW, Albert Herbert Sydney
3 Mote Hall Villas
Parents Adam and Emily Goodhew
Married
Wife Lavinia (née Peckham)
Children Edward and Laurence
Service Number M/339536
Royal Army Service Corps, Military Transport
Western Front

GOODHEW, Harry
Royal Navy
Harry's service included duties on board a minesweeper

GOODHEW, Richard
Royal Navy
Chief Petty Officer
HMS Sir Thomas Picton
Croix-de-Guerre, Italian Order

GOODWIN, Arthur Wallace *
Tower Lane, Roseacre
Single
West Kent Yeomanry (Queen's Own)
later 11th (Service) (Lewisham) Battalion, The Queen's Own (Royal West Kent Regiment)
Service Number G/7785 Private
Killed in action 20 September 1917
Commemorated Panel 106 to 108, Tyne Cot Memorial, Zonnebeke, West Vlaanderen, Belgium

Arthur enlisted in Maidstone. He is also mentioned on the Otham village war memorial and on a memorial plaque originally in St John's church, Willington, now located in St Nicholas church, Otham.

Reproduced courtesy of Jean Jones

A transcript of the report from the Kent Messenger, 10 August 1918:

Pte. A. W. Goodwin (Otham)
Royal West Kent Regiment

KILLED IN ACTION

Pte. A. W. Goodwin had been missing since the 20th September 1917. His parents have recently received the sad news that he was killed on that date. Joining up on May 24th, he was in England 18 months before being sent to France. He was out there nine months when reported missing, at the age of 25. Before entering the Army he was employed at Sir Louis Mallet, Ward's, Otham and was a highly respected member of the Church Choir for 15 years. His parents, brother and sister wish to thank all friends, for kind sympathy in their sad bereavement.

Reproduced courtesy of Kent Messenger newspaper group

First World War: 1914 to 1918

GORHAM, Walter William
Oliver's Row
Married
January 1916 1st Battalion, The Queen's Own (Royal West Kent Regiment)
later 10th (Service) (Kent County) Battalion, The Queen's Own (Royal West Kent Regiment)
France December 1916
Italy 1918
Germany 1919
Vimy, Achiet, Bapaume
Wounded
Demobilised 27 September 1919

GRANT, George
Chapel Lane
Service Number 67377 Private
199th Labour Company

GRANT, George Walter
Ware Street
Married
Wife Elizabeth (née Wood)
Children Katie Florence, Margaret, Georgina, Frederick, Bertie and Frank
25 May 1915
Service Numbers G6597, 64107, and 67377 Private
Posted overseas 24 February 1917, British Expeditionary Force, France and Western Front
Service: Army Service Corps, King's Own Yorkshire Light Infantry
            113 and 148 Labour Companies, Labour Corps
Discharged Wimbledon Dispersal Station 22 February 1919

GRANT, John William
1/1st Kent Battalion, Army Cyclist Corps
India

GREEN, Walter Charles
Army
Sergeant

GROUT, Frederick William Collins
Milgate Park
Single
Service Number 226860 Chief Mechanic 1st Class
Royal Flying Corps, Royal Air Force
France

Frederick was Chairman of Bearsted Parish Council 1949-1952

GROUT, William
Milgate Park
Married
1918 Mechanical Transport, Army Service Corps
Service Number M402491 Private
Demobilised 17 February 1919

First World War: 1914 to 1918

GUEST, Walter William
Thurnham Court Cottages, Thurnham Court Farm
Married
Wife Rose (née Robinson)
Children Lucy, Robert, Winifred, Walter and Alfred
20th (Light) Division, Army Service Corps

Walter was highly-skilled with horses and so he was deployed to look after them. This photograph shows him in his army uniform, note the spurs on his boots.

Reproduced courtesy of Winifred Harris

In 1917, Walter sent his family an official Christmas card from the 20th (Light) Division. The front and inside are reproduced:

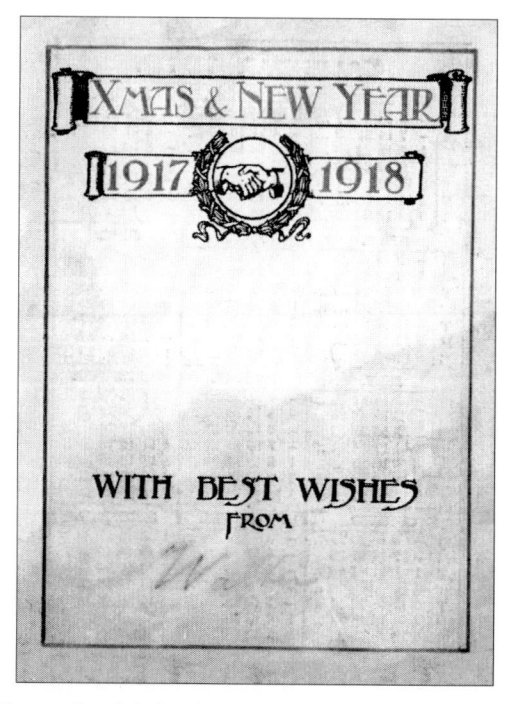

Both reproduced courtesy of Margaret Peat (née Lang)

First World War: 1914 to 1918

HAISMAN, William Prebble
Roseacre
Service Number 35530 Private
2nd (Garrison) Battalion, Bedfordshire Regiment

HALLETT, George Thomas
Ware Street
Parents Frank and Eliza Hallett (née Bottle)
Single
Bedfordshire Regiment, Western Front

HALLETT, William Henry
Ware Street
Parents Frank and Eliza Hallett (née Bottle)
Single
The Queens Own (Royal West Kent Regiment)
Western Front

HAMPSON, Dennys Francis
The Court
Lieutenant
Rifle Brigade (The Prince Consort's Own)

This photograph of Dennys Hampson was taken in 1935:

HAMPSON, John Nicholl
Common Wood
Lieutenant
Royal Dublin Fusiliers

This photograph of John Hampson was taken in 1935:

Both reproduced courtesy of Chris and Sue Hunt

43

First World War: 1914 to 1918

HANNAN, George Madder *
24 Abingdon Villas, Kensington, Middlesex
Married
Wife Mary (née Carlisle)
Major
9th (Service) Battalion, Cameronians (Scottish Rifles)
Died 13 October 1915, The Green, aged 55
Buried in north west corner of Holy Cross churchyard

George was born in Dublin, Ireland and before the outbreak of the war was an Army Major with the Special Reserve

HANNINGTON, Charles
Invicta Villas
Married
November 1914 10th (Canadians) Battalion, Canadian Infantry
Sergeant
Posted overseas 27 April 1915
France April 1915 to 1918
Lieutenant 7th (1st British Columbia Regiment) Battalion, Canadian Infantry
Captain Headquarters Staff in Germany
Second Battle of Ypres, Festubert, Givenchy, Ploegsteert, Somme, Vimy
Three times wounded
Demobilised August 1919

HANNINGTON, William James
Invicta Villas
Married
22 May 1896 19th (Queen Alexandra's Own Royal) Hussars
1897 12th (Prince of Wales Royal) Lancers
Sergeant 1901
Staff Sergeant Major 1912
South Africa, India and South African War
Long Service Medal, Gold Medal of Saint George (Russia) 2nd class
France October 1914 to March 1915
Palestine September 1917 to February 1919
Regimental Sergeant Major 1917
7th Division
Ypres, Neuve Chapelle
Distinguished Conduct Medal, 1914 Star
Demobilised 27 April 1919

HARBORD, Godfrey
Royal Field Artillery
Ceylon Mounted Rifles
Lieutenant then Major

HARDWELL, William Alfred
Keeper's Cottage, Thurnham Lane
Service Number 38788 Driver
Army Service Corps attached to H & Y Battalion, Royal Garrison Artillery

First World War: 1914 to 1918

HARMAN, Percival Brooks
Rusaker
Single
11 November 1915 Royal Army Medical Corps
Service Number 77128 Private
Posted overseas 3 August 1916
Attached No 31 Casualty Clearing Station
Macedonia and Bulgaria August 1916 to April 1919
Discharged 10 May 1919

Thinking of You

During the First World War, it became very popular to wear a 'sweetheart brooch'. These were small items of jewellery, and often comprised a miniature version of a regimental insignia or device worn as lapel brooch or badge. They were frequently used to indicate a military connection, such a family member serving their country. A wide variety of designs were executed in many different materials including precious metals, enamel and paste, fragments of shell casings and uniform buttons. These are some examples.

First Row (left to right)   Royal West Kent Regiment; brooch made from a Royal Navy uniform button
Second Row   Royal Flying Corps

Sweetheart Handkerchiefs were also popular and this photograph shows the hand-embroidered detail on an example in cotton lawn. Printed designs were also available.

All reproduced courtesy of Malcolm Kersey

First World War: 1914 to 1918

HARNETT, Arthur Norman
Otteridge House
Parents Frank and Kate Harnett (née Furber)
Single
22 October 1915   28th (Reserve) Battalion (University & Public Schools), Royal Fusiliers (City of London Regiment)
transferred to 104th Training Reserve Battalion
and 53rd Young Soldier Battalion, Royal Fusiliers (City of London Regiment)
England and Scotland   1915 to 1919
Lance Corporal May 1916
Discharged   1 February 1919

HARNETT, Dorothea Kate
Otteridge House
Parents Frank and Kate Harnett (née Furber)
Single
4 August 1917   Queen Mary's Army Auxiliary Corps   Driver
Posted overseas   13 January 1918 to August 1919

Dorothea was one of the first girls from Bearsted to volunteer for military service.

HARNETT, Frank Furber Erskine
Otteridge House
Parents Frank and Kate Harnett (née Furber)
Single
4 November 1914   2/5th Battalion, Queen's (Royal West Surrey Regiment), Territorial Force   Private
Commissioned Second Lieutenant 11 August 1915, 9th (Service) Battalion, The Queen's Own (Royal West Kent Regiment)
Posted overseas   31 May 1916
Lieutenant 10 September 1916
178 Trench M Battery
France and Belgium   May 1916 to November 1917
Italy   November 1917 to February 1918
France   February 1918 to February 1919
Germany   February 1919
Somme 1916, Passchendaele 1917, Kemmel Hill 1918

Below and on the next page is a transcript of the report from The South Eastern Gazette, 29 August 1916:

FOR KING AND COUNTRY

Mr and Mrs F E D Harnett of Otteridge House, Bearsted, have two sons, patriotically serving King and Country. Second Lieu. Frank Furber Erskine Harnett, the elder son, will be 20 years of age next October. He was educated at Maidstone Grammar School where he was in the Officers Training Corps.

Frank F. E. Harnett

At the time war broke out, he was a pupil in a nursery business at Woking. He was prompt to answer the call of patriotism and in September joined the 2/5th Queen's West Surrey Regiment. He received his first training at Windsor and then came to Tunbridge Wells at the latter place he was recommended for a commission, and on August 11th, 1915, was gazetted to the 9th Battalion Royal West Kent Regiment, then at Shoreham, Sussex. He made a speciality in signalling and passed top in the Morse code.

He was then sent to Tilbury as an instructor. In May of this year he went to the Front, being attached to another Battalion of the Royal West Kent Regiment. After a good deal of experience of trenches and wire entanglements he took a course in the use of trench mortars and is now attached to a Trench Mortar Battery

Arthur N. Harnett

Arthur Norman Harnett, second son of Mr and Mrs Harnett, attained his 17th birthday only last May, yet he is but one inch short of six feet in stature. Like his elder brother, he was educated at Maidstone Grammar School and was also in the O.T.C. there. He held Corporal's stripes and was solo bugler in the band. In October of last year he found the lure of military service too strong to resist and straightaway offered himself for the Public Schools Battalion (Royal Fusiliers) at Epsom, and was accepted. For about four months he was at Oxford, and was ready for the Front when the order came that he was to go to Edinburgh instead. He is now stationed at Holyrood, and though disappointed at not being in the firing line, is content with the duties allotted to him, as every good solider should be. At school, young Harnett won the Monckton Swimming Cup three times. He was only twelve when he secured the trophy for the first time, being the youngest boy who had ever proved successful.

Reproduced courtesy of Kent Messenger newspaper group

HAYDN, ------
In July 1917, it was reported in the parish magazine[1] that Private Haydn was on board the ship *Tyndareus* when it was sunk, but he was saved.

HAYES-SADLER, Walter
Friningham Lodge
Parents Colonel James Hayes-Sadler KCMG and Sophia Jane (née Taylor)
Single
Army
Home Service Reserve of Officers, Western Approaches Training Instructors Depot

HAZELDEN, Basil
Crismill Farm
Single
11 October 1912 1st Household Cavalry, Field Ambulance, Territorial Force, Royal Army Medical Corps
August 1914 81st Field Ambulance, 27th Division
Service Number 493083
Posted overseas 21 December 1914
Belgium and France December 1914 to November 1915
Macedonia December 1915 to January 1919
Caucasus January to June 1919
Second Battle of Ypres 1915, Vardar, Struma
Demobilised 7 July 1919

HEPDEN, George
Parsonage Farm
Married
10 December 1915 Suffolk Regiment
transferred 1/8th Battalion, Royal Warwickshire Regiment, Territorial Force 1917
Posted overseas 14 June 1917
France and Belgium June to August 1917
Italy November 1917 to September 1918
France September 1918 to February 1919
Demobilised 16 March 1919

This photograph was taken in 1935:

Reproduced courtesy of Chris and Sue Hunt

HEPTON, George *
Bearsted Spot
Single
Sister Louisa Page of Bearsted Spot
March 1896
Rejoined 19 May 1915 10th Heavy Battery, Royal Garrison Artillery
Service Number 6634
Posted overseas October 1915
Royal Horse Artillery Driver
Serbia, Egypt
Died in hospital 1 July 1917, aged 42, from cancer
Buried in grave D 151, Alexandria (Hadra) War Memorial Cemetery, Egypt

George was born in Otham and enlisted in Maidstone

First World War: 1914 to 1918

HEPTON, John Frank
Bearsted
Parents Frank and Helen Matilda Hepton formerly of Maidstone, now Colchester
Married
1st Battalion, Coldstream Guards
Service Number 16619 Private
Posted overseas 8 June 1916
France June 1916 to September 1917
Died of wounds 22 September 1917, aged 36
Buried in grave VI B 4A, Wimereux Communal Cemetery, Pas de Calais, France

A transcript of the report from the Kent Messenger, 13 October 1917:

**Pte. J. F. Hepton (Maidstone)
Coldstream Guards**

Pte. John Frank Hepton, twin son of Mr and Mrs Frank Hepton, late of Maidstone and Bearsted, now residing at 42 Hythe Hill, Colchester, has died from wounds. He was born in the parish of St Paul's, Maidstone, and started his education under Mr J. B. Groom, finishing under Mr John Day at Bearsted. He then took up a situation with Messrs Leveritt, Frye and Page, where he served for upwards of four years, leaving there for Surbiton. After sixteen years at the latter place with Messrs Williamson and Co. he left to join the 1st Battalion Coldstream Guards, finishing his training at Windsor where on the occasion of the King's visit to the Castle, he was one of the picked men to form 'King's Guard', a fact of which he was very proud. He left Windsor for France on June 8th 1916, and was severely wounded in the head and admitted to hospital on September 18th last, passing away on September 22nd. Taking up the cause of the Church of England Missionary Society, he was an ardent worker in the parish of St Matthew's, Surbiton, where he will be sadly missed. He leaves a widow and two children to mourn their loss.

Reproduced courtesy of Kent Messenger newspaper group

HICKMOTT, Arthur
The Street
Single
24 October 1915 Army Service Corps
Service Number B185514 Private
Egypt, Palestine
Demobilised 21 March 1919

HILLS, Charles Edward
Ty Fry
Parents John and Philadelphia Hills of Friars Place
Single
15 February 1915, Canterbury
Service Number 265379 Acting Corporal
Regimental Number 36802
A Company, Kent Cyclist Battalion, 7th Battalion, 4th Reserve Battalion, The Buffs, East Kent Regiment
British Expeditionary Force, France 26 July 1916 to 15 January 1917
Demobilised 22 February 1919

In December 1916 Charles contracted pneumonia. He was sent to a military hospital in Camiers followed by admittance to United Volunteer Force hospitals in Belfast and Gilford in Craigavon for treatment and recuperation.

Before volunteering to serve in the army, Charles was a landscape gardener and was employed by the General Cemetery Company at Kensal Green.

HIRST, Arthur
Roseacre Terrace
Single
4 January 1917 Inland Waterways and Docks, Royal Engineers
Service Number 321658 Sapper

HODGES, George
Ware Street
Parents Harry and Ellen Hodges
The Queen's Own (Royal West Kent Regiment)

George reached the rank of Sergeant Major in the army and his service included a spell in India. This photograph of George in tropical uniform is undated but was taken during the First World War. Note the long service stripes on his sleeve.

Reproduced courtesy of Jean Jones

First World War: 1914 to 1918

HODGES, Harry
Ware Street
Labour Company

HODGES, Henry
Ware Street
Parents Harry and Ellen Hodges
The Buffs (East Kent Regiment)
Private

Badly gassed and invalided out of the army, Henry returned to Thurnham and assisted his family in running Rosemount Dairy farm, Ware Street. This photograph shows Henry in his uniform.

HODGES, William
The Plantation public house
Wife Emily Sarah
Service Number R2727 Able Seaman
HMS Perham

William was the landlord of The Plantation public house. After his death in 1920 their son, also called William, assisted Emily Sarah to run the business.

HODGES, William Ernest
The Plantation public house
Parents William and Emily Sarah Hodges
Single
West Kent Yeomanry (Queen's Own)
Salonika

This undated photograph shows William Ernest Hodges as a young man:

Both reproduced courtesy of Jean Jones

First World War: 1914 to 1918

HOLMES, George William Verney *†
60 Ware Street
Parents Richard and Lavinia Holmes of Ware Street
Married
Wife Gertrude Cecilia Dorothy (formerly Tolhurst, née Holmes) of Caring Farm, Leeds
Grandfather to Les, Jacqui and Neville
2nd Battalion, The Buffs (East Kent Regiment)
Service Number G/4679
Killed in action 3 May 1915, aged 29
Commemorated Panel 12 and 14, Ypres (Menin Gate) Memorial

Note: the war memorial in St Mary's church gives an incorrect name: George Vernon Holmes

HOLMES, Richard
Army, Royal Defence Corps
Home Service

HOLMWOOD, George Walter
Coldharbour
Service Number 226245 Private
692nd Agricultural Company, Army Service Corps

HOLNESS, Louis
Parents Alfred and Minnie Holness (née Cheeseman)
Army
Western Front

HOLNESS, Percy Henry
Ware Street
Parents Alfred and Minnie Holness (née Cheeseman)
Service Number 63071 Gunner
D Battery, Royal Horse Artillery

A transcript of the report from the Kent Messenger, 31 July 1915:

Gunner P. H. Holness R.H.A

WHO HAS RECEIVED THE RUSSIAN ORDER OF ST. GEORGE

Gunner Percy Henry Holness, eldest son of the late Sergeant Holness of the K.C.C., and of Mrs. Holness, of Ware Street, Thurnham, has been awarded the Russian Order of St. George for bravery in the field. Having been in the R.H.A. for four or five years. Gunner Holness has been at the Front since the outbreak of the war, with the exception of a short break at Christmas. He has been once wounded but has recovered and is again in the trenches.

Reproduced courtesy of Kent Messenger newspaper group

First World War: 1914 to 1918

HOLTUM, Arthur Henry
West Lake, Hastings Road, Maidstone, later Sunnycot, Roseacre Lane
April 1908
Service Number 493007 Sergeant
Territorials, later 81st unit, Field Ambulance, Royal Army Medical Corps
France, Salonika, Balkans, south Russia

Mentioned in Secretary of State's Despatches 1 January 1916, 25 November 1917 and 9 March 1919
Distinguished Conduct Medal 9 March 1919, gazetted 3 June 1919
Territorial Force Efficiency Medal
Serbian Silver Medal for Zealous Service
Serbian Gold Medal for Zealous Service
Demobilised Crystal Palace 4 July 1919

Later, Arthur was a key figure in the Bearsted branch of the British Legion.

HOOD, Victor
1/1st Kent Battalion, Army Cyclist Corps
India

HOPPERTON, William Angus
Thurnham Mill
Single
31 March 1915
Service Number G/12276
10th (Service) (Kent County) Battalion, The Queen's Own (Royal West Kent Regiment)

HOWELL, William
Royal Navy
HMS Inflexible

HUMPHREY, Charles Thomas
Army
Western Front

HUMPHREY, George
Army
Western Front

HUMPHREY, Leonard George
Ware Street
Single
Parents George and Mary Humphrey (née Farewell) of Ware Street
2 November 1914
Service Number 2526
Field Ambulance, Royal Army Medical Corps

Leonard was discharged from service as medically unfit but of good character, 13 March 1915

HUMPHREY, Percy
Parents George and Mary Humphrey (née Farewell) of Ware Street
Army
Western Front

First World War: 1914 to 1918

HUMPHREYS, Alfred
Roseacre Terrace
Married
Rejoined 6 October 1914 9th (Reserve) Battalion, The Buffs (East Kent Regiment)
later 3rd (Reserve) Battalion, The Buffs (East Kent Regiment)
Service Number S720 Sergeant

HUNT, Alfred George
Roseacre
Single
11 December 1915 The Queen's Own (Royal West Kent Regiment) later Essex Regiment
Service Number 201586 Private
Egypt July 1916 to April 1919
Palestine 1919
Sudan, Gaza, Jerusalem
Military Medal 1917
Demobilised 15 September 1919

A transcript of the report from the Kent Messenger, 23 June 1917:

Pte. Alfred G. Hunt (Boxley) Royal West Kent Regiment

AWARDED THE MILITARY MEDAL

Pte. Hunt, who is a son of Mr and Mrs W. Hunt of Boxley, has been awarded the Military Medal in Egypt.

Reproduced courtesy of Kent Messenger newspaper group

HUNT, Edward Springfield
Roseacre
Devonshire Regiment
Private

HUNT, George
Ashford Road
Single
1914 18th (Western Ontario) Battalion, Canadian Infantry
France September 1915
Wounded and invalided back to Canada November 1917

HUNT, George
Ivy Cottage
Parents Alfred and Emma Hunt
9 December 1915 West Kent Yeomanry (Queen's Own)
Service Number 528454 Private
273rd Agricultural Company, Army Service Corps

George was exceptionally skilled with horses. During the war, the army put him in charge of two stallions that were on a stud circuit in Kent, Essex and Sussex. He used the stallions to produce a bloodline of horses that were suitable for the war effort.

First World War: 1914 to 1918

HUNT, Herbert William
Parsonage Farm
Married
December 1917 Canadian Reserve Battalion
Posted overseas 26 March 1918

HUNT, Leonard Robert
Ashford Road
Mother Mrs E Hunt
Single
20 April 1915 35th Battalion, Canadian Infantry
France March 1916
Invalided back to Canada 1917

Leonard had emigrated but joined the Canadian Overseas Expeditionary Force

HUNT, Raymond James
5 Fancy Row Cottages, later Parsonage Farm
Married
Wife Violet Emma (née Wanfor)
7 July 1916
5 May 1917 Lance Corporal
Service Numbers 46632 and 177124
1st and 53rd Works Companies of Royal Fusiliers, 328th Home Service Works Company, Labour Corps
Discharged 12 February 1919, Crystal Palace

HUNT, William
Ivy Cottage
Parents Alfred and Emma Hunt
March 1915 Mechanical Transport, Army Service Corps,
            24th Division
Posted overseas 1 September 1915

This photograph of William is undated:

Reproduced courtesy of Chris and Sue Hunt

HUTCHINS, Walter Martin
Royal Field Artillery and Royal Naval Air Service
Home Service

HUTCHINSON, Alfred Thomas
Fauchons Farm
Single
October 1915 72nd Field Company, Royal Engineers Driver
Mesopotamia 1916 to 1919
Kut, Baghdad, Persia, Caucasus
Demobilised 1 September 1919

HUTCHINSON, Helen May
Fauchons Farm
Single
29 June 1917 Queen Mary's Army Auxiliary Corps
Posted overseas 15 January 1918
France January 1918 to February 1919
Gassed and then discharged 15 February 1919

HUTCHINSON, Walter Edward Arthur
Fauchons Farm
Single
6 May 1915 Queen's (Royal West Surrey Regiment)
Posted overseas 22 September 1915
France 1915 to 1918
Wounded 11 October 1918
Lance Corporal 5 June 1919
Discharged 28 June 1919

HYDE, Sydney Philip *
Acacia Villas, Willington Road
Father Robert Lough Hyde
Single
December 1914 1st Battalion, The Queen's Own (Royal West Kent Regiment)
Service number G/5024 Private
Posted overseas 22 April 1915
France and Belgium April to May 1915
Killed in action Voormezeele 30 May 1915, aged 23
Buried in grave I A 10, Voormezeele Enclosures No 1 and No 2, Ieper, West Vlaanderen, Belgium

Sydney was born in Gravesend and enlisted in Bromley.

JAMES, Richard
Oliver's Row
Married
Volunteer Training Corps later 2nd Volunteer Brigade, Royal West Kent

JACKSON, Claud
Mote Hall
Single
Army Service Corps
Captain
Lieutenant 65th Training Squadron
Later Royal Air Force

First World War: 1914 to 1918

JEFFREY, William Ernest *
6 Invicta Villas, The Green
Parents Edward and Mary Risely Jeffrey of 6 Invicta Villas
Single
10 August 1914 2nd Battalion, Queen's (Royal West Surrey Regiment)
Service Number G/211 Private
France August 1915 to September 1917
Loos, Somme, Ypres
Missing, presumed killed in action, 25 September 1917, aged 26
Commemorated Panel 14-17 or 162-162a, Tyne Cot Memorial, Zonnebeke, West Vlaanderen, Belgium

A transcript of the report from the Kent Messenger, 24 November 1917:

Information Wanted

Pte. W. E. Jeffrey (Bearsted) Queen's Surrey Regiment

REPORTED MISSING

Mr and Mrs Jeffery, of 6 Invicta Villas, Bearsted, have received official news that their son, Pte. W. E Jeffrey, Queen's R.W. Surrey Regiment, was reported missing, 25th September. If any of his chums could give them any further information, they would be very grateful. He enlisted on August 10th, 1914, up to which he was a male attendant at Farnham Workhouse, Surrey.

Reproduced courtesy of Kent Messenger newspaper group

JENNER, Harold *
Mote Lodge, School Lane, Maidstone
Parents Herbert W and Edith A Jenner of North Lodge, Mote Park
Single
11 August 1915 123rd Field Company, Royal Engineers
Service Number 38841 Driver
Posted overseas 16 March 1916
France and Belgium March 1916 to July 1917
Killed in action Yser Canal 31 July 1917, aged 20
Buried in grave I M 26, Bard Cottage Cemetery, Ieper, West Vlaanderen, Belgium
Harold is also commemorated on the war memorial plaque at St Nicholas church, Otham.

JENNER, Percy Leonard *
Mote Lodge, School Lane, Maidstone
Parents Herbert W and Edith A Jenner of North Lodge, Mote Park
Married
Wife Eunice Alice of Bridge Lodge, Mote Park
5 December 1916 594th Mechanical Transport Company, Army Service Corps attached to X Corps Heavy Artillery later attached 228th Siege Battery
Service Number 273355 Private
Posted overseas 16 January 1917
France and Belgium
Zillebeke
Killed in action 23 September 1917, aged 22
Buried in grave I O 5, Spoilbank Cemetery, Ieper, West Vlaanderen, Belgium
Percy is also commemorated on the war memorial plaque at St Nicholas church, Otham.

First World War: 1914 to 1918

Below is a transcript of a report from the Kent Messenger, 27 October 1917, concerning Percy and Harold Jenner:

Pte. P. L. Jenner (Maidstone)
A.S.C. (M.T.)

KILLED IN ACTION

Mrs Jenner, of the Lodge, Ashford Road, Maidstone, has had the distressing experience of having lost two sons in the war in two months, viz: Pte. P. L. Jenner, A.S.C. (M.T.) on September 23rd, and Pte. H. Jenner, R.E. (Transport Section) on July 31st. Pte. P. L. Jenner joined the Forces on December 5th, 1916, and went to France January 26th. He was employed for several years before by Messrs. G. E. Wakefield and Sons before enlisting, and formerly lived at 13, Brunswick Street East. He was 22 years of age and leaves a widow and one child. His Lieutenant, who has been invalided home, in a letter expressing his sympathy with the relatives says of the deceased: "I was as attached to him as much as it is possible for an officer to be attached to one of his men...He was one of the best men I had - always reliable and keen - so much so that I had intended making him a corporal directly an opportunity occurred. If I can be of service to you in any way I sincerely trust you will not hesitate to count me your friend." Private Jenner's particular friend, who was with him, also writes a touching letter. He was with the deceased when he met his death, which was instantaneous. "I picked him up and took him to the nearest dressing station as quickly as possible," says the writer, "but they could only tell me what I knew. He was a good lad, well liked by everyone in the column."

Driver, H. Jenner (Maidstone)
Royal Engineers

KILLED IN ACTION

Driver Harold Jenner was the youngest son. He enlisted August 11th, 1915, and went to France seven months later, being killed on July 31st of this year. He was formerly employed by Mr. Woolley, of Pudding Lane, and was 20 years of age. It is believed he is laid to rest in the same cemetery as his brother. His Captain has written expressing his deepest sympathy with the mother and saying: "Your son was always willing to do his utmost, and I feel that the company has lost a willing worker." His Sergeant, in a letter of consolation, says: "It happened whilst taking up stores the morning of an attack. He was struck by a piece of shell and death was instantaneous – pain was entirely absent." "Words at this juncture," adds the Sergeant, "are but empty symbols, but it is the wish of all the boys (poor Harold's colleagues) that I should convey to you their individual sympathies, for your son had endeared himself to each of us. He was always cheery - and after all, it is sometimes difficult to be cheery out here - and could be relied on to do everything to the best of his ability. He was indeed the type of lad we could ill afford to lose."

Reproduced courtesy of Kent Messenger newspaper group

First World War: 1914 to 1918

JORDAN, Charles Edward
Byfrance, Otham Lane
Single
August 1916 Royal Field Artillery France

JORDAN, Robert James
Byfrance, Otham Lane
Single
25 October 1915 71st Field Company, Royal Engineers
Service Number 136688 Driver
Posted overseas 12 May 1916
Mesopotamia April 1916 to February 1919
India February to March 1919
Kut Relief Force 1916 to 1917, Capture of Baghdad, Kifri 1917, Kirkuk 1918
Discharged 28 April 1919

JURY, Horace Henry
Black Horse Inn
Married
Wife: Louisa Olive (née Hughes)
The Queen's Own (Royal West Kent Regiment)
Service Number G690 Colour Sergeant, Warrant Officer Class 2
Recalled 1914 Drill Instructor, Maidstone Depot of the Royal West Kent Regiment
24 September 1914, Acting Company Sergeant Major; later Company Sergeant Major
Discharged 10 May 1919

Horace had originally served in the Royal West Kent Regiment from 1891 as a professional soldier, Service Number 3050. His military campaigns included Egypt, South Africa, the North West Frontier in India, Ceylon and China. Louisa his fiancée, travelled out to Ceylon and they were married there. Later, their first child was born in China. By 1914, the family had returned and Horace was the landlord of the Black Horse public house. At the outbreak of hostilities, he was recalled to military duties.

KEMSLEY, George Alfred William
The Royal Oak
Motor Mechanic
HMS Vanguard

KITCHENHAM, Henry John
Binbury Cottage
Grenadier Guards
Service Number 25634 Private

KITNEY, Fred
Army
Western Front

KITNEY, Samuel
Army
Western Front

KNIGHT, Howard John
The Green
Army

Howard married Edith Annie Jones at Holy Cross on 26 October 1919

First World War: 1914 to 1918

Christmas in War Time

In November 1914, contributions were invited for a Soldiers and Sailors Christmas Gift Fund. The fund was the idea of Princess Mary, the daughter of King George V and Queen Mary. The intention was to provide everyone in the armed forces serving overseas on Christmas Day 1914 with "a gift from the nation". The contents varied but this box contained tobacco, cigarettes and some chocolate, together with a greetings card and photograph of Princess Mary. The design of the box lid shows the head of the princess and her monogram:

Reproduced courtesy of Malcolm Kersey

During December 1914, there was a dilemma within many families with members serving in the armed forces: was it patriotic or appropriate to celebrate Christmas? One local store offered a practical solution, as shown in this advertisement, Kent Messenger, 12 December:

In 1915, many clubs that supported the armed forces, arranged collections of donated items for Christmas gift parcels containing 'home comforts'. These included tobacco, cigarettes, chocolate, knitted socks and balaclavas, which were sent to men serving at the front. There is no mention about the collection in the log books for Bearsted School, but the certificate reproduced below records a donation made by Sidney Hunt:

Reproduced courtesy of Kent Messenger newspaper group

Reproduced courtesy of Chris and Sue Hunt

60

First World War: 1914 to 1918

LEIGH, ------

LENOISE, Vivian
Roseacre
Service Number M7373
Royal Navy, *HMS Pembroke II*

LIDYARD, John Robert
The Street
Married
18 June 1917 Mechanical Transport, Army Service Corps
France July 1917

LISSENDEN, Anthony John
The Street
1st Battalion, The Buffs (East Kent Regiment)
Service Number 4825 Private

LUSHINGTON, Godfrey Lionel Law
Cobham House
1st Battalion, The Buffs (East Kent Regiment)
Lieutenant

LUSHINGTON, Lionel Edward Law
Married
Wife Ada (née Merriman)
Children Betty Mary and Joan Christian
Lieutenant Colonel
Recruiting Officer Labour Corps and Agricultural Commandant, Maidstone, 1915 to 1918

MACE, Leonard
Church Cottages
Married
Wife Frances Mary (née Rose)
Service Number 92417 Driver
68th Field Company, Royal Engineers

Leonard and Mary married at Holy Cross church, 24 February 1916

MacONEGAL, Roy
Orchards, Landway
Royal Flying Corps

MACQUEEN, Ronald Brodie
Little Milgate
Single
April 1918 Indian Army from Royal Military College, Sandhurst Second Lieutenant
India, North West Frontier 1919
Lieutenant 24 April 1919
Afghan War 1918 to 1919, Musa Khel
Mentioned in Secretary of State's Despatches

First World War: 1914 to 1918

MACQUEEN, William James
Little Milgate
Married
1886 Alexandra, Princess of Wales's Own (Yorkshire Regiment)
Major, British South African Police
Matabele War, Mashonaland Rebellion 1896 to 1897, South African War 1899 to 1902
Retired March 1914
Rejoined 16 October 1914
18th (Service) Battalion (1st Public Schools), Royal Fusiliers (City of London Regiment)
transferred to 150th Reserve Company, Royal Defence Corps 1 May 1916
England October 1914 to April 1919
Demobilised 16 April 1919

MANKELOW, Edgar
Willows Cottage, Chapel Lane
Service Number TR 13/77818 Company Sergeant Major
52nd Graduated Battalion, Rifle Brigade (The Prince Consort's Own)

MANNERINGS, Charles
The Street
Married
September 1917 Royal Field Artillery Driver
France, Italy, Belgium
Demobilised December 1918

MANNERINGS, Edgar *
The Street
Parents John and Malvina A Mannerings of The Street
Single
7 December 1917 4th Battalion, Northamptonshire Regiment, Territorial Force
transferred 1st Battalion, Norfolk Regiment
Service Number 41503 Private
Posted overseas 15 May 1918
Killed in action Beugny 2 September 1918, aged 18
Commemorated Panel 4, Vis-en Artois Memorial, Pas de Calais, France

Edgar was one of six sons that served in the army. His parents received a letter of congratulations from the King for this achievement. He enlisted in Maidstone.

MANNERINGS, George
The Street
Married
September 1914 Army Service Corps Driver
Sergeant
Salonika 1916

MANNERINGS, Harry
The Street
Married
September 1914 11th (Service) Battalion, Durham Light Infantry
Sergeant
France August 1915
Wounded 1916
Invalided out 1917

First World War: 1914 to 1918

MANNERINGS, John Anthony
Oliver's Row
Married
25 January 1904 Army Service Corps
Service Number T21788 Driver
later 528th Company, Army Service Corps
Posted overseas 9 August 1914
France and Belgium August 1914 to December 1918
Germany December 1918 to June 1919
Mons, La Cateau, Ypres, Somme, Marne, Lens, Arras, Cambrai, Maubeuge
Military Medal
Demobilised 10 June 1919

MANNERINGS, Sidney
The Street
Single
23 November 1914 Horse Transport, Army Service Corps, 10th Division Farrier
Posted overseas 1 March 1915
Egypt March to October 1915
Salonika October 1915 to March 1918
France October 1918 to March 1919
Serbian Retreat, Dorian, Vardar
Invalided 1 March 1919

MANNERINGS, Thomas
The Street
Single
March 1907 2nd Battalion, The Queen's Own (Royal West Kent Regiment)
India 1909 to 1914
Mesopotamia 1916 to 1919
North West Frontier 1919
Meritorious Service Medal

MANSFIELD, Frederick
Chapel Lane
Service Number W R/10314
Pioneer 332nd Road Corps Company, Royal Engineers

MANSFIELD, George
2 Chapel Lane
13th (Transport Workers) Battalion, Bedfordshire Regiment
Service Number 39281 Private

MARSHAM, Francis William Bullock
Bearsted Court
Single
1911 19th (Queen Alexandra's Own Royal) Hussars
Captain
France September 1914 to February 1919
Military Cross (London Gazette, June 1916), Distinguished Service Order (London Gazette, June 1918)
Twice mentioned in Secretary of State's Despatches

MARTIN, James William

First World War: 1914 to 1918

MAXTED, William Sutton
Crismill
Single
25 October 1915 Royal Field Artillery
1917 2/1st Battalion, Warwickshire Royal Horse Artillery Second Lieutenant
Lieutenant

William was usually called Sutton. This photograph of Sutton was taken in 1935:

Reproduced courtesy of Chris and Sue Hunt

In 1918 he sent this postcard of Mons to his mother. Note that the message had to be passed by the censor even though it was written after the Armistice.

30/11/18

No letter again today. I hope you're well. My hand is going on alright. Quite well fondest love. Hope to write letter tomorrow.

Sutton

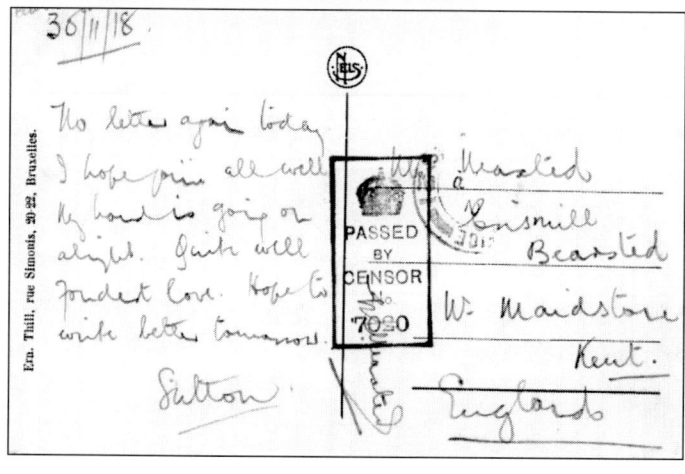

Both reproduced courtesy of Malcolm Kersey

64

First World War: 1914 to 1918

MEDHURST, John Alfred
Parents James and Rachel Medhurst of The Lord Raglan, Slade Green, Erith
1st Battalion, The Buffs (East Kent Regiment)
Service Number G/10572
Killed in action 19 June 1915, aged 19
Buried in grave B10, Potijze Chateau Wood Cemetery, Ieper, West Vlaanderen, Belgium

From the Kent Messenger, 30 June 1917:

For King and Country

IN MEMORIAM

> MEDHURST - In ever loving memory of our dear son, Pte. John Alfred Medhurst, the Buffs, who was killed in action by a shell on June 19th, 1915, son of Mr and Mrs J Medhurst of Lord Raglan, Slade Green, late of Bearsted
>
> Sick, dying, in a foreign land
> No father by to take his hand,
> No mother near to close his eyes,
> Far from his native land he lies.

Reproduced courtesy of Kent Messenger newspaper group

MELLOR, Harold
Roseacre Terrace
Single
8 July 1913 Royal Navy
HMS Victorious and *HMS Cedric*
Ordinary Seaman on *HMS Lightfoot*
Able Bodied Seaman on *HMS Waterhen*
Battle of Jutland

MELLOR, Robert *
Roseacre Terrace
Parents Fanny Mellor of 3 Crisfield Cottages and the late William Mellor
Single
3 November 1914, Maidstone 83rd Field Ambulance, Royal Army Medical Corps, 27th Division
Service Number 497639 Private
Posted overseas 25 December 1914
France December 1914 to December 1915
Salonika December 1915
Lost at Sea in Mediterranean 21 February 1917 aged 23
Commemorated Mikra Memorial, Kalamaria, Greece

Robert was lost at sea when Fleet Messenger *SS Princess Alberta* was sunk in Mudros Bay in the Aegean Sea by a mine laid by the German submarine *U-23* while on a voyage from Styros Island to Mudros.

First World War: 1914 to 1918

MESSAGE, Frederick Christian *
Single
24 February 1916 7th (Service) Battalion, The Queen's Own (Royal West Kent Regiment)
Service Number G/12309 Private
Posted overseas 4 July 1916
France July to September 1916
Killed in action Thiepval 29 September 1916
Buried in grave I A 19, Mill Road Cemetery Thiepval, Somme, France

Frederick was born in Yalding and enlisted in Maidstone.

A transcript of the report from the Kent Messenger, 11 Nov 1916

Pte. F.C. Message (Bearsted) Royal West Kent Regiment

KILLED IN ACTION

No 12309 Pte. F. C. Message, Royal West Kents, eldest son of Mr and Mrs Message, of Rose Acre, Bearsted, aged 20, was killed in action, September 29th. He joined up in February 1916 and went out to France, July 4th, being transferred to the 7th Battalion. Should any of his comrades see this, who saw him at the last, news would be most gratefully received by his mother and dad.

Reproduced courtesy of Kent Messenger newspaper group

MESSAGE, Harry Thomas
Roseacre
Single
21 April 1915 2/1 Household Cavalry Field Ambulance
transferred 54th Field Ambulance 1917
Posted overseas 1 January 1917
France January 1917 to July 1919
Beaulincourt, Ypres, Passchendaele, Vimy Ridge, Trones Wood
Wounded September 1918
Demobilised 7 July 1919

MITCHELL, Ernest George
Howe Court
Service Number 47385 Gunner
Royal Garrison Artillery

MITCHELL, Lewis
Milgate Park
Single
25 October 1915 Royal Field Artillery

MITCHELL, William Gordon
The Green
Married
20 September 1915 Royal Army Veterinary Corps
Service Number 1385 Sergeant
TTO 67th Ammunition Column, Royal Field Artillery
North Russia October 1918 to August 1919
Demobilised September 26 1919

MOON, Edmund
The Street
Single
Parents Alfred and Eliza Moon
19 October 1916 3/4th Battalion, Queen's (Royal West Surrey Regiment), Territorial Force
Service Number 202852 Private
Posted overseas 30 May 1917 France
Severely wounded August 1917
Invalided 14 December 1918

This photograph shows Edmund whilst undergoing rehabilitation for injuries received during the war when a shell exploded nearby. He is wearing a uniform that became known as 'hospital blues':

Reproduced courtesy of John Mills

MOON, Frederick William
Colegate Cottages
Single
6 January 1915 Army Service Corps attached to 76th Brigade, Royal Field Artillery
Service Number 041194 Private
463rd Company Army Service Company
Posted overseas 29 July 1915

First World War: 1914 to 1918

MOORE, Thomas
Crisfield Cottages
Married
September 1914 8th (Service) Battalion, The Queen's Own (Royal West Kent Regiment)
Service Number 718 Private
Posted overseas 30 September 1915

MORGAN, Arthur
Thurnham
Service Number 13055 Private
426th Agricultural Company, Army Service Corps

MOSS, William Joseph
Ivy Dene, Thurnham Lane
Royal Flying Corps

NAYLOR, Frederick
The Street
Single
June 1918 52nd Graduated Battalion, Duke of Cambridge's Own (Middlesex Regiment)
Signaller
Germany 1919

OTTAWAY, Alfred George
Friningham
Service Number 107948 Private
50th Battalion, Machine Gun Corps

OVENDEN, ------
Romney's Hill
Single
Women's Army Auxiliary Corps

OVENDEN, Arthur George
Romney's Hill
Single
1 March 1915 11th Canadian Mounted Regiment
Wounded
Invalided to Canada 1918

OVENDEN, George
The Homestead, Romney's Hill
Married
London Air Defences 1917, London Electrical Engineers
28 June 1917 22nd Company, Royal Engineers
Service Number 299813 Sapper
Posted overseas 28 July 1918
France July 1918 to March 1919
Demobilised 16 April 1919

This photograph of George was taken in 1935:

Reproduced courtesy of Chris and Sue Hunt

First World War: 1914 to 1918

OVENDEN, Herbert
Romney's Hill
Single
19 September 1914 West Kent Yeomanry (Queen's Own)
Prisoner of War 1918

OVENDEN, John
Romney's Hill
Married
5 April 1918 Royal Marine Engineers Sapper
Demobilised 25 November 1918

PAGE, Albert William *
Bearsted Spot
Single
Parents Albert and Louisa (née Hepton) of Bearsted Spot
14 June 1915 The Queen's Own (Royal West Kent Regiment)
Service Number 8513 Private
Posted overseas 6 January 1917 France
Died of wounds 16 September 1917, aged 18
Buried in grave G VI A 28, Duisans British Cemetery Etrun, Pas de Calais, France

Note: Louisa also lost a brother during the war - see the entry for **HEPTON, George**.

A transcript of the report from the Kent Messenger, 22 September 1917:

BEARSTED

SAD NEWS - Mr Albert Page, of Bearsted Spot, who has worked at Messrs Fremlin's Brewery, Maidstone for many years, received news early this week that his son, Pte. Bert Page, Royal West Kent Regiment, formerly a servant in the household of Sir Reginald MacLeod at Vinters Park, has been badly wounded. The family were expecting him on Wednesday but instead of his arrival they had the sad intelligence that the poor lad, who was only about 19, had succumbed. Much sympathy goes out to the bereaved family.

Reproduced courtesy of Kent Messenger newspaper group

PAGE, Alfred
Acacia Villas, Willington Road
Single
March 1915 12th Labour Company, Army Service Corps
Lance Corporal
Posted overseas March 1915

Women's Land Army

By 1917, food shortages became a distinct possibility so the government, decided to increase the cultivation of food crops. War Agricultural Committees were set up on a local basis and were directed to maximise the potential of farms and other areas of land, having powers to compel landowners to undertake cultivation. Waste ground and gardens were turned into allotments and poultry was kept wherever there was space. Over two and half million acres of land was taken into agricultural use, and by the end of the war, Britain had an extra three million acres of farming land.[2]

Agriculture was regarded as a 'reserved occupation' and therefore farm labourers were exempt from conscription but men volunteered to serve in the armed forces anyway. Farming was still labour-intensive and largely powered by horses although some routine tasks were mechanised. There was a shortfall in the number of people working on the land so it was decided that women might be called up to fill the gap. The work force became known as the Women's Land Army or 'Land Girls' and a practical uniform was devised of white smocks, breeches and gaiters. The women undertook all the jobs required on a farm and this included threshing, ploughing, tractor driving, land reclamation and drainage.[3]

There was an agreed maximum working week; 50 hours in the summer and 48 hours in the winter. A normal week would comprise five and a half days but did not include Saturday afternoon and Sunday. However during busy times such as lambing or harvest time, many girls worked all day and easily exceeded their 50 hour week.[4]

Reproduced courtesy of Malcolm Kersey

The pay for the Women's Land Army was set by the Agricultural Wages Board: for girls aged over 18 the wages were £1 12d a week (after deductions for food and lodgings). All girls who were posted more than twenty miles away from home would also receive a warrant for a free rail trip to enable them to visit their home once every six months.

By 1918, it was estimated that over two hundred Land Girls were working on the land in Kent and East Sussex.[5] This undated photograph shows some of them working at Chapel Lane farm:

Reproduced courtesy of Tony and Sheila Foster

Such was the success of the scheme that at the outbreak of the Second World War, Britain resurrected it and girls once more worked on the land and in the woods to great effect.

First World War: 1914 to 1918

PAGE, Thomas Frank
Acacia Villas, Willington Road
Single
9 October 1916
Royal Navy
HMS Juno
Service Number K36933 Stoker 2nd Class
Demobilised June 1919

PANKHURST, Bernard William
North Gate, Friningham
Service Number SS 1011 Sergeant
Royal Army Service Corps

PANKHURST, Edwin George
Single
12 August 1914
Service Number M/23340
Sergeant
1st Brigade Motorised Torpedo Boat, Royal Army Service Corps

PANKHURST, William John
Red Lodge, Friningham
Service Number 68651 Private
24th (Service) Battalion (2nd Sportsman's), Royal Fusiliers (City of London Regiment)

PARKES, Charles David
Parsonage Farm
Married
3 November 1904 14th (King's) Hussars also 20th Hussars
Posted overseas 12 August 1914
France and Belgium 1914 to 1915
Mons, Marne
Wounded
Invalided out 9 April 1916

PAULL, John
Shaw's Cottages
Single
13 October 1915 Army Ordnance Corps
Posted overseas 18 May 1916
Salonika May 1916
Demobilised 14 August 1919

PEARSON, Walter
Rosemount
Married
Wife Emma Kathleen (née Swift)
Lieutenant Royal Army Medical Corps

Walter married Emma on 12 February 1916; she was serving as an Army Nursing Sister.

PENDRY, Josiah

First World War: 1914 to 1918

PENFOLD, George Henry †
Station House, Bearsted and Thurnham railway station, Ware Street
Father George Penfold of Southborough
Married
Wife Kathleen Agate
Royal Navy *HMS Hawke*
Service Number 164841 Chief Petty Officer
Killed 15 October 1914, aged 37
Commemorated Panel 1 Column 2, Chatham Naval Memorial

HMS Hawke was a cruiser built at Chatham Dockyard and launched in 1891. It was torpedoed and sunk by U-boat *U.9* in the North Sea on 15 October 1914.

PERRIN, Albert Sidney
Woodbury
Married
Volunteer Training Corps later 2nd Volunteer Brigade, Royal West Kent

PILE, Stephen
The Buffs, East Kent Regiment

PLAYFOOT, Frederick
Triangle Cottage
Single
April 1902 Royal Navy Petty Officer
HMS Vanguard

PLAYFOOT, George
Invicta Villas
Married
Suffolk Regiment

PLUMMER, Clarence
Service Number 19202
Driver Royal Field Artillery
France 1915

POLLARD, Arthur
Invicta Villas
Single
12 December 1914 Army Service Corps
Service Number S 4/036160 Corporal
24th Lines of Communication (Supply) Company
Egypt September 1915
Demobilised 7 July 1919

POLLARD, Charles
Invicta Villas
Single
14 December 1914 Royal Engineers Driver
Posted overseas September 1915

First World War: 1914 to 1918

POLLARD, Frederick
Invicta Villas
Single
10 December 1914 Army Service Corps
Service Number A202195 Driver
12th (County of London) Battalion, London Regiment (The Rangers), Territorial Force
also attached to 1st Battalion, Prince Albert's (Somerset Light Infantry)
Posted overseas 10 December 1914

POLLARD, James Edwin
Aldington Cottages
Service Number 496646 Private
697th Agricultural Company, Army Service Corps

POLLARD, Leonard
Invicta Villas
Single
10 December 1914 Army Service Corps Driver
Service Number T3 029142 Private
Posted overseas December 1914
Demobilised 28 April 1919

POLLARD, Percy
Invicta Villas
Single
9 November 1915 Army Service Corps
Service Number 145661 Driver
Posted overseas January 1916

POLLARD, Victor
Invicta Villas
Single
November 1915 Mechanical Transport, Army Service Corps
Service Number 148862
Salonika

POTTER, Harry
Romney's Hill
Married
15 November 1915 Mechanical Transport, Army Service Corps
Staff Car Driver General Headquarters and III Corps Headquarters
France and Belgium August 1916 to 1919
Cambrai, St Quentin, La Fere, Amiens, Lille, Albert, Tournai
Demobilised August 1919

POULTENEY, ------
Roseacre
Married

POUND, Henry Samuel
Ware Street
1st Battalion, King's Royal Rifle Corps

First World War: 1914 to 1918

PRESLAND, Thomas
5 Mote Hall Villas
Widower
February 1886 Royal Navy Able Seaman
Royal Fleet Reserve 1903 to 1914
Rejoined 2 August 1914
Service Number 136322 Able Seaman
HMS Victorious
North Sea 1914 to 1915
Admiralty Office Chatham April 1915 to February 1919
Demobilised 16 February 1919

PRESLAND, Thomas
Mote Villas
Single
March 1918 Royal Navy Armoury Mate
HMS Dragon 1919

RAGGETT, Herbert Edward
The Green
Married
July 1917 1/14th (County of London) Battalion, London Regiment (London Scottish), Territorial Force
later 697th Labour Company
Service Number 517070 Private
France November 1917 to April 1918
Cambrai, Oppywood
Gassed
Demobilised 15 September 1919

READY, Michael
Crisfield Cottage
Service Number 66396 Private
186th Labour Company

The Blue Cross Charity

During the war countless animals were deployed in the conflict and became casualties alongside the armed forces. Amongst those which assisted animals affected by war was the Blue Cross Charity, originally founded in 1897 as Our Dumb Friends League. This advertisement for the charity appeared in The War Budget, published by the Daily Chronicle, in 1915:

Reproduced courtesy of Roger Vidler

First World War: 1914 to 1918

RICE, Frank
Triangle Cottages
Single
Parents William and Martha Rice
7 October 1916 2/6th (Cyclist) Battalion, Suffolk Regiment, Territorial Force
Service Number 265815 Private
Lance Corporal

RICE, George
Triangle Cottages
Married
August 1914 24th (County of London) Battalion, London Regiment (The Queen's), Territorial Force
Transport

RICE, Thomas Merrall
Triangle Cottages
Parents William and Martha Rice of Triangle Cottages
Married 17 June 1916
Wife   Annie Elizabeth Jane (née Rix),
          1 Willenhall Road, Plumstead and 4 Locket Road, Wealdstone, Harrow
Son Albert Thomas
1 November 1916
14th (County of London) Battalion, London Regiment (London Scottish), Territorial Force
Service Number 514487 Private
Gassed
Died 15 January 1920, aged 26
Buried in north west corner of Holy Cross churchyard

In 1917 Thomas sent this postcard to Annie. The message reads:

> 1st Battalion London Scottish
> No 78 B D 14th Camp
> B E F France
>
> Darling One
> Arrived quite safe Wednesday morning, shall be at the above address for a week or two, will send a letter tomorrow, hope both baby and your dear self are keeping well, felt a bit tired today took us four hours to get here
> From your loving husband
> Tom

Reproduced courtesy of Sally Hook and family

First World War: 1914 to 1918

This transcript is a report from the Kent Messenger, 24 January 1920, together with an undated photograph of Thomas wearing the uniform of the 14th London Regiment (London Scottish):

Pte. T. M. Rice (Bearsted)
Late 14th London Scottish

DIED JANUARY 15TH, AGED 26

The village of Bearsted was impressively touched on Monday by the military funeral obsequies which attended the last tokens of respect and honour to Private Thomas Merrall Rice of Triangle Cottages, Bearsted, who passed away at Hollingbourne on Thursday last. The deceased, who was only 26 years of age, was gassed, during the Great War, in which he served with the 14th London Scottish Regiment, and after being demobbed was never able to follow any employment. He was married and leaves a sorrowing widow and one little son.

He was buried near his father, who recently predeceased him, in Bearsted Churchyard. A gun carriage from Chatham conveyed the coffin, covered by a Union Jack and surmounted by deceased's sporran and other military accoutrements and a firing party and a couple of buglers attended from the Maidstone Barracks. The vicar, the Rev F J Blamire Brown conducted the service. There was a large gathering of villagers. After the committal, the impressive sounding of The Last Post by the buglers was followed by the firing of the usual three volleys.

Among those present were - Mrs T M Rice (widow); Mrs W Rice (mother); Messrs H F L A and F Rice (brothers); Miss G Rice and Mrs Hughes (sisters); Mrs Rix (mother in law); Mrs Fred Rix (sister in law); Mr and Mrs William Walkling (uncle and aunt); Mr B Walkling (cousin); Mr Apps, Mrs Rolf, Mr Raggett (late of the London Scottish).

Beautiful floral tributes were sent by; His little son; his loving wife; his loving mother and sister; brother and sister Harry and Ethel; brothers Fred, Frank, Len and Albert, his brothers; Will and Arthur and Hack (abroad); brother Charlie; sister Emma; Mrs Rix; brother in law; brother and sister in law; nephew; brother and sister; Oswald Higgins; Mrs Deakins; Mr C Brooke Wright, (Turkey Court); Miss D Hills; Mr Apps and friends at Hollingbourne; nephews; uncle and aunt and family.

Reproduced courtesy of Kent Messenger newspaper group

Reproduced courtesy of Sally Hook and family

RIXON, Bert
Roundwell
Single
1914 Royal Naval Reserve
HMS Bacchante, *HMS Chester* and *HMS Pembroke*

RIXON, Charles
Roundwell
Married
21 January 1910 The Buffs (East Kent Regiment)
transferred to Machine Gun Corps February 1916
Service Number 28397 Sergeant
Posted overseas 17 March 1916
France March to October 1916
Wounded at Somme 2 October 1916
England December 1916 to March 1919
Invalided out 10 March 1919

First World War: 1914 to 1918

RIXON, Frederick
Roundwell
Married
Royal Navy
First Officer Light Vessel, Calcutta, Mombassa
Second Lieutenant 29 March 1918
Labour Battalion, Indian Army

RIXON, William
Roundwell
Married
1902 Royal Garrison Artillery

ROGERS, William Robert
Friar's Place
Service Number M2/120817 Lance Corporal
14th Military Ambulance, Mechanical Transport, Army Service Corps

ROSE, Robert Richard †
Church Cottages, Ware Street
Parents Sarah Rose and the late Robert Rose
Single
23 February 1916 7th (Service) Battalion, The Queen's Own (Royal West Kent Regiment)
Service Number G/12307 Private
France July 1916
Killed in action 30 September 1916, aged 19
Buried in grave X H 15, Serre Road Cemetery, Number 2, Somme, France

Note: Robert first volunteered to serve with the Royal Army Medical Corps, 19 April 1915
Service Number 2858 Private
3/1st Home Counties Field Ambulance
Robert only served eight days, 19 to 27 April 1915, before being discharged as medically unfit to serve with the ambulance which comprised a mobile medical unit rather than a vehicle.

This is a transcript of the report from the Kent Messenger, 18 November 1916:

Pte. R. R. Rose (Bearsted)
Royal West Kent Regiment

KILLED IN ACTION

Pte. Robert R. Rose, Royal West Kent Regiment, was killed in action, September 30th, 1916, aged 19. He joined up February 23rd 1916 and went to the Front July last. Before enlisting, he worked for Mr Bradley, Rose Acre Farm, Bearsted. His widowed mother and sisters live at Church Cottages, Ware Street, Thurnham and he has an elder brother serving in the Army Veterinary Corps.

Reproduced courtesy of Kent Messenger newspaper group

ROSE, William
Church Cottages, Ware Street
Parents Sarah Rose and the late Robert Rose
Single
Royal Army Veterinary Corps

First World War: 1914 to 1918

ROWLAND, Alfred William
The Bakery, The Green
Parents William and Sarah Rowland
Single
Service Number 53684 Private
May 1913 2nd Signal Company, Royal Engineers
Posted overseas August 1914
Service Number 24345 Lance Corporal
Demobilised 12 April 1919

A transcript of the report from the Kent Messenger, 5 December 1914:

Pte. A.W. Rowlands, R.E.

Pte. A.W.Rowlands, Second Signal Company, R.E., is recuperating at the Royal Infirmary, Glasgow, after having been wounded at the front. A former resident of Maidstone, he is a son of Mr W. Rowland, now of the Bearsted Green Bakery, and will be remembered as an old member of the Kent Cyclists' Brigade, and of the Maidstone Swimming Club. He has kept up his natatory *(swimming)* practices while with the Army, and was last season, a member of the team which was at the head of the Inter-Unit League at Aldershot.

In a letter home Pte. Rowlands writes:- "Would you believe it. I landed in England on the 21st, and got sent to Scotland to a big hospital in Glasgow, where we are living like lords, and I am looking well on it. My head and knees are going on very well, and it will not be long before I am out of it. Altogether this makes the seventh hospital I've been in, and had my name taken about a thousand times. I expect next time I have it taken it will be for Bearsted. Roll on! I have got a holiday to come, and may be lucky enough to get it for Christmas. You talk about doing it in style. You ought to have seen three of us going through Glasgow to the hospital in an open private motor car! Swank wasn't in it - kiddies cheering and the men raising their hats.

Where I got wounded was about the hottest place I have ever been in. It's about four miles the other side of Ypres; the most forward point of our line at the time. When I got hit in the head a bombardier was with me, and he lost his head and soon as he was hit first time, and tried to run away, and it made a terrible mess of him. I bobbed down and kept there until the storm was over. When I looked up, I saw a flame, or it looked like one! I made a dash for it, and was going to run wide, as I thought, to get out of the road, and came in contact with another one. It made a clean dive and dropped about ten yards behind me. I was beginning to think I had got to go. It gives you a lovely feeling, but I think I have nearly got it off my nerves now. I will tell you more when I get home."

Reproduced courtesy of Kent Messenger newspaper group

ROWLAND, Reginald
The Bakery, The Green
Parents William and Sarah Rowland
Single

First World War: 1914 to 1918

ROWLAND, Thomas
The Bakery, The Green
Parents William and Sarah Rowland
Single
April 1914 1/1st Kent Cyclist Battalion
February 1917 Alexandra, Princess of Wales's Own (Yorkshire Regiment)
June 1917 Prince Albert's (Somerset Light Infantry)
September 1917 2nd Garrison Battalion, Northumberland Fusiliers Bugler
Service Number 53684 Private
India February 1916 to September 1917, Mesopotamia September 1917 to March 1919
Demobilised 14 March 1919

RUCK, George Henry
Friningham Farm
Service Number 45568
Suffolk Regiment

RUSSELL, John Henry
The Street
Married
Horse Transport, Army Service Corps
Service Number 143227 Driver

SAGE, Bertie
South Budds Farm
General Base Depot, Royal Engineers
Service Number 163100 Driver

SAGE, John William †
Little Budds Farm, Cold Blow Lane
9th (Service) Battalion, Royal Sussex Regiment
Service Number SD/5681 Private
Killed 31 August 1916
Commemorated Pier and Face 7C, Thiepval Memorial, Somme, France

SEAGER, Lewis
Ware Street
Royal Navy
Service Number 161507 Petty Officer
HMS Actaeon and Royal Naval Barracks, Chatham

SEARS, George Thomas
Married
Wife Dorothy Ellen (née Hughes)
1907 Royal Navy *HMS Natal*
Service Number 311686 Stoker Petty Officer
Killed 30 December 1915
Commemorated Panel 11 Column 1, Chatham Naval Memorial

HMS Natal was a cruiser built in Barrow-in-Furness and launched in 1905. It was destroyed by an internal explosion in Cromarty Firth on 30 December 1915.

George and Dorothy married 30 January 1915 at Holy Cross church. The parish magazine[6] reported George's loss in February 1916 and sadly commented that his daughter was born four days after his death.

First World War: 1914 to 1918

SELVES, Annie Elizabeth
6 Park Row, Aylesford
Parents Henry and Elizabeth Selves of Roseacre
Single
17 March 1918, aged 18, Womens Army Auxiliary Corps
Service Number 86473 Private
Service included 601st Company, also First Wales Borderers and the Queen Mary's Army Auxiliary Corps Depot at Chatham
Demobilised and discharged 8 September 1919

Annie was born in Thurnham and is shown on the 1901 census return as living in Ware Street. Her family later moved to Roseacre. She was employed as a housemaid before working in a munitions factory owned by The Cotton Powder Company, Faversham for sixteen months. Annie received thirty shillings a week to blend cordite and explosives. When she volunteered, her father was serving as a Private in 12th Battalion Bedfordshire Regiment.

SELVES, Arthur John
Roseacre
Married
2 January 1917 Labour Battalion, Royal Engineers
Service Number 504568 Sapper
Posted overseas 12 February 1917
also Minesweeping and Inland Water Transport
Demobilised 3 May 1919

SELVES, Henry
Roseacre
Married
Wife Elizabeth
12th Battalion, Bedfordshire Regiment

Henry was a farm labourer before he joined the army as a Private. The 12th Battalion of the Bedfordshire Regiment, was raised December 1916 and disbanded in September 1919. It was based in Croydon and, although the soldiers wore Infantry uniform, they were not armed. The Battalion worked in the ports of Folkestone, Rochester (which included Chatham and Sittingbourne) Weymouth and Newhaven.

SENT, Arthur
Sutton Street
Single
25 October 1915 3/1st Home Counties Divisional Train, Army Service Corps
transferred 799th Company, Army Service Corps 29 October 1917
Service Number 211199 Driver
Posted overseas 19 August 1916
Salonika August 1916 to March 1919
Dorian and Vardar Front April 1917, August to September 1918
Demobilised 13 April 1919

This photograph of Arthur was taken in 1935:

Reproduced courtesy of
Chris and Sue Hunt

First World War: 1914 to 1918

SHARP, Stuart Forbes
Woodside
Major Seaforth Highlanders (Ross-shire Buffs, The Duke of Albany's)

SHERWOOD, Percy Douglas
Shaw's Cottages
Married
Hampshire Cycling Corps
later 24th (County of London) Battalion, London Regiment (The Queen's), Territorial Force
Service Number 295285

SHORTER, George

SHORTER, Harold William
Shaw's Cottages
Single
8 August 1909 5th (Princess Charlotte of Wales's) Dragoon Guards
later City of London Yeomanry (Rough Riders)
Service Number D 3547 Private
France and Belgium August 1914 to March 1917
Mons, wounded at Charleroi
Egypt, Palestine March 1917 to June 1918
France June 1918
King's Corporal

SIMMONDS, Frederick
Bearsted Spot
Single
Volunteer Training Corps later 2nd Volunteer Brigade, Royal West Kent

SIMPSON, Thomas Richard †
Parents James and Rebecca Simpson
Single
1st Battalion, The Buffs (East Kent Regiment)
Service Number G/495 Corporal
Killed 15 September 1916, aged 23
Buried in grave XIII B 7, Guillemont Road Cemetery, Guillemont, Somme, France

SLENDER, Charles Lewis
Roundwell
Parents Thomas and Louisa Lucy Slender of Roundwell
Single
1 November 1915
Service Number G/10706
Royal West Kent Regiment
Charles was discharged from service as medically unfit, 16 March 1916

Note: his name is given as Lewis Charles Slender on the Roll of Honour at St Mary's church

SLENDER, Thomas George †
Roundwell Cottage, Roundwell
Parents Thomas and Louisa Lucy Slender of Roundwell
Single
November 1914 24th Signal Company, Royal Engineers
Service Number 60010 Driver
France September 1915 to February 1916
Killed in action 12 February 1916, aged 32
Buried in grave I E 28, Poperinghe New Military Cemetery, Poperinghe, West Vlaanderen, Belgium

A transcript of the report from the Kent Messenger, 1 April 1916:

Driver Slender (Bearsted)
24th Signalling Co., R.E., 13th Signal Co., R.E.

KILLED IN ACTION BY HOSTILE AIRCRAFT

Mr and Mrs Slender, of Round Well, Bearsted, have received the sad news from his Captain (and the War Office) that their eldest son, Thomas George Slender, was killed on February 12th 1916 in France by a bomb from an enemy aeroplane. The Captain, in the course of a sympathetic letter said the deceased would be greatly missed by all his regiment - he was so well liked by all who knew him. The burial took place in a cemetery in France. Driver Slender enlisted in November 1914, and set sail for France in September 1915. He was 32 years of age and greatly respected, and much sympathy is felt with Mr and Mrs Slender and family in their sorrow.

Reproduced courtesy of Kent Messenger newspaper group

Under Fire During The War

It is not generally acknowledged that there was a sustained German bombing campaign over Britain in the war because many accounts concentrate on the prolonged land offensives on the Western and Eastern Fronts. The German air offensive, sometimes known as 'the Fire Plan' aimed to devastate London by fire, causing the collapse of British morale and the will to continue the war. Parts of Kent were attacked in air raids undertaken by Zeppelins and aircraft; the first bomb fell on 24 December 1914 in Dover. Later Chatham, Deal, Folkestone, Hythe, Margate, Ramsgate, Sheerness, the Isle of Sheppey, Thanet and London all suffered destruction and casualties caused by shelling and bombs.[7]

The public needed to be aware of what could happen and so regular notices appeared in the local newspapers about the raids. On the next page is shown a typical notice from the pages of the Kent Messenger newspaper, 13 February 1915.

First World War: 1914 to 1918

PUBLIC WARNING

The public are advised to familiarise themselves with the appearance of British and German Airships and Aeroplanes, so that they may not be alarmed by British aircraft, and may take shelter if German aircraft appear. **Should hostile aircraft be seen,** take shelter **immediately** in the nearest available shelter. Remain there until the aircraft have left the vicinity: do not stand about in crowds **and do not touch unexploded bombs.**

In the event of **HOSTILE** aircraft being seen in country districts the nearest Naval, Military or Police Authorities should, if possible, be advised immediately by telephone of the **time of appearance,** the **direction of flight** and **whether the aircraft is an Airship or an Aeroplane.**

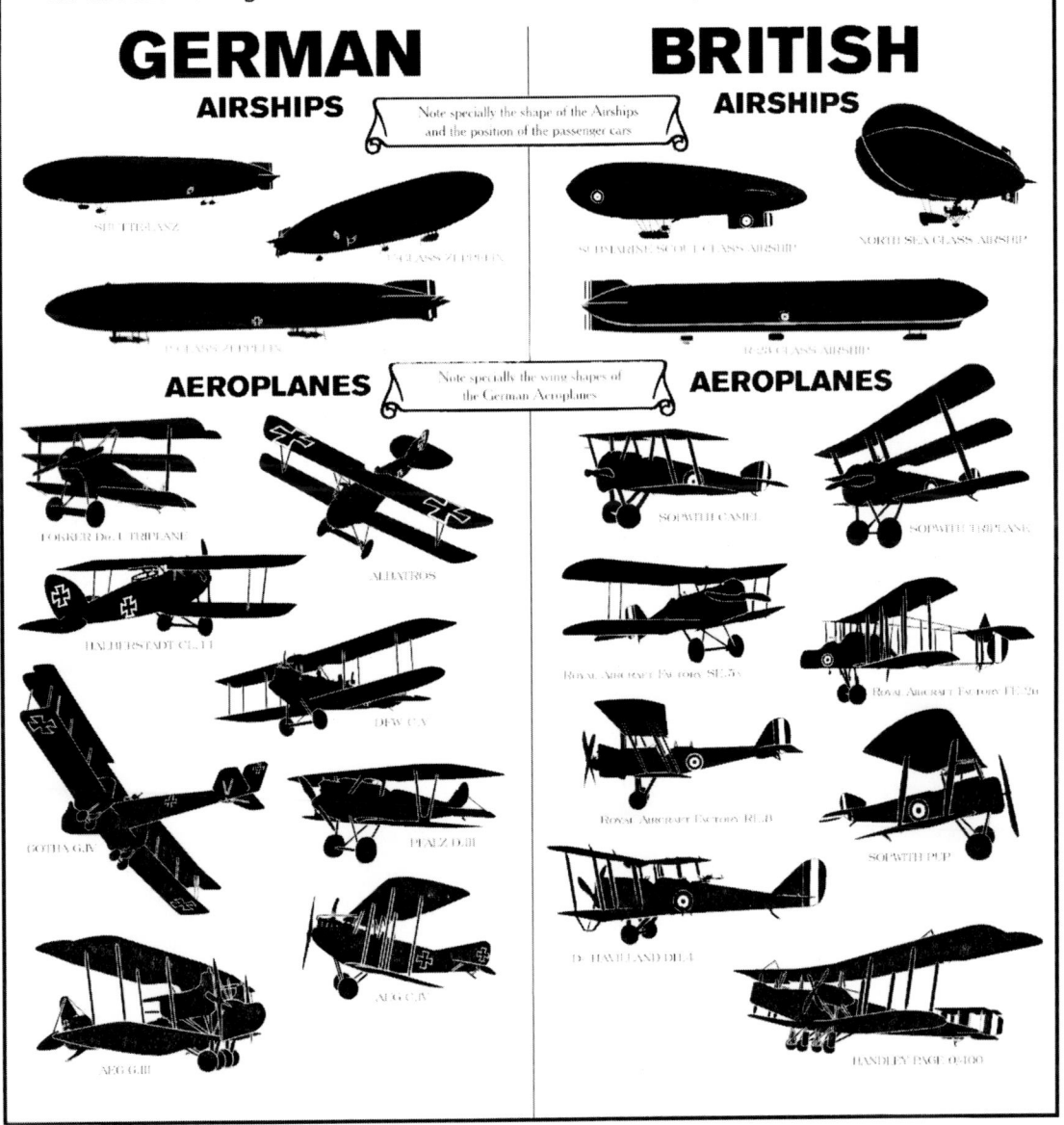

GERMAN AIRSHIPS / BRITISH AIRSHIPS

Note specially the shape of the Airships and the position of the passenger cars

AEROPLANES

Note specially the wing shapes of the German Aeroplanes

Reproduced courtesy of Kent Messenger newspaper group

At first, there was little that could be done to stop the raids; defence against air warfare, observation and early warning communication arrangements were still being developed and many people simply did not realise that they needed to seek shelter during an air raid. Limited directions for blackouts had been ordered by the Home Secretary on 1 October 1914; illuminated signs, shops and street lighting were all partially obscured but a full blackout took some time to achieve mainly because of problems with gas street lighting.[8]

83

First World War: 1914 to 1918

It was not until 1916 that the engineering used in Allied aircraft was sufficiently developed to work at a greater height and speed and so gave some defence against the German raids. There was some successful defence during daytime air raids, but this was not matched at night time.[9]

During September and early October 1917, London was particularly targeted in what became known as 'the Blitz of the Harvest Moon raids'. Many people had been completely unprepared for aggression against civilians, and casualties mounted. It is surprising, given that Maidstone was a garrison town, that it was not regarded as an apparent target. A reduction in the attendance at Bearsted school was attributed to the raids. On 5 October, the Master, Mr Goodman also recorded in the log book he had received a request from a parent that her children be sent home in the event of a raid.

There was certainly cause for concern; sixty three air raid warnings occurred before one which took place on 19 October 1917. This raid involved seven airships which ran into fog and most were destroyed across the channel but one of the airships flew across Maidstone and three bombs were dropped. Two fell onto the cricket ground at Milgate Park, the home of Walter Fremlin. As they fell, the bombs were clearly audible, the noise was later described as similar to that of steam escaping from an engine at high pressure. The detonations occurred within a few seconds at 10.45pm. The damage included a large crater in the park and many windows in Milgate House were shattered. It was reported that another bomb had been dropped just before this onto an open field in Chapel Lane, Ware Street; a few windows were shattered and tiles clattered to the ground but fortunately, there was little other damage. The bomb craters were measured and found to be nearly twenty feet in diameter and had scooped out earth to a depth of eight or nine feet.[10]

The public rapidly learned the importance of strategic shelter; dug outs were constructed, and for the first time, people took cover in Underground railway stations. Taking shelter during air raids undoubtedly saved many lives but there was widespread social and political unrest as morale became dented. The British government was in danger of being regarded as ineffectual in defending civilians in their own country.[11]

However, what probably saved London and avoided a collapse in support for the government, was the evolution of a coherent defence system. In time, this system included efficient communications with airfields, fire brigades on permanent stand-by and anti-aircraft gun batteries. These advancements were supplemented by the installation of balloon barrages. Both the anti-aircraft gun batteries and balloon cables disrupted the altitude of the German bomber aircraft, forcing them to heights where bomb-aiming would be less accurate yet anti-aircraft fire could achieve a reasonable degrees of success.[12]

The Air Force Bill became law on 29 November 1917 and under this legislation, the Air Ministry was established in January 1918. In April, the two air forces, previously known as the Royal Flying Corps and the Royal Naval Air Service, became the Royal Air Force.[13] These were usually known by their initials as RFC, RNAS and RAF.

By mid May, the air fighter zones of the new RAF operations had been completely reorganised. Squadrons were now close to every possible attack route from the Kent coast to Suffolk, including 143 Squadron of Sopwith Camel aircraft which was based at Detling under the leadership of Major Frederick Sowrey.

German air raids continued into 1918. On the evening of 18 May Major Sowrey substantially damaged two Gotha aircraft over Maidstone, although he was unable to shoot them down.[14]

RAF operations introduced systematically planned reconnaissance manoeuvres, taking photographs of the land offensives and targets. As a result of the information which had been gathered, they subsequently carried out air raids over the occupied countries and Germany. The German war effort, which had been boosted by the Russian withdrawal from the war, was disrupted. The timing was crucial: the raids took place as Allied advances, supplemented by American forces, began to take effect. A German plan to fire-bomb both London and Paris during September 1918 was postponed at the very last moment. London was not bombed again for the rest of the war but Paris suffered heavy damage through substantial raids. If London and Paris had been engulfed by flames in the summer of 1918, the outcome of the war may have been very different.[15]

First World War: 1914 to 1918

SMITH, Albert Septimus
Parsonage Farm
Married
Wife Ellen (née Myles)
Royal Navy 12 March 1896
Royal Fleet Reserve Royal Navy 1911 to 1914
Rejoined 2 August 1914
Leading Seaman *HMS Campania*
Petty Officer with North Sea Fleet 1914 to 1918
Cuxhaven Raid 25 December 1914, Destroyer Action 1 September 1917
Invalided 19 January 1918, Died 4 March 1921

A slightly edited transcript of the report from the Kent Messenger, 12 March 1921:

> **NAVAL FUNERAL**
>
> General sorrow was expressed on Friday, when it became known the ex-Petty Officer Gun Layer Albert Septimus Smith had passed away at Parsonage Farm, after an illness that dates from his experiences in the Great War. He was early in the Navy as a lad and…became a Swimming Instructor at the Maidstone Baths till war broke out.
>
> He suffered hardships in the Jutland and other naval engagements, from which he never recovered, being eventually invalided from the Navy in January 1918, suffering from tuberculosis contracted in the North Sea, where he spent an active two years hard service. So he had a crowded life of only thirty nine years, and the utmost sympathy goes out to his sorrowing widow and four young children.
>
> The funeral took place on Wednesday in Bearsted churchyard. A funeral party from the Royal Naval Barracks at Chatham consisting of two Officers, a Chief Petty Officer, Bugler and twenty four Seamen drew the gun carriage bearing the coffin covered by the Union Jack. The Comrades of the Great War (Bearsted and Thurnham Post) commanded by Tom Presland, R.N., of which the deceased was a member were in attendance. The Rev F J Blamire Brown, Vicar, conducted the service, at the conclusion of which the bugler sounded The Last Post.
>
> Among the beautiful floral tributes ere those sent by his loving Wife and Mother, who also deposited the deceased's naval cap, H.M.S. Parker, on the grave.

Reproduced courtesy of Kent Messenger newspaper group

SMITH, Edward John
Colegate's Cottages
Single
21 October 1915 Royal Navy Division
Service Number 3547 Able Seaman
transferred Royal Naval Volunteer Reserve November 1915
Naval Air Defences Dover February 1916 to July 1918
HMS Attention II
HMS Excellent July to November 1918
HMS Vestal November 1918 to January 1919
Demobilised 20 January 1919

First World War: 1914 to 1918

SMITH, Frank
Colegate's Cottages
Single
Palestine

This photograph of Frank was taken in 1935:

Reproduced courtesy of Chris and Sue Hunt

SOLE, Ernest
Royal Marines Artillery and *HMS Endeavour*

STAPLEY, William
Roseacre
Single
Volunteer Training Corps later 2nd Volunteer Brigade, Royal West Kent

STEMP, George
White Horse
Married
23 October 1916 Mechanical Transport, Army Service Corps
Posted overseas 20 October 1916 France

STERN, Leopold Grahame *†
North Down, Church Lane
Parents Leopold John and Lilias Mary Stern (née Dunlop) of Red Oaks, Henfield, Sussex
Single
October 1917 99th Squadron, Royal Flying Corps Cadet
Second Lieutenant
France, Germany
Killed in air action 26 September 1918, aged 18
Buried in grave Plot 379, Chambieres French National Cemetery Metz, Moselle, France

Leopold was the pilot of De Havilland DH9 Bomber D5573, from 99 Squadron, Independent Force, RAF. He was accompanied by his Observer/Gunner Lieutenant Frederick Oliver Cook. On 26 September 1918, the squadron undertook bombing raids, supporting French and American forces around Verdun. Leopold was re-routed from railway targets at Thionille. His aircraft was one of six that were attacked by thirty to forty enemy aircraft over Metz-Sablon around 5.10pm. Leopold's airplane was shot down and both of the occupants were killed.

Parachutes were not generally used prior to January 1917. The early designs and packing of parachutes made them bulky and there was very little space for them in a tight cockpit. The authorities decided that the availability of parachutes might tempt a pilot to abandon his aircraft and crew before it was strictly necessary, so they were only useable in very limited circumstances. The aircrew casualty figures during the last two years of the conflict, ensured that this policy was soon changed. Parachutes were sanctioned for general use during 1918, but before they could be widely distributed, the war ended.[16]

First World War: 1914 to 1918

SWIFT, Edgar Earl †
Ware Street
Single
8th (Service) Battalion, King's (Shropshire Light Infantry)
Service Number 16897 Lance Corporal
Died of wounds 17 January 1918, Salonika
Buried in grave V E 17, Doiran Military Cemetery, Greece

Edgar is buried next to Frank White who died the following day. See entry under **WHITE, Frank** for further details

SWIFT, Stephen
Egypt Cottages
Married
14 February 1916 Army Service Corps
Service Number 126514 Private
31st Squadron Remounts
France

TANNER, Ernest
Chapel Lane
Service Number 48798 Private
1st Battalion, Prince of Wales's (North Staffordshire Regiment)

TAYLOR, Edward Cunningham
Stonefield, Ashford Road, near Maidstone
Royal Flying Corps

TAYLOR, Elgar George
Triangle Cottages
Married
10 December 1914 61st Company, Mechanical Transport, Army Service Corps attached to 2nd Division
Posted overseas 16 December 1914

TAYLOR, Ernest George
Ware Street
Service Number 021774 Private
Mechanical Transport, Army Service Corps

First World War: 1914 to 1918

TAYLOR, George *
Mount Cottages
Parents George and Alice Mary Taylor of Danefield Cottage
Single
18 January 1915 13th Signal Company, Royal Engineers
Service Number 60574
Posted overseas 26 June 1915
Gallipoli June to August 1915
Cape Helles, Anzac
Killed in action 29 August 1915, aged 19
Commemorated Panels 23-25 or 325-328, Helles Memorial, Turkey

George was born in Meopham and enlisted at Chatham. He was the brother of Edward Taylor who later ran the village newsagents in Bearsted. His father was a verger and sexton at Holy Cross church.

A transcript of the report from the Kent Messenger, 3 October 1915:

60574 Driv. G. Taylor (Bearsted)
13th Signal Co., R.E.

KILLED IN ACTION AT GALLIPOLI

Driver G. E. Taylor, R.E., was the son of Mr and Mrs George Taylor, of Bearsted, and his death came as a surprise to his friends. A driver in the 13th Signal Company, he was killed in the action of August 29th at Gallipoli, but notification was not received by his parents until late in September. Meanwhile, several letters which he had written had arrived, and a postcard dated August 28th, the day before his death, saying that he was all right. The news of his untimely end therefore was quite unexpected.

Joining up on January 18th, he went though his training and set out for the Dardanelles on June 26th. He had consequently landed less than two months when he was cut off, within a few weeks of his 20th birthday (which would have been on October 6th). Every sympathy has been evinced towards the bereaved parents by friends and acquaintances near and far, for the deceased was a very popular young fellow, esteemed for his bright and buoyant manner.

Mr and Mrs Taylor and family wish to sincerely acknowledge the many marks of sympathy shown towards them in their sorrow. They would also be most grateful if any member of the 13th Signal Company who might be able to give any particulars of their son's death would communicate with them at Mount Cottages, Bearsted.

Reproduced courtesy of Kent Messenger newspaper group

First World War: 1914 to 1918

TAYLOR, Louis
White Horse
Single
7 July 1908 19th (Queen Alexandra's Own Royal) Hussars
Posted overseas 21 August 1914
France and Belgium 1914 to 1918
Germany 1919
Demobilised 29 April 1919

TAYLOR, Percy Walter
White Horse
Married
Wife Esther Grace (née Wingate)
17 February 1915 Mechanical Transport, Army Service Corps attached 25th Field Ambulance
Posted overseas 10 March 1915
France and Belgium 1915 to 1919
Demobilised 17 February 1919

Percy married Esther Wingate on 23 January 1916 at Holy Cross church. It was reported in the parish magazine in February[17] that Percy came home from the Front on Thursday and they were married by special licence on Sunday. The following Friday, he returned to the Front. This was not an uncommon timetable; during the war, many engaged couples were only able to marry when leave was permitted, often at short notice.

TAYLOR, Stephen
White Horse
Single
1 May 1916 Mechanical Transport, Army Service Corps attached 25th Field Ambulance
Posted overseas 17 May 1916
France and Belgium 1916
Prisoner of War May to November 1918
Demobilised 26 August 1919

A transcript of the report from the Kent Messenger, 20 July 1918

<u>**Information Wanted**</u>

Stephen Taylor (Bearsted)
Motor Field Ambulance

MISSING

Mr and Mrs W. W. Taylor of the White Horse, Bearsted, have been officially notified by the War Office that their son, Stephen Taylor, 25th Motor Field Ambulance, 8th Division, has been missing since May 27th 1918. He joined up on May 6th 1916 (having previously been chauffeur to Lieut. Colonel A. Wood-Martyn) and went over to France on the 15th. He was home on his last leave in October 1917. Three other sons and a son in law of Mr and Mrs Taylor are all serving in France and it was Stephen's brother Percy, (who himself had a 'narrow escape' from being captured), who first reported home that he believed Stephen to have been taken prisoner. If anyone can furnish any information respecting him, the family would be deeply grateful.

Reproduced courtesy of Kent Messenger newspaper group

First World War: 1914 to 1918

TAYLOR, Walter James
Ware Street
Service Number M2 143131 Private
46th Divisional Motor Transport Company, Army Service Corps

TAYLOR, William James
Royal Field Artillery

TAYLOR, William Louis
White Horse
Married
9 November 1910 9th (Queen's Royal) Lancers
transferred Machine Gun Corps (Cavalry) May 1917 later 19th (Queen Alexandra's Own Royal) Hussars
Service Number 2677 Private
Posted overseas 15 August 1914
France August 1914 to January 1917, March 1917 to February 1919
Ireland January to March 1917
Mons, Marne, Aisne, Ypres, Cambrai, Somme
Wounded
Demobilised 13 March 1919

TESTER, Charles
Forge Cottages
Married
Volunteer Training Corps later 2nd Volunteer Brigade, Royal West Kent

Charles was a blacksmith and farrier. He served for some of the war with the 5th (Reserve) Battalion, King's Royal Rifle Corps, Transport Division. This photograph shows him in the middle of the back row.

Reproduced courtesy of John Mills

THOMPSON, Wilfred Arthur
Tollgate
Married
September 1895 Royal Navy
Lieutenant-Commander *HMS Glasgow*
Commander *HMS Roberts, HMS Martin*
Falkland Island Battle

First World War: 1914 to 1918

Food in Wartime

During the war Britain continued to import food, largely from America and Canada, so merchant ships that crossed the Atlantic Ocean were subject to attacks by German U-boats. The U-boat offensive was so successful that by April 1916, the government reckoned that Britain had only enough wheat to meet the national level of consumption for six weeks. 1916 was a grim time for many families: the armed forces casualty rate rose steeply because of military offensives at the Somme and at home, food shortages began. There were frequent allegations of hoarding supplies and profiteering.[18]

In August, the government established a Food Department. Eventually there were several sub-departments including Food and Food Production, overseen by a Food Controller, Lord Devonport.[19] By October 1916, food prices had risen and coal was in such short supply that its purchase was limited by an allowance based on the number of rooms occupied in a property by a family.

The Food Department became aware that there was a real danger of starvation. It attempted to implement a code of rationing whereby people voluntarily imposed upon themselves a limit to the amount of food they should eat, called 'Eat Less Bread'.[20] It soon became apparent that these measures were not appropriate. Nutrition was still poorly understood and few government officials recognised that bread comprised an essential food for families with a limited income. People became caught between supporting the patriotic gesture of eating less but incurring hunger. Eventually it was realised that this dilemma was affecting factory workers supporting the war effort and leading to the inefficient production of munitions. It also became clear that anyone with sufficient funds could obtain foodstuffs on the black market. In an attempt to redress these issues, the government introduced local Food Control Committees during December 1916.

It was also recognised that parts of Kent faced particular difficulties; the population continually fluctuated as sections of the armed forces moved backwards and forwards to the continent across the county.[21]

It may have been because of the food shortages and difficulties that a pig club was set up for Bearsted and Thurnham. This is a slightly edited transcript of a report about the club which appeared in 13 April 1918 edition of the Kent Messenger:

A PIG CLUB FOR BEARSTED AND THURNHAM

A largely-attended meeting, under the presidency of Mr H V Lushington, was held at the Village Hall, Bearsted on Tuesday, when it was decided to form a Pig Club for those villages under the auspices of the Rural League. The meeting elected a Committee consisting of Mr H V Lushington (chairman), Mr F E D Harnett, the Misses Green, Scarth and Shipley, and Messrs J Brown, F White, Tooley, Moon, C Foster and J Datson, with Mr W H Whitehead as Hon. Treasurer, and Miss Day, Hon. Secretary.

A generous offer by the Chairman to supply to members of the Club 20 young pigs at 20s each payable by such instalments as best suited the members was heartily appreciated, and before the meeting closed 15 of such pigs were disposed of in this manner.

Reproduced courtesy of Kent Messenger newspaper group

Despite these measures, food prices continued to rise and were eventually to double between 1914 and 1918. Malnutrition became readily apparent in poorer communities and the government became concerned that conscripted men would not be fit to fight.

It was clear that further state action was required; mandatory rationing was introduced during 1917. It was decided that in order to be fair, the same quantities of food would be available for everyone. Rationing was introduced at different stages for various commodities on both a national 'General Scheme', and a local scale. Cards or books to record the amounts people received were issued and everyone had to register with a butcher and a grocer. Retailers received supplies in proportion to the number of people registered with a business or shop.[22]

First World War: 1914 to 1918

To make the rationing scheme work, government control of imports and home grown produce was introduced and a Ministry of Food replaced the Food Department. Rationing was abandoned after restrictions were lifted in 1921. The malnutrition which had been apparent in the poorer communities disappeared and as in World War Two, although food was limited, it was widely acknowledged that no one actually starved in Britain under the ration scheme during the war.[23]

Here are the nationally rationed items and the weekly amount permitted for one adult: [24]

Sugar Rationed from 31 December 1917 to 29 November 1920.
Initially this was 8oz sugar

Fat Butter was rationed from 14 July 1918 to 30 May 1920
Margarine was rationed from 14 July 1918 to 16 February 1919
Lard was rationed from 14 July to 16 December 1918
Initially, this was a total of 4oz fat

Beef, Mutton or Lamb from the butcher
Rationing under the Meat Scheme from 7 April 1918
Rationing under the General Scheme from 14 July to 28 July 1918
Initially this was for a total of 15oz uncooked meat

Bacon and Ham
Rationing under the Meat Scheme from 7 April 1918
Rationing under the General Scheme from 14 July to 28 July 1918
Initially this was for a total of 5oz bacon or ham

Jam Rationed from 2 November 1918 to 15 April 1919
Initial quantity not known

Tea This was not rationed nationally but its distribution was controlled by national registration of customers and was based on an allocation of 2oz per person from 14 July to 2 December 1918.

The themes of rising prices and food shortages took on comic overtones in these postcards, produced around 1917:

Both reproduced courtesy of Malcolm Kersey

First World War: 1914 to 1918

TOLHURST, Friend
Crisfield Cottage
Married
5 July 1918 Army Service Corps attached 178th Tunnelling Company, Royal Engineers
Posted overseas 5 November 1918
France November 1918 to June 1919
Demobilised 18 June 1919

TOMPSETT, Franklyn
Royal West Kent
Home Service

TOMPSETT, William James
Kings Liverpool Regiment and Labour Corps
Home Service

TOMSETT, William Thomas
1 Fancy Row
Service Number 171563 Private
309th (Home Service) Works Company, Army Service Corps

TOWN, Stephen
The Street
Single
31 October 1914 Royal Army Medical Corps, Territorial Force
Service Number 49370 Private
Posted overseas 16 August 1916
Salonika August 1916 to December 1918
Struma Valley
Demobilised 9 January 1919

TOWN, Thomas Charles
The Street
Single
April 1915 Army Service Corps
Lance Corporal
Posted overseas July 1915

TREE, Alfred Edward
The Green
Single
July 1918 51st Graduated Battalion, Queen's (Royal West Surrey Regiment)

TROWELL, William Henry
Detling Hill
Royal Navy
Service Number 2842536 Chief Stoker
HMS Bacchante

TUDD, Thomas
Roseacre
Inland Waterways & Docks, Royal Engineers
Service Number 333551

First World War: 1914 to 1918

TURVEY, Arthur
Ware Street
1st Battalion, Grenadier Guards
Service Number 24857 Private

WALKER, Arthur Francis Gregory
Tollgate
Married
1 January 1915 8th Battalion, East Lancashire Regiment
Posted overseas 24 July 1915 France
Staff Captain 112th Infantry Brigade
General Staff Officer 3rd Grade, 33rd Division March 1917
Wounded at Ypres 1917
Brigade Major 1918
11th Cyclist Brigade 1919
Deputy Assistant Adjutant General Eastern Command
Arras 1917, Ypres
Military Cross (London Gazette, January 1918)
Mentioned in Secretary of State's Despatches
Demobilised 31 March 1919

WALKLING, Albert
3 Egypt Place
Married
1 June 1915 21st (County of London) Battalion, London Regiment (1st Surrey Rifles), Territorial Force
Service Number 64026 Private
Posted overseas 28 December 1916 France
Attached to Balloon Section, Royal Air Force Italy 1 November 1917
France 4 February 1918
Ypres, Messines, Passchendaele, Merville
Demobilised April 1919

WALKLING, Alfred Thomas
The Street
Service Number T4 211223 Wheeler Corporal
Base Depot, Army Service Corps

WALKLING, Frank Charles
South View
Single
7 October 1915 Suffolk Regiment later 8th (Service) Battalion, King's Own Yorkshire Light Infantry
Service Number 37610 Private

WALKLING, Thomas
South View
Single
October 1915 Army Service Corps
Corporal
France
Demobilised 4 June 1919

First World War: 1914 to 1918

WALKLING, William
318 Arnold Avenue, Fort Rouge, Winnipeg, Manitoba, Canada
later, 46R Carlaw Avenue, Fort Rouge, Winnipeg, Manitoba, Canada
Parents Henry and Kate Walkling
Single
Fiancée Miss Wye
26 July 1915
Service Number 153333 Corporal
43rd Battalion, Canadian Infantry
Posted overseas February 1916; Canadian Expeditionary Force, Regina Trench, Monchy, Arras, France
Wounded 1916
Killed 28 August 1918, aged 23
Commemorated Vimy Memorial, Pas de Calais, France
Distinguished Conduct Medal

William was born at Chapel Lane Cottages. By 1911, his family had moved to 95 Melville Road, Maidstone, and William was employed as a grocer's assistant. On 20 March 1913, he emigrated from Southampton to Canada via Portland, Maine, on board *SS Ausonia*, Cunard Line, to join his parents who had left England in 1911. Other members of the family also emigrated later on in 1913. William enlisted in Winnipeg and returned to Britain to serve with the Canadian Expeditionary Force.

A transcript of a report which appeared in the Kent Messenger, 2 November 1918:

Cpl. W. Walkling (Maidstone)
Canadian Infantry
KILLED IN ACTION

The many friends of Cpl W Walkling, 43rd Canadians, will regret to hear of his death in action at Monchy on August 28th, after experiencing some of the severe fighting before Cambrai. Born at Thurnham some 23 years ago, he came to Maidstone and finished his school days at All Saints'. Prior to emigrating to Winnipeg, he was employed at the Home and Colonial Stores, Week Street. Miss Wye, his fiancée, has received a letter from his Captain, who says: "It will possibly be of some consolation to you to know that he was considered one of the finest men in this company and battalion. On August 8th he came out of the battle in charge of his platoon after his officer and senior n.c.o. had been killed. His work was of the best, and he headed the list from the company for decorations. A recommendation was put in by me for the D.C.M., and we are expecting it through daily. On August 16th he again went over the top and again did fine work. August 27th and 28th saw him in action again and he came through the show successfully. However, while the relief was coming through the village of Monachy, just east of Arras, he was killed by a shell. By the men he was considered one of the finest, and by his officers one of the most trustworthy reliable and capable. It was indeed a loss to us when he went, and we miss him." He and the late Pte. J. Randall joined up at the same time and proceeded overseas in February 1916. Corpl. Walkling was wounded at Regina Trench on October 8th, 1916, and after recovering from his injuries at home, he returned to France on November 19th last.

Reproduced courtesy of Kent Messenger newspaper group

WALTER, Alfred Jesse
Oliver's Row
Married
July 1915 Mechanical Transport, Army Service Corps
Lance Corporal
Posted overseas August 1915 France
Somme, Messines, Cambrai, Lille, Tournai
Demobilised 29 May 1919

WATCHAM, Alfred John
Golf House
Married
Wife Susan
Service Number 400931
27 October 1916 Essex Regiment
Discharged as medically unfit for service, 27 February 1918

Alfred was the groundsman for Bearsted Golf Club. After being called up for service, his wife took over the post until he was able to resume his duties having been discharged from the army.

WATCHAM, Frederick
Church Cottage
Married
15 October 1915 Royal Navy Division, Anti Aircraft Defences Dover
Royal Naval Volunteer Reserve 1916 Able Seaman
Defensively Armed Merchant Ships
Seaman on *SS Corinthian* wrecked off Nova Scotia December 1918
HMS Victory 1919

WATKINS, A
Royal Naval Division and *HMS Miranda*
Croix-de Guerre

WATKINS, Bertie Simpson
3 Chapel Lane Cottages, Ware Street
Parents Alfred and Elizabeth Watkins of Ware Street
Married
Wife Emma Elizabeth (née Spenceley)
Children Vera Elizabeth and Leslie Bert
3 June 1915
Service Number G8116 Private
Posted overseas 3 August 1915, British Expeditionary Force, France, Italy and Western Front
10th Battalion, Royal West Kent Regiment

Before joining the army, Bertie was a boot repairer. He married Emma in Gillingham on 23 June 1915.

He was wounded in action on 7 May 1918 and returned to Etaples 17 May 1918. He was then posted for a short stay in an army rest camp in Maidstone before being judged fit for service and returning to the Front. He was demobilised 2 May 1919 at Hounslow, Middlesex.

First World War: 1914 to 1918

WATKINS, Leslie †
3 Ware Street
Parents Alfred and Elizabeth Watkins of Ware Street
Single
7th (Service) Battalion, The Queen's Own (Royal West Kent Regiment)
Service Number G/20607 Private
Posted as Missing, presumed killed, 21 March 1918
Commemorated Panel 58 and 59, Pozieres Memorial, Albert, Somme

A report which appeared in the Kent Messenger, 1 June 1918:

Reproduced courtesy of Ann Lampard and Lynda Copsey

Pte. Leslie Watkins (Bearsted) Royal West Kent Regiment

MISSING

Leslie Watkins, aged 19, is the youngest of the six fighting sons of Mr and Mrs Alfred Watkins of Station Hill, Bearsted. He was, on attaining the age of 18, called up from his employment at the Japanese Embassy, London, when the youngest boy of the family, Albert, took his position. Leslie went out to France early in the present year with a draft of the Royal West Kents, and has been missing since the 21st March. Letters and cigarettes sent to him since have been returned intact. In reply to inquiries by his parents, the War Office, his commanding officer, and the chaplain, all say they can only report him as missing. Any information with regard to him would be most gratefully received by his parents at the above address.

Reproduced courtesy of Kent Messenger newspaper group

WATKINS, Percy Arthur Cummings
Ware Street
Parents Alfred and Elizabeth Watkins of Ware Street
Single
Army Service Corps

This undated photograph shows an unidentified member of the Watkins family in the uniform of The Buffs (East Kent Regiment).

Reproduced courtesy of Jean Jones

WATKINS, Sidney
Ware Street
Parents Alfred and Elizabeth Watkins of Ware Street
Royal Field Artillery, Western Front

WATKINS, Spencer
Army
Devon Yeomanry, Western Front

WATTS, Henry Herbert Eric
Holmleigh
Single
25 January 1915 3/1st City of London Field Ambulance
later 2/1st Field Ambulance, Royal Army Medical Corps
Service Number 508368 Private
Posted overseas 21 February 1916
France and Belgium February 1916 to March 1919
Somme, First, Second, Third Battle of Arras, Third Battle of Ypres, Bullecourt, Cambrai, Mons 1918
Demobilised 20 March 1919

WEBB, Frederick
Royal Navy

WELLARD, Charles William *
South View
Parents Charles and Louisa Wellard
Single
March 1918 1/8th Battalion, Duke of Cambridge's Own (Middlesex Regiment), Territorial Force
Service Number 54745 Lance Corporal
Posted overseas August 1918 France
Killed on active service 12 October 1918, aged 18
Buried in grave ID 12, Cagnicourt British Cemetery, Pas de Calais, France

Charles was born at Frinsted and enlisted in Maidstone. His father was village Police Constable in Bearsted for a time.

A transcript of the report from the Kent Messenger, 2 November 1918:

Lce-Cpl. C. W. Wellard (Bearsted) Middlesex Regiment

KILLED IN ACTION

Lce-Corpl. C. W. Wellard, elder son of P.C. and Mrs Wellard of Bearsted, was killed in action on October 12th. He was 18 years of age, an old Volunteer, and was formerly employed at the Kent County Council Offices at Maidstone.

Reproduced courtesy of Kent Messenger newspaper group

First World War: 1914 to 1918

WHEATLEY, Horace Gordon
Bearsted
Married
Wife Edith Hannah (née Hunt)
Private
Army Cyclist Corps

Horace and Edith were married at Holy Cross church on 13 August 1918

WHITE, Alfred
Ware Street
Service Number 10798 Lance Corporal
11th (Service) Battalion, King's Royal Rifle Corps

WHITE, Carie
Honor Oak
Single
June 1917 Women's Army Auxiliary Corps
Demobilised 15 April 1919

WHITE, Ernest Albert †
2 Chapel Lane, Ware Street
Parents Frederick Horace and Emma Jane White of Ware Street
Married
Wife Agnes Elizabeth
Children Agnes and Ernest
2nd Battalion, Royal Fusiliers (City of London Regiment)
Service Number 46714 Private
Killed 19 August 1918, aged 26
Buried in grave II E 60, Rue-Petillon Military Cemetery, Fleurbaix, Pas de Calais, France

Ernest was tragically killed in the final two months of the war and before his second child was born. The White family took care of his widow and children, who were known as Little Agnes and Little Ernest.

Recognition of Services Rendered

By 1916, many men apparently eligible for military service but not in uniform, were being targeted by organisations such as the Order of the White Feather. The Order, in particular encouraged the public distribution of white feathers by young women as a symbol of cowardice. The white feather quickly became a powerful symbol, but there were frequent instances where they were inappropriately distributed, including to a recipient of the Victoria Cross who was not in uniform but on the way to a public reception for his award.

The government realised that some sort of symbol or badge was required which could be worn by men in exempted professions or occupations, those home on leave and wearing civilian clothes or already wounded. Several badges and armbands were therefore devised.

An example of a War Badge is shown here on the right. From September 1916, this sterling silver badge was issued to servicemen honourably discharged due to wounds and was worn on the right lapel of civilian clothes. Each badge was stamped with a unique identification number on the reverse.

Reproduced courtesy of
Malcolm Kersey

WHITE, Frank †
Neatherton Cottages, Ware Street
Parents Clara and the late Albert White
Single
1915 8th (Service) Battalion, King's (Shropshire Light Infantry)
Service Number 16898 Private
Died of wounds 18 January 1918, aged 26
Buried in grave V E 18, Doiran Military Cemetery, Greece

A partial transcript of the report from the Kent Messenger, 23 February 1918:

Pte. Frank White (Thurnham)
Shropshire Light Infantry

Mrs C White, of Ware Street, Thurnham, has received the sad news of the death of her son, Private Frank White, of the Shropshire Light Infantry, at the front at Salonika. He was badly wounded by a shell on January 18th and only lived about two and a half hours after. He had been in the Army three years, of which he was in Salonika two years and four months. Before he joined he was under gardener for Mr W. R. Prosser, Ardenlee, Sittingbourne Road, Maidstone for four years and afterwards for Sir Reginald MacLeod, K.C.B., at Vinters Park.

Frank White was much esteemed during his career as a soldier as well as in private life as the sympathetic letters to his widowed mother from his Colonel and his Captain amply testify. Mrs White, whose husband died at Netley Hospital during the Boer War, has also had several letters from comrades of her son, Frank, speaking most highly of him and deploring his death. It appears that the same shell that killed him also killed Edgar Swift, the son of a neighbour in Ware Street. They had been schoolmates together, worked together, joined up and went out together, fought side by side, died together and were buried together. Frank White was 26 years of age. At home he had always taken a keen interest in cricket, football and other sports and was most highly esteemed.

Reproduced courtesy of Kent Messenger newspaper group

WHITE, Frederick
2 West View
Married
8 May 1916 Royal Field Artillery
Service Number 145737 Gunner
13th Division GAAS
Posted overseas 13 September 1916
Mesopotamia October 1916 to August 1918
Recapture of Kut, Baghdad to Kirkuk
Demobilised 13 February 1919

First World War: 1914 to 1918

WHITE, Frederick Horace
Ware Street
1st Battalion, The Queen's Own (Royal West Kent Regiment)
Service Number 265289 Lance Corporal

WHITE, Percy George
Honor Oak
Single
10 November 1915 2nd County of London Yeomanry (Westminster Dragoons)
1916 Royal Field Artillery Gunner
Service Number 945053
Posted overseas 6 February 1917
France February 1917 to September 1918
Arras 1917, March Retreat, Marne, Somme 1918
Wounded
Demobilised 10 January 1919

WHITE, Philip Henry
14 St Peter's Street, Maidstone
Married
2/4th Battalion, The Queen's Own (Royal West Kent Regiment), Territorial Force
Service Number TF/3582
Posted overseas 19 July 1915
Died 21 September 1915 of enteric fever
Buried in grave B XIII 5, Pieta Military Cemetery, Malta

A transcript of the report from the Kent Messenger, 26 February 1916:

Pte P. H. White (Maidstone)
Royal West Kent Regiment

DIED AT MALTA

Pte. P. H. White of the 2/4th Royal West Kent Regiment, which left Bedford July 19th for the Dardanelles, died of enteric fever at Malta September 21st 1915. He was born at Bearsted, and before enlisting was in the gardens of Mr R. J. Balston, for 12 years. He leaves a widow and six children (the eldest 12 years of age) at 14 St Peter's Street, Maidstone, to mourn their loss.

Reproduced courtesy of Kent Messenger newspaper group

WHITE, Stanley Thomas
Honor Oak
Single
20 January 1915 Royal Naval Air Service and Royal Air Force
Chief Mechanic
Service Number 203192 Petty Officer
France August 1916 to May 1917
Italy May 1917 to February 1918
Dunkirk, Piave
Demobilised February 1919

WHITE, Walter Frederick
Honor Oak
Single
14 August 1914 1/1st Kent Cyclist Battalion
Posted overseas November 1914
Second Lieutenant later Lieutenant The Queen's Own (Royal West Kent Regiment)

WHITE, Walter Victor
Ware Street
Enlisted 20 April 1914
1st Battalion, The Queen's Own (Royal West Kent Regiment)
Service Number 265290 Lance Corporal
Western Front 9 February 1916
India (including Ferozpore, Dagshai and Bombay)

Whilst serving in India, he sustained a knee injury in Ferozpore jumping a ditch. He was initially hospitalised for three weeks during which he was on 'light duties only' but then contracted dysentery, from which it took him nine weeks to recover.

Walter had an unusual pastime; he spent a great deal of time unravelling the tops of worn out woollen socks to crochet an enormous blanket. It was made up of many different shades of grey and khaki but was very warm and lasted for years!

He returned to England on 8 November 1919 on board *SS Derbyshire*. Walter married Elsie Sent in 1924 at Holy Cross church and this photograph was taken after the ceremony. Elsie's wedding dress was made of silk that he had brought back from India.

Reproduced courtesy of Evelyn Fridd and Margaret Plowright

WHITEHEAD, Dorothy
The Mount
Married
Husband William Whitehead
Children Frances, Charles and William
Voluntary Aid Detachment, Kent 12, Maidstone

Kent 12 Detachment had been formed and registered in 1910. The detachment was mobilised 14 October 1914 at the Howard de Walden Institute; Maidstone.[25]

First World War: 1914 to 1918

WHITEHEAD, William Hingeston
The Mount
Married
Wife Dorothy (née Parkin)
Children Frances, Charles and William
1915 Lieutenant The Queen's Own (Royal West Kent Regiment) Reserve Training
Retired 1918

William was a solicitor and involved in many organisations. His appointments included Under Sheriff of Kent and he was Chairman of Bearsted Parish Council 1909-1949.

WICKENS, George Arthur
The Street
Married
14 October 1914 West Kent Yeomanry (Queen's Own)
Service Number 492063 Private
later 684th Agricultural Company, Army Service Corps
France
Demobilised 5 March 1919

WILKINSON, Arthur *
1 Mote Villas
Single
Service Number 4846
2nd also 9th (Service) Battalion, Royal Fusiliers (City of London Regiment)
France
Missing, presumed killed 4 August 1916
Buried in grave IV J 36, Pozieres British Cemetery Ovillers la Boisselle, Somme, France
Bearsted war memorial date is 4 August 1918

Arthur was born at Mote Hall Villas. He resided and enlisted in East Ham. His father Charles was an Old Scholar and Manager of Bearsted School. Charles was a builder and undertaker.

WILKINSON, Charles
1 Mote Villas
Single
2 November 1915 Royal Engineers
Service Number 140150 Sapper
Posted overseas 31 July 1916
Mesopotamia August 1916 to July 1918
Persia June to December 1918
Caucasus December 1918 to April 1919
Recapture of Kut, Capture of Baghdad, Dunsterville Expedition in Persia.
Demobilised 24 June 1919

WILKINSON, Frederick *
1 Mote Villas
Single
11th (Service) (Cambridgeshire) Battalion, Suffolk Regiment
Service Number 41446
Lance Corporal
France February 1917 Training Reserve Battalion
Killed in action 22 March 1918
Commemorated Bay 4, Arras Memorial, Pas de Calais, France

First World War: 1914 to 1918

WILKINSON, Wilfred
1 Mote Villas
Single
2 November 1915 Royal Engineers Driver
Service Number 141023
Demobilised 8 January 1919

Wilfred was born in 1891. He married Florence Sent at Holy Cross church in October 1922

WILKINSON, William Jesse
The Street
Married
26 October 1916 King's Royal Rifle Corps
Service Number 31857
Demobilised 22 February 1919

WISDOM, Albert John *
3 Acacia Villas, Willington Road
Parents Solomon and Elizabeth Wisdom
Single
May 1915 Royal Naval Volunteer Reserve
Service Number London Z/2197 Able Seaman
HMS Nottingham and *HMS Laurentic*
Lost at Sea on 25 January 1917 aged 19, when *HMS Laurentic* struck two mines near Lough Swilly off the northern Irish coast.
Commemorated   Panel 27 Column 3, Chatham Naval Memorial;
        war memorial plaque at St Nicholas church, Otham

SS Laurentic was an ocean liner of the White Star Line built in Belfast and launched in 1908. It was commissioned as a troop transport for the Canadian Expeditionary Force and renamed *HMS Laurentic* at the outbreak of the war.

WISDOM, George Solomon
3 Acacia Villas, Willington Road
Parents Solomon and Elizabeth Wisdom
Single
1906 Royal Navy
Service Number 236381 Leading Seaman
HMS Apollo, HMS Bat

WISDOM, Solomon
4 Willington Road
Married
23 March 1915 5th Battalion, The Queen's Own (Royal West Kent Regiment), Territorial Force
later 162nd Company, Royal Defence Corps
Service Number 1801 Private
Demobilised 11 March 1919

WISDOM, William Henry
3 Acacia Villas, Willington Road
Parents Solomon and Elizabeth Wisdom
Single
1913 Royal Navy
Service Number K 19272 Stoker 1st Class
HMS Africa

Memories of the First World War

It is curious that although the First World War, or Great War, as it was known at the time, was an almost universal experience, there are remarkably few eye witness accounts from residents of Bearsted and Thurnham of the hostilities and the impact of wartime on local everyday life. In the light of this, sparse details are all the more valuable, so here are some experiences and recollections of local people and children.

These accounts begin with some information compiled by Albert Baker about his wartime service, together with some other recollections which involve his siblings in wartime, originally written down around 1978. Thomas Gilbert's memories which follow, were recorded when he was around ninety years old. Thomas was usually known as Tom, and was interviewed by James Moore from the former Thurnham History Group.

Albert Baker

Albert Baker was part of a large family who are probably best remembered in recent times as living at Bell farmhouse in Bell Lane, Ware Street, and operating a wood yard there. The Baker family comprised Richard and Lucy Baker (née Mannering) and they had five sons and six daughters - a large family! In order of appearance in the world they were: Richard (usually known as Fred), Elizabeth (usually known as Ciss), John, William (usually known as Bill), Albert, Jesse, Henrietta (usually known as Hettie), Hilda, Daisy, Grace and Mabel.

All five brothers served and happily survived the war, but it is probably worth noting that only one of them was married at the outbreak of the hostilities: Fred had married Mabel in early 1914. At the time of their marriage, could they have imagined that the first year of their life together would be marked by war and separation?

Fred had inherited his father's skills and was an exceptionally talented thatcher and although he volunteered to serve, the Royal Army Service Corps preferred to keep him in Britain to undertake essential maintenance. These undated photographs show an example of his work and an image which is believed to show members of the Service Corps. Fred is third from the left in the back row:

Both reproduced courtesy of Beryl Doig and Margaret Tomalin

105

Until the outbreak of war, Bill's occupation reflected his name as he had been working as a baker. Albert was a valet, employed by the branch of the Lushington family who lived at Oakwood Park; a large house and estate, Maidstone. At the start of August, Albert was enjoying a month's holiday with full board and lodging in Chislehurst. The brothers went to London and were in the throng of people gathered outside 10 Downing Street when war was declared. Bill later recalled that the crowd was fired with patriotism and so he decided straightaway that he was going to join the army, like thousands of other young men.

But such were the numbers of men wanting to join up, that Bill had great difficulty in finding a unit which would accept him. The military authorities were flooded with applicants and were reduced to taking down details and then sending the volunteers home until they were notified that they were required. But Bill was impatient. He got on his bicycle and toured round from one recruiting office to another until he found one that would take him on straightaway. Years later, Bill admitted that his action had been foolish but war had been declared and many young men were in a similar position; desperate to make a contribution and defend the country.

Albert took over Bill's job and also worked as a baker until, as he later expressed it, 'his feet began to itch'. Here are some of his recollections:

> By February 1915, I decided that I wanted a share in this soldiering lark, so I went to Woolwich and joined up. It wasn't many days before I was on my way to France. I did the little training I received at the base in France. They must have been mighty short of men! I volunteered for a course of shoeing and breaking-in of horses, knowing it carried an extra payment of eight pence a day Proficiency Pay, once you had passed the course, so my pay rose to one shilling and eight pence a day. After a while, this began to pall, so I put in for a transfer and found my true niche.
>
> I was sent to join the 122H Battery Royal Garrison Artillery, a sixty-pounder horse drawn unit, and a finer bunch of men you couldn't beat. I stayed with them until the end. Of course, during the three years with them we suffered many casualties, including three Commanding Officers, dozens of gunners, drivers, captains and lieutenants. I was the youngest in the Battery and one of the lucky ones. I received a few slight injuries, and have the scars to prove it. At times, I think the only clever thing I did was to stay alive; I must have had a guardian angel because there were only a few who survived in our outfit. We had reinforcements almost daily, but they went the same way as so many others.

Food was always rather a mixed blessing. Our rations included a pound of bread a day; around ten slices. Breakfast was some of the bread ration with a slice of streaky bacon (or you could dip your bread in the fat, but not both) and a pint of sweet tea. You used half the bread for this meal and saved the other half for teatime. For dinner, there was usually bully beef stew or on rare occasions, a tin of Maconochie's, which was a name given to a sealed tin of meat, vegetables and gravy which was heated up.

This advertisement gives further information about the Maconochie ration. Note that the advertisement includes soldiers from Britain, France, Russia and Italy all depicted as happily gathered together round steaming cans of the stew!

Reproduced courtesy of Peter Sauer
http://joyoffieldrations.blogspot.co.uk

> At times, there was also a ladle of boiled rice to which could be added a handful of dried fruit such as sultanas. For tea, there was the balance of the bread ration and a share of a tin of mixed fruit jam (normally allocated as a one pound tin for every ten men) or, very occasionally, some small bits of cheese, and another pint of tea to drink. I remember that all of the above was consumed in good conditions and when you were lucky. There were times when the supply wagons did not get through the lines and all that was available for days was a monotony of biscuits and bully beef.

We also had an issue of rum; three tablespoonfuls every day. Goodness, did we need it! At first, I didn't care much for it as it was very strong, but after a while I came to like it. Perhaps it was a distraction from the conditions, being knee deep in mud and freezing cold, soaked to the bone for days on end with no change of clothes. Few of us even contemplated whether there would be a tomorrow. The horrendous sights and misery I both witnessed, and took part in, are still just too horrible to begin to describe. I lost so many friends and remember vividly so many incidents.

I was once placed on light duties for a month to help recover from slight wounds, and was made Battery postman. All letters had to be censored by the Commanding Officer so a letter was never sealed down. But once a fortnight everyone was issued with a green envelope which could be sealed and signed to the effect that it contained no military information. You put your name, number and unit on it and just accepted that it was liable to be opened at base. But your officers never knew of your intimate affairs, so these envelopes were always in demand by the men wishing to write to wives and sweethearts. My job as postman was to collect all mail each day from the Commanding Officer dugout and drive back to the advanced field post office, collect mail and return it to the Battery.

One needed a sense of humour to keep going! The guns in our unit were known as 'the hearses'; they were horse-drawn, and six to eight horses were required for each gun. Being classed as 'heavy artillery' we were attached to whatever division was holding the trenches ahead. Sometimes we were in a position for weeks and weeks; it was a slow-moving war, sometimes involving only a few yards a day. Firing our shells, seemed at times, like all hell let loose. We also undertook 'agony shots' during which a gun was elevated to full height and fired behind the enemy lines, at other times they were aimed on the trenches and barbed wire. Our army scouts used to signal back to the guns about the correct direction for firing.

Every day a number of men would have to ride back to the nearest railhead for rations. Shells were always carried in slings and as each of these weighed sixty pounds, this was no light job. The fuses were separate and had to be set and screwed in before firing. There were different fuses; high explosive, shrapnel and delayed action. Our gunners were always busy; during some offensives we must have fired many thousands of shells.

My service included Ypres, Passchendaele, moving right through the Somme twice, Bapaume and Cambrai. During one of my spells on the Somme, Baroness Orczy sent a parcel of cigarettes and tobacco to each member of the forces from Bearsted. I wrote and thanked her as this was very welcome and most generous, but I was upset to hear later on she had told people that she had not received any acknowledgments.

When the Germans withdrew from Russia, they launched a big offensive and drove us back from Cambrai to Albert, a nice cathedral city. This involved retreating many kilometres. What had taken us three years to capture, they retook in as many weeks. Back at Albert, there was a large Madonna and Child statue perched on the top of the cathedral. Everything was in ruins except the Madonna which had been fixed by the engineers, hanging sideways on. Superstition had it that once it fell, the war would end in so many weeks. Strange to say that proved to be true, but not before many more months of carnage and slaughter.

The image of the Madonna and Child statue perched precariously on the ruins of the Albert cathedral proved to be a popular one which was reproduced on many postcards sent home by British troops. This example was sent during 1916; note the smudged pencil marks made by the postal censor.

Reproduced courtesy of Brenda Iacovides

When we fought for the Somme again, the Germans over-ran themselves; our men dug in and during the fighting, the guns stood almost wheel to wheel. When the firing began, it was beyond deafening. Thunder today sounds like the tick of a tiny watch compared to the roar of those guns in actions. I was in the Death Valley and the resulting carnage is just impossible to describe...

But there were lighter periods and during my service, I had three spells of leave from the Front. Like many men, faced with the conditions of trench warfare, and widespread shortages involved in the struggle to survive, I became rather adept at scrounging and learning some of the 'dodges' which were taking place. Some of the latter took place with the connivance of the administration clerks and officers and I was able to use one of these with good effect!

During my first spell of leave I asked for my travel warrant to be made out to enable me to travel to Crewe in Cheshire. Before the war, I had been seeing one of the maids who had worked for the Cazelet family from Tonbridge but after her mother died, she had returned home to Crewe to keep house for her father. She was working at Crewe station serving tea and cakes to the soldiers passing through, but seemed pleased to see me and arranged some accommodation for me during my ten days leave. Whilst serving, I did not draw on my weekly pay but saved it all up for my leave when it was granted, so I was able to fund afternoon teas and trips to the theatre and cinemas etc. The time went quickly, and at the end of it, I caught the train to Euston.

However, I had not given up my rail pass, and by this time, it did not seem fair not to visit home, so I made my way to Victoria and bought a ticket to Bearsted. Mother was delighted to see me. I did not tell her I had already had my leave, but said I had ten days and stayed that time, very quietly enjoying it.

After my time in Bearsted was up, I bought a ticket to Victoria but I still had not surrendered my pass, so returned to Crewe before finally heading back to London.

By now, I was seventeen days overdue and knew that this would need some explanation. I bought a ticket to Dover and asked for an interview with the Embarkment Officer. There was a solution: some of the clerks were prepared, for a cost, to supply stamped and dated forms advising that the above-named soldier was unable to sail today. I then bought seventeen of them which cost me £1.00 (around £260 today) but it was money well spent. On arrival back at the Battery, I handed in the forms and all was well, although our Sergeant Major tore me off a strip. But it was he who had put me up to the ruse! He said he thought that I had overdone it, but all was well.

My second leave was around Christmas time and on the way over the Channel, there was a scare as it was thought U-boats were around our vessel. We sat for hours in the middle of the Channel and so were very late running into Dover. Although my rail pass was for Bearsted, we reached Victoria just in time for me to catch the last train to Maidstone, but there it finished. It was then 1.30am and I could not get a conveyance of any kind. I was invited to spend the night in the waiting room or to walk it. I decided to walk.

Before I left the Battery, I had been issued with new boots and they were still a bit stiff. When I reached Maidstone, five inches of snow had fallen. About a mile from Maidstone, the boots were rubbing and blistering my heels so I took them off and slung them around my neck and plodded on. By the time I reached Weavering Street, my socks were going flip-flop, so they also came off. I made my way barefoot through the village leaving large imprints in the middle of the road, all the way to Cross Keys and through the door. Mother came down and soon got busy. Early next morning, there was a knock on the door; a friend had seen the footprints and followed them. When my mother opened the door, the friend started laughing as my feet seemed like nothing on earth; after mother had bathed and bandaged them, she had totally swathed them in dressings.

I also had some short-lived escapades in France. Once with a few slight wounds and bad abscess I was put on a Red Cross train, taken to base hospital and soon made well again. Whilst there, one of the doctors asked me if I would like to transfer to become his batman; good food, no danger and always under cover in bad weather. I thought it over and decided that despite the attractions of the post, I would rejoin my friends.

The return journey involved changing trains at Rouen. Miss Young, who used to run a bible class I had attended in Bearsted, ran a cafe with a friend, for soldiers in Rouen. She used to write to me every month sending thirst tablets, meat cubes, chocolate and cigarettes well wrapped in religious tracts. I knew her address and decided to see her, but this involved passing the military police, which could be difficult. However, my problem was solved as I noticed an outgoing wagon nearby and hid under the tarpaulin and so was safely away. After about a mile, I dropped off and made my way to her cafe. Miss Young was so pleased to see me as I was the only man from Bearsted who had visited her. I told her I was returning from hospital, and decided to call, so had escaped from the station in the back of a lorry. She was horrified and wanted to take me back, advising me that as she was well-known for her good work so could get me safely through. I told her not to worry; that I would return the same way. Before we parted though, she packed me six hard-boiled egg sandwiches, cakes, chocolate and cigarettes; these were all most welcome.

Despite these slight respites, the war went on and on until something had to give. In the end when it finished and an Armistice announced, I was near Mons in Belgium. They gave out the news and there was just total silence whilst the news sunk in, until the announcement of a double issue of rum, then loud cheers. After a while, we slowly drew back towards the coast and home, but then it was all spit and polish and not my idea of being a soldier. After a short time, and with huge relief, I was demobilised.

Now, many years later, still bearing the scars of battle and of life in general, I agree with these lines which always featured on Charlie Chester's regular radio programmes: 'Do good in this world and it will do you the world of good'. How true.

All five Baker brothers survived the First World War and in May 1971, over fifty years after the war ended held a reunion. The following report featured in the Kent Messenger newspaper:

Old comrades' lunch reunion

FIVE brothers who fought together during the First World War sat round the table for lunch together on Sunday—more than 50 years after the war ended.

Youngest of the bunch was 72-year-old Jesse Baker, from Bromley, who served in France with the Suffolk Regiment.

Next in line was Albert, from Tooting, who served with an artillery regiment in France, and is now a cheerful 75.

Brother Bill, from Beddington in Surrey, is 77 and served with the Royal Army Service Corps in France, and then there is the instigator of the party, another RASC man, Mr. John Baker who lives at Hockers Lane, Weavering and looks very sprightly for his 79 years.

Oldest of the five was Richard, 82, who lives at Plantation Lane, Bearsted, and was in the Middlesex Regiment.

They all met at the home of John's daughter, Mrs. Thelma Brown, at Pembury Gardens, Maidstone, for a celebration lunch and then were joined later by other members of the family for tea.

Left to right: Bill, Jesse, Albert, John and seated; Richard.

Reproduced courtesy of Kent Messenger newspaper group

Thomas Gilbert

The Gilbert family moved to Ware Street in the early 1900s. Tom recalled that during the first decade of the twentieth century some local men had emigrated to Canada and joined the armed forces there once war was declared. Relatives of the emigrants continued to live in Ware Street and received money that was sent home. For many men, joining the army seemed an attractive option: in addition to the chance for adventure, a ready supply of food and accommodation was guaranteed.

On 27 May 1915, there was a major explosion in Sheerness dockyard which was heard over a long distance. Tom particularly recalled that he certainly heard a detonation in Ware Street. It was some time before it was learned that the cause was the explosion of a Canadian Pacific liner called *HMS Princess Irene* which had been converted for mine-laying. Debris from the ship blew far and wide in the explosion; paper fragments fell in Detling and Thurnham. The blast blew open the doors and windows of Hollingbourne School and in Maidstone windows were broken and bottles and jars jolted from shelves. An eye witness recalled that a pall of smoke and flame over two miles high immediately arose from the wreckage.[1] An inquiry was held into the disaster. It established that there were over four hundred people, including eighty Petty Officers from Chatham naval base and seventy six workers from Sheerness dockyard on board, completing tasks prior to the ship departing to lay the mines on 29 May. It was admitted that the men priming the mines had received little training, primarily due to a lack of time, but the explosion itself was ascribed to a faulty primer mechanism.[2]

This dramatic photograph of *HMS Princess Irene* was taken approximately a mile away from the vessel and forty five seconds after the explosion.

Photograph (ADM1/8422/147) courtesy of The National Archives

There were occasions during the war when six small airships would appear over Thurnham Hill for bombing practice. A series of trenches had been dug along the top of the Downs in preparation for possible invasion. At the top of Thurnham parish was Detling aerodrome. Parts of the Medway estuary were less than four miles away from Thurnham and Stockbury, so there were at least two reasons why the area was deemed vulnerable. One airship looked like three joined together and earned the nickname 'the three sausages' although Tom thought that the real name might have been 'blimps'. Tom used to join his friends exploring the trenches. One favourite place was a covered dugout which the troops had named 'Ginger Beer Redoubt'.

In the spring of 1916, Tom Gilbert's father was in the Army. However, the pay was very low. There was an additional separation allowance that was paid to some families but it was not very much, so money was scarce. During the war, temporary exemptions from attending school for up to three months were allowed to address the shortage of labour but it was decided that Tom should leave school. He was nearly thirteen when he went to work. His first wages were six shillings a week. In the absence of his father, he was regarded as the 'man of the house'. The chores he had to perform included tending the garden and allotment. Tom's experience of leaving his childhood behind to assume adult responsibilities and work in agriculture was a common one for many local children during the war.

Michael Perring has been able to confirm and corroborate some of Tom's memories about the trenches. The earthworks formed part of the Chatham first line of defence but they were put to other uses. They were dug by the Kent Fortress Royal Engineers and Infantrymen along the northern side of Detling Hill and the Stockbury valley. The earthworks passed through the northernmost parts of Thurnham parish at Binbury and Beaux Aires. The Maidstone Peace Souvenir published in 1919 mentions that during 1915 to 1916 there was a camp behind St Mary's church in West Meadow, which accommodated a unit of the Royal Engineers and another is known to have been pitched at Detling. This may well have been to house men who were constructing trenches at Binbury.

The log books for both Bearsted and Thurnham schools record two day closures in January 1915 to afford accommodation for soldiers. On 19 August, Frank Goodman, the Master of Bearsted school, noted that poor attendance was probably due to manoeuvres in connection with the camp.[3] This photograph is from a postcard sent on 13 August 1916 and is believed to show a Royal Engineers camp at Detling. Note the number of bell tents and larger marquees on the site:

Reproduced courtesy of Malcolm Kersey

In addition to a line of defence, the trenches were also used to test the effectiveness of bombs dropped from aircraft to attack enemy forces that were deeply entrenched. Maidstone residents were able to witness this bombardment from the air, which took place in the presence of Lord Kitchener, at a safe distance. The destruction wrought by the bombs from high in the air, first by aircraft and then by airships from the Chatham district, could not be seen, but the huge volume of earth which was thrown up by each explosion was easily visible from the different assembly points.[4]

Mr Cornford, a former resident of Detling, recalled that when he was a boy in 1915, soldiers from the 12th Battalion, Royal Sussex Regiment, set up a tented camp on the Pilgrims Way, between Detling and Thurnham. A few yards behind the field gate, a soldier was on guard. He wore a khaki uniform and carried an Enfield rifle. During the summer and for many weeks, the soldiers marched up Thurnham Lane to Detling Hill in one column, four abreast, led by a brass band. He believed that the trenches were used by the men to learn the art of trench warfare so it is possible that they also used the earthworks constructed by the Royal Engineers. Mrs Sybil Trowell also recalled that the soldiers even constructed a facility that could be used as an underground hospital.[5]

The trenches were also used for Volunteer Training as indicated in this report, from the Kent Messenger, 20 October 1917:

> **MAIDSTONE VOLUNTEERS**
> **NIGHT OPERATIONS AT DETLING**
>
> The Headquarter Company ('A') of the 5th Battalion Kent Volunteer Regiment, composed more particularly of men living in and around Maidstone, had a quite unique experience last Saturday night, and early - very early - last Sunday morning. Captain Rhodes, who commands A Company, with a view to further instructing the men under his command in the work which they have undertaken, made arrangements for operations at night on an elementary scale.
>
> It should be stated that these operations had been arranged to take place on the night of 29-30 September, but the scheme was, sad to relate, abandoned, since German airmen took the opportunity of having their night operations then! Which shows once more how necessary it is to beat the Germans before they can beat you.
>
> Saturday night's scheme was first a night march, then the manning of trenches, and a grand finale of a night attack. The exercise was arranged mainly with a view to exhibiting to the Volunteers what it looks like to be entrenching at night, to keep perfectly quiet, to seek out your enemy and to destroy him. By kind permission of the General Officer Commanding Chatham Garrison, a section of the trenches near Maidstone was allotted to Captain Rhodes and his Company for the operations.
>
> A scheme was prepared and approved by the Brigade Major at Sittingbourne (Captain D Chesney) who went over the proposed operation on the spot, accompanied by Captain Rhodes and the Battalion Adjutant. Subsequently, Officers and Non Commissioned Officers of the company were taken by their commander on a visit to the trenches by daylight and Captain Rhodes allotted the various duties.

Michael has also discovered that another part of Thurnham was involved in defence research. Airship raids on the Humber and Thames estuaries in May 1915 had made it clear that there was an urgent need for some sort of early warning system. Experiments with sound mirrors had taken place elsewhere in 1914, but in July 1915 further trials were started at Binbury, in the north western extremity of Thurnham (Ordnance Survey grid reference TQ 813605). It is not clear why Binbury was chosen and despite the close proximity of Detling aerodrome, the aircraft used in the tests were flown in from other locations.[6]

Professor Mather of the City and Guilds Engineering College in South Kensington, arranged for a sound mirror, approximately sixteen feet in diameter, to be constructed at Binbury Farm, then owned by Mr Murray. A section of the vertical cliff face was hollowed out to an almost spherical shape but tilted upwards and a sound collector was mounted on a pivot at the focal point. The apparatus was rather like a stethoscope whereby a person could listen to sounds detected by a trumpet shaped cone. The collector could be moved across the face of the mirror to establish where the sound was loudest. It was envisaged that the reflector could sweep up to thirty degrees of the horizon. Bearings to the target could then be read from vertical and horizontal scales on the collector.[7]

In the subsequent report it was claimed: [8]

> It is extremely probable that a Zeppelin with its very large engines and gearing would be easily heard at a distance of twenty miles. We think a concrete reflector of sixteen feet diameter would be superior to one of chalk as the reflecting surface would be harder…

Both reproduced courtesy of Kent Messenger newspaper group

Memories of the First World War

This photograph shows the hollow spherical shape cut into the cliff face and was taken at the time of the experiments in 1915. A good indication of the size of the sphere can be gained from the man standing on the platform, believed to be Professor Mather: [9]

Photograph (AIR1/121/15/40/105) courtesy of The National Archives

Despite disappointing results in subsequent experiments carried out by the Army in Wiltshire, several mirrors lined with concrete were constructed around the south-east coast. These later mirrors were evidently able to successfully detect enemy aircraft as the reports were sent to a central command centre to assist defensive measures during raids in 1917 and 1918. All of these experiments were forerunners of the technology which would ultimately lead to the development and successful deployment of radar in the Second World War.[10]

This photograph of the sound mirror site at Binbury was taken in May 2013; only a small scar in the landscape remains to indicate the land was ever disturbed.

Reproduced courtesy of Michael Perring

Memories of the First World War

Grace Dibble

At the start of the war, Grace Dibble's family lived at The Poplars, Roseacre Lane before later moving to Ware Street. These slightly edited recollections give an impression of the impact of war on the younger generation of the community: [11]

> At home in Bearsted there had been murmurs of the possibility of war with Germany. But it was an unpleasant shock on August 4th, when I came out of the railway station in the early evening to be told by a neighbour, "It's war!" I was returning from a birthday party in the home of a school friend in Lenham, where we had enjoyed ourselves and there was no talk of war. Aged only twelve years, I could not appreciate all the incomprehensible horrors of the future.
>
> After the initial shock, it was soon brought home to us what it meant to the village as men enlisted, then appeared briefly in khaki before embarkation. These were young men whom we knew and many whom mother had taught in the village school. Women were organised, very quickly, to knit and sew, with khaki wool and materials provided. My sister and I had learned to knit father's long cycling stockings and our own stockings, so we knitted socks for the Forces. In the nearby Mission Room there were women cutting up materials for pyjamas or three-tailed bandages. The latter we found puzzling at first. We wound endless skeins of wool. I particularly hated knitting the very long stockings in natural greasy wool which were worn with rubber boots.
>
> An Appeals Committee was soon organised under Mrs Tasker. Over 100 garments were sent to the depot in Maidstone following a special appeal by Fleet Surgeon A G P Gipps for wounded soldiers in Dieppe. Then there was a special fund for the Belgian refugees who had escaped to the United Kingdom. It was the Prince of Wales who made an appeal for a National Relief Fund.
>
> We could hear the German aircraft flying over our area to raid London. During daytime air raids, we were assembled in the corridors in the Maidstone Grammar School for Girls. Once I was spending a weekend with a school friend in East Malling, we went down into the cellar during a raid. This was the first time I had this frightening experience. Later in the war we had to go down into our own damp, cold and dark cellar during raids. One bomb did drop not far off, in Chapel Lane. Up on the North Downs was Detling aerodrome, for military purposes.
>
> My father became a sergeant in the Volunteer Training Corps in Bearsted. He was proud of his khaki uniform and little cane. Men who were over thirty-eight years or unfit for active service met in a hall behind the White Horse Inn for rifle shooting on three days in the week. Then there was attendance at a camp near Canterbury for training: father conscientiously studied the special handbook. Once father organised the billeting of soldiers in Bearsted and Thurnham, on their way to France; our house was full and our beds were given up to the troops, while we slept on the floor. We fed them in relays, with roast beef and apple pie for dinner. The men were from a brigade of the Royal Sussex Regiment, so for a long time afterwards we frequently sang "Sussex by the Sea", after we had bought a copy of the song. Some of them were in a tented camp in Detling at the foot of the North Downs. We soon learned other songs: "It's a long way to Tipperary", "Keep the Home fires burning" and "Pack up your troubles in your old Kit Bag".

This undated photograph shows one of the tented camps. Although officially described as located in Detling, the 10th Battalion of the (Kent County) Royal West Kent Regiment was actually camping on part of Penenden Heath. As mentioned previously, training manoeuvres were undertaken with the 12th Battalion, Royal Sussex Regiment, in Detling and on the slopes of the North Downs.

Reproduced courtesy of Kent Messenger newspaper group

The daily newspapers kept us informed about events beyond Bearsted and overseas. It was a shock to many families when conscription was made compulsory in 1915. Though we were young, my sister and I were interested in the leadership of Earl Haig on the Western Front and of T E Lawrence in the Near East. We could share the sorrow of those lost in 1915 when the *Lusitania* was sunk and we could realise the sinister menace of the U-boats and mines. It was not so easy to appreciate the great horrors in 1916 when the Zeppelins bombed London. We kept a copy of the newspaper picture of a Zeppelin being brought down at Cuffley.

We were proud to read of the visits King George made overseas during the war. Many British people were sorry to learn that Prince Louis of Battenburg was forced to resign as First Lord of the Admiralty. In Bearsted and Thurnham there was some anti-Baroness Orczy feeling by a few people, because she was Hungarian. The year 1917 brought the introduction of shipping convoys and the revolution in Russia; though then the far reaching results could not be visualised. We were shocked by the murder of the Czar, because he was a cousin of our King.

Of course, there came rationing of foods. We were fortunate in that Auntie Lucy in Gloucestershire regularly sent us a pound of her farm butter in a tin. I remember how we hated maize pudding, as a substitute for rice. We also disliked the shortage of sugar. The members of the Women's Institute certainly gained a reputation for their skilfully produced jams and marmalades.

On one occasion a troop-train broke down in the cutting opposite to our house in Ware Street; the train stretched back as far as the bridge. It was too heavy to cope with the incline of 1 in 60 up to Bearsted Station. From Maidstone there is a rise of 150 feet in the two and three-quarter miles. It was in early autumn, so we loaded up baths with Beauty of Bath apples, taking them across the road and through Mr Hodges' garden to lower down the bank to the train. We were accustomed to seeing the troop-trains crossing the bridge on their way to the coast. We used to wave to them. We hated to see these young men going overseas, especially after casualties were announced in church and printed in the parish magazine, and local newspapers.

Many people in Britain were put in touch with prisoners of war in German prisons. We adopted one in Berlin and used to send him parcels of socks and food which we could spare, in tins. When his little girl was born in Kent, I was asked to choose a name for her. This took much consideration, but finally I wrote to him and to his wife, suggesting Katharine. I was disappointed to learn later that she was christened Kate.

As Grace mentions, people were encouraged to contact and adopt British prisoners of war that were in German prisons, sending them tinned food and other comforts but there were also other fund-raising efforts which also took place throughout the war. In 1916, a Kentish Prisoners of War Fund had been set up and the following year, advertisements about donations appeared in the local press.

A typical advertisement which appeared in the Kent Messenger, 17 November 1917:

KENTISH PRISONERS OF WAR FUND
Registered under War Charities Act, 1916.

Committee—Chairman, Lord Harris, G.C.S.I., G.C.I.E.; The Marquis Camden (Lord Lieutenant of Kent); Lt.-Col. J. P. Dalison (Depot the Royal West Kents); Major A. H. Tylden-Pattenson, D.S.O. (Depot the Buffs); J. L. Spoor, Esq., J.P.
Regimental Care Committee—THE BUFFS, ROYAL WEST KENTS.
Hon. Treasurer—D. J. WILLIAMS, ESQ., London and Provincial Bank, Rochester. Hon. Secretary—J. L. SPOOR, ESQ., J.P.

THE COMMITTEE has on its books over 1,200 men, Prisoners of War in Germany and Turkey.

The cost of Food Parcels sent out is £3,500 per MONTH, which has to be provided by the Committee and its local Branches in the County.

Donations and Subscriptions will be welcomed and acknowledged by the Hon. Secretary.

Mr. SPOOR,
REDE COURT, ROCHESTER.

Reproduced courtesy of Kent Messenger newspaper group

The first local death was George Taylor in Gallipoli, in August 1915. Later that year came the news of the death of our curate, Captain W. M. Benton, who had at once joined up as a fighting officer and not as a chaplain. As we would have expected, he was killed while rescuing a wounded soldier. The next year we were distressed to hear that Arthur Wilkinson, Christian Message and Robert Rose had been killed in action. At sea, Reggie Ball lost his life. In Ware Street, the inhumanity of war was emphasised when our milkman, Harry Hodges, had to return after suffering a very bad gas attack - something from which he never really recovered.

But there were cheerful occasions when we were especially proud of our men from Bearsted and Thurnham. In 1916, James Frazier was awarded the Distinguished Conduct Medal. Two years later our baker, Lance Corporal Lionel Datson was awarded the Military Medal. Showing great courage, he brought his ambulance three times through a village which was being shelled, thus enabling a dressing station to be cleared of wounded. Major Daniell was awarded the Russian Order of St.Stanislav of the 2nd Class in 1918.

We were also proud of Dora Harnett who had joined the Women's Army Auxiliary Corps, and was sent to France, as a driver, attached to Army Service Corps. There were ripples of pride when Mr and Mrs Mannerings of The Street received a letter from King George V, congratulating them on having six sons in the army…

The war had many long-lasting effects on British Women. As early as 1914, women began to work in factories to release men, especially those producing munitions. The following year saw about 600 women typists in Whitehall. All spheres became open to women, including the police force, where they wore long navy skirts. This had the effect of bringing about a real levelling of society. In 1918, at last, came the 'Qualification of Women Act', giving the vote to women over thirty years of age! In the Auxiliary Army Corps, the women played an important part in backing up the Forces.

It was natural that clothes became much more practical. When bobbed hair became fashionable it was a disappointment to my sister and me that father would not permit us to have our long hair bobbed!

Below is a transcript of a notice which appeared in the Kent Messenger, 14 September 1918, about a fund-raising cricket match which took place on the Green organised by Pelham Warner, usually known as Plum. This would have undoubtedly been attended by Grace's father, George, as he was a stalwart of Bearsted Cricket Club, acting as their Honorary Secretary for over twenty years. Plum was an England test cricketer who lived in Caring Lane. He was later knighted for his services to the sport.

CRICKET

Captain P F Warner writes us from Caring House, Leeds, that a cricket match has been arranged to take place on Bearsted Green this Saturday between the Royal West Kent Regiment and his XI in aid of the Bearsted and Thurnham Wounded and Prisoners of War Fund. Today, he adds, when the existence of our Country and Empire so largely depends upon our magnificent sailors, soldiers and airmen, he confidently relies on the sympathy and help of the public. It is for those men, their grit and their courage, their hardships, and their battles and their heroic lives, that he appeals. Several prominent cricketers have promised to play (including Major C H B Marsham, J Douglas and J W Hearne) and by kind permission of Colonel Dalison the band of the Royal West Kent Regiment will play during the afternoon. The game will begin at 11.45 and stumps will be drawn at 6 o'clock.

Reproduced courtesy of Kent Messenger newspaper group

The worlds of business, and finance, were of course, at the centre of the war effort and were directly affected. The conflict certainly ushered in two new bank notes to supplement the five pound notes. These were introduced after the August Bank Holiday in 1914. The one pound note was intended to replace gold sovereigns and the ten shilling note was intended to replace the half-sovereign.[12]

Perhaps one of the most successful fund-raising schemes was that promoted by the government which encouraged people to invest in War Bonds. These allowed the government to borrow money and astonishing amounts were raised in this scheme.

Advertisements for the War Bonds featured in the local press. This notice appeared in the Kent Messenger, 15 December 1917, just in time for Christmas:

> FEED YOUR HORSES ON ENGLISH OATS and SAVE
> £1 per Quarter and
> invest the saving in
> **NATIONAL WAR BONDS.**
> We can supply the Oats the Post Office the Bonds.
> **R. WAKEFIELD & SONS,**
> 59, Stone Street and 13, Middle Row, Maidstone.

Reproduced courtesy of Kent Messenger newspaper group

Local companies and businesses were also called upon to invest in War Bonds. A report from the Kent Messenger, 16 March 1918, concerning a Business Men's War Bond Week shows that Maidstone raised £305,817: three times the amount which the borough had been called upon to raise and around £10,700,000 today. Sir Marcus Samuel of Mote Park also gave three generous donations. But such an effort was not without other popular marketing inducements; the bonds were sold from a tramway shelter in the High Street and were stamped on board an aeroplane, either by the members of the RFC or by Boy Scouts, who were seated in the cockpit of the night fighter!

Eventually, though, after four years of war, there came the Armistice, as Grace concluded:

> I shall never forget Armistice Day on November 11th, 1918. At the Maidstone Girls' Grammar School, we were all in the playground waiting for Miss Jones to return on her bicycle to hear if it was really true that the war had at last ended. When the joyful news was brought, we trooped into the hall and sang, "Praise my soul, the King of Heaven".
>
> In Bearsted, like so many other villages, the end of hostilities was celebrated by dances. We had a fancy dress dance when I wore a long white voile dress with a Greek Key design embroidered in yellow wool, which took me a long time to sew. On my 'golden' crown I had painted the word, Peace. I carried a sheaf of Madonna lilies.

A number of postcards were produced to mark the end of the First World War. Here are two examples:

Both reproduced courtesy of Roger Vidler

Keeping In Touch

The First World War marked the end of the 'Golden Age' of postcards! Cards were a popular means of quick and easy communication and their convenience had been boosted by the introduction of the 'divided back layout' which enabled messages and addresses to be written on the reverse side of postcards, thereby freeing the whole front of the card for an illustration. Cards sold in millions and collecting them became very popular.

The value of receiving and sending letters and cards as a boost to morale was soon recognised by the armed service. For many men serving abroad in difficult conditions, it was frequently easier to write a brief message than to write a letter. Pre-printed cards were produced to make it easy to send a communication even in difficult circumstances - all that was required was the address of the recipient and the deletion of the sentences which did not apply. Those for the army were officially known as Army Form A2042, Field Service Post Card, but were widely known as 'Quick Firers', and gave basic information to a soldier's family. An unused example is shown on the right. All letters and cards were subject to censorship before being collected by battalions and sent across the Channel to be posted in Britain. Censorship prevented details of precise locations or activities, but that was of little concern since the real point was simply to do one's best to stay in touch, to keep spirits up, to make light of worries and to reinforce those bonds of love, friendship and affection that were put under such severe strain by the war.

```
NOTHING is to be written on this side except
the date and signature of the sender. Sentences
not required may be erased. If anything else is
added the post card will be destroyed.
────────────────────────────────────
I am quite well.
I have been admitted into hospital
  { sick    } and am going on well.
  { wounded } and hope to be discharged soon.
I am being sent down to the base.
                        { letter dated_____
I have received your    { telegram ,,_____
                        { parcel   ,,_____
Letter follows at first opportunity.
I have received no letter from you
  { lately.
  { for a long time.
Signature }
only.     }
Date_____
[Postage must be prepaid on any letter or post card
 addressed to the sender of this card.]
(93871) Wt. W3497-293 4.500m. 7.16 J. J. K. & Co., Ltd.
```

Some messages were very brief, often domestic, but invariably moving. Here are extracts from a series of cards an officer wrote to his wife during 1915. The first one was sent in May:

> My darling wife,
> Have at last got a decent coat, but there are no chevrons to be had. Will you ask Albert to go up to Hobsons and purchase two sets; send one to me and keep one at home.
>
> From your loving Percy

On 11 August, Percy had another request to make:

> Am sorry it was not possible to write to you fully this evening as I have a beastly headache and to make things worse have had the misfortune to break both lenses of my specs. Am sending them home by Cpl Alsop to save time and delay. He will post them at Waterloo Station tomorrow. Will you please get them put right and returned without delay? The expense will be borne by deductions from my pay.

In early September 1915 Percy sent another card:

> Am delighted my letter of 29 August was so cheerful. Didn't know it was possible to be so these days. It often so happens when one least feels like writing one does best...

All reproduced courtesy of Roger Vidler

Keeping In Touch

During the war, postcards were used to bolster morale, promote propaganda, lionise leaders, champion heroic deeds, record major events, illustrate the destruction wrought by war and even provide glamour and pin-up cards. Both sides in the conflict invoked religion and religious images in their support, examples include the famous 'Angels of Mons' shown on the left, drawings of patron saints protecting soldiers in battle, and images of the fallen cradled in the arms of the Lord. Christ was also depicted comforting those who had lost husbands, brothers or sons in battle:

Sentiment played an important part in the illustrations used in cards; soldiers dreaming of their loved ones back home; mothers, wives, sweethearts and children all praying for the safe return of their son, dearest boy or father. These are two examples:

All reproduced courtesy of Roger Vidler

Keeping In Touch

Cards which showed entire units and companies of soldiers became an easy means of reference to many families whose members were serving in the armed forces. Pictures were often taken alongside their horses, vehicles, tanks, guns, shops and increasingly as the war progressed, aircraft. Some cards were sold specifically to raise money for charitable causes. Song cards were popular too, reproducing the words of favourite songs of the time over deeply sentimental illustrations. They were often sold in packs of four or six, featuring one verse on each card.

Here are shown two instances of some of the rarest cards sought by collectors because they include specific aspects of the war. The first postcard is believed to show part of an Army Service Corps convoy at an unidentified location but superficially similar to the Green at Bearsted!

In this image, there are drivers and vehicles from the Royal Army Medical Corps. Note the hospital wagons for wounded troops in the background:

Both reproduced courtesy of Roger Vidler

Silk cards proved particularly popular for adding to family collections of cards. These were often embroidered designs, largely hand sewn by French women onto strips of silk fabric and then cut and mounted on to card. They bore patriotic and sentimental designs - the forget-me-not flower was a favourite motif - and some cards even included pockets into which smaller cards could be inserted. So attractive were these cards that they were often sent unused and in special envelopes to protect the delicate fabric. Two examples of these cards are shown here:

Both reproduced courtesy of Malcolm Kersey

Keeping In Touch

Whilst many of the themes used for the cards were common on both sides of the conflict, only the British used wry humour to lighten the danger, privations, frustration and misery of war. This shared sense of humour between the British soldier and civilian has been described as one of the most under-played winning factors in the war. The prime exponent of this approach was Bruce Bairnsfather. He had been at the second battle of Ypres, and later became an office-cartoonist in the Intelligence Corps. Bairnsfather produced what many consider the most famous postcard of the war, shown here:

"Well if you knows of a better 'ole, go to it."

Other artists who frequently produced comic images used for postcards include Dudley Buxton, Reg Carter, Frederick Gothard, Reg Maurice, Donald McGill, Fred Spurgin, Doug Tempest and Lawson Wood; their work is now all widely collected. Here is an example by Donald McGill:

Art thou weary
Art thou languid?

Both reproduced courtesy of Roger Vidler

The First World War undoubtedly marked a high spot of the postcard as a means of communication. After 1918, with the wider availability of cameras and telephones, a doubling of postage rates (to 1d!) and less frequent deliveries, the long decline of postcard sales began as people found other means of convenient communication.

Roger Vidler

Armistice, Peace and Aftermath

The Armistice was declared and then signed in a railway carriage halted at Compiègne Forest in France on 11 November 1918, after 1,559 days of war. This is a French postcard showing the Allied and German commanders just after the Armistice was signed:

Reproduced courtesy of Malcolm Kersey

It was not the end of the First World War; it was to be regarded as a pause in the conflict during which attempts were made to negotiate peace. A lasting peace was subsequently established through the Paris Peace Conference and the signing of the Treaty of Versailles in 1919.[1]

Although news of the Armistice, had been widely distributed to the armed forces during the morning of 11 November, it also included the advice that it was due to take effect from 11am, so it was decided that fighting should continue right up until that time. There were many reasons for this, including a belief that if the Armistice subsequently failed, gaining a favourable position before cessation was important if fighting restarted. As a result, even at 10.58am, gas shells were still being dropped, and over two thousand men died on the last day of the war.[2] For some, the news of the Armistice and a suspension of fighting, took time to sink in. A British army officer commented: [3]

> ...It took some time getting used to, this knowledge. There was a future ahead; something I had not imagined for some years...No more slaughter, no more maiming, no more mud and blood, and no more killing...no more of those hopeless dawns with the rain chilling the spirits, no more crouching in inadequate dugouts scooped out of the trench walls, no more dodging of snipers' bullets, no more of that terrible shell-fire. No more shovelling up bits of men's bodies and dumping them into sandbags...and no more writing of those deadly difficult letters to the next of kin of the dead...

And an American soldier later recorded his mixed reaction: [4]

> ...you can imagine - no you *can't imagine*, it is impossible for anyone to imagine who did not experience it, the sense of relief and pure joy that came into our hearts... At first we took it quietly. The feeling of gratitude was too deep for noisy expression. Instead of running out in the street yelling...we felt like stealing away into some lonely spot and crying for sheer joy...

The following is a slightly edited transcript of a report giving details of how Maidstone received the news of the Armistice. This appeared on 16 November 1918 edition, Kent Messenger:

PEACE!!!

MONDAY'S MAGNIFICENT NEWS

HOW IT WAS RECEIVED IN KENT

THE REJOICINGS

JOY IN THE COUNTY TOWN

Maidstone received the joyful news just before the 'ceasefire' was due to sound on the Western Front. All through the weekend, of course, it had been anticipated. Yet there was a certain subduing doubt - due, perhaps, partly to the influenza, and partly due to incredulity that the Germans would even in such a hopeless hour, ignominiously yield to the drastic terms which it was presumed we had presented to them. For the 'flu, gripping not only our friends, but ourselves, seemed to have been more patient in producing a sober restraint than Big Bertha was when there was a chance of her muzzle being turned towards Kent. Even the concurrence of municipal events on Saturday with the imminence of peace failed to lift us into ecstasy. And Monday dawned with a chastened faith in the inevitable. The fact of peace seemed so enormous that the dull human brain seemed incapable of appreciating it. We wanted another faculty to help us to assimilate it. So little had we risen to the occasion that we even argued that an armistice does not necessarily mean peace; it was possibly only a temporary cessation of the grim carnage of war.

All this was before 11 o'clock, when the Kent Messenger had the satisfaction of communicating official news of the armistice to the townspeople and the authorities.

Then the whole atmosphere changed; and we realised to the full, as with one swift and indisputable revelation, that the war had indeed come to an end - that we could watch the moon rise this week without trepidation; that again we should soon be children of the light instead of human moles groping about in the darkness; that our lads at the front, millions of them, could lift their eyes to the autumn skies and find them clear of the devastating Boche - that they would lie down that night without the lullaby of the roaring cannon, either far or near.

And what was our outward and visible manifestation of this feeling? We had evidently not prepared for the occasion. How could we improvise? At first out came the flags - the public flags over the Town Hall, the church and various other buildings. Then the tradespeople produced similar symbols and arrayed the fronts of their premises. Then scurrying motor-cars appeared, apparently from nowhere, similarly decorated; and meanwhile the pedestrian was making a frantic raid on a well-known emporium near the Post Office, so that the colours of England and the Allies, in all sizes, soon dominated the scene. But we were still voiceless. We seemed to be acting a hymn without a tune. Some great musician was needed to touch the chords of our emotions and draw out the music. And more and more we felt that this was an occasion to vociferate as the crowds swelled and swelled. Every shop turned out its staff, and the men and boys, women and girls, from every large establishment, poured forth into the Broadway, over the Bridge and into the High Street.

Armistice, Peace and Aftermath

But hark! Music, surely. Yes, the Gloucester Band had come to the rescue. Its lively strains came nearer and nearer, from the direction of the Bridge and never was music more welcome. It played gaily, the hearts of the boys were in the notes; the crowd responded to the pulsations of the music. People marched in step with the band, they danced, they became excited and ecstatic, and within half an hour the scene was as demonstrative and vociferous as could be desired.

We have said nothing of the shriek of the steam whistles from the various factories, or of the siren of the Electric Works - that ominous sound which has so often filled the stoutest spirits with fear. But these were about 11 o'clock, let off at full blast, and inharmonious as they were they were welcomed; they seemed to supply that fierce shriek of joy which everybody yearned to give. But which to human throats seemed impossible.

In course of time the spontaneous demonstrations of democracy were somewhat diverted by the call of Authority. Events had somehow moved to the top of the street and the band had halted below the Queen's statue, with a dancing throng around, when the inspiring strains of 'Who Killed Cock Robin?' suddenly ceased. The Mayor was speaking. His Worship, robed, stood in the doorway of the Town Hall and was talking to an attentive crowd bent on catching is words. To many, however, the words were inaudible. But it was sufficient for them that those within hearing were quite in agreement with his Worships patriotic declarations...the upshot of the speech was that the Mayor declared a public holiday and forthwith business was suspended for the day - or at least part of it...

It had been contemplated that in the afternoon Authority would again take a hand in the celebration, and even show itself in procession to an admiring town, but the rain intervened and while the Mayor and Corporation manfully faced the elements on a hastily erected platform in the High Street, from which further speeches were made, they sensible decided that the procession could be dispensed with. This was supplied however by the band and lads and lasses whose exuberance had not been exhausted found a further outlet for it in marching exercise. To detail the further proceedings of the day would only be to repeat what has already been said. People came and went, so that there was always a crowd in the main part of the town, and they enjoyed the experience, not known for four years, of seeing themselves under the glare of gas and electricity, for the street lights shone with unusual brilliance, and the Gas Company produced its familiar illumination. Many private citizens who had been compulsorily saving light during these years, now also put the rays on and in places Maidstone was its old self again.

At the meeting in the afternoon, already referred to, the Mayor called for the National Anthem, and this having been honoured, the Vicar led three cheers for the King. The Mayor remembered 'Our Boys at The Front', and 'Our Sailors' and they were given three times three in return.

Never in the history of Maidstone had such a crowd assembled in its ancient High Street, His Worship ventured to remark, and certainly never on such an auspicious occasion. When the local Press went out to our boys at the Front, it was his great desire that the first message of Maidstone should be one of gratitude to them. They had had horrible times to endure with much suffering and it was only their magnificent and indomitable spirit that had carried them to final triumph "We have fought for love of our own country; we have fought for something even more than that," said the Mayor, "for the love of life and the liberties of the whole world. And we older men and women ought to go down on our knees and thank God for the spirit of the young men of our race." To those who had passed through years of anxiety and dread suspense, His Worship offered the solace that their loved ones would soon home again...

The following message was received on Tuesday by the Mayor of Maidstone "Lambeth Palace", The Mayor, Maidstone - I share your rejoicings today and join my thanksgiving and prayers with yours- Archbishop of Canterbury. The Mayor replied - "His Grace the Archbishop of Canterbury, Lambeth Palace - Your gracious message during our rejoicings and thanksgivings is deeply appreciated by myself and all the inhabitants of Maidstone - Foster Clark, Mayor.

The bells of All Saints and St Michael's were rung merrily at intervals during the day.

Reproduced courtesy of Kent Messenger newspaper group

A further report in the same edition of the Kent Messenger mentioned that Bearsted and Thurnham had held Armistice celebrations on the Green. These included fireworks and the lighting of a huge bonfire complete with an effigy of the Kaiser on top, before a peal of the church bells was rung and a service of Thanksgiving at Holy Cross church.

Armistice, Peace and Aftermath

Both Bearsted and Thurnham Schools were closed on Armistice Day, but for a rather more practical reasons than marking the end of the war; there was an outbreak of influenza in the communities.[5]

Walter Fremlin of Milgate Park, also decided to commemorate the end of the war. He and his wife, Lilias, had no children, but they had been immensely distressed by the number of casualties in the war and the effect of the losses upon local families. He therefore gave to every child of his estate workers, a War Savings Certificate, worth fifteen shillings and sixpence. This certificate and compliments card was given to Eileen Blandford. Note his added words to the latter: 'After the world's greatest and saddest war'.

Both reproduced courtesy of Jenni Hudson

It was popularly believed that full demobilisation would be quickly achieved and, indeed, this process started on 9 December, barely four weeks after Armistice Day. But delays crept into the system and movements to demobilisation camps, which were initially intended as holding points for a maximum of twenty four hours, commonly lasted for several weeks. Upon demobilisation, soldiers were provided with railway coupons, a ration book, a clothes allowance and a weekly pension of thirty eight shillings which was paid for twenty weeks.[6]

There were other reasons for the delay; British troops were still being deployed in the Rhine, in France and supporting the White Army in Russia following the revolution. There was widespread public unrest about this in Britain during January 1919 and so the Prime Minister, Lloyd George turned to the Secretary of State for War and Air, Winston Churchill, for advice. He suggested that a reserve army should be made up of those men who had joined late in the war. Three men out of four would therefore be released and the Government would pay the fourth man double wages. It was a solution, of sorts, but the majority of people just wanted to return to their families and resume their ordinary life.[7]

After six months of hard negotiation, and five years after the assassination of the Archduke Franz Ferdinand, the Versailles Peace Settlement was signed on 28 June 1919. It was time finally to mark the dearly-bought and achieved Peace but many people thought it should be a commemoration rather than a celebration. King George V approved a plan to hold a Peace Day on 19 July 1919.[8]

Bearsted was slightly ahead of national events as a series of dinners was held at the White Horse to welcome back returned members of the armed forces. On the next page is a transcript of the report from the Kent Messenger, June 1919:

BEARSTED AND THE WAR

Entertaining the Returned Heroes

'Bearsted bears her blushing honours thick upon her with a modesty well becoming her present prestige in the annals of England's glory' as some most interesting details that came out on Thursday evening go to show. The occasion was a friendly smoking concert got up amongst 'the boys' themselves who have been 'demobbed' and held at the White Horse Assembly Rooms which had been tastefully decorated for the occasion. Mr Thomas Presland, R.N., occupied the chair, and the guests, with a few invited friends numbered about 150, the proceedings being characterised throughout with much patriotic enthusiasm and gusto. Mr Presland thanked the people of Bearsted very heartily for their thoughtful kindliness in sending parcels and comforts to the sick, wounded, prisoners and others, and stated that the number of men from the village who joined up was approximately 100, killed or died of wounds 27, wounded 40 per cent.

The honours gained had been as follows:- James Frazier D.C.M., Lionel Datson and Sergeant Sid Attwood the M.M., Chief Petty Officer Dick Goodhew, the Croix-de-Guerre and the Italian Order, A Watkins, the Croix-de-Guerre, P Holmes, the Russian Order, and Harold Shorter had been made a King's Corporal.

The village had good cause to be very proud of such a fine record, and it was a great pleasure to him to present, on behalf of those of his comrades, a handsome watch with suitable inscription: 'to James Frazier in recognition of the noble exploit in the field that had gained him the D.C.M.'. Mr James Frazier, in acknowledging the gift, said he had certainly gained the D.C.M., but they had all been fighting alike for the old folks at home, and had each been doing his bit.

His joy was somewhat marred by the sorrowful reflection, that during the ten years he had been on service, he had lost both father and mother, who would today have felt so proud to see him honoured by his King and fellow villagers alike. His emotion would not permit him to say more than to thank them all (applause).

Mr John Baker proposed the toast of 'absent friends', among whom he included those who were unable to be present for various reasons, those who are still doing their bit, and those sacred ones who had fallen and made the great sacrifice. The company drank the toast standing in silence.

Mr E G Taylor, of Thurnham, proposed the toast of 'The good friends of the village, who did so much for us in the war', in the way of parcels of necessaries and comforts, of which good work, he said, the White Horse appeared to have been the grand headquarters. (applause). He referred with regret to the death of Mr W W Taylor, and expressed sympathy with Mrs Taylor and the bereaved family. Mr George White responded.

Mr Doughty, Maidstone Secretary of the Comrades of the Great War, spoke briefly on the aims and objects of his society. Mr B Pearce of Maidstone, presided at the piano, and among those who contributed to the harmony of the evening were Messrs Harry Pearce, Tom Walkling, John Watson, Mr Doughty, Harry Apps, A Selves, F Pratt, W Frazer, James Frazier (by special request 'Neuve Chapelle'), Albert Baker, Tom Presland, Harold Shorter, C Peck, Ernest Farewell, E G Taylor and others.

Reproduced courtesy of Kent Messenger newspaper group

A committee, headed by Lord Curzon, agreed that the national events for Peace Day would include a Victory March through London. The march would go past a symbol of those who had died in the conflict. Edwin Lutyens, an architect, was asked to design the monument and produced some sketches for a 'cenotaph', a word meaning a monument or memorial to someone buried elsewhere. The thinking behind it was that it resembled an empty tomb in which a body could be laid. As it had to be produced urgently, the Cenotaph was made from wood.[9]

Armistice, Peace and Aftermath

A partial transcript of a report about the proceedings in London taken from the Sunday Times, 20 July 1919: [10]

> Standing in the centre of Whitehall, the memorial was most impressive, with its summit crowned by a great laurel wreath, holding in place a Union Jack that was draped loosely above the monument. The sides were adorned with the White Ensign, the Red Ensign and the Union Jack representing the Navy, the Mercantile Marine, and the Army...
>
> ...On the steps were a number of tiny home-made wreaths and humble garden flowers, placed there by loving hands. A very pathetic instance occurred just before the arrival of the procession. A lady, richly attired in the deepest mourning, emerged from the crowd. Silence immediately fell upon the huge assemblage. Slowly advancing to the Cenotaph, she reverently laid a beautiful wreath at its base. She remained for a few moments with head bowed in sorrow and pride before again disappearing among the people.

Reproduced courtesy of The Times and Sunday Times newspapers

Despite the inconvenience of the location in Whitehall where it interrupted the flow of six lanes of traffic, and although originally intended to be a temporary structure, the monument rapidly formed a focus for war widows and bereaved families throughout Britain. Somehow the Cenotaph seemed to be the silence of grief made visible, marking the absence of the missing men. Floral tributes continued to be laid at the base of the monument throughout the year. Plans to remove the monument to another location such as Parliament Square, were quietly dropped.[11]

There were many local festivities to mark Peace Day. Maidstone's celebrations were opened by a parade of school children which assembled by the Town Hall in the afternoon in front of His Worship the Mayor, Councillor G Foster Clark, members of the Corporation and the Town Clerk. After the public reading of a message from the King and a speech from the Mayor, a procession, headed by the bands of the Grammar School, the Officers Training Corps, and the Cadets, 2nd Battalion Royal West Kent Regiment, marched to Mote Park where Sir Marcus and Lady Samuel received them. After tea, each child was presented with a brand new sixpence and a tin of Sharps Kreemy Toffee. This was followed by a programme of sports and games. It was later estimated that around six thousand people were in Mote Park that afternoon.[12] This is the scene outside the town hall during the occasion:

Reproduced courtesy of Kent Messenger newspaper group

The communities of Bearsted and Thurnham combined to mark Peace Day. An edited transcript of the report from Kent Messenger, 26 July 1919:

> **BEARSTED AND THURNHAM**
>
> Bearsted and Thurnham, being so intermixed, joined up for their Peace Celebrations at historic Bearsted Green. Most people were awakened in the early morning by bell ringing and at 7 o'clock came the sound of an old Crimean cannon in Milgate Park. From the main turret of the church floated a flag. The band of the 2nd Battalion Royal West Kents under Band Sergt J Coombes, played selections of music, and there were sports of all kinds for children, women and men, many of which were sources of immense amusement, and the beauty of it was that class distinctions were dropped and all joined together in the various competitions. In the tug-of-war competition the women of Thurnham defeated Bearsted, but in the men's final tussle, Bearsted became victorious. 230 school children were entertained to a substantial tea in the White Horse Hall, which had been tastefully decorated and later some 204 people were similarly entertained, while coffee, tea, tobacco and other luxuries were sent to such as were unable to attend. The fancy dress carnival was a great success and then came a grand march past, headed by the amusing Bearsted Fancy Dress Band, the distribution of prizes, the magnificent firework display and the huge bonfire which could be seen for miles around.
>
> Major McQueen had an arduous task as Chairman of the various Committees and he was assisted by Messrs W H Whitehead, Dibble and Dewhurst, Colonel and Mr H V Lushington and many others, while Mr W Prime Jones had his hands full as M C over the day's doings as a whole. Amid the throng on the Green moved Mr and Mrs Walter T Fremlin and party, the Baroness Orczy, Mr Montague Barstow, Mr Jack Barstow and friends, who took a lively interest in the gay festivities. Mrs H Brook and Mrs A Spence were mainly responsible, with much willing help at the tea. Over £50 had been subscribed voluntarily for the celebrations and Mr Walter Fremlin defrayed the cost of the fireworks, etc., which were under the direction of Mr Stanley Johnson. Everyone voted the Celebration an unqualified success.

In 1919, Maidstone Council published, in association with the South Eastern Gazette, a booklet called the Maidstone Peace Souvenir.[13] Maidstone's part in the Great War was recorded. The booklet also encompassed some of the work undertaken by nearby villages and this photograph of wounded soldiers from Voluntary Aided Detachments being entertained on Bearsted Green was included. Unfortunately there are no further details.

Both reproduced courtesy of Kent Messenger newspaper group

Armistice, Peace and Aftermath

At the first Remembrance Sunday, held on 11 November 1919, King George V asked that the public to observe a short silence at 11am. This tradition continues today both on 11 November and on the Sunday nearest to that date.

In addition to the Cenotaph, the tomb of the Unknown Soldier became another focus for individual and national grief. The idea had been inspired by Rev David Railton, an army chaplain who had been a curate at Ashford, later Folkestone and then vicar of Margate. During the war he had seen a grave marked by a wooden cross which had the words 'An Unknown Soldier' written across it in black pencil. He wondered if one of these unidentified men would serve as a symbol of comfort and courage to those relatives left behind who had had no funeral to attend and no body to bury. What if one body could be brought out of the mud of France, never to be identified, was given the equivalent of a state funeral. Would this somehow fill the gap left by the loss of a loved one? The idea was agreed upon and promoted by the Dean of Westminster and the Prime Minister.[14]

One body retrieved from the battlefields carrying no identifying mark other than the uniform of a British soldier was selected and sealed in a coffin made from an English oak tree felled in the grounds of Hampton Court. One of King George V's personal swords was laid on the top as a tribute during the journey back to Britain. The cortege travelled back to Dover on *HMS Verdun* and continued by train in a specially decorated railway carriage to Victoria Station. On 11 November 1920, the funeral procession made its way through Grosvenor Place to Hyde Park Corner, then Constitution Hill to the Mall, under the Admiralty Arch and on to Whitehall. It then stopped at the Cenotaph and the king unveiled the permanent replacement of the previous wooden structure. It was thirty five feet high and made of stone. After what seemed to be an eternity of absolute silence which had followed Big Ben sounding eleven o'clock, the procession resumed its route to Westminster Abbey.[15] This postcard shows the Cenotaph shortly after the unveiling:

The funeral service for the Unknown Soldier was simple and brief. The coffin was lowered into the floor of the Abbey and packed around it was earth which had been brought from Flanders. A last handful of the earth was scattered on to the coffin by the king. A slab of York stone was laid on the top of the grave as a temporary measure. Later, a slab of Tournai black marble would be placed on the top of the grave and inscribed with brass lettering made from melted down ammunition. The location was deliberately sited in the abbey to ensure that, for ever after, no one, especially a monarch approaching the altar at their coronation, would be able to avoid side-stepping the grave of a man who had given his life for his country.[16]

This is a recent photograph of the tomb of the Unknown Soldier:

Both reproduced courtesy of Malcolm Kersey

Armistice, Peace and Aftermath

During the war, it had become very clear that organisations were needed to look after the welfare of ex-Servicemen. Today, the best known of these, of course, is the British Legion, but a number of small charitably-based organisations also arose. The majority of these smaller enterprises aimed to act as bases for re-unions and were attempts to address issues of welfare. However, given the great number of former Servicemen in need of help, many of these organisations were really far too small to promote their work and eventually merged with the British Legion, which received the status of 'Royal' in 1971.

In Bearsted, a branch of the Comrades of the Great War Society was founded and the first meeting took place in November 1919. A report which appeared in the Holy Cross parish magazine:

Comrades of the Great War Society

It may be of interest to our readers to hear that this Society has now come to Bearsted. It is non-sectarian and non-political and has as a fundamental principle a policy of close association with its various organisations throughout the Empire, so that a member of any Post or branch is assured a welcome. Comradeship and all advantages of mutual benefit wherever he may be. The primary unit of the organisation is the Post, the secondary unit (a hundred members or more) the Branch, and the County unit is the Division.

The idea of the Society is to form Assistance Bureaux to keep in touch with local employers, trade unions, employment exchanges and local advisory committees, so as to be able to assist and advise Comrades on questions concerning their welfare; another aim is the provision of Clubs and organising a system of medical and legal aid for Comrades; a further idea is eventually to promote facilities for seaside and country holidays for Comrades and their dependents by a system of holiday exchanges between Branches and Posts; and among many other activities it is desired to organise, where possible, cricket, football, athletic sports etc and to promote inter-Post, Branch and Divisional competitions.

On Wednesday November 19th, a meeting of those who have served in the Great War was called by Mr J Hampson and fifty or sixty men turned up. This meeting was addressed by Mr J A Clarke for Kent Divisional Headquarters, Ashford, and decided to form a Post of the Comrades of the Great War in Bearsted. Before leaving the room, about thirty five men enrolled themselves as Comrades and then proceeded to elect a Committee with the following officers: Captain Brigadier-General Allen; Treasurer Mr G Mercer; Secretary Mr T Presland.

On Thursday 11th December, a General Meeting of the Post was held at 7pm in the Village Hall. The meeting confirmed the previous election of Committee and Officers and added two more names to the Committee. The next business was to elect a delegate to the meeting of delegates, which is to be held in Maidstone on Saturday 13th and for this Comrade H H Jury was unanimously chosen. The Meeting then decided that the monthly general meetings shall be held on the first Thursday on each month at 7pm during the winter and after some further discussion broke up, but before leaving, fourteen Comrades enrolled themselves as Members, bringing the total up to over fifty.

In conclusion, it is desirable to point out that in this Society there are no ranks; all are equal as Comrades whether they be Dukes, Generals or Privates and all will not only assist each other, but the Society as well.

Reproduced courtesy of Holy Cross church

The work of the Royal British Legion, is now known and recognised throughout the world; its foundation and the adoption of a red poppy as its symbol were the result of many elements which coincided shortly after the war.[17] Flanders and Picardy were the sites of some of the biggest offensives and a result of the fighting, buildings, trees and roads simply disappeared. Where once there were homes and farms there was mud and apparent desolation. However, by a quirk of natural history, countless poppy plants germinated and bloomed; huge areas of land turned scarlet. The symbolism was readily apparent.

Armistice, Peace and Aftermath

In 1915, a doctor called John McCrae, was working with the Canadian Armed Forces. He had seen the phenomenon of the poppies whilst posted to a casualty clearing station during the second Battle of Ypres to oversee burials. The experience led him to write a poem later published in Punch magazine: [18]

> In Flanders fields the poppies blow
> Between the crosses, row on row,
> That mark our place; and in the sky
> The larks, still bravely singing, fly
> Scarce heard amid the guns below.
>
> We are the dead. Short days ago
> We lived, felt dawn, saw sunset glow
> Loved and were loved, and now we lie
> In Flanders' field.
>
> Take up our quarrel with the foe;
> To you from failing hands we throw
> The torch; be yours to hold it high,
> If ye break faith with us who die
> We shall not sleep, though poppies grow
> In Flanders fields.

The symbolism of the poppy began to spread. In 1918 the poem was reprinted in the American Ladies' Home Journal and caught the eye of Moina Michael who was working with the Young Mens Christian Association War Secretaries headquarters. Two days before the Armistice was signed, Moina attended a conference in New York. With a small donation given by the delegates as a thank you for her work and inspired by the poem, she bought twenty five red silk poppies from a local shop. She wore one on her coat and gave the rest to the delegates in memory of the fallen. In France, Anne Guerin had been thinking along very similar lines. She realised that if a sufficient number of artificial poppies were made, they could be sold. Funds raised through the sales of the flowers could help people who had been involved in the war and who now required financial and other assistance.[19]

In Britain, Major George Howson also wanted to help people who had been hurt in the war and had formed the Disabled Society. George had met Anne Guerin. He was impressed by the simple idea of a buying a flower; a simple gesture, yet one which could help so many in need. He quickly realised that the people who worked in his society could make the poppies in Britain. He was assisted by the British Legion and together, members of both organisations worked to make paper flowers for the first Poppy Day which was held on 11 November 1921. Samuel Green from Bromley drew up a simple yet effective design for the flower.[20] The tradition of selling poppies had begun.

Eventually the Disabled Society became part of the British Legion. King George V was impressed with the work of the Legion and offered Patronage. A factory was established and to this day it employs many disabled people to make the poppies that are sold to mark Remembrance Sunday. Every poppy and every poppy wreath that is worn or laid at a war memorial in this country and the Commonwealth is made in a Royal British Legion poppy factory. The main base for the Royal British Legion in Kent is at Aylesford but the poppies are manufactured in Richmond, Yorkshire. Today, nearly everyone has heard of the Poppy Appeal. More than 36 million poppies, 98,000 wreaths and 730,000 small Remembrance crosses are made by hand every year.[21]

Armistice, Peace and Aftermath

For many years there was a Bearsted and Thurnham branch of the British Legion. This photograph of the members was taken on 6 May 1935:

Reproduced courtesy of Chris and Sue Hunt

Back Row (left to right): W W Guest, A Sent, S Goodenough, S Curtis, W J Hawkins, E J Jordan, G Ovenden, A G Hunt, E Weaver

Third Row from front: T Boddy, E A Abery, A V Pearson, J Baldwin, F Smith, H W Smith, W Rigden, G Apps, W G Apps, R Gregory, R C Holliday, E Wilkinson

Second row from front: A Holtum, F Gatland, S Plumb, A J Bishop, Dr J C Fisher, F Bevis, W Foster, G Hepden, H Relf, T W Swain, C M Stack, E C Bodiam

Front row: S Sackett, J N Hampson, D F Hampson, A Barker, W S Maxted, T Presland, Rev A O S Scutt, L S Monckton, H E Chapman, Rev G A M Griffiths, F May

On ground in front: E Moon

Second World War: 1939 to 1945

By the end of August 1939, it was evident that the warm summer weather enjoyed by much of Britain's population stood in deeply marked contrast to the strained diplomatic and political relationship between the nation and Germany. Many people perceived that after a series of crises, another war was almost inevitable. Newspapers began to publish advice in an effort to calm widespread apprehensions.

A transcript from the Kent Messenger, 2 September 1939:

If the Crisis Breaks....
POINTS YOU SHOULD REMEMBER
THEY SPELL SAFETY

We all hope that the present crisis will pass over as it has on previous occasions, but should it break, readers are reminded of the following points:

1   Gas masks should be handy - they should be carried to work. Everybody should already have fitted their gas masks so that they are comfortable to wear and so that if a newspaper or card is put over the bottom of the cylinder it is impossible to breathe: this shows that the gas mask is fitting correctly.

Remember time is the essence of the contract. It should be possible to find, put on and adjust your gas mask in six seconds. Try it on your family and on yourself!

One other point: don't take a long breath before putting your gas mask on - you might breathe in poisonous gas. When the gas mask is on, breathe out to eject any poisonous gas which may be inside the mask before you get it on.

2   Windows should be covered with a good thickness of cellophane paper or criss-crossed with gummed paper. If you haven't this, pasted brown paper will do. This will not prevent the window breaking but it will prevent the splinters flying. Skylights should be covered inside with wire netting so that glass doesn't fall on people below.

3   Bombs. Don't worry about high explosives. In one ten-thousandth of a second you will either be dead or alive. If you are dead there is nothing to worry about - if alive, thank God for it.

Gas Bombs. Probably very little gas will be used - the chief danger is from incendiary bombs. These should be tackled either by pouring sand on them or with a fine spray of water to make it burn out quickly. It will be up to those living in detached houses to see to the incendiary bombs themselves, for the fire brigade will specialise on the congested areas where there is danger of fire spreading. If an incendiary bomb falls in the garden, let it stop there and burn out of its own accord - it will be quite harmless.

In your dug out there should be a pick and shovel in case you should get trapped; wireless to keep you happy; and a loud gong or bell to attract attention should you be unable to get out. Of course, if there are two entrances, escape should be easy

4   Last of all, don't panic: the people in Spain got quite used to war dangers - it is always the first week which is the worst.

After All, It May Never Happen

Reproduced courtesy of Kent Messenger newspaper group

Second World War: 1939 to 1945

War was officially declared on 3 September 1939. The announcement was made at 11.15am during a radio broadcast by the Prime Minister, Neville Chamberlain. He had almost visibly aged under the strain caused as the situation worsened and advised the nation that an ultimatum given to Hitler to withdraw from its invasion of Poland had been ignored and the failure of negotiations as 'a bitter blow'.

Below and on the next page are transcripts of the main reports which appeared in the Daily Mirror, 4 September 1939:

BRITAIN'S FIRST DAY OF WAR; CHURCHILL IS NEW NAVY CHIEF

BRITAIN AND GERMANY HAVE BEEN AT WAR SINCE ELEVEN O'CLOCK YESTERDAY MORNING. FRANCE AND GERMANY HAVE BEEN AT WAR SINCE YESTERDAY AT 5pm

A British War Cabinet of nine members was set up last night. Mr Winston Churchill, who was First Lord of the Admiralty when Britain last went to war, returns to that post.

Full list of the War Cabinet is:-

PRIME MINISTER	Mr Neville Chamberlain
CHANCELLOR OF THE EXCHEQUER	Sir John Simon
FOREIGN SECRETARY	Viscount Halifax
DEFENCE MINISTER	Lord Chatfield
FIRST LORD	Mr Winston Churchill
SECRETARY FOR WAR	Mr Leslie Hore-Belisha
SECRETARY FOR AIR	Sir Kingsley Wood
LORD PRIVY SEAL	Sir Samuel Hoare
MINISTER WITHOUT PORTFOLIO	Lord Hankey

There are other Ministerial changes. Mr Eden becomes Dominions Secretary, Sir Thomas Inskip goes to the House of Lords as Lord Chancellor, Lord Stanhope, ex-First Lord, becomes Lord President of the Council, Sir John Anderson is the Home Secretary and Minister of Home Security - a new title. None of these is in the Cabinet, which is restricted to the Big Nine. These are the men who will be responsible for carrying on the war. But Mr Eden is to have special access to the Cabinet. The Liberal Party explained last night that although Sir Archibald Sinclair had been offered a ministerial post, the Party had decided at this moment not to enter the Government.

The first meeting of the new war Cabinet took place last night. Mr Churchill was the first to leave and the crowd broke into a cheer as he walked out. Mr Hore-Belisha was driven away by a woman chauffeur in uniform. The Premier went from Downing Street to Buckingham Palace where he stayed with the King for three quarters of an hour.

It was announced last night that as from September 16 all petrol will be rationed. In the meantime all car owners are asked not to use their cars more than is vitally necessary.

Today all banks throughout Britain will be closed

Australia yesterday declared war on Germany. "Where Britain stands, stand the people of the Empire and the British world," said Prime Minister Menzies in a broadcast message last night.

New Zealand has cabled her full support to Britain. There is a rush of recruits in Canada. At Toronto a queue of 2,000 men lined outside the Recruiting Office. Japan has assured Britain of her neutrality in the present war.

Britain's last two-hour ultimatum to Germany was revealed to the people of Britain in a memorable broadcast from Downing Street by Mr Chamberlain at 11.15 yesterday morning. By that time Britain had been at war for fifteen minutes.

The House of Commons met at noon. The Premier spoke quietly to a grave, resolute House. He told of the ultimatum delivered in Berlin three hours before, of the assurances demanded from Germany before 11 am.

"No such undertaking was received by the time stipulated." Mr Chamberlain said, "Consequently his country is now at war with Germany."

Only once the Premier's voice trembled. "For no one," he said, with a trace of emotion in his voice, "has it been a sadder day than for me. Everything I worked for, everything I hoped for, everything I believed through my public life has crashed in ruins!" But now he was able to speak freely. "I trust I may live," he said, as the cheers resounded through the House, "To see the day when Hitlerism has been destroyed so as to restore the liberty of Europe."

Reproduced courtesy of Mirror newspaper group

"STAND CALM, UNITED WE SHALL PREVAIL":

THE KING

Seated alone in his study in Buckingham Palace, the King broadcast to his people last evening. In serious, measured tone, he said: "In this grave hour, perhaps the most fateful in our history, I send to every household of my people, both at home and overseas, this message, spoken with the same depth of feeling for each one of you as if I were able to cross your threshold and speak to you myself.

For the second time in the lives of most of us we are at war. Over and over again we have tried to find a peaceful way out of the differences between ourselves and those who are now our enemies.

"But it has been in vain. We have been forced into a conflict.

For we are called, with our allies, to meet the challenges of a principle which, if it were to prevail, would be fatal to any civilised order in the world. It is the principle which permits a State, in the selfish pursuit of power, to disregard its treaties and its solemn pledges; which sanctions the use of force, or threat of force, against the sovereignty, and independence of other States."

His voice rose a little, the pace of his words increased, as he declared: "Such a principle, stripped of all disguise, is surely the mere primitive doctrine that might is right; and if this principle were established throughout the world, the freedom of our country and of the whole British Commonwealth of Nations would be in danger.

Breaking Bondage of Fear

"But far more than this - the peoples of the world would be kept in the bondage of fear and all hopes of settled peace and of the security of justice and liberty among nations would be ended.

This is it the ultimate issue which confronts us. For the sake of all that we ourselves hold dear, and of the world's order and peace, it is unthinkable that we should refuse to meet the challenge.

It is to this high purpose that I now call my people at home and my peoples across the seas, who will make our cause their own. I ask them to stand calm and firm and united in this time of trial.

The task will be hard. There may be dark days ahead, and war can no longer be confined to the battlefield. But we can only do the right as we see the right, and reverently commit our cause to God of one and all. If we keep resolutely faithful to it, ready for whatever service or sacrifice it may demand, then, with God's help, we shall prevail. May He bless and keep us all."

The King wore the dark blue un-dress uniform of an Admiral of the Fleet. As he spoke, the Queen listened in another room. When Britain entered the war at eleven o'clock, the King and Queen were together in their private rooms at the Palace.

Reproduced courtesy of Mirror newspaper group

Second World War: 1939 to 1945

The Daily Mirror also gave this advice on 4 September 1939:

DON'T...

This is intended for YOU. Read it, remember it, pass it on to your friends. First, and most important of all things is

Don't Listen to Rumours

You will get all the news that matters—bad or good—in your newspapers. Disbelieve anything else you hear — particularly alarmist news. Next thing to remember is

Don't Broadcast Information

You may know that there is an anti-aircraft gun cunningly concealed in the field next to your garden. But that's no reason for passing on the information. It may reach someone who should not know it.

Don't Lose Your Head

IN OTHER WORDS—KEEP SMILING. THERE'S NOTHING TO BE GAINED BY GOING ABOUT WITH THE CORNERS OF YOUR MOUTH TURNED DOWN, AND IT HAS A BAD EFFECT ON PEOPLE WHOSE NERVES ARE NOT SO GOOD AS YOURS.

SO EVEN IF A BOMB FALLS IN YOUR STREET—WHICH IS UNLIKELY—KEEP SMILING.

Don't Listen to Scaremongers

You will always find scaremongers about. Just treat them as you would a smallpox case—move on quickly. The enemy loves to spread rumours. Part of his campaign was to panic Britain—and he will still try it, hopeless although it is.

Don't Cause Crowds to Assemble

THE POLICE HAVE ENOUGH TO DO. IF YOU SEE PEOPLE GATHERING AND THERE IS NO REASON FOR YOU TO JOIN THEM—WALK ON. IN OTHER WORDS—MIND YOUR OWN BUSINESS.

AND ABOVE ALL DON'T FORGET THE OLD ARMY ADAGE.

Be silent, be discreet, enemy ears are listening to you.

NOW GET AHEAD, DO YOUR JOB AND DON'T WORRY.

Reproduced courtesy of Mirror newspaper group

A transcript from the Kent Messenger, 9 September 1939:

WE CAN ALL HELP WIN THIS WAR

The war in which since Sunday the British Empire has been engaged will be won, or lost, not only in the field of battle, but in the homes of the people.

That is why, although we cannot all serve in the armed forces, every one of us can contribute in very real measure towards the victory which we are confident will be ours.

We can contribute by carrying on quietly with our jobs, being cheerful and keeping our heads.

The Germans have started this war with their people ignorant, bewildered, and hungry.

We have met their challenge with a stout heart, not only because we understand the issues and know we are fighting in a just cause, but because our larders are full, our resources plentiful.

We do not expect our lives to go on as usual. We are prepared to suffer inconvenience and danger, and we are proud to think that in some small measure we can in our own homes share the perils and hardships of our men who wage our war on land and sea and in the air.

By meeting our own problems with equanimity and cheerfulness, we are making their task more easy and doing our duty to our country and our cause.

Reproduced courtesy of Kent Messenger newspaper group

Second World War: 1939 to 1945

ABEL, W A
Cavendish, The Grove
Married
8 October 1937 19 Group, Romeo 2, Bearsted
Royal Observer Corps

This photograph shows Mr Abel in his Royal Observer Corps uniform:

Reproduced courtesy of Evelyn Pearce

ABERY, E A
Head of Special Constabulary and Assistant Billeting Officer
Received medal in 1942

ADAMS, Robert
1 Yew Tree Villas, Plantation Lane
Royal Navy

AKEHURST, Harold
Hollebeke, Ashford Road
Married
Wife Mary (née Anderson) of Royal Air Force Hospital, Lochmaw, Stranraer, Scotland
Royal Air Force
Service Number 1156865 Sergeant

Harold married Mary on 16 January 1945 at Holy Cross church. Mary was serving as an Aircraft Woman, Women's Auxiliary Air Force.

ALLEN, Thomas James Whitacre
Upper Barty
Father Alfred James Whitacre Allen, Brigadier-General
Born 1 March 1918
Single
Adopted three sons
Awarded Military Cross 1943
Captain, later Major

Royal Military College, Sandhurst
Duke of Cornwall Light Infantry 1938
Service included 1st Battalion, Duke of Cornwall Light Infantry
1st Battalion, 5th Royal Gurkha Rifles
6th Gurkha Rifles (later 6th Queen Elizabeth's Own Gurkha Rifles)
Postings Lahore, Mozzagrogna in Italy, Penang, Gurkha Depot, HQ Far East Land Forces

Died 19 June 2005

Second World War: 1939 to 1945

Part of an obituary from an undated edition of the Daily Telegraph:

MAJOR TOM ALLEN

Won an MC with the Gurkhas

MAJOR TOM ALLEN who has died aged 87, won a Military Cross with the Gurkhas in Italy in 1943 and, after the war, devoted himself to philanthropic projects in Nepal.

On the night of 27 November 1943, the 1st Battalion 5th Royal Gurkha Rifles (Frontier Force), part of 17th Indian Infantry Brigade, 8th Indian Division, advanced in heavy rain on the village of Mozzagrogna, north of the River Sangro, Italy. When the artillery barrage was lifted, the Germans emerged from their underground positions and raked the forward slopes up which the Gurkhas were scrambling, sliding and slithering as they did so. Allen, then a captain, was in command of one of the two leading companies in the attack. They broke through the enemy defences but the Germans fought back fiercely and turned each house into a strong-point. By midnight, his company held part of the village but he was then wounded during a fierce counter-attack. When the commander of the other forward company was also wounded, Allen took command of them both and organised the defence of the village. He was wounded again during successive counter-attacks but he stayed at his post, encouraging his men and sending back vital reports.

Two companies of 1st Battalion Royal Fusiliers (1RF) were ordered into support the Gurkhas and parties of both battalions soon found themselves under siege from enemy tanks, flame-throwers and snipers. At first light, when their ammunition was almost exhausted, Allen undertook a hazardous journey through a part of the village that was still occupied by enemy snipers in order to replenish supplies. He refused to wait while his wounds were being dressed but instead led the relief party straight back to his men. Shortly after 8am, 1/5 RGR and 1RF were ordered to withdraw but some of the troops did not receive the order and a grim game of hide and seek began among the ruins of the village. Allen was twice wounded again before being evacuated. The citation for the award of an immediate Military Cross paid tribute to the great personal courage that he had shown.

Thomas James Whiteacre Allen was born on 1 March 1918 at Bearsted, Kent. His father, Brigadier-General Alfred Allen was commissioned into the Buffs and fought in the Zulu War and on the North West Frontier.

Young Tom was educated at Malvern before going to the RMC Sandhurst. He was commissioned into the Duke of Cornwall's Light Infantry in 1938 and posted to the 1st Battalion at Lahore.

He transferred the following year to 1/5 RGR and saw active service in West Iran and then in Italy. In 1947 when India achieved Independence, 5th Royal Gurkha Rifles remained part of the new Indian Army and Allen transferred to the 6th Gurkha Rifles (later 6th Queen Elizabeth's own Gurkha Rifles) and was subsequently posted to Penang, Malaysia, with the 1st Battalion. Allen had two spells at the Gurkha Depot before moving to HQ Far East Land Forces. He retired from the Army in 1951 in the rank of major and settled in Penang.

During the next 40 years, Allen involved himself in many philanthropic projects in Nepal, supervising and financing them in person. These included road improvement and water storage schemes and building village schools and health centres.

In the years 1961 to 1965, Allen organised the planting of 8,000 trees at Baidichhap Kayakmi to prevent soil erosion. Seedlings were imported from Scotland and nurtured locally before being planted. He returned to England in 1988 to settle in Kent and remained active until well into his eighties, swimming at least a mile every day. Tom Allen died on 19 June 2005. He never married but he adopted three sons and brought them up as members of his family. He educated them and they looked after him devotedly in his old age.

Reproduced courtesy of the Daily Telegraph

Second World War: 1939 to 1945

AMOS, Marjorie Daisy
Winona, Ashford Road
Married
Husband Eli Alfred Frederick Cork of 17 Prestledge Avenue, Ramsgate
Message Writer Civil Defence

Marjorie married Eli on 25 July 1944 at Holy Cross church. Eli was a serving as a Corporal in the Royal Air Force.

ANDERSON, Einar Ralph
Married
Wife Audrey Monica (née Prescott) of Share Donard, Ashford Road
Home Forces, Bearsted
Corporal Canadian Army

Einar married Audrey on 6 December 1941; she was a nurse. 'Home Forces' was the name for a group of people, usually men, who were considered to be unfit for overseas and front line service, but still wanted to serve their country in an active role. Their duties often involved acting as a guard for important utility sites such as electric or gas installations.

APPLETON, Charles Routledge
5 Council Houses, The Street
Married
Wife Irene Mary Veronica (née Keay) of 5 Council Houses, The Street
Lance Sergeant Army

APPS, William G
2 The Cottages, Chapel Lane, Ware Street

ASHBEE, Paul
Four Walls, Spot Farm Estate
Born 23 June 1918
Married
Wife Richmal (née Disher)
Children Edward and Kate
1939 Royal West Kent Regiment
Lance Corporal 1940

Died 19 August 2009

Paul was one of the most distinguished archaeologists which Kent has ever produced. He was interested in archaeology from childhood, and aged only 15 in 1933, oversaw the first excavation of Thurnham Roman villa. He shone at history and geography at school and later at the German language, although reaching six feet in height when he was 12 years old, generated a lot of comment! In 1939 war intervened and he joined the Royal West Kent Regiment, gaining a lance corporal's stripe the following year. His ability with languages was deemed useful and from 1946 to 1949, he was deployed in the Control Commission for Germany, although he later commented that his English accent sometimes intervened! His acute addiction to books probably saved his life during the war. He was unable to resist the sight of a bookcase crammed with intriguing texts and entered a ruined house in the northern Rhineland to investigate: a shell landed directly outside the window where he had stood but a moment before! After the war, he studied for a diploma at the University of London Institute of Archaeology. Subsequently, he undertook excavations for the Ministry of Works for over thirty years, including Sutton Hoo and was a Patron of the Kent Archaeological Society from 2002 until his death in 2009.

ATKINS, Daphne M
Sunways, The Grove

Second World War: 1939 to 1945

ATTWOOD, Lewis

AUSTIN, N E
Little Budds
Royal Artillery

AVARD, John A G G
23 Royston Road

AYRES, Arthur
Ware Street

AYRES, C R
Glencoe, Royston Road
Army

AYRES, Herbert T
Rose Cottages, Ware Street

BACON, Geoffrey
Edensor, Ashford Road
Royal Marines

BACON, Stewart C J
Conrace, Ashford Road
Royal Air Force

BACON, William

BAILY, Kenneth L M
Hill House, Ware Street

BAKER, Anthony Hugh Randall
Olde Highgate
Father William Archie Nicholls Baker, Lieutenant Colonel
Married
Wife Margaret (née Fairbrother)
Captain Royal Artillery

Anthony married Margaret on 26 April 1947 at Holy Cross church. Margaret was working as a radiographer at Lymington and District Hospital, Hampshire, when they married.

BAKER, Anthony Richards
East Len, Spot Lane
Parents Violet Ellen Baker (née Cook) and the late William Baker
Single
Coldstream Guards

Second World War: 1939 to 1945

Protection and Shelter

As the international situation deteriorated and war looked increasingly likely, companies began to produce goods that would be of use should war be declared. There were many different types of air raid shelter and window protection products that were available to buy, as these three advertisements which appeared in the Kent Messenger, 11 November 1939 show. These shelters were still very expensive to purchase for many households, so people used Anderson and Morrison shelters at home instead, and these became the best known designs against air raids.

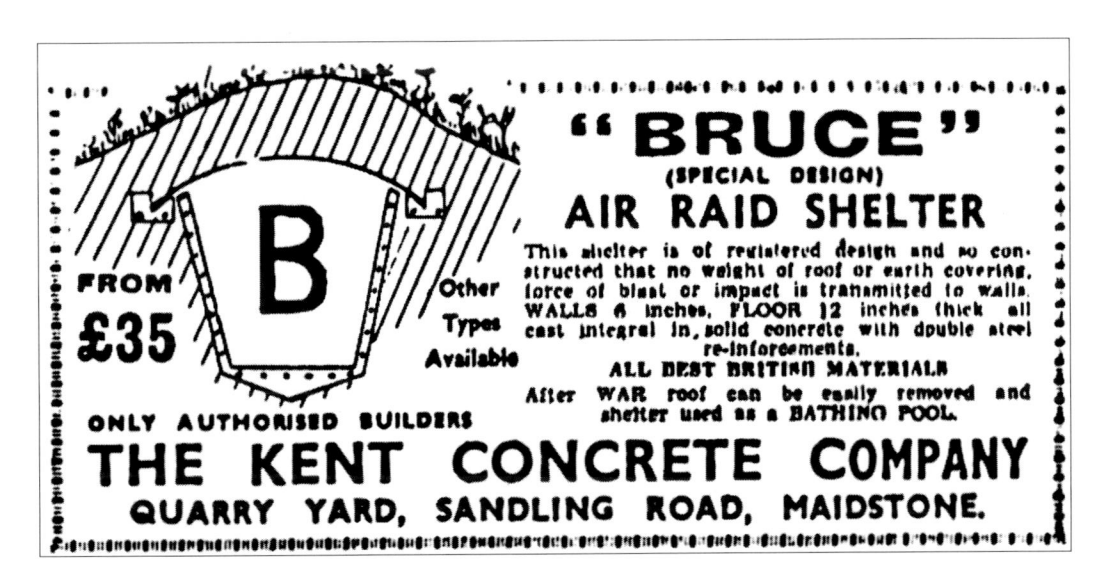

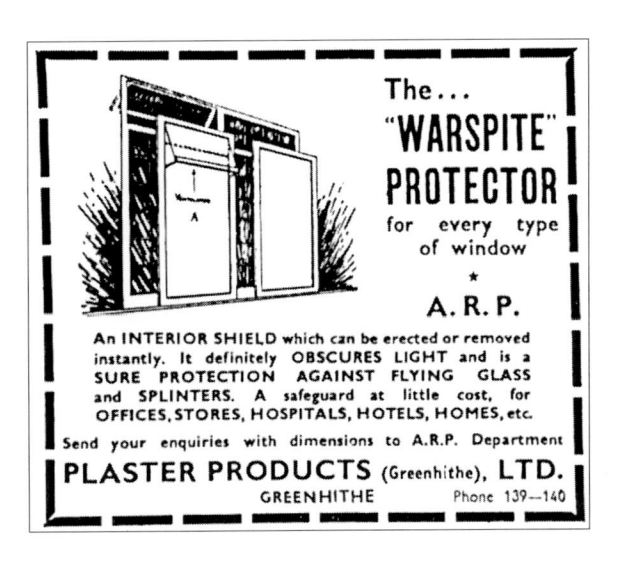

Reproduced courtesy of Kent Messenger newspaper group

Richard Kresja could recall that there was a public air raid shelter in the middle of the road in Cavendish Way. It is understood that there were others in Bearsted and Thurnham although the specific locations of many of them may have now been forgotten.

Other precautions were also taken: the windows of Bearsted school were protected with very fine gauge wire netting and the foundation stone was covered up as it included the names of local villages: Bearsted, Thurnham, Boxley and Detling.[1] An air raid shelter was not built at the school until November 1940.

Second World War: 1939 to 1945

BAKER, Claude
Swaylands, Yeoman Lane
Married
Wife Elizabeth West (née Campbell)
Yeoman of Signals Royal Navy

Claude married Elizabeth on 5 October 1946 at Holy Cross church

BAKER, Ernest J
Holly Tree Cottage, Weavering Street

BAKER, Ethel Violet
East Len, Spot Lane
Parents Violet Ellen Baker (née Cook) and the late William Baker
Single
Auxiliary Territorial Service

Ethel was usually known as Susan or Sue

BAKER, H R
Olde Highgate, Plantation Lane

BAKER, Jack

BAKER, Kenneth Frederick
Binwell, Plantation Lane
Married
Wife Patricia Helen (née Locker) of Coleman's Hotel, East Grinstead
Corporal Royal Army Service Corps
Captain Royal Artillery

Kenneth married Patricia on 4 May 1944 at Holy Cross church. Patricia was serving as a Private in the Auxiliary Territorial Service.

BAKER, Robert F
The Leas, Lord Romney's Hill
Captain Royal Artillery

BAKER, William H
East Len, Spot Lane
Parents Violet Ellen Baker (née Cook) and the late William Baker
Single
Royal Marines

BALDERSTONE, Bernard G
170 Royston Road

BALDWIN, John
Married
Fauchons Lane, Ashford Road, Maidstone
19 Group, Romeo 2, Bearsted
Royal Observer Corps

This photograph shows John in his Royal Observer Corps uniform:

Reproduced courtesy of Evelyn Pearce

Petrol Rationing

When war was declared, petrol rationing was also announced. Only essential workers in the community, such as doctors, would be entitled to a petrol ration, so many families put away their cars 'for the duration', little realising that it would be many years before the vehicles would be used again.

This advertisement appeared in the Kent Messenger, 30 September 1939 and highlighted the idea that the petrol ration would go further if vehicles were adequately maintained:

The rationing brought increased administration as petrol pumps had to be read daily to ascertain sales, ration coupons had to be accounted and a daily form returned to the Ministry of Transport. Some garages took on contracts from local companies which assisted the war effort. Shorts Brothers of Rochester agreed contracts with garages with machine shops. Parts for flying boats and other aircraft could be prepared, machined and assembled before being returned to the factory premises in the Medway area. The dispersed nature of these arrangements meant less disruption of production in the event of a factory being bombed.

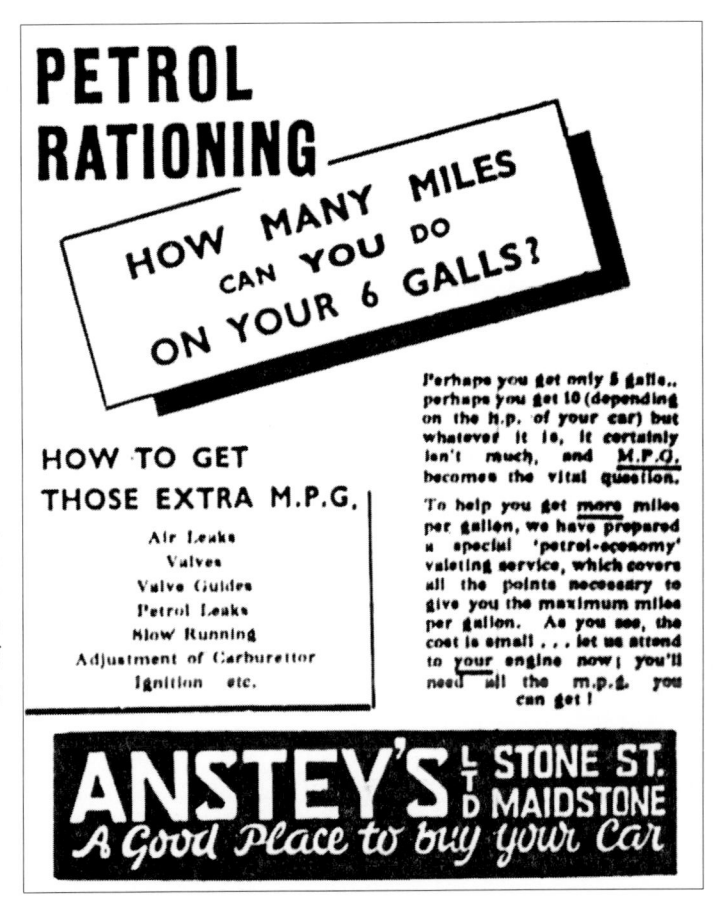

Reproduced courtesy of Kent Messenger newspaper group

Second World War: 1939 to 1945

BANNER, Bernard
Married
Wife Vera Rose (née Croucher)
Gunner Royal Artillery

Bernard married Vera on 30 October 1943, at Holy Cross church

BARHAM, Albert E
Sweetbriars, Yeoman Lane
Royal Corps of Signals
Service Number 14726641 Signalman

BARKER, Albert
Little Snowfield
Air Raid Precautions Warden Civil Defence

BARNES, Walter Brenchley
Neidspath, Roseacre Lane
Married
8 October 1937 19 Group, Romeo 2, Bearsted
Royal Observer Corps

BARRATT, Florence Annie May
Court Farm Cottages, Thurnham Lane
Married
Husband Jack William Johnson
Aircraft Woman Women's Auxiliary Air Force

Florence married Jack Johnson of Eyhorne Farm, Hollingbourne on 23 September 1944 at Mary's church.

BARRETT, Leslie D
Wooded Slopes, Detling

BARTON, Ernest H
5 Council Cottages, Spot Lane

BASELEY, Henry W
Bermuda, Royston Road

BATCHELLER, Richard

BATCHELLER, Robert M
The Little House, Roseacre Lane

BATES, Stanley
Father Mr T Bates
Chaplain Royal Air Force

BEALE, Stanley
40 Royston Road

144

Second World War: 1939 to 1945

BEDFORD, Reginald C F
Leevale, Ashford Road

BEDFORD, Rex

BEDOW, Stanley G C
217 Winifred Road

BEECHING, ------
Bydews, Weavering Street
Corps of Military Police

BEECHING, R J
Bydews, Weavering Street
Royal Air Force

BEER, Edward
2 Golf View Cottages, Ware Street

BENCE, Eric Wilfred John
Milgate Park
Father Frederick H Bence, Physician and Surgeon
Born Clerkenwell London, 1894
Married
Wife Dorothy (née Grace)
Royal Artillery
Service Number 123459

During the First World War Eric was commissioned as a Second Lieutenant with 87th Brigade, Royal Field Artillery on 2 December 1914. He subsequently served in the Middle East and was promoted to Captain. He was awarded the Military Cross on 1 January 1919 whilst resident at Wrotham Heath House, Wrotham Heath.

On 7 September 1920 he joined the Auxiliary Division of Royal Irish Constabulary, Service Number 518

Between the wars, Eric and Dorothy purchased Milgate Park. They travelled to New York 21 July 1926 and returned 10 October 1929. Eric then travelled alone to Canada 18 August 1933, returning to Britain via New York 30 October 1933, and to New York, 20 September 1935, and returned to Britain via Rio de Janeiro, on 7 May 1936.

In 1940, Eric rejoined the Royal Artillery as a Major, then promoted to Lieutenant. On 1 January 1953, Lieutenant-Colonel Eric Bence was awarded Order of the British Empire, retired and in 1957 was appointed Deputy Lieutenant of Kent. Eric died, 8 September 1965

BENNY, Raymond

BENTLEY, Stanley C
Haifa, Roseacre Lane
Royal Air Force

Stanley qualified as a pilot. His service with the RAF included postings to St Austell and Wales.

BETTS, Albert S
Cobham Cottage, Water Lane

BETTS, Frank

Second World War: 1939 to 1945

BETTS, Sidney

BEXON, Constance Audrey
Sunset, Lord Romney's Hill
Married
Husband Ronald London of Leaverel, West Street, Rottingdean
Section Officer Women's Auxiliary Air Force

Constance married Ronald on 25 March 1944 at Holy Cross church. Ronald was serving as a Flying Officer in the Royal Air Force.

BIRCH, John Percy
Aldington Court Cottages
Royal Engineers

BISHOP, John S
Cobbins, The Grove

BLACK, Donald William
Married
Mandor, Landway
1940 19 Group, Romeo 2, Bearsted
Royal Observer Corps

BLAMIRE BROWN, Christopher
Southfield, Tower Lane

BLAMIRE BROWN, John
Southfield, Tower Lane
Royal Marines

BLANDFORD, Cyril E
The Green
Royal Army Medical Corps

BLANDFORD, William

BODIAM, Ellen F
1 Triangle Cottages, Yeoman Lane

BODIAM, Robert W H
211 Winifred Road

BOOTE, Stella Doreen see entry under **HOUNSELL**

BOTTLE, Henley A
Maydene, Weavering Street

BOX, George W A
Droglands, Ashford Road

Second World War: 1939 to 1945

BRADBEER, Henry J
Coombatch, The Landway

BRADLEY, Cyril B
Roseacre Farm

BRADLEY, Dennis R
Roseacre Farm

BRADLEY, Reginald

BRANSBY, Frederick
Hazeldene, Spot Lane
Royal Air Force

BRIMSTEAD, Edward E
The Green

BRIMSTEAD, Jean Frances May
The Green
Married
Husband James Parren of The Green
Women's Auxiliary Police Force

Jean married James on 26 December 1944 at Holy Cross church. James was serving as a Leading Aircraftman Royal Air Force.

BRITCHER, Thomas
The Queen's Own (Royal West Kent Regiment)

Thomas served as part of the British Army of the Rhine.

BROOK, Benjamin B
White Horse Inn

BROOK, Brian

BROOKER, Elsie Margaret see entry under **HARRISON**

BROWN, Arthur

BROWN, D J
6 Council Houses, The Street
Royal Navy

BROWN, Daisy Muriel
Court Farm
Married
Husband Alan Temple of 7 Bond End, Knaresborough, Yorkshire
Charge Hand, Navy Army and Air Force Institute

Daisy married Alan on 13 March 1945 at St Mary's church. Alan was serving as a Sapper, Royal Engineers, Service Number 1744437

BROWN, Hilda

BROWN, Laurie

BROWN, Lucy

BROWN, Muriel Beatrice
6 Council Houses
Married
Husband John Keith Frisken of Wellesley House, Broadstairs Kent
Auxiliary Territorial Service
Service Number W/251654 Lance Corporal

Muriel married John on 16 May 1945 at Holy Cross church. John was serving in the Second New Zealand Expeditionary Force, Service Number 10445 Private

BUCK, Roy D
Felderland, Ashford Road

BUCK, Terence

BURCH, Albert

BURGESS, Flora Eileen Winifred
4 Invicta Villas, The Green
Parents Nelson Henry and Ada Elsie Burgess
Married
Husband Melvin Crapp of Glen Doone, Royston Road

Eileen, usually known as Winnie, worked for the council where she was known as Miss Flora Burgess. She met her husband, Melvin Crapp, soon after starting work when a letter was mis-delivered to another address two doors along. However shortly afterwards, Melvin was drafted into the army.

Winnie had a highly responsible job during the war: she worked in the Civil Defence office in the Maidstone Rural District Council office at 26 Tonbridge Road.

Winnie and Melvin were married on 13 July 1946 at Holy Cross church.

This photograph shows Winnie before her marriage:

Reproduced courtesy of Winnie Crapp

Second World War: 1939 to 1945

BURGESS, Frederick William *
4 Invicta Villas, The Green
Parents Nelson Henry and Ada Elsie Burgess
Single
Royal Army Ordnance Corps
Service Number 7663330 Private
Died 28 August 1943, aged 26
Prisoner of War at Kuie Camp, Thailand
Buried in grave 6 B 45, Kancanaburi War Cemetery, Thailand

Frederick was sent to Thailand in a party of prisoners known as F Force which departed from Singapore on 29 April 1943. He worked on the Burma railway. This photograph shows Frederick in army uniform during the last leave he spent with his family in 1941:

BURGESS, Ronald N J
4 Invicta Villas, The Green
Parents Nelson Henry and Ada Elsie Burgess
Married
Wife Joan (née Comney)
Royal Air Force - service included Poona

This photograph of Ronald was taken in 1947:

Both reproduced courtesy of Winnie Crapp

BURNYEAT, Diana

BUTLER, Roy

BUTLER, Violet
Thyley, Weavering Street
Married
Husband Alan Ernest Tomlinson of Sandbanks, Cliff Road, Felixstowe
Cook Women's Royal Naval Service

Violet married Alan on 21 November 1942 at Holy Cross church. Alan was serving as a wireless operator.

BYAM, Arthur A
Triangle Cottages, Yeoman Lane

CALCUTT, P F
Sellindge, Plantation Lane
Royal Naval Volunteer Reserve

CAPELING, Frederick E
Dromore, Cavendish Way

CARR, Ernest R
Ormonde, 215 Winifred Road
Royal Air Force

CARR, Harold
Ashley, Ashford Road

CASTLE, F
53rd Reconnaissance Regiment
Service Number 4104959

CHAINEY, Charles A
Weston House, Spot Lane

CHANTLER, John

CHANTLER, William Ernest *
Baristone, Manor Rise
Parents Edmund William and Olive Orpah Avery Chantler
Married
Wife Iris May
Royal Artillery and 198th Light Anti Aircraft Regiment
Service Number 166849 Lieutenant
Killed 15 February 1943, aged 30
Commemorated Panel 2, Column 2, Brookwood Memorial, Surrey

CHAPLIN, Chas. H A
199 Winifred Road

CHAPMAN, Harry Ernest
Milgate Park Estate
Chief Constable of Kent 1921-1940

Order of the British Empire 1920; Commander of the British Empire 1939
Previously Deputy Chief Constable; also a Major in the Border Regiment

CHAPMAN, Jean M N
Sidcoombe, Ashford Road
Auxiliary Territorial Service

CHAWNER, Harry
1 Mays Cottages, Ware Street

CHAWNER, Sidney
1 Mays Cottages, Ware Street
Royal Engineers

Second World War: 1939 to 1945

CHUBB, Alfred J
Brydale, Plantation Lane

CHUBB, James

CLIFTON, Charles B
Forteviot, Yeoman Lane

CLOUT, Vallance
Little Dunkeld, Fauchons Lane

COALES, John William *+
Briardene, Ashford Road
Parents   Edith and Herbert Coales
Single
Royal Air Force Volunteer Reserve
35 Squadron
Service Number   1806859   Flight Sergeant (Pilot)
Killed 27 June 1946, aged 21
Buried in grave   14 F2, Hanover War Cemetery, Niedersachsen, Germany

John was Captain of Bearsted school and Captain of Bartie House in 1938.[2] He went into accountancy in Maidstone after leaving school. Before the war, he joined the Royal Air Force Association which was aimed at people interested in aviation, but not specifically geared for wartime flying. After John joined the Volunteer Reserve he began flying in Tiger Moths before moving to Spitfire V, Meteor and Tempest aircraft. His service included duty in the Mediterranean and Bloemfontein in South Africa. He took part in the Victory Fly Past over Buckingham Palace with Douglas Bader on 8 June 1946, and paraded through Maidstone for the V J Celebrations. John was killed instantly in a crash during an exercise which involved formation cross-country and low altitude flying, in a Tempest V, over Wunsdorf, north of Osnabruck, Germany.

This photograph shows John proudly showing his 'wings badge', after qualifying as a pilot:

Reproduced courtesy of Edith Coales

COBB, R Anthony
Beechdene, Ashford Road

COLEGATE, Charles E
4 Fancy Row, Thurnham Lane

COLEGATE, Herbert George
Smarts Cottages, The Green
Married
Wife   Alice Ellen (née Bonner) of The Bell Inn
Royal Army Service Corps

Herbert married Alice on 27 September 1944 at Holy Cross church.

COLEGATE, John A
Smarts Cottages, The Green

Second World War: 1939 to 1945

COLES, Thomas
1939 19 Group, Romeo 2, Bearsted
Royal Observer Corps

COLLINS, Harry
4 Cavendish Way

COLLOR, Gladys Margaret
2 Chapel Lane
Married
Husband Stanley Roland Delves of 6 Mote Hall Villas
Private Auxiliary Territorial Services

Gladys married Stanley on 18 October 1944 at St Mary's church.

COOK, Philip W
4 Egypt Place

COOKSON, Walker †
Married
Wife Joan (née Earl) of 6 Fancy Row
1/4th Battalion, Essex Regiment
Service Number 5569750 Corporal
Killed in action 20 February 1944, aged 23
Buried in grave VII K 8, Cassino War Cemetery, Italy
Note: the memorial in St Mary's church incorrectly shows his first name as Walter.

Walker married Joan on 2 May 1942 at St Mary's church. This photograph was taken at their wedding:

Reproduced courtesy of Louie Smith

Left to right: Jack Smith, Janet Smith, Walker Cookson, Joan Cookson (née Earl) and Nellie King (née Earl)

Second World War: 1939 to 1945

COOPER, Charles E
2 West View, Roseacre Lane

COOPER, Charles F
15 Pine Grove, Caring Lane
Royal Air Force

COOPER, Donald George
Eartham, Ashford Road
Married
8 October 1937 19 Group, Romeo 2, Bearsted
Royal Observer Corps

CORAM, Leslie
6 Cavendish Way

CORFE, Roger

CORK, Marjorie Daisy see entry under **AMOS**

CORKE, Stanley

COSTIN, Horn Edward A
The Cot, near Black Horse public house
Major Royal Engineers

COX, Alan E
1 The Gables, Lord Romney's Hill

COX, Molly Matilda see entry under **FRAZER**

COX, Stephen
5 Mays Cottages, Ware Street

COX, William

CRAMPTON, Cyril
1 Holly Villas, The Street
Royal Air Force

CRANE, Arthur T
11 Cavendish Way

CRAPP, Flora Eileen Winifred see entry under **BURGESS**

CRAPP, Melvin
Melvin went into the army shortly after the war began. In May 1940 he was one of the troops evacuated from the beaches at Dunkirk in Operation Dynamo.

In 1946, Melvin married Flora Burgess (usually known as Winnie).

Second World War: 1939 to 1945

CRASKE, W L
The Haven, Lord Romney's Hill
Royal Engineers
Service Number 2196463 Lance Corporal

CRAVEN, G
Manor Rise
Stoker Royal Navy

He was posted Missing, presumed killed, when *HMS Electrum* was sunk, but arrived in England, having been invalided home after a minor injury.

CRELLIN, Jennifer Lane see entry under **SMITH**

CROUCH, Les
This undated photograph shows Les on the right with his friend, John Gilbert wearing Army uniform. They enlisted on the same day.

Reproduced courtesy of John E Gilbert

CROUCHER, Alfred H
44 Sandling Lane, Maidstone

CROWSLEY, Ernest G H
Newlands, Cavendish Way

CURTIS, Edith
4 Council Houses, The Street
Married
Husband Charles Victor Sedge of 115 Old Tovil Road, Maidstone
Private Auxiliary Territorial Services

Edith married Charles on 8 May 1943 at Holy Cross church. Charles was serving in the Royal Army Medical Corps.

CURTIS, Sydney
4 Council Houses, The Street

DALLEY, Annie Ida see entry under **MARTIN**

Second World War: 1939 to 1945

DANIELL, John
Parents Oswald and May Daniell
Born 1903
Royal Artillery 1923
Second Lieutenant
Colonel Commandant Royal Artillery 1956-1966
World War Two service included Middle East, Iraq and Burma

DARLINGTON, Peggy
173 Royston Road
Women's Royal Naval Service

Peggy married Kenneth Walter Head of The Briars, Kings Avenue, Broadstairs on 21 January 1943 at Holy Cross church. Kenneth was serving as an Able Seaman, Royal Navy.

DATSON, Laurence
1939 19 Group, Romeo 2, Bearsted
Royal Observer Corps

Laurence was usually known as Larry. His family ran Datson's Bakery in The Street.

DAVEY, Lionel
Yeoman House, Ashford Road
Royal Air Force

DAVIS, Harold
2 Hill Cottages, Roseacre Lane

DAVIS, Terence
Clover Rise, Fauchons Lane

DAWE, Jean D
Vicarage Cottages

DEARING, Norman Arthur
Bryanstone, Roseacre Lane
Married
8 October 1937 19 Group, Romeo 2, Bearsted
Royal Observer Corps

DELVES, Gladys see entry under **COLLOR**

DELVES, Stanley Roland
6 Mote Villas
Married
Wife Gladys Margaret (née Collor) of 2 Chapel Lane
Petty Officer Royal Navy

Stanley married Gladys on 18 October 1944 at St Mary's church.

DENNIS, W F

Second World War: 1939 to 1945

DICKENSEN, Chas. J
3 Oliver's Row
Royal Engineers

DICKER, Stanley J
5 Pine Grove

DONALDSON, Allen

DRAKE, Cyril Stanley
The Poplars, Roseacre Lane
Parents Stanley and May Drake
Royal Navy

Cyril was usually known as Bill. He recorded some of his wartime experiences and naval service. These are included in the *Memories of the Second World War* chapter.

DRAKE, Stanley
The Poplars, Roseacre Lane
Married
Wife May
Children Cyril and June
Home Guard

DRAPER, Cyril

DRUMMOND, Kingsley
Ashley House, Bell Field, Weavering

DUMBRELL, Raymond
Ladybank
Lord Romney's Hill

Raymond was injured during an air raid on 2 October 1940

DUNK, Edward
178 Royston Road
2/5th Battalion, Leicestershire Regiment
Service Number 5789086 Private

Edward saw service in Tunisia - Kasserine Gap, Cap Bon.
He was involved in the Italy-Salerno landing, Volturno and Garigliano rivers, the Gothic line and also served in Egypt and Palestine.
He was demobilised 1946

This photograph of Edward was taken during his service with the Army:

Reproduced courtesy of Terence Dunk

DUNLAP, Michael L
Oaklands, Thurnham Lane
Army

Michael was held as a prisoner of war at Lambinowice, Poland

Second World War: 1939 to 1945

DURBAN, Harry E
Milgate Lodge, Ashford Road

EALHAM, G F
Corporal Royal Army Medical Corps

EARL, Harold

EARL, Henry George
6 Fancy Row, Thurnham Lane

EARL, Sidney F
Ware Street
Royal Artillery

EATON-SHORE, Eileen Venables see entry under **LEWIS**

EAVES, Thomas D
Ashmore, Ashford Road

EDMONDS, Frank
Church Farm, Ashford Road

EGAN, John
Lisgibbon, Ashford Road

ELGAR, Charles Robinson *
Bearsted Lodge, Tower Lane
Parents Walter Robinson and Lilian Elgar
Married
Wife Esme of Swanage, Dorset
Royal Air Force (Auxiliary Air Force)
Service Number 90009 Squadron Leader (Pilot)
Killed 22 May 1943, aged 32
Buried in grave 4, Row 9, St Bartholomew's churchyard, Bobbing

Charles was a gifted musician and an organist at Holy Cross church

ELLIS, Basil H
Roysden, Roundwell
The Queen's Own (Royal West Kent Regiment)

ELSWOOD, Albert L
3 Egypt Place

ELVES, Stanley R
6 Mote Villas, The Green
Royal Navy

Second World War: 1939 to 1945

ENGLISH, Richard Gerald
Crismill Oast House, Crismill Lane
Married
Wife Elizabeth (née Gilfillan)
Flight Lieutenant Royal Air Force

Richard married Elizabeth on 12 May 1941 at Holy Cross church

EVERSDEN, Richard A
Holly House, The Street

EVERSDEN, Stephen H
Holly House, The Street
Royal Army Service Corps

FARMER, John E A
Babbacombe, The Grove

FAULKENER, Leonard S B
Yonder Cottage, Tower Lane

FAULKENER, Mrs W M
Yonder Cottage, Tower Lane
Women's Auxiliary Air Force

Mrs Faulkener is believed to be the first woman to leave Bearsted on 4 September 1939 to join the armed forces after war was declared.

FELLOWES, Sidney Hubert
Mill Cottage, Willington

FILMER, William G
Sutton Street

FINNEGAN, James P
2 West View, Roseacre Lane

FINNIS, Cyril F
Morningside, The Grove
Royal Army Ordnance Corps

FLOOD, Albert

FLOOD, B W
Ware Street

FLOOD, George
2 Neatherton Cottages, Ware Street

Second World War: 1939 to 1945

FOGG-ELLIOTT, Mark
Danedale, Church Lane
Royal Navy
Commander *HMS Delight*
Companion to Distinguished Service Order 1940 (London Gazette, July 1940)

FORWARD, Stanley J
Oak Cottage

FOSTER, Violet L
Rosherville, The Green

FOX, Charles
4 The Cottages, Chapel Lane
The Buffs (East Kent Regiment)

FOX, James

FRANKLIN-BATES, Ronald H
2 Yew Tree Villas, Plantation Lane
The Buffs
Eighth Armoured Brigade

FRAZER, Molly Matilda
The Green
Married
Husband Leonard Victor Cox of 70 Harold Road, Sittingbourne
Women's Land Army

Molly married Leonard on 31 March 1945 at Holy Cross church

FREEMAN, Alfred Percy
Dunbolyn
156 Ashford Road

Air Raid Precautions Warden Civil Defence

Alfred was usually called 'Tich' on account of his height of five feet, two inches. Before retirement, he had been a first class cricketer with twelve Test appearances for England. He then played for Bearsted cricket club. Deirdre Leadbetter, recalled that during the war her grandfather served as an ARP warden. He was on duty one night on his front lawn, when two bombs fell in the Lilk valley adjacent to Otham Lane and opposite Major's Lake; fortunately, they did not explode.

FREESTONE, William G
Milford, Lord Romney's Hill

FRENCH, James S
Glennifer, Roseacre Lane
1939 19 Group, Romeo 2, Bearsted
Royal Observer Corps

Second World War: 1939 to 1945

FRISKEN, Muriel Beatrice see entry under **BROWN**

FROST, Charles Henry Dennis *
Ribblesdale, Ashford Road
Parents William Henry and Dorothy Beaumont Frost
Single
Royal Air Force Volunteer Reserve
Service Number 910014 Sergeant (Wireless Operator, Air Commander)
Killed 27 March 1941, aged 22 when his aircraft crashed at Wroxton, Banbury, Oxfordshire
Buried in grave K40, Holy Cross churchyard, 3 March 1940, but subsequently exhumed and cremated during July 1947 in accordance with his expressed wishes.
Charles is also commemorated on a panel, west pavilion of Charing crematorium.

A transcript of the report from the Kent Messenger, 5 April 1941:

Death of Sergeant C.H.D. Frost

Great sympathy is felt for Mr W.H. Frost, Estates Manager to Maidstone Corporation, and with Mrs Frost, in the loss of their only son, Sergt. Charles Henry Dennis Frost, R.A.F., on Thursday of last week, of which they have received official news. Sergt. Frost, who was 22 years of age, joined the Royal Air Force December 19th 1939, and had therefore been on war service for the past 15 months. Educated at Maidstone Grammar School, he left about five years ago and entered the service department of the Maidstone Corporation Electricity Undertaking.

The funeral took place on Thursday from his home at Ribblesdale, Milgate, Bearsted, for interment at Bearsted Church. The service was conducted by the Rev R A Parsons, Vicar of Bearsted.

Reproduced courtesy of Kent Messenger newspaper group

FRY, Trevor
Single
85 Night Fighter Squadron, West Malling also Bomber Command
Royal Air Force.
Distinguished Flying Cross

FULLAGER, Hubert H
4 West View, Roseacre Lane

Second World War: 1939 to 1945

FULLER, Albert W
Cherwell, Ashford Road

GARDNER, Reginald George *
Ware Street
Parents Samuel and Agnes Gardner
Married
Wife Nancy
Royal Air Force Volunteer Reserve
608 Squadron
Service Number 68776 Flight Lieutenant (Pilot)
Killed 9 October 1944, aged 31
Buried in grave 184, Section N, Holy Cross churchyard

Flight Lieutenant Gardner was flying with O C Sweetman, Navigator (Distinguished Flying Medal) in a Mosquito aircraft which was returning from Germany. As they neared their Norfolk base, Downham Market, the aircraft started to fall at a thousand feet and exploded on the ground at 21.30 hours. O C Sweetman was buried in Newcastle upon Tyne.

A partial transcript of the report from the Kent Messenger, 20 October 1944:

FLT.-LIEUT. REGINALD GARDNER

Funeral at Bearsted

The funeral took place on Monday, at Holy Cross Church, Bearsted, of Flt. Lieut. Reginald George Gardner, aged 31. The Rev E M Hughes (priest in charge and a late R.A.F. chaplain) conducted the service.

Chief mourners were: Mrs R Gardner (widow), Mrs F Gardner (mother), Mrs J Sorrell (sister), Mr and Mrs A Williamson and Mrs L Secker (cousins). Flt. Lieut. Lilley represented his R.A.F. station and Mr R Smith represented the Puck-a-Pu band.

Flt. Lieut. Gardner's brother, Corporal J Gardner, was unable to attend the funeral owing to the fact that he is on active service on north west Europe.

Reproduced courtesy of Kent Messenger newspaper group

Second World War: 1939 to 1945

GAULD, Kenneth M
Puckscroft, The Landway
Suffolk Regiment

GEE, Daniel S
Ware Street

GEE, Sidney

GIBBENS, Ernest W
Crompton, Fauchons Lane

GILBERT, Cyril

GILBERT, Frank W
Parks Cottages, Ware Street

GILBERT, John Alan †*+
7 Mays Cottages, Ware Street
Parents Charles Edward and Amy Gilbert
Married
Wife Bessie Letitia of Hollingbourne
Son John Edward
4th Battalion, The Queen's Own (Royal West Kent Regiment)
Service Number 6346570 Lance Corporal
Died 10 January 1944, aged 25
Buried in grave 12 B 11, Taukkyan War Cemetery, Burma (now Myanmar)
John is also commemorated on the war memorial at Hollingbourne.

These photographs show John and Bessie on their wedding day and John's grave where the Gilbert family arrange for a cross or wreath of poppies to be laid every year.

John Edward was only two when his father died.

Both reproduced courtesy of John E Gilbert

Second World War: 1939 to 1945

GILBERT, William A
Parks Cottages, Ware Street
Bombardier

GILES, William Montague Charles
3 Golf View Cottages, Ware Street
Bombardier

After the war, William helped to organise the Welcome Home arrangements for Bearsted and Thurnham. Later, he was Chairman of Thurnham parish council 1964-1966.

GODDARD, Norman E
Three Stacks, Landway

GOLDSMITH, Leonard

GOLDTHORPE, Gavin

GOLDUP, Nellie
4 Roseacre Terrace, Tower Lane
Auxiliary Territorial Service

GOODHEW, John H
The Clayton, The Grove

GOODMAN, Gerald
Hill Top, Tower Lane

GOOSEMAN, John F
Hyeres, The Landway

GRAINGER, Stuart

GRANT, Albert R
1 The Cottages, Chapel Lane

GRANT, Douglas
1 The Cottages, Chapel Lane
Royal Marines

GRANT, Frederick G C
Sunny Villa, Manor Rise

GREGORY, R
Hill View

Mr Gregory trained many members of the Local Defence Corps, later Home Guard.

GRIFFITHS, Daphne A
Moorings, Lord Romney's Hill

GRIFFITHS, Hugh

GROUT, Frederick William
Married
West View, Thurnham Road
8 October 1937 19 Group, Romeo 2, Bearsted
Royal Observer Corps

Freddie owned Yeoman Garage on the Ashford Road which was the central collection point in Bearsted for scrap and salvage. This photograph shows Frederick in his Royal Observer Corps uniform:

Reproduced courtesy of Evelyn Pearce

GROUT, Gordon W T
West View, Thurnham Lane
Army

GUEST, Alfred Herbert
Keeper's Cottage, Thurnham Lane
Parents Walter and Rose Guest
Single

GUEST, Ernest John
Keeper's Cottage, Thurnham Lane
Parents Walter and Rose Guest
Single

Second World War: 1939 to 1945

GUEST, Reginald James
Keeper's Cottage, Thurnham Lane
Parents Walter and Rose Guest
Single
Royal Army Medical Corps

Before the war, Reginald was the Professional at Bearsted Golf Club. This report, which was featured in the Kent Messenger, 19 January 1945, shows that Reginald was adept at using the limited resources available to him during the war:

Wounded Men Cheered by Kent Golf 'Pro's' Ingenuity

Through the ingenuity of a Kent RAMC private, all the wards and departments of a casualty clearing station in Italy have daily radio programmes. He is Private Reginald Guest, 27 year old son of Mr and Mrs W W Guest, of Keeper's Cottages, Thurnham.

With, originally only a 6-valve receiver donated by the Red Cross to work with, he has with odds and ends, built up an efficient receiving and relay station. In addition, there is an intercom outfit, also constructed by this budding radio engineer who was a golf professional in 'civvy street'.

PROGRAMMES RELAYED

Private Guest picks up the most popular programmes and these are relayed to the patients and staff. Pinned on the wall are autographed photographs of two of the Forces 'sweethearts' Jean Metcalf and Avis Scutt - and, of course, Mrs Guest.

The whole relay system has only a 6-volt battery which last four days, for power. Private Guest says his great needs are an electric turntable to enable gramophone records to be relayed and a main spring for portable Columbia gramophone.

A former Boy Scout, Private Guest served his apprenticeship as a golf professional on Bearsted links.

Reproduced courtesy of Kent Messenger newspaper group

Second World War: 1939 to 1945

GUEST, Robert George †
Parents Walter and Rose Guest of Thurnham
Married
Wife Cissy Lily of Catford, London
Son Robert, usually known as Bobby
Royal Navy
Service Number C/JX 127267 Able Seaman
His Majesty's Motor Torpedo Boat 310
Killed 14 September 1942, aged 31 when *MTB 310* was attacked and sunk by Italian aircraft at Tobruk, Libya.
Commemorated Panel 54 Column 2, Chatham Naval Memorial
Distinguished Service Medal.

Robert joined the Royal Navy in December 1927. He had a particularly distinguished career in the Royal Navy, marked by his transfer to the Motor Torpedo Boat section.

Torpedo boats were used for operations which involved silent search and ambushes of German shipping routes in the North Sea travelling in channels bristling with enemy shipping and aircraft. They sailed on moonless winter nights, running with no lights, moving in a diamond formation at an average speed of twenty knots or by day, used fog banks for concealment. The boats were long and narrow with shallow draughts which enabled them to move very fast, leaping over oncoming waves, rapidly becoming known as 'grey ladies'. They were fitted with powerful engines which were early experiments in jet-engine technology. The engines were used to enable the boat to escape at a very fast speed. Each boat carried two torpedoes and four machine guns. Warfare with this type of boat was rapid and intense: success often hinged on a split-second decision in storm force conditions. Many of the crews were awarded medals for their selfless actions and bravery.[3]

These two undated photographs show (left) Robert in his naval uniform and (right) his family; Walter Guest, Cissy Guest, Cissy Guest's mother, Rose Guest and Bobby Guest, outside Buckingham Palace having collected his Distinguished Service Medal.

Both reproduced courtesy of Margaret Peat

HADLEY, Henry
Otteridge Cottage, Yeoman Lane

HAGGER, Gilbert

HALLETT, Alfred E
4 Mays Cottages, Ware Street
Royal Artillery

Second World War: 1939 to 1945

HALMETT, A

HAMMERTON, Kenneth William
Car-Trav, Ashford Road
Single
Highland Light Infantry
Service Number 14646267
Prisoner of War Number 91966

Kenneth was held at Stalag XII-A, Limberg, Baden-Württemberg, Germany.

HAMMOND, Charles W H
Meadow View, Lord Romney's Hill

HAMMOND, Ebenezer *
Triangle Cottages, St Faith's Lane
Married
Wife Alice Amelia
Civilian drayman at Maidstone West Station
Killed 3 August 1944, aged 57, during an air raid
Listed on the civilian section of the Roll of Honour for the Municipal Borough of Maidstone

HAMMOND, Frank H
The Rose Inn, Ashford Road

HAMPSON, Sir Dennys Francis
The Court

Head Air Raid Precautions Warden Civil Defence

HAMPTON, Walter James
Married
Wife Maney Violet (née Fardyce) of St Faith's Home
Royal Army Pay Corps

Walter married Maney at Holy Cross church, 2 December 1939

HAMSON, Ernest

HARDING, Alfred G
Holly Tree Cottage, Weavering
Royal Engineers

HARDY, John K
Home Cottage, Roundwell
Royal Electrical and Mechanical Engineers

HARNETT, Charles H
Rockies, Yeoman Lane

HARNETT, Edward F
Roseridge, Roseacre Lane
Army Lieutenant

Second World War: 1939 to 1945

HARNETT, Frank Furber Erskine
Roseridge, Roseacre Lane
Married
8 October 1937 19 Group, Romeo 2, Bearsted
Royal Observer Corps

Frank was a partner in Harnett's Nurseries.
This photograph shows Frank in his Royal Observer Corps uniform:

Reproduced courtesy of Evelyn Pearce

HARRIS, Eric S
Mooltan, Ashford Road
Royal Artillery

HARRIS, Faith S
Cherrydene, Roseacre Lane

HARRIS, Montague
Frantom, Plantation Lane

HARRISON, Betty Frances
Bearsted House, The Green
Married
Husband Rowland Albert Vaughan of 42 Unity Street, Sittingbourne
Voluntary Aid Detachment
Service Number W/557374 Cook, Bearsted House

Betty married Rowland on 8 September 1945 at Holy Cross church. Rowland was serving as a Bombardier, Royal Artillery, Service Number 1530629.

HARRISON, Elsie Margaret
Bearsted House, The Green
Married
Husband Charles Wallace Brooker of 10 Central Street, Holmewood, Chesterfield, Derbyshire
Voluntary Aid Detachment
Service Number 132036 Bearsted House

Elsie married Charles on 19 January 1946 at Holy Cross church. Charles was serving as a Fusilier, Royal Welch Regiment, Service Number 4199812.

HARRISON, Thomas †
Nine Elms, Hockers Lane

Second World War: 1939 to 1945

Black Out!

In the early stages of the war, the government placed great emphasis on achieving thoroughly darkened streets. It was hoped that it would therefore be difficult for enemy planes to gain bearings from landmarks, outlines of urban areas, and other significant buildings or structures on the ground. Lessons had been clearly learned from the bombing raids in the previous conflict and so 'blackout regulations' to restrict lighting were imposed again. However, nothing could be done about the distinctive shape of the river Thames as it led a way up to London from the sea!

If there was a breach of 'black-out' regulations, households were liable to fines. One of the simplest ways of blocking out light was to put up curtains or panels made from black-out fabric at twilight.

This advertisement for black-out material appeared in the Kent Messenger, 30 September 1939:

> **STOCK AVAILABLE**
>
> **HEAVY QUALITY BLACK-OUT SERGE, 54in. wide**
>
> IN
>
> **DARK GREEN, DARK BROWN, BLUE & BLACK**
>
> AT **4/6** YD.
>
> **THIS FABRIC IS FIRE-PROOF**
>
> Make your Black-out trouble-free AND PERMANENT.
>
> You are advised to order quickly. Post or Phone.
>
> Also, HEAVY BLACK FELT PAPER, 36in. wide,
> Proof against Light, Damp, Moth, etc., 4½d. yard.
>
> **HAYWOOD ROWLAND, Ltd.**
> **14 MILL STREET MAIDSTONE**
> PHONE 3036   PHONE 3036

Reproduced courtesy of Kent Messenger newspaper group

HARVEY, Henry W
42 Roseacre Lane

HAWKINS, Eric
The Bungalow, Mote Hall
Royal Air Force

HEAD, Peggy see entry under **DARLINGTON**

HEARD, Anthony J C
Cherisy, Ashford Road

HEARD, Rowley
The Willows

Second World War: 1939 to 1945

HEIGHTON, Ronald A
Plumstones, The Grove

HEWETSON, Brian G
203 Winifred Road

HEWETSON, Peter A
Holmleigh, Roseacre Lane

HEWETT, F L
Clarendon, Roseacre Lane

HICKMOTT, Desmond J
1 Egypt Place
Prisoner of War

HICKMOTT, Ronald H
1 Egypt Place

HIGGENS, Henry B
Amesbury, Spot Farm Estate
Royal Navy

HILL, William J
Earlsfield House, Spot Lane
Royal Air Force

HILL, William R
Toys Hill, Spot Farm Estate
Royal Electrical and Mechanical Engineers

HILLS, Arthur A
The Orchard, Lord Romney's Hill

HIRST, Bernard E
6 Roseacre Terrace, Tower Lane

HOBDEN, H

HOLMES, George R
Coronel, Royston Road
Royal Navy

HOLTUM, Arthur John
Sunnycot, Roseacre Lane
Parents Arthur and Daisy Holtum
Single
Royal Army Medical Corps

Arthur was usually called John

Second World War: 1939 to 1945

HOLTUM, Arthur Henry
Sunnycot, Roseacre Lane
Married
Wife: Daisy (née Goodenough)
Children Arthur and Robert
Special Constabulary Sergeant

Arthur's earlier service is recorded in the First World War chapter of this book.

HOLTUM, Robert Keith
Sunnycot, Roseacre Lane
Parents Arthur and Daisy Holtum
Single
HMS Royal Arthur
ARP Boy Messenger and Home Guard
Later Engine Room Mechanic then Aircraft Mechanic, Fleet Air Arm

Robert was usually called Keith; this photograph shows Keith in his Home Guard uniform:

Reproduced courtesy of Bill Drake

HORN, ------
Triangle Cottages
Auxiliary Territorial Services

HORN, Dudley Crofton *
Triangle Cottages
Parents Cyril Roland and Sarah Marion Horn
Single
Royal Air Force Volunteer Reserve
247 Squadron
Service Number 1333758 Flight Sergeant (Pilot)
Killed 14 January 1945, aged 21
Buried in the south west corner of Bergharen Protestant churchyard, Gelderland, Netherlands

HOUNSELL, Stella Doreen
Swaylands, Yeoman Lane
Married
Husband James Walleden Boote, 110 Mount Pleasant, Wallasey
Officer Auxiliary Territorial Services

Stella married James on 8 March 1941 at Holy Cross church. James was an Aircraft Engineer.

HOWARD, Cecil
Homeleigh, Yeoman Lane
Royal Air Force

Second World War: 1939 to 1945

HOWARD, Henry Charles
Leeds Castle Gardens, Leeds
Married
Wife Eileen Dorothy (née Blandford) of The Retreat
Engine Room Assistant Royal Navy

Henry was usually known as Harry. He married Eileen Blandford on 26 August 1944 at Holy Cross church. Harry's naval service included *HMS Chitral*, His Majesty's Motor Torpedo Boats in Malta 1943 and *HMS Gadfly* 1945 before being discharged in 1946. For further details about motor torpedo boats see the entry for Robert Guest.

This photograph shows Harry as a Chief Petty Officer when serving in Malta:

Reproduced courtesy of Jenni Hudson

HUBDEN, N

HUBER, W
10 Council Houses, The Street
Army

HUGHES, Oswald
195 Winifred Road
Married
Wife Alice Rose but usually called Daisy (née Britcher)

Oswald had a distinguished career in aviation for forty five years. In May 1917 he joined the RFC, aged 16. He then served with the RAF until 1925 before becoming a civilian member of staff at the Air Ministry Headquarters in London until retirement in 1962. This department was responsible for the provision and maintenance of airfields and accommodation for the RAF throughout the world. During the war Oswald's job also concerned the security of airfields. Oswald remained employed in the Directorate-General of Works for the rest of his working life. He flew in many types of aircraft including the Avro Bristol Fighter, the De Havilland 9A, Handley Page Bomber and Vickers Vimy. He was awarded the MBE in 1951.

This photograph was taken of Oswald between 1918 and 1923 and shows the outfit he wore for flying:

Reproduced courtesy of Christine Hughes

HULKS, John C
191 Winifred Road
Royal Navy

HUMPHREY, Joseph T
La France, Roseacre Lane

Second World War: 1939 to 1945

Rationed Fashion

In June 1941 the Board of Trade published regulations for clothing and introduced a scheme called Civilian Clothing Control 1941; clothes were now subject to ration coupons. The allowances, deemed to be sufficient to provide one new outfit for everyone in a year and were based on statistics about sales of clothes before the war. Purchasing rationed garments now required coupons and money and until specific ones could be issued, spare margarine coupons from ration books were used.

Adults were initially allocated sixty six coupons but this quantity was considerably reduced by the end of the war. In addition, all new garments were to be sold bearing 'Clothing Control 1941 labels'; this became known as the CC41 mark, shown here on the right. The scheme was perceived to be fair by the public and deemed a success. It did not finally end until March 1949.

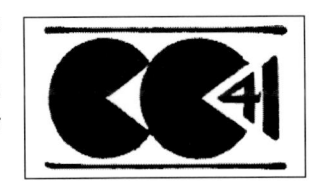

The population was also urged to 'Make Do and Mend' in a series of government booklets which featured Mrs Sew and Sew, giving hints and handy tips on repairing and renovating clothes. The booklets tried to try to ensure that people were making the best of the clothes they already possessed. Readers were urged to consider home dressmaking, refurbishing and renovating old garments and other crafts; although many of the materials required were still subject to wartime restrictions. This photograph appeared in a contemporary dressmaking manual advertising Bestway Dressmaking Patterns and depicted a fashionable young woman enjoying a worthwhile pastime:

Both reproduced courtesy of Malcolm Kersey

A new 'utility' range of clothes was also introduced by the government following a project with the Incorporated Society of London Fashion which included designs from Norman Hartnell and Hardy Amies. Expert pattern cutting and minimal cloth usage was essential to these designs, buttons were limited to three and no turn up cuffs or hems were allowed. Skirts were now a regulation length. The first utility dress to be produced was a Hartnell design. With great foresight, the government was aware of the historic nature of the dress and donated it to the Victoria and Albert museum, where it is still regularly displayed. Even with the Utility scheme, couture garments were available for those who could afford them but they were still subject to coupons. The wealthy also had their uniforms adapted at the best tailors they could afford instead of wearing standard issue. Many women were employed in war work and factories, so there was a great demand for sensible clothing. Chiesmans store in Maidstone was quick to respond to their customers requirements as indicated in this advertisement which appeared in the Kent Messenger, 15 August 1941.

Reproduced courtesy of
Kent Messenger newspaper group

Second World War: 1939 to 1945

HUMPHREYS, Marise Jacqueline
Marise, Spot Lane
Married
Husband Robert Arthur Relf of 58 Postley Road, Maidstone
Women's Land Army
Service Number 135607

Marise married Robert on 27 October 1945 at Holy Cross church. Robert was serving a Staff Sergeant, Royal Electrical and Mechanical Engineers, Service Number 145115643.

HUNT, Anthony G
Egypt House, The Green

HUNT, George
Egypt House, The Green
Married
8 October 1937 19 Group, Romeo 2, Bearsted
Royal Observer Corps

This photograph shows George in his Royal Observer Corps uniform:

Reproduced courtesy of Evelyn Pearce

HUNT, Hubert A
Tower Cottage, Tower Lane

HUNT, Jesse George †
Friningham Cottages
Father George Thomas Hunt of Cobham Cottage
Civilian War Dead
Killed 13 August 1940, aged 37 during an air raid at RAF station Detling
Commemorated on Civilian Roll of Honour, Rural District of Hollingbourne

HUNT, Vera May
Aldington Cottages
Married
Husband Frank John Twining of 68 Perry Hill, Catford
Army Territorial Services
Service Number 93417 Private

Vera married Frank on 31 March 1945 at St Mary's church.

Second World War: 1939 to 1945

HUNT, William F
Ivy House, The Green
Army

HUNTER, George A
Marie Paule, The Landway

HUNTLEY, William S
The Kentish Yeoman

HURSEY, Cecil Roy
Sulby, Cavendish Way, Ashford Road

Cecil was injured during an air raid on 27 September 1940 and was later admitted to the Royal West Kent Hospital, Maidstone

HURST, Clifton E S
Yeoman House, Ashford Road

HUTTON, Stanley J
Green Bank, Fauchons Lane

INGRAM, James

IRWIN, Bromley F S
The Green

JAMES, Arthur G
Northgate, Ashford Road

JAMES, Kenneth A
14 Spot Farm Estate
Royal Electrical and Mechanical Engineers

JESSEL, Richard F
Mote Hall
Married
Wife Winnie
Children Oliver, Peggy, Toby and Camilla
Commander Royal Navy
DSO, OBE, DSC and Bar, Knighthood (First Class) Order of St Olav

Richard Jessel was usually known as Dick and he had a most distinguished and unusual career in the Royal Navy. In 1940 he was posted to Plymouth and then Glasgow. He participated in the siege of Malta, before his own ship, *HMS Legion*, was sunk in Malta harbour. He sustained a broken leg and was taken prisoner on the way home. He arrived at a prison camp in the Sahara as a sick man; jaundiced, and trying to recover from his broken leg. He was the most senior of the allied officers at the camp and so was nominally in charge of the rest of the prisoners, steering a diplomatic path with the authorities. He was in the camp for seven months before a release was arranged.

Dick was awarded a Distinguished Service Cross in January 1942 and was later reunited with his family. He arrived home in a curious combination of clothes: an army Private's uniform and a naval Commander's hat. It was all the uniform he possessed, but the hat was unusually distinguished; whilst in the camp, his men decided that it lacked the usual gold braid so they supplied a replacement which they had fashioned out of some sardine tins!

Dick was subsequently posted as a training commander at *HMS King Alfred*, Brighton, before becoming captain of the training house at Lancing College but soon he was back at sea, serving on the Arctic convoys. He was awarded a Knighthood First Class of the Order of St Olav.

The following details are taken from obituaries for Dick which appeared in The Times, 16 February 1988 and The Guardian, 17 February 1988:

Commander Richard Jessel

Reproduced courtesy of The Guardian newspaper

Commander Richard Jessel, DSO, OBE, DSC and Bar, who died on February 14, aged 85, was a Second World War destroyer captain of outstanding dash and heroism. His sheaf of decorations marked long arduous service in Malta and Arctic convoys, with all the hazards which that entailed.

After the Royal Naval Colleges at Osborne and Dartmouth, Jessel's pre-war service took him to the China, Malta and New Zealand stations. He played an incidental part in history when, as captain of *HMS Glow-worm*, he escorted King Edward VIII on the famous Mediterranean cruise in the summer of 1936 which the King made in the yacht *Nahlin* with Mrs Simpson.

Jessel's career nearly came to a premature and disastrous end: taking an evening swim while they were at anchor he was run over by the King's motorboat and his legs were caught in the propeller. The episode is described in *The Rainbow Comes and Goes*, by Lady Diana Cooper, who was a guest on the cruise. He was later visited in hospital by the King and by Queen Mary.

Considered, unfit for service at sea, after the accident, Jessel made do with shore jobs including the training of cadets in *HMS Erebus*. But early in the war he joined the battle-cruiser *Hood* as first lieutenant. Shortly before she was sunk, with almost all hands, he had left her to take command of his favourite ship, the destroyer, *Legion*. This was the time of the siege of Malta. The convoys which supplied the beleaguered island saw some of the most testing fighting of the war.

In January 1942 Jessel was awarded the DSC for 'skill and enterprise in action against enemy submarines'. He gained a mention in despatches - one of three he won - when the aircraft carrier *Ark Royal* was sunk and he steered the *Legion* alongside to rescue 1,834 officers and crew. His DSO recognised a brilliant night action in which two Italian cruisers and an E-boat were destroyed. The *Legion*, having inflicted so much damage on the enemy, finally perished herself. Bombed at sea, she limped into harbour in Malta, where, bombed again, she sank. Jessel who had sustained a broken leg - yet again - saw to the safety of his crew and was the last to leave his ship. He was invalided home, but another adventure overtook him. The hospital ship, harassed by enemy bombers, went aground on the North African coast. All on board were taken prisoner by the Vichy French.

Jessel's character as the senior allied officer in Laghoust Prison in Algeria was included in Commander Charles Lamb's book, *War in a String Bag*. In the book, Lamb described Jessel as an exceptional leader, taking lessons from Jessel on how to handle 500 mutinous and angry men whom another officer had punished misguidedly by stopping their coffee ration. It did not take Jessel long to find out that the men were furious because a guard had taken a bribe to let some men escape and then shot them in the back. "Tell the men that I am sorry that their coffee was stopped", Jessel told me, "explain that it was a mistake, and it won't happen again. At the same time, tell them that I would like to address them after tomorrow's Appel."

When I turned the men about at the Appel, Jessel's black beard was jutting out aggressively. He was an arresting spectacle with one leg in plaster of Paris and the other looking more like an elephant's trunk. He studied them quietly for a pregnant moment. Then he said: "We are on display here, all the time, like animals at the zoo with a lot of bloody Frogs and Arabs looking at us through the bars of our cage, hoping that we will crack up. If we can't behave like disciplined men, so that our spectators recognise that we are British and proud of it, then we should be ashamed of ourselves." He said to me, "You will oblige me by taking them in Physical Training for 20 minutes."

"He stalked away on two stiff legs and I signed to the men to form their usual circle around me and wondered how they would react. A few minutes before they had been sullen and angry. Now they were grinning, and they did their Physical Training as though they were enjoying it."

Released in the American advance across North Africa, Jessel resumed his career. It was now that he saw service with the Arctic convoys. Just before the end of the war he won a further decoration, the Knighthood 1st Class of the Order of St Olav, to mark the evacuation from a fjord of Norwegian resistance fighters.

After the war, Jessel was on the Directing Staff of the Royal Naval Staff College at Greenwich, where his work was recognised with an OBE. In 1952 Earl Mountbatten recognised his qualities of tact and modesty; he was selected to teach the Indian Navy tactics and strategy as head of the naval wing of the Joint Services Staff College at Wellington, South India. After independence, a whole generation of Indian naval offices regarded him as a friend.

Reproduced courtesy of The Times and The Guardian newspapers

JOHNSON, Edward Charles
Keeper's Cottage, Friningham Manor
Married
Wife Gertrude Ellen
Royal Air Force

JOHNSON, Florence see entry under BARRATT

JOHNSON, Walter J
Friningham Cottages

JONES, Margaret Oswald
Snowfield Cottage
Women's Royal Naval Service

JONES, Ronald R
167 Royston Road

KEAY, Edward Thomas Joseph *+
5 Council Houses, The Street
Parents Edward William and Elizabeth Keay
Single
Royal Air Force Volunteer Reserve
195 Squadron
Service Number 1896361 Sergeant
Posted as Missing, presumed killed 23 November 1944, aged 20
Commemorated Panel 232, Runnymede Memorial, Surrey

Eddie was Captain of Fludd House and Bearsted school for two years.[4] He joined the Royal Air Force Volunteer Reserve and became a Flight Engineer with 195 Squadron.

His squadron had originally been formed at Duxford, Cambridgeshire, November 1942. It was re-formed in October 1944, and from the following month it was based at RAF station Witchford, Wratting Common, Cambridgeshire.

Eddie's Lancaster Bomber took off on 23 November from RAF station Witchford at 1256hrs for a raid on Gelsenkirchen, Germany. On the way to Germany the aircraft caught fire and crashed into the sea, west of the Dutch island of Walcheren. All the crew members were reported as Missing.

From the Bomber Command diary:

> 23 November 1944
> 168 Lancaster planes of No. 3 Group carried out a GH (*anti-radar*) bombing raid through cloud on the Nordstein oil plant at Gelsenkirchen (*near Essen, Germany*). The bombing appeared to be accurate. One Lancaster plane was lost, registration HK683.

This photograph of Edward accompanied an undated press cutting which reported his loss:

Reproduced courtesy of Irene Bourne

Second World War: 1939 to 1945

Robert Skinner, headmaster of Bearsted school wrote this tribute when Eddie was posted Missing. It was published in the Parish Magazine: [5]

> **EDDIE KEAY - A TRIBUTE**
>
> Eddie Keay, one of the most popular of Bearsted school head boys and captains, is reported missing from an operational flight over enemy territory.
>
> Eddie Keay was one of the finest and most likeable characters at Bearsted school, which he attended from 1933 to 1939. Always courteous and considerate, and as captain for two very successful pre-war years, he was an inspiration to the school and a great help to the staff. A terrific worker, and with a magnificent physique, at the age of 13, he led his sports teams to victory, and during those two years Bearsted School more than held its own with the schools in the district.
>
> His school work was as outstanding as his physical activities. Always thorough and painstaking, he was quick to grasp new matters, and was one of the best scholars. It was no surprise to us who knew him that he was able to pass all his difficult Flight Engineer's examinations and pass into the Air Force a member of an air crew. Eddie never lost contact with us; on every leave he would visit the school to glance at the old groups in which he was such a prominent figure and to take his cheerful and confident smile through the rooms. His old fellow scholars will always remember that smile and the quiet confidence behind it.
>
> The school prays that he may be returned to continue a life which is so full of promise. If that cannot be, we know that Eddie met whatever happened as he always met other things with a quiet calm - and without complaint.

Reproduced courtesy of Holy Cross church

There is a prize in Eddie's name, donated by his sister, Mrs Irene Bourne, which was first awarded at Roseacre School in 2003.

KEAY, Edward William
5 Council Houses, The Street
Married
Wife Elizabeth Rose (née Martin)
Royal Marine Light Infantry

Edward was usually known as Ted. Before the war, Ted had served as a Leading Stoker in the Royal Navy before entering the Royal Naval Reserve. When war broke out, he was still a reservist and was immediately called up entering the Royal Marine Light Infantry. His wartime service included Scapa Flow and undertaking escort duties for shipping convoys around Iceland. Shipping convoys were part of the Battle of the Atlantic; the longest continuous military campaign during the Second World War.

KEAY, Gordon Alan Richard
5 Council Houses, The Street
Parents Edward William and Elizabeth Keay
Married
Wife Joan (née Brown)
Royal Air Force
Service Number B 4033602 Aircraftman Second Class

Gordon married Joan Brown on 30 January 1950 at Holy Cross church. Joan was serving as an Aircraft Woman Second Class, Women's Royal Air Force, Service Number 2811336. Gordon and Joan emigrated in 1959 and he was employed on a railroad then at Diamond Match in Clocquet, Minnesota. Later employment was with the Minnesota Power and Light Company until retirement in 1989. Gordon and his second wife, Pat, then moved to Apache Junction, Arizona in 1991. Gordon died on 24 December 2008, aged 78.

Second World War: 1939 to 1945

KEMBALL, Vero

KENNEDY, Norman W
Orchardene, The Grove

KENNETT, Frank Edward
Crisfield Cottage
Married
Wife Dorothy Hilda (née Shorter)
Corporal Royal Air Force

Frank married Dorothy on 24 June 1941 at Holy Cross church

KING, Donald G
4 Castle Cottages
Stoker Royal Navy

KING, Edward Arthur
4 Castle Cottages
Royal Navy

Edward married Joyce Lowain Harvey, Women's Auxiliary Air Force of 12 Cranston Gardens, Chadwell, Romford, on 7 March 1942 at Holy Cross church.

KING, Gordon D
4 Castle Cottages
Royal Navy

KING, John S
4 Castle Cottages
Royal Navy

KING, Leonard Charles
4a Fancy Row, Thurnham Lane
Married
Wife Nellie (née Earl)
Signaller Army

KING, Percy M
Kaypers, Royston Road

KING, Philip W
Paget, Spot Lane
Royal Navy Captain

KINNE, Cecil
St Mary's, Ashford Road

KIRBY, William E
1 Cavendish Way

Second World War: 1939 to 1945

KITCATTE, Charles Frederick *
6 Mallings Lane, The Street
Parents Robert George and Bertha Sarah Kitcatte (née Waller)
Married
Wife Gwendolyn Edith (née Jones) of Bearsted Green
1st Battalion, Suffolk Regiment
Service Number 5825322 Sergeant
Killed 4 June 1943, aged 30
Buried in grave 42, Plot 9, Row 3, Oostende New Communal Cemetery, West-Vlaanderen, Belgium

Charles married Gwendolyn on 20 September 1939 at Holy Cross church.

KNIGHT, Albert W
1 Rosemary Road
Royal Artillery

KNIGHT, Stanley G
1 Rosemary Road

KREJSA, Sidney R H
Carsphairn, The Grove

LAMLEY, Frank P
1 Golf View Cottages, Ware Street

LAMSLEY, Arthur H
Bengalah, 206 Winifred Road

LANG, Francis H

LATTIN, Charles H
Applegarth, The Landway

LAWRENCE, George Henry
Lilk Mount, Otham Lane
Married
Wife Pamela Ianthe (née Thorpe)

Further information about George can be found in *Pamela and George: two lives interrupted by war*.

LAWRENCE, Pamela Ianthe * see entry under **THORPE**

LEADBETER, Percy
Bredgar, The Grove

Second World War: 1939 to 1945

LEE, Thomas R
The Retreat, The Green
2nd Battalion, Royal Warwickshire Regiment
Company Quarter Master Sergeant
Thomas was a Prisoner of War in Stalag VIII B, Germany 1940 to 1945

This photograph shows Thomas in his uniform:

Reproduced courtesy of Jenni Hudson

LEWIS, Eileen Venables
Drayton House, Spot Lane
Married
Husband John Holt Eaton-Shore of Smallwood Vicarage, Sandbach, Cheshire
Leading Aircraft Woman Women's Auxiliary Air Force

Eileen married John on 19 September 1945 at Holy Cross church. John was serving as a Flight Lieutenant, Royal Air Force.

LEWIS, John
Hilltop Cottage, Roseacre Lane

LEWIS, Pamela

LEWIS, Richard

LIELL, John

LIELL, Lawrence J
Yelverton, Plantation Lane

LING, Edward A
Sarum, Roseacre Lane

LITCHFIELD, Frederick P
Snowfield
Parents   Cecilia Litchfield-Speer (née Sandys) and the late Rear Admiral Frederick Shirley,
          (Companion of the Order of St Michael and St George, Distinguished Service Order)
Married
Royal Navy

Frederick was usually known as Jim.

This photograph was taken in August 1934:

LITCHFIELD, Laurence
Snowfield
Parents   Cecilia Litchfield-Speer (née Sandys) and the late Rear Admiral Frederick Shirley,
          (Companion of the Order of St Michael and St George, Distinguished Service Order)
Single
Royal Air Force

Laurence was usually known as Buster.

This photograph was taken in August 1934:

Both reproduced courtesy of Mark Litchfield

Second World War: 1939 to 1945

LITCHFIELD, Oliver
Snowfield
Parents   Cecilia Litchfield-Speer (née Sandys) and the late Rear Admiral Frederick Shirley,
              (Companion of the Order of St Michael and St George, Distinguished Service Order)
Single
Coldstream Guards

Oliver was usually known as Noll. His twin brother was Richard.

This photograph was taken in August 1934:

LITCHFIELD, Richard Hill Sandys *
Snowfield
Parents   Cecilia Litchfield-Speer (née Sandys) and the late Rear Admiral Frederick Shirley,
              (Companion of the Order of St Michael and St George, Distinguished Service Order)
Single
Royal Navy Lieutenant
Killed 27 November 1941, aged 26 en route to Tobruk
Commemorated Panel 41 Column 1, Chatham Naval Memorial

Richard was usually known as Dick. His twin brother was Oliver. The Litchfield family planted a mulberry tree as a memorial to him in the grounds of Snowfield.

This photograph was taken in August 1934:

Both reproduced courtesy of Mark Litchfield

Second World War: 1939 to 1945

LITCHFIELD-SPEER, John Shirley Sandys
Snowfield
Parents   Cecilia Litchfield-Speer (née Sandys) and the late Rear Admiral Frederick Shirley,
            (Companion of the Order of St Michael and St George, Distinguished Service Order)
Married
Wife Margaret Cecilia (née Portal)
Royal Navy *HMS Norfolk* Commander

This photograph of John Litchfield-Speer was taken in 1939 before promotion to Commander:

At the start of the war, John was in command of a destroyer. He was posted to *HMS Norfolk* as second in command. *Norfolk* was deployed as part of the escort to the Icelandic and Russian convoys. This photograph shows John on deck in the Arctic during escort duty. Note the thick clothing he is wearing to counteract the low temperatures, and the heavy icing on the rails:

Both reproduced courtesy of Mark Litchfield

John was posted for stints at the Admiralty and was involved in both the intelligence department and the planning for D Day. He also served in Western Approaches Command at Liverpool. John was appointed as Captain of *HMS Vanguard*, the biggest battleship built for the Royal Navy, towards the end of 1951, just before the formal announcement of a royal cruise. He was appointed to command a ship on a cruise to South Africa with King George VI in 1952. However, in February 1952, the King died, and the cruise was immediately cancelled. John later became Director of Operations before finally retiring from the navy. He was elected as the Conservative MP for Chelsea and represented the constituency from 1959 to 1966.

Second World War: 1939 to 1945

Comforts for the Troops

Throughout the war, people of all ages in Britain, both male and female, knitted and stitched to assist the war effort. They produced a variety of items such as hats, gloves scarves and socks. These generally became known as 'Comforts for the Troops' but in reality were produced for members of all the armed forces in schemes organised by the voluntary services. Wool was supplied in appropriate colours, so dark blue was used for the Royal Navy, a lighter blue for the RAF and khaki for the Army.

Knitting, in particular, was very popular as needles and wool could be easily carried into a shelter during air raids; it was viewed as a patriotic activity. Companies produced specialist patterns. This is an example of a typical booklet which was available:

Reproduced courtesy of Malcolm Kersey

LOCKYER, Frederick †
Married
Wife Cicely Nellie
Mother Gertrude Lockyer of 8 Hardy Street, Maidstone, formerly of The Rose Inn
53rd Tipper Company, Royal Army Service Corps
Service Number T/14668408 Driver
Killed 28 January 1946, aged 36
Buried in grave X 33 28, Brussels Town Cemetery, Evere, Vlaams-Brabant, Belgium

A transcript of the report from Kent Messenger, 9 February 1946:

DIED IN BRUSSELS
Pte. F. H. Lockyer, R.A.S.C.

Official news of the death in Brussels of Pte. Frederick Henry Lockyer, R.A.S.C. on January 29th has been received by Mrs Lockyer, 8 Hardy Street, Maidstone. He was the son of the late Mr and Mrs Lockyer of the Rose Inn, Bearsted, where he was born.

Pte. Lockyer who was 36, spent all his two years service in the Army overseas. He left for the continent three weeks after D-Day.

Before joining the forces he worked at the Mid-Kent Laundry, Boxley Road. He was also an agent for the Liverpool Victoria Insurance Co., King Street. A widow and two daughters are bereaved.

Reproduced courtesy of Kent Messenger newspaper group

Second World War: 1939 to 1945

LONDON, Constance Audrey see entry under **BEXON**

LONG, Irene Ursula Peggy see entry under **RING**

LONG, John

LONKHURST, Stanley L
Eryl, Roseacre Lane

LOWETH, S H
Air Raid Precautions Warden Civil Defence

LOYD, John C
Wendings, Roseacre Lane

LURCOCK, Bernard Charles
Primrose Bank
Married
Wife Alice Louise (née Camfield) of Maesfar
Aircraft Fitter

Bernard married Alice on 10 June 1939 at Holy Cross church.

LUXFORD, A
Bell Lane, Ware Street
Women's Auxiliary Air Force

LUXFORD, Charles
Bell Lane, Ware Street
Royal Artillery

MACKELDEN, Lester A
Vicarage Cottage, Thurnham Lane

MACIVER, John Christian *
9 Downside Crescent, Hampstead, London
Parents Reverend Peter and Mrs MacIver of Bowmore, Islay, Argyllshire, Scotland
Married
Wife Joyce
Killed 20 April 1941, aged 47 at Aldington South Court
Listed on Civilian Section of the Roll of Honour for the District of Hollingbourne

MACKIE, Ramsey W M
Shenstone, Ashford Road

MACKNAY, Basil R F
Carnlea, Lord Romney's Hill

MacONEGAL, Roy
Orchards, Landway
Married
8 October 1937 19 Group, Romeo 2, Bearsted
Royal Observer Corps

MANNING, Sidney F
Mansfield, The Grove

MARGETTS, Joan
3 Church Lane
Auxiliary Territorial Service

MARSH, Ernest
Home Forces, Bearsted
Married
Wife Sylvia (née Hardcastle) of 102 Leeds Road, Dutiwood, Wakefield
Private Royal Army Ordnance Corps

Ernest married Sylvia on 3 January 1942 at Holy Cross church.

MARSHALL, John C
Sellindge, Plantation Lane

MARTIN, Annie Ida
The Limes
Married
Husband Dorman James Dalley of Bourne Grange, Hadlow, Kent
Sergeant Auxiliary Territorial Service

Annie married Dorman on 15 March 1943 at Holy Cross church. Dorman was a serving as a Gunner.

MARTIN, Frederick Edwin
Glenwood, Yeoman Lane
Married
Wife Vera Elizabeth (née Watkins) of Station Hill
Corporal Royal Army Service Corps

Martin married Vera on 8 March 1944 at Holy Cross church

MARTIN, William W
Amesbury, Lord Romney's Hill

MARWOOD, Ernest W
Llewellyn, Spot Farm Estate

Second World War: 1939 to 1945

MATTHEWS, Denis J
Roseacre Stores and Post Office, Ashford Road
Married
Wife June
Radio Electrical Artificer, Royal Navy

Denis joined the Royal Navy in 1943, just before his sixteenth birthday, as an apprentice to become an Electrical Artificer in the Fleet Air Arm. The apprenticeship took four years, so the war had finished by the time he qualified! Further training enabled him to convert to a Radio Electrical Artificer, having been rated up to Petty Officer in the meantime. His fourteen years of service included eighteen months in the Far East during the Korean War., He left the Navy in 1957 as a Chief Radio Electrical Artificer and returned to Bearsted with his wife June and their children, to join the family business running Roseacre Stores and Post Office.

This photograph of Denis was taken in 1949 after he was promoted to Petty Officer:

MATTHEWS, Percival Victor
Roseacre Stores and Post Office, Ashford Road
Married
Flight Lieutenant, Royal Air Force

Percival was usually called Percy or Vic. Before the war he worked in the Borough Treasurer's Office, Maidstone, and in 1938 joined the Territorial Army. After mobilisation, Vic was posted to Woolwich Barracks in London as a driver in the Royal Army Service Corps. He then answered an appeal for volunteers to train as pilots and was accepted into the RAF. His training included a spell in America and he became a Sergeant Pilot flying Lancaster bombers. Vic was commissioned as a Pilot Officer.

This photograph of Vic was taken in 1943, shortly after his commission:

His service included several missions to Italy during which his aircraft was attacked and shot down in flames by a German night-fighter near Paris. He was posted Missing but three months later, to everybody's surprise and joy, he arrived home, without warning. It transpired that after bailing out from his burning Lancaster, he was rescued by members of the French Resistance, given a French identity and was passed through various "safe locations" before being flown back to England on one of the regular clandestine RAF flights which operated to and from Occupied France. He was promoted during the time he was in France and thus he flew out as a Sergeant Pilot and subsequently flew back as a Pilot Officer!!

Upon his return, Vic was posted to a unit at Cosford which test flew Horsa troop carrying gliders, in preparation for D-Day. His main role was piloting the Armstrong-Whitworth Whitley bombers, then being used as towing aircraft for the gliders.

Both reproduced courtesy of Denis Matthews

He subsequently joined the newly formed Ferry Command, which delivered aircraft around the country. Vic, now promoted to a Flight Lieutenant, flew twenty seven different types of aircraft, with only the Pilots Notes for each as a guide before take-off. He was seconded to Lossiemouth in Scotland as a Test pilot before his de-mobilisation in 1946.

After the war he returned home to Roseacre Stores Post Office, becoming Sub Postmaster in 1958 to 1984. He ran the business together with his younger brother, Denis, their wives and respective families until it was sold in 1987.

MATTHEWS, Richard

MAY, Arthur L
11 Council Houses, The Street
Married
Wife Mabel Ellen (née Seager) of Bell Lane
Royal Army Medical Corps

A transcript of a report from the Kent Messenger, 24 July 1942:

GLAD NEWS FOR WIFE
Thurnham Man Reported Missing, Now In Hospital

One of the eleven men of the Maidstone contingent of the R.A.M.C. who came back from Dunkirk, was Pte. Arthur May. He is 26 and in February last year, he married Miss M Seager of Bell Lane, Thurnham.

Recently his wife received news that he was missing in the Middle East since June 14th. On Wednesday of this week, Mrs May received a letter from her husband in a base hospital, dated June 25th. He joined the Maidstone Territorials in 1936 and before the war was employed at Messrs. Harnett's Nurseries, Bearsted.

Reproduced courtesy of Kent Messenger newspaper group

McDOWELL, Norah Gladys see entry under **NOAKES**

McDOWELL, Reginald George Henry
The Limes
Married
Wife Norah Gladys (née Noakes)
Royal Navy
Service Number CSP R/300362 Stoker

Reginald married Norah on 7 November 1944 at Holy Cross church. Norah was serving as a Leading Aircraftwoman with the Women's Auxiliary Air Force.

McKEOUGH, Raymond A
Rostrevor, Ashford Road
Royal Navy

MELLOR, Harold

MERRITT, Horace G
Newcot, Weavering

Second World War: 1939 to 1945

MILDREN, Ernest S
Hatherill, Roseacre Lane
Parents Mr and Mrs J Mildren
Single
Royal Navy

MILDREN, Joseph Jack
Hatherill, Roseacre Lane
Parents Mr and Mrs J Mildren
Married
Wife Frances (née Smeaton)
Royal Air Force
Distinguished Flying Medal 1940

This report about Joseph appeared in the Kent Messenger during 1940:

BEARSTED AIRMAN WINS D F M

Stopped Petrol Leak in Mid Air

A FORMER patrol leader of 1st Bearsted Troop Boy Scouts, 'The Scarlet Pimpernels' has been on the recommendation of Air Officer C in C Middle East, awarded the D.F.M.

He is Sergeant Observer Joseph Mildren, elder son of Mr and Mrs J Mildren of 'Hatherill' Roseacre Lane, Bearsted.

He has the distinction of being in every raid made his squadron since the commencement of hostilities and has always been in the leading aircraft. 'On one occasion when carrying out his duties in a raid on an enemy aerodrome he continued his work despite the fact that enemy fighters had already begun to attack.

Throughout the engagement he gave a lucid, calm and very helpful description of the flight to his pilot, and when the starboard petrol feed was severed, causing the loss of half the petrol into the fuselage, he made great efforts to stop the leak and assisted the pilot with fuel calculations, which eventually resulted in the safe return of the aircraft to the base.

When an apprentice he won the silver drum sticks as champion drummer. An all round sportsman, he has won medals for running, cricket, football and swimming.

Sergeant Mildren was educated at Gillingham Welseyan School; he is 28 years of age and married Miss Frances Smeaton of Gillingham on 26 March 1938.

Reproduced courtesy of Kent Messenger newspaper group

MILES, W

MILLER, John S, Jun.
Dulwich, Royston Road

MILLER, Robert G
Neatherton Cottages, Ware Street

MILNER, Peter W A
Bandra, Royston Road

MITCHELL, Brian

MITCHELL, Jack
Married
Wife Florence Grace (née Hills) of Fairways, Ware Street
Leading Sick Beth Attendant Royal Naval Volunteer Reserve
HMS St Tudno

Jack married Florence on 12 December 1942 at St Mary's church.

MONCKTON, Francis P
Maybank, The Green

MONCKTON, John
Maybank, The Green
Father Francis P Monckton
Royal Air Force

MONCKTON, Lancelot Richard Stephen
Married
Bell House, The Green
19 Group, Romeo 2, Bearsted
Royal Observer Corps

Lance was a solicitor and later became chairman of Bearsted parish council, 1952-1960. This photograph shows Lance in his Royal Observer Corps uniform:

Reproduced courtesy of Evelyn Pearce

MOODY, Frank L J
Rougemont, Weavering Street

Second World War: 1939 to 1945

MOORE, Albert
Royal Army Service Corps
Service Number S/10668415 Corporal

MOORE, Pauline
Sutton House, Sutton Street
Women's Land Army

MOORE, Robert
Dove Row, Royston Road
Grenadier Guards

MOORY, F

MORLING, Maurice B
Two Trees, The Landway
Territorial Army

Maurice's wartime service included surviving six nights on the beaches at Dunkirk before evacuation.

MORRIS, Arthur E
194 Winifred Road

MORTIMER, Frederick
1939 19 Group, Romeo 2, Bearsted
Royal Observer Corps

MOSELEY, William E
Bletchingley, Weavering Street
Royal Artillery

MOSS, Muriel Mary
The Limes, The Green; later Ivydene, Thurnham Lane
Married
Husband William Joseph
Son Noel Robert
Assistant to Commandant Red Cross, Bearsted

This photograph shows Muriel in her Red Cross uniform:

Reproduced courtesy of Susan Imgrund (née Moss)

Second World War: 1939 to 1945

MOSS, Noel Robert
The Limes, The Green; later Ivydene, Thurnham Lane
Parents William and Muriel Moss
Born 28 December 1924
Married
Wife Anastasia (née Barsky)
Children Michael and Susan
Royal Air Force
Service Number 180589
Awarded Order of the British Empire 1977
Died 2000

This photograph of Noel is believed to have been taken in 1947:

Reproduced courtesy of Susan Imgrund

Noel began his distinguished service within the armed forces by joining the Officer Training Corps whilst at Maidstone Grammar School, he also acted as a messenger with the ARP. He then became a sergeant in 741 Squadron Air Training Corps when it formed at the school. In 1941 he joined the Home Guard before becoming Captain of School and enlisted at Euston for the RAF. Aged 17, Noel was placed on the Reserve List to finish his studies! The next year, as Warrant Officer Moss, he was awarded an RAF Short University Course with a view to receiving a commission in the RAF and a place at Selwyn College, Cambridge. On 16 October 1943 he was mobilised to the Air Crew Dispersal Centre, Manchester. It was whilst serving in the RAF that he acquired the nickname of 'Micky'. The following notes summarise his subsequent career:

<u>1944 - 1946</u>
January 1944 RAF station Heaton Park assisted other cadets clearing V1 flying bomb damage

September 1944 posted to 24 Course, RAF station Falcon Field, Mesa Arizona, America for basic flight training.

16 June 1945, Pilot Officer N R Moss received a commission and returned to Britain where postings included RAF stations Elmdon and Desford, AFU Wheaton Aston.

17 December 1945 promoted to Flying Officer. During the summer 1946, posted to 13 Operations Training Unit and then Operations Training Unit, Kinloss.

Second World War: 1939 to 1945

<u>1947 - 1949</u>
During 1947, posted to Far East including: RAF station Tebrau, Johonre, Malaya; 18 Squadron Mingaladon; 45 Squadron and 205 Squadron, Negombo, Ceylon; RAF stations Koggola and Seletar, Singapore.

<u>1949 - 1954</u>
By 15 December 1949 returned to Britain and promoted to Flight Lieutenant, qualified as a Flying Instructor 1950, then qualified as Flying Instructor (Jet) 1953. Postings included: Central Flying School, RAF station Little Rissington; RAF College Cranwell; No 207 Advanced Flying School at Full Sutton.

<u>1954 - 1961</u>
January 1954 posted to Canada, Advanced Flying Instructor and Chief Standards Officer.

October 1955 promoted to Squadron Leader. Postings included: RCAF Claresholm; RCAF Trenton; RCAF Gimli; RAF station North Luffenham, 141 Squadron at RAF station Coltishall; 152 Squadron at RAF station Stradishall; RAF stations Wattisham and Horsham St Faith; Staff College at RAF station Bracknell.

Noel met and married Anastasia (usually called Ann), a serving RCAFW, whilst at RCAF Gimli. They were married in the Protestant Chapel on the station.

<u>1962 - 1989</u>
In 1962 posted to Joint Planning Services, HQ Middle East Command, RAF Steamer Point at Aden. During early 1964 posted to Britain as the political situation in Aden deteriorated then to Ministry of Defence at Northumberland House. Postings included: RAF stations Bracknell, Biggin Hill, Binbrook and Brampton; Ministry of Defence and Staff College at RAF station Bracknell.

1969 - 1970 Personnel Selection and Training Instructor, RAF station Biggin Hill
1970 Officer Commanding, Administration Wing, RAF station Binbrook.
1971 Wing Commander
1977 Tutor, Individual Studies School, Staff College, RAF station Bracknell
1979 - 1989 retired but continued as Retired Officer, Grade 2 Individual Studies School.

MOSS, William Joseph
The Limes, The Green; later Ivydene, Thurnham Lane
Married
Wife Muriel Mary (née Ashwell)
Son Noel Robert

8 October 1937 19 Group, Romeo 2, Bearsted
Royal Observer Corps

William was usually known as Bill and had served in the Royal Flying Corps in the First World War. He was a Master Butcher and owned a shop at Chestnut Place next to Brooks Stores in Bearsted. This photograph is undated but shows Bill in his Royal Observer Corps uniform:

Reproduced courtesy of Susan Imgrund

MOTTON, John A
Ondeen, Spot Farm Estate

MOUNT, Douglas
Nine Elms, Hockers Lane
Army

MUNN, Alan V
Rosemead, Roseacre Lane

NAYLOR, Frederick
The Street
Married
8 October 1937 19 Group, Romeo 2, Bearsted
Royal Observer Corps

This undated photograph shows Frederick receiving a medal for his work with the Royal Observer Corps during a parade at Cranbrook.

Reproduced courtesy of Bryan McCarthy

NAYLOR, Margaret L
1 Sunnyside, The Street

NEIL, Frederick
184 Royston Road

NEWSHAM, Florence Margaret
Friningham Lodge, Detling
Married
Husband John Westerman of 12 Viewforth, Edinburgh, Scotland
Women's Land Army
Service Number 75055

Florence married John on 21 July 1945 at St Mary's church. John was serving as a Sergeant, in the Royal Air Force, Service Number 1349434

NOAKES, Norah Gladys
The Limes
Married
Husband Reginald George Henry McDowell of The Limes
Leading Aircraft Woman, Women's Auxiliary Air Force

Norah married Reginald on 7 November 1944 at Holy Cross church. Reginald was serving as a stoker in the Royal Navy.

NOURSE, Alexander
Cambria, Ashford Road

O'GORMAN, Mervyn John
197 Winifred Road
Married
Wife Gladys Elaine (née Bull)
Daughter Jennifer Elaine
G Troop 392 Battery 119 Light Anti-Aircraft Regiment, Royal Artillery

Mervyn was usually known as John. His service included operations and duties in Gheel, Belgium, Eindhoven and Nijmegen in the Netherlands. Jenny, his daughter, believes that he also witnessed the airborne armada en route to Eindhoven and Arnhem on 20 September 1944. His battery lost count of the number of aircraft they saw passing overhead.

This undated photograph shows John in his uniform:

Reproduced courtesy of Jenny Boniface (neé O'Gorman)

OLD, Gordon Garnett
Red Pillars, Ashford Road
Married
Wife Joyce Eileen (née Burgess) of Danefield
Lance Corporal Royal Army Service Corps

Gordon married Joyce 4 October 1941 at Holy Cross church. Joyce was a Probationer Nurse.

OSBORNE, Ronald
Chine Wood, Fauchons Lane
Royal Artillery

OSWALD, R
Nether Milgate
Army

OVENDEN, ------
Oak Dell, Weavering Street
Women's Auxiliary Air Force

OVENDEN, W

PALMER, Edward
Shirley Way

PALMER, Edward W
Glendale, Spot Lane
Royal Navy

PALMER, R A
Sergeant in Special Constabulary, received bar to medal in December 1942

PALMER, R C B
Fairview, The Green
Army

PANTING, John W
Snowfield Garage

PARKHOUSE, Charles F
1 Council Houses, The Street

Second World War: 1939 to 1945

PARKIN, William Hugh *
Parents William and Dorothy Whitehead of The Mount
Married
Son William Hugh
Royal Navy
Lieutenant Commander
Killed in action 9 June 1940, aged 33 during sinking of *HMS Glorious*
Commemorated   Bay 1, Panel 2, Lee on Solent Memorial, Hampshire;
a memorial window to *HMS Glorious* in Holy Cross church;
a memorial in St Peter's church, Martindale, Cumbria.

William came from a distinguished family: his father, also called William, was a solicitor, chairman of Bearsted parish council and the Under Sheriff of Kent. His mother, Dorothy, came from the Parkin family of Westmorland. William changed his surname to his mother's maiden name upon inheriting some of his grandfather's estate. William was a trained pilot and served on aircraft carriers before retiring in 1934. As a Royal Naval Reservist, he was recalled to active service in 1939 and posted to *HMS Glorious*.

HMS Glorious was one of the British warships that provided cover for the evacuation of British, French and Polish forces from Narvik following the German invasion of Norway. At 4.30pm on 8 June, the *Glorious* and her two escorting destroyers, *Acasata* and *Ardent*, were sighted by the German battle cruisers Gneisenau and Scharnhorst which opened fire on the British ships. The *Ardent* was soon sunk, but the *Acasta* continued to provide support for *Glorious*. Just after 6pm, *Acasta* and *Glorious* were overwhelmed. There was only one survivor from *Acasta* and fewer than forty from *Glorious*.

A memorial stained glass window dedicated to the memory of William and the crew of *HMS Glorious* is in Holy Cross church.

This photograph shows William in his naval uniform:

Reproduced courtesy of Holy Cross church

PARR, Norman H
Anfield, The Landway

Head Air Raid Precautions Warden Civil Defence

PARREN, James
The Green
Married
Wife Jean Frances May (née Brimstead) of The Green
Leading Aircraftman Royal Air Force

James married Jean on 26 December 1944 at Holy Cross church, Jean was serving with the Women's Auxiliary Police Force.

PARREN, Jean see entry under **BRIMSTEAD**

PAYNE, Arthur G
The Haven, Lord Romney's Hill

PAYNE, Robert W
Long Windows, The Grove

PEACH, Charles William
Kenbar, Manor Rise
Married
12 September 1939   19 Group, Romeo 2, Bearsted
Royal Observer Corps

This photograph shows Charles in his Royal Observer Corps uniform:

Reproduced courtesy of Evelyn Pearce

PEACH, Denis

PEARCE, Geoffrey B
Trevarno, Roseacre Lane
Royal Air Force

Second World War: 1939 to 1945

PEARSON, Albert Victor
8 Council Houses, The Street
Married
8 October 1937 19 Group, Romeo 2, Bearsted
Royal Observer Corps

This photograph shows Albert in his Royal Observer Corps uniform:

Reproduced courtesy of Evelyn Pearce

PEARSON, Frank
8 Council Houses, The Street
Royal Air Force

PEARSON, Harold Frederick
Armenia, Ashford Road
Married
Wife Esme Ellen (née Town)
Lance Corporal Corps of Military Police

Harold and Esme married on 29 April 1944 at Holy Cross church

PELLETT, Albert W
3 Invicta Villas, The Green

PELLETT, George

PELLETT, Stanley

Second World War: 1939 to 1945

National Registration and Food Rationing

The National Registration Act, passed in 1939, re-introduced an identity card scheme which had originally operated in the First World War. As in the previous conflict, all households had to register as this notice indicates.

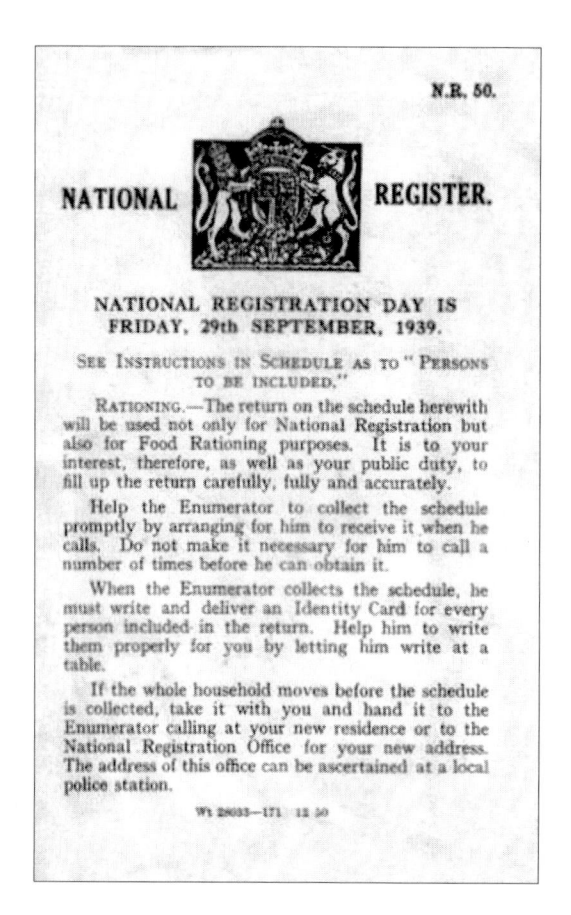

To begin with, all cards were a brown colour, but in 1943, a blue card was introduced for adults. The cards recorded the owner's name, address and previous addresses, and an individual National Registration Number. They had to be carried at all times by everyone and were only valid if they were stamped by the local registration office. Identity cards had to be produced with a ration book when shopping. A typical example of a blue card:

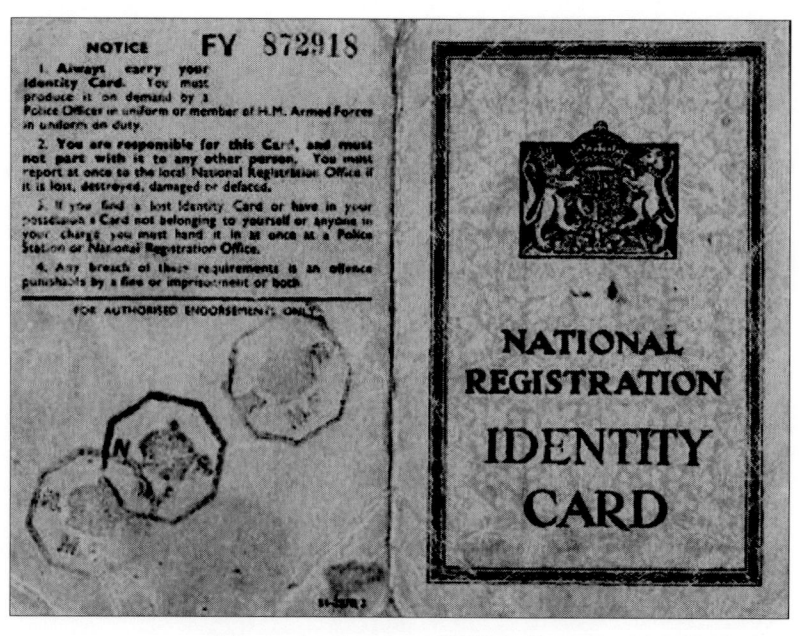

Both reproduced courtesy of Malcolm Kersey

Second World War: 1939 to 1945

Food rationing was introduced in January 1940, but preparations began the previous year and not all foodstuffs were immediately restricted. These were the basic rations as initially introduced for one adult for a week: [6]

Bacon and ham	4oz	Meat (to the value of)	1s 10d
Sugar	12oz	Tea	2oz
Cheese	1oz	Cooking fat	2oz
Butter	4oz	Butter plus margarine	6oz
Preserves	8oz (for 4 weeks)		

The 'points' system was introduced in December 1941 and initially covered canned fish, meat and beans but later came to include a range of food including dried pulses, dried fruit, biscuits and cereals. Each of these were given points values and within the limit of the allocation of points coupons, there were no other restrictions on the amount purchased. Bread was not rationed until after the war in 1946: the lessons about bread and rationing during the First World War had been learned.[7]

The ration book was the passport to getting enough food to eat. The first books were issued during October 1939. They were valid for a year and replacements were obtained by detaching and sending back a postcard. Once a book was received, everyone had to register at a shop for the groups of foods which were rationed and the retailer's details had to be entered on every page of coupons but different retailers and shops were allowed for the rations.[8]

These images are taken from a reproduction ration book but give a good impression of the original document. Original and first issue ration books are, of course, very rare!

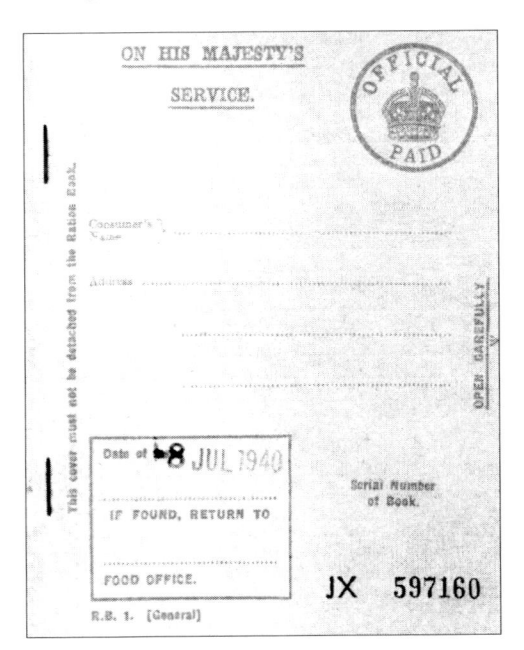

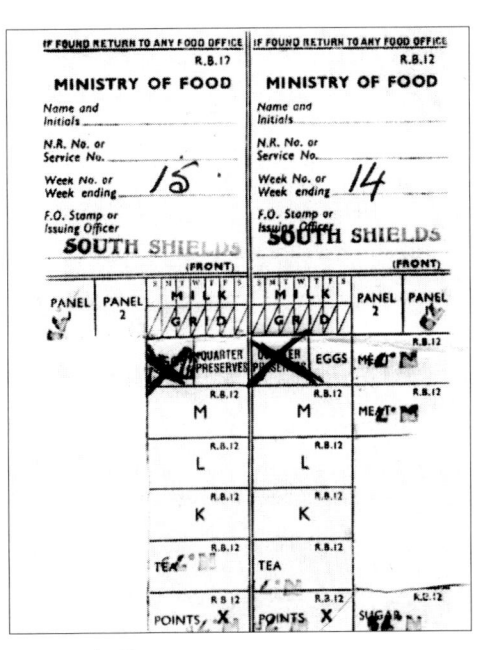

Both reproduced courtesy of Malcolm Kersey

The Ministries of Agriculture and Food worked together to ensure that the cultivation of land, food production and supply was maximised. At the outbreak of hostilities, a War Agricultural Committee was set up for each county. They were instructed by the government to increase home food production by overseeing the cultivation of many acres of land previously left unploughed or used for purposes other than growing food. The committees had sweeping powers and could either evict or dispossess farmers if their crop yields were regarded as insufficient.

By the middle of 1941, the German U-boat offensive against Allied shipping convoys in the Atlantic was significantly affecting food supplies, raw materials and other goods imported into Britain. Propaganda leaflets were also dropped by the Luftwaffe and the government realised that there was a danger of a reduction in public morale.

Here is a copy of a typical German propaganda leaflet:

> # The Battle of the Atlantic is being lost!
>
> ### The reasons why:
>
> 1. German U-boats, German bombers and the German fleet sink and seriously damage between them every month a total of 700 000 to 1 million tons of British and allied shipping.
> 2. All attempts at finding a satisfactory means of defence against the German U-boats or the German bombers have failed disastrously.
> 3. Even President Roosevelt has openly stated that for every five ships sunk by Germany, Britain and America between them can only build two new ones. All attempts to launch a larger shipbuilding programme in America have failed.
> 4. Britain is no longer in a position to secure her avenues of supply. The population of Britain has to do with about half the ration that the population of Germany gets. Britain, herself, can only support 40% of her population from her own resources in spite of the attempts made to increase the amount of land under cultivation. If the war is continued until 1942, 60% of the population of Britain will starve!
>
> All this means that starvation in Britain is not to be staved off. At the most it can be postponed, but whether starvation comes this year or at the beginning of next doesn't make a ha'porth of difference. Britain must starve because she is being cut off from her supplies.
>
> ### Britain's losing the Battle of the Atlantic means Britain's losing the war!

Reproduced courtesy of Leslie Lawson

In response, the government launched one of its most successful campaigns: 'Dig For Victory'. Everyone in the country was urged to grow as many vegetables as possible in order to release sufficient farmland to cultivate potatoes, wheat, barley and animal fodder. In June 1941, Bearsted parish council was advised that the Committee had ascertained there were two areas which could be suitable for cultivation: some waste ground on the Royston estate on the west side of Spot Lane and land at the rear of Premier House, Wrights Limited, on the east side of Spot Lane. It was recommended that they be cultivated as allotments.[9] In addition to the Committee's efforts, local landowners also offered land for cultivation. Mrs Jessel of Mote House volunteered one and half acres of her land for use as allotments in Church Landway. Mr Whitehead of The Mount also offered some orchard land for use as vegetable gardens.[10]

When administering the food rationing scheme, the Ministry of Food recognised that there were many agricultural workers, including Land Girls, who had to eat their lunch in the fields. After some debate, a special, much larger ration of cheese was allowed for these people. This varied though, so in May 1941 it was 8oz but rose to 12oz in December. The greatest amount permitted was 1lb in July 1942 (double the domestic ration) but returned to 12oz by the following year.[11]

The Ministry of Food aimed to supply at least one hot nutritious meal every day, at a reasonable price to workers everywhere, usually at a works canteen or British Restaurant. However in rural areas, access to these facilities was limited. During 1942 the Ministry decided upon what became known as the 'Rural Pie Scheme'. Centres were organised to make and supply items such as pies and sausage rolls and were usually run by voluntary organisations such as the Women's Institute or Women's Voluntary Service. The cooking was undertaken anywhere where there was a large kitchen which could be used, frequently the local bakeries lent experienced hands.[12]

Second World War: 1939 to 1945

It took some time to get the Rural Pie Scheme into operation and there were difficulties along the way. In Bearsted and Thurnham, the Women's Institute was already hard-pressed: they were running a canteen and a rest room for the troops stationed nearby and also cooking school dinners. Nevertheless, it was decided that it might still be possible for the scheme to go ahead using other organisations.[13]

Alas for well-laid plans! Somehow, the advice about distributing literature concerning the scheme became garbled. And so, Mr Skinner, the headmaster of the school wrote (with some justified exasperation), the following entry in the log book: [14]

> **13 April 1943**
> A representative from the WVS called and left pamphlets for the children to take home, explaining that those who needed them would be able to obtain 3d pies at Datson's, the Bakers. These seem entirely unnecessary for the majority of the children, and were intended in the first place for agricultural workers. Since there were forty forms short it was impossible to distribute them. The representative from the WVS called back in this afternoon and said the scheme wasn't working and asked for the pamphlets back. <u>Typical!</u>

Reproduced courtesy of Roseacre School

Despite this unfortunate hiccup, the scheme was well-received nationally and it was estimated that by the end of May 1945, workers in 5,000 villages munched their way through nearly a million pies a week.[15]

Of course, it took an immense number of staff at the Ministries of Agriculture and Food to administer the various rationing schemes. They also wrote and issued many leaflets including 'Food Facts'. The intention was to give recipes and advice on how to produce nutritious and interesting meals for the family from the range of foods and rationed amounts that were available. Although meals seemed were fairly monotonous during the war, the levels of nutrition were well balanced. As at least one person has commented, although obesity was not exactly a problem, it was due to rationing that the spectre of starvation so evident on the Continent, was effectively kept at bay in Britain.

These transcribed details from some Food Facts leaflets concern sandwich fillings and to modern tastes, appear quite startling:

> **Good sandwich fillings - have you tried these?**
>
> 1 Mashed sardines, pilchards or herring mixed with shredded fresh carrot;
>
> 2 Vegetable or meat extract and mustard and cress;
>
> 3 Chopped cold meat with mashed cooked vegetables with seasoning;
>
> 4 Brawn, shredded swede and chutney.

Under the rationing scheme, an adult was entitled to a packet of dried egg every four weeks. These are the instructions on how to use this dehydrated food:

> **How to use Dried Egg**
>
> 1 Store the tin in a cool, dry place and replace the lid after use;
>
> 2 Mix one level tablespoon of the powder with two tablespoons of water;
>
> <u>This equals one fresh egg;</u>
>
> 3 Treat this mixture as a fresh one;
> Do not waste the mixture by making up more than is necessary for the dish; beat as usual before adding to other ingredients.

Second World War: 1939 to 1945

This recipe was named after Lord Woolton, who was Minister of Food:

> **Woolton Pie**
>
> Dice and cook 1lb of each of these vegetables: Potatoes, Cauliflower, Swedes, Carrots.
>
> Strain the vegetables, but keep some of the water that was used to cook them. Place the vegetables in a large pie dish. Add a little vegetable extract and about an ounce of rolled oats or oatmeal to the vegetable liquid. Cook until liquid has thickened and pour over the vegetables.
> Add 3 - 4 spring onions.
>
> Top with potato pastry or with mashed potatoes and heat in the centre of a moderately hot oven until golden brown.
>
> Serves 4 to 6 people.

Reproduced courtesy of Malcolm Kersey

In 1943, the Bearsted and Thurnham Produce Association was formed as a local effort in the Dig for Victory Campaign. The annual subscription was one shilling and sixpence. There were forty members and the benefits included cheap seeds and fertilisers. The Committee included Lionel Datson, Mr Abery and Bill Foster. A sty was also built on the spare ground at the Kentish Yeoman public house for a Pig Club.

The British Pig Association formed the Small Pig Keepers' Council to encourage backyard pig keeping. Local Pig Clubs could exercise thrift in using kitchen waste for a purpose, and which would also increase the number of pigs kept throughout the country. The scheme was run in association with the Ministry of Agriculture and a licence was required from the Ministry of Food to keep the animals.[16] The club members included the Gregory, Harnett and Pearce families. The Harnett family were central to activities as they owned a gas-fired copper. Every Sunday, members would use the copper to prepare the swill for the pigs. This included all the unsold or old vegetables from the market gardens, allotments and vegetable plots around Bearsted and Thurnham and soon became part of the local natural economy. When the pigs were slaughtered, the pork and bacon was a welcome change to a diet controlled through rationing.

Here is a popular poster which emphasised the importance of feeding pigs from scraps and waste:

Reproduced courtesy of Trevor Hunt and www.wartimegardening.wordpress.com/

PENNELLS, Ronald Leslie
207 Winifred Road
Married
Wife Lucienne Marie Louise (née Penez)
Hampshire Regiment 27 June 1940
Transferred to 21st Army Group. Royal Army Service Corps from 20 January 1941 to 5 May 1946
Service Number S/5506938 Staff Sergeant

Ronald was born in Barton Road, Maidstone. He met his future wife in 1944 whilst he was serving as a Staff Sergeant with General Montgomery in Belgium. His Group was initially posted to a base at the Phillips factory in Holland but it was too small and so they were staying in Brussels instead. During an evening at the Hotel Metropole with some colleagues, a Belgian family on the next table noticed the servicemen and invited them to Sunday lunch. Many Belgium people invited servicemen to their homes for meals as a way of say thank you to the allied forces for liberating them from German occupation. When Ronald took up the invitation, he started to talk to Lucienne.

The couple became engaged at Easter 1945 and married in July 1945. Ronald was allowed three days leave before returning to General Montgomery's headquarters in Germany. They were married in the Town Hall followed by a religious ceremony. As the wedding was in the morning, there was a large wedding breakfast which took nearly all the afternoon. Lucienne kept a copy of the menu which shows that there were many courses, supplemented by a great deal of wine that had somehow survived the occupation.

This photograph was taken on their wedding day:

Reproduced courtesy of Lucienne Pennells

After Ronald left the army they came to live in Bearsted. He had previously bought a bungalow in Winifred Road around 1938, but had not been able to take up residence. After the war, he worked for the Kent Messenger in Canterbury for a spell before becoming a Press Association reporter for the House of Commons. This was followed by editorship of the South Eastern Gazette newspaper. During a very active retirement, he became a national publicity director and editor of the journal for the Royal British Legion. Ronald was awarded the MBE in 1978. They celebrated their Golden Wedding in 1995.

PENNEY, Reginald Leslie †
Parents Thomas and Frances Ellen Penney of Maple Bar Gate Cottage
Single
10th Battalion, Durham Light Infantry
Service Number 14688862 Private
Killed 19 August 1944, aged 18
Buried in Banneville la Campagne War Cemetery, Calvados, France

Reproduced courtesy of Trudy Johnson

PENNEY, Ronald
Keeper's Cottage, Friningham
Royal Air Force

PENNEY, Stanley
Keeper's Cottage, Friningham
Royal Artillery

PERKESS, Jack E
Tower Villa, Tower Lane

PILBEAM, N E
4 Bearsted Spot Cottages
Army

PILBEAM, R O
1 Bearsted Spot Cottages
Royal Electrical and Mechanical Engineers

PITCHFORD, Francis Edward
Timedean, Spot Lane
Married
Wife Barbara (née Kenley) of 38 Aviedale Avenue, Murton, Blackpool
Leading Aircraftman Royal Air Force

Francis married Barbara on 1 January 1942 at Holy Cross church. Barbara was a civil servant.

POCOCK, Terence R
Aldworth, 212 Winifred Road
Royal Marines

POLLARD, Ernest F
3 Council Houses, The Street
Army

POUND, Douglas

POUND, ------
Crest View, Hockers Lane
Royal Air Force

PRESCOTT-DENNIS, William F
173 Royston Road

PRESLAND, ------
Auxiliary Fire Service

PRICE, Harold

PRINCE, Joseph W T
St Albans, Plantation Lane

RAGGETT, Cecil M
Dilkoosha, Lord Romney's Hill

An Intriguing Report

This is a transcript of a report which appeared in the Kent Messenger, 6 April 1945. It is typical of the wartime press in that there are few firm details and was subject to censorship, but the information remains intriguing!

German Hid In Kent Railway Tunnel

Found Cowering In Manhole

An escaped German prisoner was captured by the police while hiding in a tunnel between Bearsted and Maidstone railway stations about 9pm on Wednesday night.

Information had been flashed to the police that the prisoner had got onto the line and had been seen making his way to Maidstone.

A sergeant and constable went to Maidstone East station and guided by Station Foreman Wright, set off in search.

They found their man in the second tunnel about halfway through.

Reproduced courtesy of Kent Messenger newspaper group

RAGGETT, Ernest Edward
Dilkoosha, Lord Romney's Hill
Parents Herbert Edward and Marguerite Jane Raggett (née Lecomte)
Single
April 1938 Kent Civil Air Guard
Killed 19 August 1939, aged 26

A transcript of the report from the Kent Messenger, 26 August 1939:

KENT CIVIL AIR GUARD PILOT KILLED

Nose Dive Caused By Attempt to Adjust Goggles?

Tragedy overtook an enthusiastic young airman, Civil Air Guard Pilot, Ernest Edward Raggett, son of Mr and Mrs H Raggett of Dilkoosha, Lord Romney's Hill, Maidstone, on Friday last week. As the plane he was flying passed over the playing field at Borough Green, at a low altitude, he was seen to wave frantically to the children below, evidently warning them to escape from danger. Then, almost immediately, the plane nose dived into an adjoining ploughed field. Witnesses of the crash rushed to the spot in order to render help, but they found the young airman, 26 years old, lifeless. He had, apparently been killed instantaneously.

MACHINE HALTED IN MID AIR

At the inquest at the Church Hall, Borough Green, on Tuesday, the suggestion was put forward by Mr G W Harrison, Chief Instructor for Maidstone and Malling Airdromes, that Mr Raggett might have been troubled by the fact that as he was taking off for the flight, which ended in the crash, his goggles fell off.

It might have been, said Mr Harrison, that he had flown on adjusting his goggles and did not know where he was. The inquest was conducted by Mr J H Soady (County Coroner) and a verdict of Accidental Death was returned. Sympathy was expressed by the jury and representatives of the airdrome with the relatives.

VERY KEEN ON FLYING

Herbert Edward Raggett identified his son, who, he said, lived with him and was a butcher with witness at Wrotham Heath.

His son as a member of the Civil Air Guard, which he joined last April. He was very keen on flying and was happy about the progress he was making. He was not at all nervous.

Dr Ralph Green, Borough Green, said that Mr Raggett had a fractured base of the skull and there were extensive injuries. Death would have been instantaneous.

Graham William Harrison, Hill View, Tonbridge Road, Teston, Chief Instructor for the Maidstone and Malling Airdromes said Mr Raggett was a pupil at his airdrome. He started training on April 19th. Up to August 16th he had had 11 hours 35 minutes dual flying and he then went up for a solo flight of ten minutes. He was flying very well. On Friday witness sent him up for half an hour's solo on practise landings.

MACHINE IN PROPER ORDER

The machine was in proper order and witness had been up in it with Mr Raggett previously on Friday evening.

When Mr Raggett took off, his goggles fell off and he rose erratically as he was trying to adjust them. This caused witness some concern and he watched for Mr Raggett to return.

EYE WITNESS STORY

George Henry Paul Greengarth, Ightham, said that on Friday evening he was in Borough Green Recreation Ground and about 7.30 saw a light airplane flying overhead at about 300-400 feet. The plane had flown from the direction of Malling and turned back. It made another turn, losing height and turned again, still dropping.

"I realised there was the possibility of a crash," said witness, "and at the time it stalled and crashed, I estimated it was about 120 feet up." The engine was operating the whole time and seemed to be functioning perfectly.

The machine seemed to halt in mid-air, its tail went up and it came crashing to earth. When he arrived at the scene of the crash he believed the goggles were on Mr Raggett's helmet. Police-Sgt Cooper, Borough Green, said the machine crashed on Whiffen's Farm. The nose was in the ground and the plane was completely smashed.

Reproduced courtesy of Kent Messenger newspaper group

RANGE, Charles David
Aldington Court Cottages
Wife Elsie Evelyn (née Hunt)
Married
Army

Charles married Elsie on 21 January 1941 at St Mary's church.
Before the war, Charles worked at a brewery.

RAVENSCROFT, James M E
Verman, Spot Lane

RAYMOND, Duncan

RAYNER, Ewin T
The Cottage, Thurnham Lane
Married
Wife Isabelle (née Hilton) of Weston House, Spot Lane
Warrant Officer and Conductor Royal Army Ordnance Corps

Ewin married Isabelle on 3 February 1945 at Holy Cross church. Isabelle, usually known as Billie, was a teacher at Bearsted school. She taught for many years there and then at Roseacre school after it relocated to The Landway. This is a transcript of the newspaper report about their wedding, which appeared in the Kent Messenger, 9 February 1945:

Warrant Officer E T Rayner (Whitstable) and Miss I Hilton (Bearsted)

Miss I (Billie) Hilton, second daughter of the later Mr and Mrs R Hilton, of Maidstone, was married on Saturday at Holy Cross church, Bearsted, to Mr E T Rayner, Warrant Officer, RAOC, son of Mr and Mrs T Rayner, Woodman Avenue, Swalecliffe, Whitstable.

The bride has been a teacher at Bearsted School for four years and is assistant commandant of the Bearsted Detachment of the Junior Red Cross. The bridegroom is home from India after four years' service.

There was a large congregation to witness the ceremony and school children were much in evidence. The Vicar of Bearsted (Rev W H Yeandle) officiated and Mr F J Cooper (Canterbury) was best man.

The bridge was given in marriage by Mr W Parker and looked very pretty in a white satin gown with veil lent by her friend, Mrs H Dearing; her flowers were pink carnations.

Miss June Dearing, a scholar at Bearsted School, was the only bridesmaid, and wore a dress of rose pink and carried a posy of violets. Her head-dress was of coloured leaves and she wore a pearl necklace, the gift of the bridegroom.

The service was choral and Miss R Hoar was at the organ. The hymns sung were 'The King of Love', and 'Love Divine, all love excelling'.

The honeymoon is being spent at Penzance, the bride travelling in a pink dress and brown coat.

Reproduced courtesy of Kent Messenger newspaper group

REATCHLOUS, Antony
Knowle Cottage, The Green

REATCHLOUS, Richard
Knowle Cottage, The Green

REEK, Ronald G
Hamilton, The Grove

REES, Alan Dorian
Mote Park
Married
Wife Joyce Kate (née Payne) of The Haven, Lord Romney's Hill
Quarter Master Sergeant Royal Engineers

Alan married Joyce on 12 June 1943 at Holy Cross church.

REES, William J
Amesbury, Spot Farm Estate
Royal Signals

REEVES, Frank E
Lunsford, Lord Romney's Hill

RELF, Marise Jacqueline see entry under **HUMPHREYS**

RICHARDSON, Jane Genny
Fairways, Spot Lane
Married
Husband William Oliver Rolls of RAF station Cardington
Flight Officer Women's Auxiliary Air Force

Jane married William on 15 July 1943 at Holy Cross church. William was serving as a Flight Lieutenant in the Royal Air Force.

RIGDEN, W
Trelawn
Lord Romney's Hill

Deputy Head Air Raid Precautions Warden Civil Defence

RING, Irene Ursula Peggy
7 Council Houses, The Street
Single
Private Auxiliary Territorial Services

Irene married Basil Norman Long of 52 Oak Villas, Dauntsey, Wiltshire on 23 November 1943 at Holy Cross church. Basil was serving as a Private with the Wiltshire Regiment.

RING, John
7 Council Houses, The Street

Second World War: 1939 to 1945

ROBBINS, Arthur S
Artily, 17 Spot Farm Estate
Married
Wife Lily
Children Patricia, Brian and Colin
Army
Captain General Staff Officer

Arthur was an insurance agent and market gardener. For many years the family ran a smallholding in Yeoman Way which included a vegetable garden, a greenhouse and an extensive orchard which extended to Spot Lane. This photograph is undated, but was taken at Artily whilst Arthur was home on leave:

Reproduced courtesy of Pat Grimes
(née Robbins)

ROLLS, Jane Genny see entry under **RICHARDSON**

RUGG, John R
17 The Grove

RUSSELL, Gordon B
Sutton House, Sutton Street

RUSSELL, John S
Rostrevor, Ashford Road
Royal Navy

RUSSELL, Robert *
Parents Adopted son of Conrad and Mabel Payne
Married
Wife Stella Rossetta of Linton
Royal Navy *HMS Hecla*
Service Number C/MX 51149 Petty Officer Supply
Killed 12 November 1942, aged 29
Commemorated Panel 64 Column 1, Chatham Naval Memorial

HMS Hecla was a destroyer depot ship launched in 1940. It was sunk off Casablanca on 12 November 1942 by the German submarine *U-515*.

SACKETT, Harold G
Thornbank, Hockers Lane

SAGE, Lilian

SAGGERS, William F
50 Royston Road

SCOTT, Thomas R †
Thornham Friars, Thurnham Lane
Parents Frederick Robert and Ethel Mary Scott
Married
Wife Yvonne Celeste
Royal Air Force Volunteer Reserve
Service Number 962240 Sergeant
Killed 30 October 1945, aged 28
Buried in grave 6254, section 18, Surbiton Cemetery, Surrey

SEDGE, Charles
4 Council Houses, The Street

SEDGE, Edith see entry under CURTIS

SELBY, William Halford
Fauchons House, Fauchons Lane
Married
Wife Hilary
Royal Navy
August 1924 Lieutenant
August 1932 Lieutenant-Commander
December 1937 Commander
December 1943 Captain
January 1953 Rear-Admiral
Retired 29 February 1956
9 February 1943 Distinguished Service Cross
9 June 1955 Companion of the Most Honourable Order of the Bath

<u>Warship Commands included:</u>

HMS Wren (D88)	(destroyer)	31 July 1939 - 13 January 1940
HMS Mashfona (F59)	(destroyer)	23 January 1940 - 28 May 1941
HMS Onslaught (G04)	(destroyer)	January 1942 - 14 February 1944 [17]

In 1946, William, who was then a Royal Navy captain, was in command of the British destroyer, *Saumarez*. The vessel was to pass through the strait between Albania and Corfu. As Albania claimed control of the waterway, the crew were told, if necessary to return fire. This was not required but *Saumarez* hit a mine and caught fire. Thirty six crew members died and William was injured. During a subsequent case at the International Court of the Hague, in which Western naval officers gave testimony, it was claimed that Albania had broken international law by secretly mining the strait. In 1949 a claim for damages was upheld, but was never paid.[18]

Second World War: 1939 to 1945

SELVES, Henry

SENT, J
Sergeant in Special Constabulary, received bar to medal in December 1942

SHARMAN, William H
Regina, Royston Road

SHARP, Ernest W
Tredene, Rosemary Road

SHAW, Henry J
Jesmond, Royston Road

SHERIFF, Francis Thomas
Married
Wife Lilian Violet (née Cooper) of 2 Westview, Roseacre Lane
Leading Seaman Royal Navy

Francis married Lilian on 14 April 1941 at Holy Cross church

SHORTER, Edward *+
3 Crisfield Cottages, The Street
Parents Alfred Charles and Edith Lilian Shorter
Single
4th Battalion, The Queen's Own (Royal West Kent Regiment)
Service Number 6346632 Private
Killed 27 May 1940, aged 21
Buried in grave 6 A 3, Le Grand Hasard Military Cemetery, Morbecque, Nord, France

Edward was the sixth child of Alfred and Edith Shorter. This undated photograph shows Edward practising his salute:

Reproduced courtesy of Rosemary Smith

SHORTER, Jack
3 Crisfield Cottages, The Street
Parents Alfred Charles and Edith Lilian Shorter
Single

SIMMONS, Cyril William
The Green
Married
8 October 1937 19 Group, Romeo 2, Bearsted
Royal Observer Corps

This photograph shows Cyril in his Royal Observer Corps uniform:

Reproduced courtesy of Evelyn Pearce

SIMMONS, D F
4 Egypt Place

SKINNER, Robert
Harangor, Ashford Road
Single
8 October 1937 19 Group, Romeo 2, Bearsted
Chief Observer Royal Observer Corps

Robert was Headmaster of Bearsted school from 1937 to 1964.

This photograph is undated but shows Robert during Royal Observer Corps duties:

Reproduced courtesy of Evelyn Pearce

SMETHURST, Monica A see entry under **THORPE**

SMITH, Albert
1939 19 Group, Romeo 2, Bearsted
Royal Observer Corps

Second World War: 1939 to 1945

SMITH, David

SMITH, Ernest
Coronel, Royston Road

SMITH, Evelyn Mary
4 Mote Villas
Married
Husband Ronald Edward Weaver of The Royal Oak public house
Women's Auxiliary Police Force

Evelyn married Ronald on 29 July 1944 at Holy Cross church. Ronald was serving as an Aircraftman Second Class in the Royal Air Force.

SMITH, Franklin W M

SMITH, Frederick A W
Reneric, The Landway
Royal Air Force

SMITH, Jennifer Lane
Stocks, Spot Lane
Married
Husband John Robert Crellin of 15 Richmond Street, near Broughton, Wallasey
Leading Aircraft Woman Women's Auxiliary Air Force

Jennifer married Robert on 4 November 1944 at Holy Cross church. Robert was serving as a Flight Sergeant in the Royal Air Force.

SMITH, Leslie T
Winter Haven, Ashford Road

SMITH, Ronald W
Thornbank, Weavering

SNOOK, Anthony John
Bracondale, Plantation Lane
Married
Wife Enid Mary Gwenllien (née Packwood) of Loiretto, South Road, Porthcawl, Glamorganshire
Royal Air Force
Service Number 1813151 Flight Sergeant

Anthony and Enid married on 10 February 1947 at Holy Cross church. Enid was serving as a Private, Auxiliary Territorial Service, Service Number 330332.

SNOOK, G W
Bracondale, Plantation Lane
Head Air Raid Precautions Warden Civil Defence

SPRINGETT, Cyril

Second World War: 1939 to 1945

SPRINGETT, James Aubrey
Ivy House
Married
Wife Joyce Elizabeth (née Eversden) of Holly House
Lance Corporal Pioneer Corps

James married Joyce on 5 April 1941 at Holy Cross church.

SQUIRRELL, Stanley A
218 Winifred Road
Army

STARNES, Albert F
205 Winifred Road

STILES, William H
The Old Water Tower, Tower Lane

STRINGER, Maurice W

STROUD, John H
Tuckenay, Spot Farm Estate

SUTTON, Charles

SWAIN, Arthur E D
193 Winifred Road
Army

Arthur and his wife, Winifred, were amongst the first residents of Winifred Road. This photograph was taken of Arthur in the 1930s:

Reproduced courtesy of Christine Hughes

SWIFT, Albert
4 Egypt Place

SWIFT, Dennis H
4 Egypt Place
Army

SWIFT, Frank
1 Council Cottages, Spot Lane

TANNER, Alfred H
Alflicot, Roseacre Lane
Royal Air Force

TAYLOR, Edward Cunningham
Married
Stonefield, Ashford Road
8 October 1937 19 Group, Romeo 2, Bearsted
Leading Observer Royal Observer Corps

This photograph shows Edward in his Royal Observer Corps uniform:

Reproduced courtesy of Evelyn Pearce

TAYLOR, G Kay
Newlands, Tower Lane

TAYLOR, J W
Fox Farm Cottages
Royal Navy

TAYLOR, James I
Glenlivet, Spot Lane

TAYLOR, Leslie J
South View, Ashford Road

TAYLOR, Rose M
Fox Farm Cottages
Auxiliary Territorial Services

TAYLOR, William
Fox Farm Cottages
Royal Electrical and Mechanical Engineers

TEBBUTT, Ann
Moorings, Ashford Road

TEMPLE, Daisy Muriel see entry under **BROWN**

Second World War: 1939 to 1945

TERRY, Douglas S
Church Farm, Ashford Road
Royal Artillery

TERRY, Frank S
Church Farm, Ashford Road
Gordon Highlanders

TERRY, Gordon
10 Pine Grove
Army

THOMAS, Edwin Guy Bambridge
San Remo, Yeoman Lane
19 Group, Romeo 2, Bearsted
Royal Observer Corps

THOMAS, May I
Hill House, Ashford Road

THORPE, Monica A
Lilk Mount, Otham Lane
Married
Husband Dennis James Smethurst of Lilk Mount
Aircraft Woman Second Class Women's Auxiliary Air Force

Monica married Dennis on 23 October 1946 at Holy Cross church.

THORPE, Pamela Ianthe *
Lilk Mount, Otham Lane
Married
Husband George Henry Lawrence

Further information about Pamela can be found in *Pamela and George: two lives interrupted by war.*

TILEY, Norman F
Woodcroft, The Grove

TILL, Reginald L J
Oddicombe, The Grove

TINNING, V M
Aldington Court Cottages
Auxiliary Territorial Service

TOLHURST, Roy
3 West View, Roseacre Lane

TOLHURST, William
Newlyn, Yeoman Lane
Royal Army Service Corps

TONE, Samuel

Second World War: 1939 to 1945

TOOMEY, A

TREE, Jack Stanley
Fancy Row, Thurnham Lane
Married
1939 19 Group, Romeo 2, Bearsted
Royal Observer Corps

TRENCH, Christopher

TREVETT, R J
Volage, Hockers Lane
Royal Navy

TROTT, George
Rosemary, Spot Farm Estate

TUBB, Charles

TUBB, George E
Amberleigh, Yeoman Lane

TUBB, John

TUCKER, Frederick
1939 19 Group, Romeo 2, Bearsted
Royal Observer Corps

TURNER, Edward G
The Laurels, Yeoman Lane

TURRELL, Leslie W C
Sutton Street

TUTT, Lionel N
The Nook, Weavering Street
Royal Air Force

TWINING, Vera see entry under **HUNT**

USMAR, Robert W
Walnut Tree Lodge, Weavering
Royal Air Force

VANE, Molly
1 Oak Villas, The Green
Women's Auxiliary Air Force

VAUGHAN, Betty Frances see entry under **HARRISON**

VAUGHAN, Reginald J
Drayton House, Spot Lane

VAUGHAN, Wilfred
The Bungalow
Married
1939 19 Group, Romeo 2, Bearsted
Royal Observer Corps

Wilfred was a chauffeur and gardener.

VICKERS, Wilfred
Orchard Lee, Ashford Road

VIDLER, Arthur J B
Polperro, The Landway

VIDLER, John

WAIGHT, Charles Francis
The Bungalow, Tower Lane
Married
8 October 1937 19 Group, Romeo 2, Bearsted
Royal Observer Corps

In addition to his duties in the Royal Observer Corps, Francis Waight owned Westwood Garage at the bottom of Thurnham Lane adjacent to the shops at Chestnut Place. This photograph shows Francis in his Royal Observer Corps uniform:

Reproduced courtesy of Evelyn Pearce

WALKER, Albert Edward
The Wilderness, Tower Lane
19 Group, Romeo 2, Bearsted
Royal Observer Corps

WALKER, Ronald H
Golf View, Ware Street

WALKLING, B
Sergeant in Special Constabulary, received bar to medal in December 1942

Second World War: 1939 to 1945

WALTERS, John H
7 Council Houses, The Street

WARLAND, Alan

WATCHAM, Walter Sidney
Church Cottage, Church Lane
Married
Wife Kathleen Georgina (née Burridge) of 28 Church Street, Maidstone
Motor Driver Royal Air Force

Walter married Kathleen 19 October 1940 at Holy Cross church

WATERS, Leslie

WATKINS, Leslie
Golf View, Ware Street

WATSON, Joan F
Quilter's Cottage, Otham turning

WATSON, John

WEAVER, Ronald Edward
The Royal Oak
Married
Wife Evelyn Mary (née Smith) of 4 Mote Villas
Aircraftman Second Class Royal Air Force

Ronald married Evelyn on 29 July 1944 at Holy Cross church. Evelyn was serving in the Women's Auxiliary Police Force. Ronald's father, Edward Weaver, was the landlord of The Royal Oak public house.

WELFARE, Desmond

WELLER, A
3 Egypt Place, The Street
Army

WELLS, Sidney J
Spot Farm

WESTERMAN, Florence Margaret see entry under **NEWSHAM**

WHITE, Charles D
Denby, Fauchons Lane

WHITE, Graham W
Little Dane

Second World War: 1939 to 1945

WHITE, Herbert Lionel *+
Madginford Farm
Parents George and Ellen White (née Chapman)
Single
Royal Army Service Corps
Service Number T/84868 Driver
Killed between 29 - 31 May 1940, aged 20
Note On the Bearsted war memorial the date of his death date is shown as 31 May 1940

Herbert was born 2 January 1920 at Manor Farm, Bredhurst. He was the eighth child and sixth son. He was baptized at St Peter's, Bredhurst on 25 May 1920. The family moved to The Harrow public house, Lidsing, until 1928. His father, George, was the tenant at Madginford Farm in the 1930s. The farm was a fruit tree nursery. Later, some of the land became the site of the Madginford schools.

Herbert attended Bearsted school and Holy Cross Sunday school. All his family: grandmothers, great aunts and brothers lived in Bearsted. Herbert left school in 1935. By 1939 he was a cold store engineer and a member of the Territorial Army. He was called up with two brothers in 1939 and served in the British Expeditionary Force in Belgium, driving large supply lorries.

He re-enlisted in the Royal Army Service Corps. It is believed that Herbert embarked on a ship which was torpedoed or blown up sometime between 29 - 31 May 1940, so there are differences in dates on official records. His parents thought he was a prisoner of war until his water-damaged belongings were returned to them.

An inscription to Herbert is to be found on the grave of his brother, Horace, in Holy Cross churchyard.

WHITE, Jack C
Denby, Fauchons Lane

WHITE, Leslie A
Denby, Fauchons Lane
Royal Army Service Corps

WHITE, Percy
Denby, Fauchons Lane

WHITE, Philip B
The Cottage, Thurnham Lane

WHITEHEAD, Charles

WICKS, Warden Arthur †*
3 Chapel Lane
The Queen's Own (Royal West Kent Regiment)
Attached to 13th (Labour) Battalion, Queen's (Royal West Surrey Regiment)
Service Number 14858994 Private
Killed 8 March 1945
Buried in grave 904, New churchyard (situated at Lower Green), St Peter's church, Pembury

WIDDOWSON, Vincent
Willington Road
Royal Air Force

Second World War: 1939 to 1945

WILKINSON, George
The Green
Married Phyllis Adelaide (née Costin)
Third Officer Merchant Navy

George married Phyllis of 50 Sandling Lane, Penenden Heath on 7 August 1943 at Holy Cross church

WILLIAMS, Alfred L
5 Pine Grove

WILLIAMS, A
Oakedeane, Firs Lane, Ashford Road
Royal Artillery

WILLIAMS, G T
1 Mays Cottages, Ware Street
Royal Engineers

WILLIAMS, Henry J
Little Orchard, Royston Road

WILSON, Albert E
Winton, Fauchons Lane

WILSON, Frank
Married
Wife Barbara Kate Edith (née Greensted) of Boxley
Major, Army

Frank married Barbara on 4 May 1944 at Holy Cross church. Barbara was serving as a Subaltern with the Auxiliary Territorial Service.

WILSON, Robert

WILSON, Thomas

WISE, J

WOOD, Herbert C
Holmbury, Royston Road
Royal Corps of Signals

WORLEY, Philip G
163 Royston Road

WORTH, Donald
165 Royston Road
Royal Air Force

WRAIGHT, H J
The Queen's Own (Royal West Kent Regiment)
Service Number 6096089 Sergeant

WYE, Anthony V P
Old Tiles, Roundwell

WYNDHAM-GREEN, G A
1 Roseacre Terrace, Tower Lane
Royal Army Service Corps

YUILL, Ronald
Renfrew, Cavendish Way

ZEE, Reginald

Pamela and George: two lives interrupted by war

On the war memorial in Holy Cross churchyard, amongst the names of the casualties there is the name of a young lady:

Pamela Ianthe Lawrence (née Thorpe) 16 January 1943

Towards the end of 2003, this caught the eye of John Franklin. He then found Pamela's grave in the churchyard and a memorial stone to her husband, George Lawrence on her grave. It was a chance encounter which set him on a quest and this is his account of what followed.

> **LAWRENCE, Pamela Ianthe (née Thorpe)**
>
> Lilk Mount, Otham Lane
> Married
> Husband George Henry Lawrence
> Parents Charles and Ettie Ianthe Thorpe (née Chattey) of Lilk Mount
> Women's Auxiliary Air Force, Dumfries, Scotland
> Service Number 384 Flight Officer and Senior Cypher Officer
> Died 16 January 1943, aged 22
> Buried in grave 23, Section J, Holy Cross churchyard

> **LAWRENCE, George Henry**
>
> Lilk Mount, Otham Lane
> Married
> Wife Pamela Ianthe (née Thorpe)
> Parents Julia Lawrence (née Pearson-Remedios) and the late Henry Lawrence
>   of 106 Ferry Road, APT1, Shanghai
> Royal Canadian Air Force
> B Flight 357 Squadron, later 628 Squadron (Royal Air Force) Squadron
> Service Number J/5674 Flight Lieutenant
> Missing, presumed dead, 3 March 1944, aged 27
> Commemorated Column 441, Kranji War Cemetery, Singapore
> George is also commemorated on a separate memorial stone on Pamela's grave

I suppose that I am rather typical of many readers of this book in that having been born towards the end of 1938, my recollections of World War Two are limited. The little I can remember includes my father, Leslie Franklin, hoisting his kitbag and rifle onto his shoulder as he left my family in 1942. My mother Gladys, had no inkling that he would not return until September 1945, and it would not be until 1946 before he was finally deemed sufficiently fit to be discharged.

I also have vague memories of an aircraft chasing a V1 'doddlebug' as it flew over our house in Bexleyheath and of nights spent with my mother either under the dining room table or down the Anderson shelter once she had carried me there in darkness down our garden. Like many of my generation I have always had a deep respect and admiration for the men and women who went to war in those dark days and for the many who made the ultimate sacrifice.

Prior to, and during retirement, one of my hobbies has been painting in watercolours. It was a chance encounter, resulting from the love of watercolours, which set me on a quest which was to take the best part of six years! I live near Gravesend, but Bearsted attracted me as there are so many wonderful buildings to paint. On this occasion though, I decided to visit the church and on entry to the churchyard I noted the unusual use of the full name of a lady on the official war memorial. Also, she had a very striking middle name, Ianthe, a Greek name describing a small flower that grows beside a stream.

Pamela and George: two lives interrupted by war

At the time I thought this was just unusual, but, further down the pathway, my eye was drawn to a headstone with the inscription picked out in red; again this is not very common. This turned out to be the headstone for Pamela and at the foot of her grave was a memorial stone to her husband, George as these recent photographs show:

IN PROUD AND LOVING MEMORY
OF
PAMELA IANTHE
FLIGHT OFFICER W.A.A.F.
ELDER DAUGHTER OF
CHARLES & ETTIE THORPE
DEARLY BELOVED WIFE OF
FLT LIEUT GEORGE H LAWRENCE
ROYAL CANADIAN AIR FORCE
KILLED ON ACTIVE SERVICE
10TH JANUARY 1945 AGED 23

FLT LIEUT GEORGE H LAWRENCE
R.C.A.F.
KILLED ON ACTIVE SERVICE
THE FAR EAST 3RD MARCH 19..
AGED 28 YEARS

All reproduced courtesy of Malcolm Kersey

I continued with my deliberations about what angles could be used for painting and thought no more about what I had noticed. It was only the following morning that 'the coin dropped'. I was sure there had been a difference between the date of death shown for Pamela on the memorial to that on her own headstone. Intrigued, I decided to check - I needed to make a second visit to Holy Cross church to continue my work, and whilst there, I followed this up. I found that there really was a difference of six days! I was to find later that the information about the age of George was also in error. How could this have happened?

It did not take long to confirm the details of Pamela's birth and marriage, and so I thought, here we have a young couple who met during the rigours of war time, married on 15 August 1942 and tragically, within nineteen months both were killed in separate flying accidents whilst on active service. At the time, our son Christopher, was of a similar age to George and I could imagine Pamela and George having all the expectations of a young couple entering marriage, children growing up and sharing life together, perhaps at some future date, even the arrival of grandchildren. Clearly the war years hung heavily over such plans but now, with my experience of researching Pamela and George over an extended period, I am sure they would have put such concerns to one side.

A slightly edited report from the Kent Messenger, 29 January 1943:

> ### W.A.A.F.'s TRIBUTE AT FUNERAL
> ### Late Flight Officer Pamela Lawrence
>
> Widespread regret is caused by the death of Flight Officer Pamela I Lawrence, W.A.A.F., the 22 years-old daughter of Mr and Mrs C T Thorpe, of Lilk Mount, Ashford Road, near Maidstone, whose funeral took place on Friday at Bearsted, the Rev R A F Parsons (vicar of Bearsted) and Squadron Leader the Rev Richard M Taylor, R.A.F. officiating.
>
> The funeral was held with full military honours, and quite a number of W.A.A.F.s in their smart blue uniforms were standing around the grave when the three volleys were fired.
>
> The chief mourners were: Flight Lt. G H Lawrence (husband), Mr and Mrs Charles T Thorpe (mother and father), A.C.W.2 Monica Thorpe and John Thorpe (sister and brother), Mr Arthur Chattey and Miss Avis Chattey (aunt and uncle) and Srgt. Obs. H H Lawrence, R.A.F.

Reproduced courtesy of Kent Messenger newspaper group

Looking at this information, almost sixty years after the death of Pamela and George, it seemed appropriate that in recognition of their ultimate sacrifice, the details should be corrected, if this was possible. Prior to leaving, I spoke with a member of the church who then confirmed that any physical alterations could only be requested by family members. However, the church could amend their records once the correct details were confirmed.

I then made enquiries with the RAF concerning Pamela's war record; it was sometime before a reply arrived. Meanwhile, I was already aware that George had been a serving officer with the Royal Canadian Air Force.

There was also some information published in the London Gazette and I found that Canada had more records freely available, so I approached the National Archives of Canada and also spoke to the Canadian High Commission in London. Fairly swiftly, I established that George's postings included 415 'Swordfish' Squadron RCAF and he had been attached to 628 Squadron RAF. His service number was J/5674, and that he had held the rank of Flight Lieutenant. The National Archives of Canada were able to supply his complete career records from birth in Shanghai, China until his death in March 1944!

Pamela and George: two lives interrupted by war

This undated photograph shows 415 Squadron RCAF in front of a Bristol Beaufort aircraft; George is seated in the front row, second from right:

Reproduced courtesy of Mark Lawrence

The Canadian paperwork mentioned a Mark H Lawrence, George's nephew. Perhaps he could be traced? The Rev John Corbyn and his staff at Holy Cross, and Jodi Ann Eskritt, Curator at the Royal Canadian Air Force Memorial Museum, then offered assistance in contacting relatives of George and the Lawrence family. I made enquiries with the telephone directory service in Canada and eventually a Mark Lawrence of CBC Television, but could not locate the Mark who was related to George. By August 2004, Kate Kersey, a community historian for Bearsted and Thurnham, was aware of my research and enquiries, and we met to share our knowledge. She was able to answer several queries about localities and offer further assistance.

It proved to be a busy time! I now knew that George had been awarded the 1939-45 Star, the Burma Star, the Defence Medal, Canadian Volunteer Service Medal with Clasp and War Medal 1939-45. The Lawrence family had also received the silver memorial cross that the Canadians issued to relatives of servicemen who died on active duty, engraved with the name, rank and service number. Also, and most intriguingly, the Canadian papers included details of a relative; Mark Henry Lawrence had been in Surrey during 1984. Twenty years later, it might be worth investigating, so I wrote a letter to the address. Sadly, there was to be no reply.

My research on Pamela was now progressing too. Pamela had been a member of the Women's Auxiliary Air Force and so Florence Mahoney of the WAAF Association assisted my enquiries. Slowly, I began to build up some details about the local community in which Pamela's family lived: the Centre for Kentish Studies in Maidstone was able to provide access to Holy Cross parish magazines which were published during the war.

Further information arrived: the Air Historical Branch RAF Bentley Priory was able to provide the AM1180 air crash report card. This gave only brief details about the crash of Pamela's plane on 16 January 1943. A copy of the full air crash report could not be supplied, but the card said that the flight was a Blenheim bomber, conveying personnel and that the aircraft was:

> ...proceeding to Dumfries from Jurby (Isle of Man). Flew into hill. Weather at location extremely poor. Investigation a/c struck ground whilst in sharp turn to port and caught fire and exploded. Consider flight not sufficiently urgent to be undertaken in this weather. Flight should have been abandoned earlier...

The crash site was recorded as three miles south west of Caulkerbush in Kirkcudbright, Scotland. Bainloch and Laggan, two neighbouring hills in the vicinity, were also mentioned. After more research, I contacted David Reid of Dumfries and Galloway Aviation Museum. Jean and I subsequently stayed in the area. Our visit included a trip to the crash site and, through David's kindness, a very late night visit to the museum. I was amassing information on what might have occurred.

I continued to make enquiries about incorrect inscriptions and contacted the Royal British Legion and the Commonwealth War Graves Commission. Sadly, neither were able to assist regarding corrections to headstones. By now, I was also reading extensively in a bid for further information. I can recommend *Bomber Command Losses of World War 2* by W R Chorley and *The Bristol Blenheim - a complete history* by Graham A Warner. The latter is the definitive book on the Blenheim aircraft and the 654 pages record all Blenheim losses during the war.

I now knew that at the time of the crash, Pamela was returning to the Dumfries area where she held the post of Senior Cypher Clerk and the rank of Flight Officer. There was also one civilian passenger on board, Mr Thomas Edward Perks, who worked for the Royal Aircraft Establishment in Farnborough. When Blenheim Z7313 crashed, there were six souls on board, twice the normal complement. I studied every crash reported in Graham Warner's book to see if this number was excessive. It transpired that many flights had carried six or more; several had carried ten crew and passengers in what could be regarded as a light-medium bomber!

I also visited a Blenheim restoration project at Duxford being undertaken by The Aircraft Restoration Company at the invitation of Project Manager Colin Swann. This was really by way of a practical exercise to see just how so many people could fit into what is a fairly small aircraft. I later joined the Blenheim Society and was advised by the late Graham Warner, then President of the Society, that he was aware of some flights which had carried fourteen people!

Details about Pamela's military work were beginning to unfold; I found that she had worked as telephonist before enlisting in the WAAF on 27 July 1939. Her experience was of considerable use and she was posted to communications. She was evidently very able, and rose through the ranks being promoted to the rank of Flight Officer on 1 September 1942.

Whilst undertaking more reading, I came across *Kent Airfields in the Second World War* by Robin J Brooks. This mentions the raid on RAF station Detling by German bombers which took place on Tuesday, 13 August 1940, when, it was said, 'the airfield was bombed beyond recognition'. In this raid, sixty seven people were killed and ninety four were injured. At the time of the raid, Pamela was based at Detling. I discovered that she had written to her friend, Ann Tebbutt:

> I expect that you heard of the awful raid of the 13th August. I was just leaving the ops block and posting a letter when suddenly out of a blue sky they swooped. There were about 50 or 60 'huns' and they let all hell loose. Never have I heard such a noise. I ran like fury with two airmen, they, poor dears got killed by bullets in the back as we were machine-gunned as we ran. I have never been so utterly terrified. I was hit by some flying wood so I threw myself on the ground while everything blew up as they dive-bombed.
>
> All of 'B' flight went up including planes just near to me. Afterwards I got cracking and cleared the road by the sick bay with my hands so that the ambulances could pass.
>
> After that raid it has been continual, in fact we spent night and day underground and work went to blazes. Fortunately only one WAAF was seriously hurt. At last everyone had moved off camp and it is only used for flying, a damn good job! We are all billeted out, which is fine and we work 'somewhere in England'.
>
> The poor old WAAF quarters got somewhat bashed about, our new messing hut caught a packet and every window was smashed. I worked for 48 hours after the main raid without sleep and carried on with little for three weeks and then got three weeks leave...

But, I felt, there was still more to be uncovered; in many ways, I seemed to be working backwards! Perhaps it would all take time… I took up the research again in early 2005 and renewed my contacts in Bearsted and Thurnham, including Kate and also Roger Vidler. Further afield, I also contacted Errol Martyn in New Zealand who had an interest in Pamela's crash and Fred Aldworth of the Air Force Association of Canada. The Association published a magazine and so I advertised in it for anyone who had known George.

Pamela and George: two lives interrupted by war

I was also able to meet a wonderful lady, Doris Britcher, in Bearsted. Doris had been in the Bearsted Brownie Pack, re-started by Pamela in 1936. In fact, Pamela had been her Brown Owl and her crystal clear memories evoked particularly happy times, attending Brownie events at Pamela's home as she was growing up. Doris could also vividly recall the air raid on Detling as she had been about to enjoy a family picnic on Bearsted green; delight on a summer's day had so quickly turned to terror as they sought shelter.

I also turned my attention once more to the matter of the headstone inscriptions and what could be done if I was unsuccessful in finding any relatives. The Royal British Legion had suggested I contact The Friends of War Memorials but I found that whilst they campaign for the restoration of war memorials countrywide, work related to gravestones falls outside their remit.

By this time I had assembled a great deal of information concerning Pamela and George and all this I happily shared with Kate. She was able to include a great deal of it in the first edition of this book, which aimed to accurately record details of all those who gave wartime services in the community. I subsequently attended the book launch during an Open Day at Holy Cross on 21 May 2005, hosted by the Friends of Holy Cross with their chairman Roger Vidler.

My researches continued, and I came into contact with Peter Connon in Carlisle. Peter is a prolific aviation author and has researched every military aircraft crash in Scotland during the Second World War! I found that not only had he previously undertaken research on Pamela, but he had also visited the Kranji War Cemetery. The names of 24,313 identified war casualties are recorded at the cemetery, and it is here that George Henry Lawrence is remembered on Column 441.

The following day, which was very wet and miserable, Jean and I visited the general area of Kirkcudbright where Pamela's aircraft had crashed. It was helpful to finally see the topography of the area and we encountered several people. First of these were Alan and Kathleen Cleasby, who live in the area. Pamela, as a Senior Cypher Clerk in the WAAF, had been based at Cargen House near Cargenbridge for a while. It transpired that in 1943, Kathleen was then a young girl, aged around nineteen and had been on Administration and Catering duties there, although she was unable to throw much light on events given the passage of time. Whilst in the area we also met a local man who had witnessed an aircraft crash but it was clearly not Pamela's plane.

I continued to research and then in 2007, purely by chance, I looked at the website, *Veterans Affairs Canada*, which maintains the records of many Canadians killed in conflict. I obtained a copy of the memorial page for George Henry Lawrence, and there the research stopped; it seemed that I could not make any further progress. I set the research aside to concentrate instead on watercolours and other matters.

So matters lay in abeyance and then…a newspaper feature in *Kent On Sunday* during August 2008, caught my eye. It concerned a soldier from Kent who had been killed in the Second World War and I contacted the author, Jemma Pudelek; an action that was to kick-start my own enquiry. Another story appeared in the paper on 28 September 2008, under the title "Taking On A Grave Mission" and describing my endeavours to locate relatives of Pamela.

Within days of publication I received a call from Peggy Hammond and a meeting was arranged. She is related to Pamela through her father Ivan; a cousin to Pamela. Peggy had little knowledge of Pamela and wanted to know more. I was able to provide her with over 50 pages of documents that answered many questions. At our first meeting, I also advised her that she only had to let me know if the family preferred me not to proceed with any further research.

I then wondered if similar action in Surrey would equally bear fruit and I would be able to find some local relatives of George. I travelled over to Woking and visited the Surrey History Centre but drew a blank. I then wrote to the *Woking News and Mail* and another article written by the news editor, Nicola Rider, appeared under the title "I'm Searching for Mark Henry Lawrence". Once again, within days my telephone rang. At 10.30pm, a voice said "I'm Mark Henry Lawrence, I understand that you are looking for me" George's nephew had been found!

Pamela and George: two lives interrupted by war

The conversation with Mark Henry Lawrence was a long one, but I learned that Mark's father was George's brother. Further, both of his parents were also in the same room listening to the conversation. It was wonderful to be able to actually speak to people so directly involved with the man who until then had simply been a name on paper!

Mark and his family had little knowledge about the disappearance of Uncle George's aircraft other than it went missing over the Bay of Bengal in early 1944. At their request, I copied a complete set of the information sent over to me from Canada and sent it on to Mark and the family. And as I had done when I first spoke with Peggy, I said that I would not continue my researches if the family would prefer it.

My contact with the Lawrence family developed and as a gesture of thanks, Mark copied some family photographs and gave them to me with a disk. This image of Pamela and George shows them leaving Holy Cross church after their wedding. Note that George's 'wings' are clearly visible on his uniform and a WAAF Guard of Honour is in the background:

Reproduced courtesy of Mark Lawrence

A slightly edited report of the wedding from the Kent Messenger, 21 August 1942:

Flying Officer G. H. Lawrence, R. C. A. F.
Section Officer P. I. Thorpe, W. A. A. F. (Bearsted)

The wedding took place at Holy Cross Church, Bearsted, on Saturday of F/O George Henry Lawrence, R.C.A.F., son of the late Mr G H Lawrence and Mrs F R Crank, of Shanghai, China, and Section Officer P I Thorpe, W.A.A.F., daughter of Mr and Mrs Charles Thorpe, of Lilk Mount, Bearsted. The Rev. R A F Parsons officiated. The hymns sung were:- 'Lead us, Heavenly Father', 'Praise my soul, the King of Heaven', and 'O Perfect Love'. Mr Ealham was at the organ. Given away by her father, Mr Charles Thorpe, the bride wore a gown of ivory satin…was attended by her sister, Miss Monica Thorpe, and Miss Eileen Lewis and little Miss Anne Lewis. Pilot Officer K Maffre, R.C.A.F., was best man and the ushers were Mr John C Thorpe, brother of the bride, Fl./Lt. Armstrong, P/O. L Sharpe and Fl./Sgt. Vokey.

The reception was held in the gardens of Lilk Mount. F/O and Mrs G H Lawrence left for their honeymoon at Liphook. The church was tastefully decorated by Mrs Charles Ambrose and friends. A guard of honour of W.A.A.F. was formed outside the church.

Reproduced courtesy of Kent Messenger newspaper group

The disk turned out to contain a short, but infinitely precious, film, which had been taken at the wedding of Pamela and George! To see this beautiful young couple, captured in the footage, so full of life and happiness on their wedding day, was truly amazing. The reception had been held at the Thorpe family home at Lilk Mount in Otham Lane and almost astonishingly, included a flypast of Blenheim aircraft by crews from RAF station Detling! I was later to copy the film for Peggy and also show the film to Doris.

The majority of my mission was now becoming resolved; I had made contact with Pamela and George's relatives but what to do next? When I first began my investigations and research, my thoughts had been to correct the erroneous information on Pamela and George's memorials. Pickard and Beale of Maidstone, had originally supplied them. That company is now part of Dignity plc, but their staff confirmed that once the approval of the relatives had been obtained, they would be prepared to undertake a survey of the stone to see if it were possible to make the alterations. There would be no charge. John Corbyn also said that the Church would waive any charges that would normally apply.

So, now, with all my evidence in their hands, I put the question to Peggy and Mark, did they want correct particulars to appear on the headstone and memorial? I reminded them that I had said when I first spoke to each of them that I would be happy to abide by the wishes of their families. They asked for time to think about the matter. Peggy later rang me to say she would prefer things be left as they are, and Mark decided to agree with this view. So the original inscriptions remain but the written records held by Holy Cross church and this book now reflect the correct information concerning both Pamela and George. I hope my investigations and information have in some way brought closure to both families, particularly the Lawrence family as Mark's parents have now passed away.

And so there the matter of the incorrect details and inscription, which started all of this, rests. But almost inevitably there are some mysteries which remain.

Uncertainty still surrounds the disappearance of the aircraft on which George was a passenger. The Catalina 1B FP161 was on a flight from Calcutta to China Bay in what was then Ceylon (now Sri Lanka). An extensive search was conducted when the aircraft failed to arrive at China Bay and this is detailed in a two page report dated 19 June 1944 to which are attached two addenda. One of these is a list of the personnel on board other than the names of five passengers *'whose names cannot be disclosed'*. George's details are intriguingly inserted in hand, so was he posted to the flight at the last minute - and just who were those five passengers?

A further mystery is contained in the main report in that the Catalina was making the flight for *'an unnamed organisation in Calcutta, an Officer of whom watched the aircraft take off on time at 1730 hours'*. It *'took off from a 231 Group Station'* and was *'flying into a 222 Group Station'*. There is a comment by the report author that as such, very little information about the flight is available at 628 Squadron.

We will probably never know either why, given the atrocious weather conditions, Pamela's flight was deemed too important to abandon, nor the exact role of Mr Perks.

What is clear is that Pamela and George were a beautiful young couple, who met during the war, almost certainly, as Mark's family understand, at RAF station Detling. It is likely, given the logistics involved in their individual wartime service and various postings, that their time together was even shorter than the five months between their marriage and Pamela's death. Their married life may have been little more than a handful of weeks.

During the war, many young couples met and married. Some of them just could not, perhaps, *dared* not even think of the possibility of a long marriage or the arrival of children. Perhaps, what was important to Pamela and George was this: that they cared sufficiently for their country to offer active service during a war when it was not at all certain who would win. They also cared so deeply for each other that they entered into a personal and public commitment, in the full knowledge that the ultimate sacrifice may have to be made. We all owe them a great deal.

'May they rest in peace'

John E Franklin

They Also Served

Civil Defence, Parish Councils and Emergency Planning Committees

The phrase, Civil Defence, came into use in the late 1930s to refer to a group of services which were under development to counter the effects of a possible war involving Britain. As mentioned in another chapter, many of these; air raid warnings, shelters, gas masks, searchlights and anti aircraft guns had all been developed in the Great War. As the international situation rapidly deteriorated and another war became inevitable, there was every chance that air raids and bombing might once more take place.[1]

In March 1933, the government decided that the local authorities would be the most suitable agency to be in charge of Britain's Air Raid Precautions services, usually known by the initials ARP.[2] A specific ARP Department was formed by the Home Office and an appeal was launched early in 1937 for volunteers.[3]

On 1 January 1938, the Air Raid Precautions Act came into force. As part of the legislation, a Minister of Home Defence was created with direct control of Civil Defence. The Act compelled local authorities to introduce an ARP scheme and required them to set up wardens, first aid posts, emergency ambulance, gas cleansing and casualty clearing stations. They were also obliged to expand local fire services by forming and equipping an Auxiliary Fire Service. A radio appeal asked for a million volunteers for all this work.[4]

As Germany moved inexorably towards war, the planning and implementation of local ARP schemes moved at great speed; a series of trial blackouts and exercises which involved all the Civil Defence services took place. The first real task for the ARP wardens though was the compilation of a gas mask census followed by the fitting and distribution of them.[5]

For some time before the outbreak of war, the parish councils for Bearsted and Thurnham acted in an advisory capacity for the Rural District Councils under the local authority arrangements for the ARP schemes.[6] In June 1939, Maidstone Rural District Council confirmed that there was a fire brigade for emergencies in its area, but this may well have been rather a formality for Bearsted as the community already had a small fire appliance which was kept in a hut in Church Lane.

On 1 September 1939, Germany invaded Poland. The same day, blackout restrictions were imposed in Britain and the Auxiliary Fire Service was mobilised. Over the next two days and before a state of war with Germany was formally declared on 3 September, the local ARP schemes came into operation. First aid posts, rescue, decontamination and ambulance depots and wardens' posts also began to function, and although it took a while for specific buildings to be constructed in some areas, nearly all were immediately staffed full time.[7]

For many volunteers, and for quite some time, the uniform was very basic: a silver ARP badge, a whistle, an armband and a helmet. The latter was frequently, but not always marked with the letter W, to denote the wearer's service. Often there was also an indication of rank on the helmet and stripes or diamonds. In the latter, one diamond denoted a head warden and two, a divisional warden. In 1941, the phrase ARP was phased out in favour of 'Civil Defence' and some uniform was distributed. Frequently, the uniform took the form of overalls which were also informally called 'bluettes'. However, with wartime shortages, for many volunteers, it was a case of carrying on in civilian clothes with the correct helmet and badges.[8] The following illustrations show a selection of equipment and badges which were issued, starting with a metal lapel badge and whistle:

Reproduced courtesy of Malcolm Kersey

They Also Served

A tin helmet with W lettering to denote the service and (right) a wooden gas rattle which was to be used to warn of gas attacks. A hand bell was also issued.

Cloth uniform badge, printed armband and shoulder flashes:

All reproduced courtesy of Malcolm Kersey

The Civil Defence office for the Maidstone Rural District Council was at 26 Tonbridge Road, Maidstone. This photograph was taken in 2009 shortly before the building was demolished. The office covered 14 parishes including Otham and Bearsted. (Thurnham came under Hollingbourne Rural District Council). The staff reported to County Hall on wartime incidents and activity taking place in the area. Each Parish had a Head Warden; in Bearsted it was Mr Stanley Johnson who lived at Bearsted House by the Green.

Reproduced courtesy of Winnie Crapp

They Also Served

The office staff received notifications of air raid messages which were then relayed to the Head Warden of each area. Winnie Crapp (née Burgess) who worked in the office recalled it was a simple system which was nonetheless effective; the notification of air raids and warnings took around 3-4 minutes. The office was also advised by the wardens of any war damage, such as crashed aircraft, and unexploded bombs.

Colonel Scott was the Chief Civil Defence Officer and Winnie's boss. She accompanied him when he went out to inspect downed aircraft, bomb damage, and record all the unexploded bombs and shells. They had to record all the details including the weight of unexploded bombs the measurements of bomb craters, plot where they had fallen and then submit a report to Control based at County Hall.

Details of the air raid warnings given and the initial reports of incidents were all recorded in a standard office diary. After the war, Winnie was given one of the diaries as a small souvenir. Reproduced below are typical diary pages from 16 and 18 August 1940. As enemy action increased, the entries for each day exceeded each page and spilled over into the only space available - earlier pages in the volume.

The terminology used was as follows:

ARM	Air Raid Message	ARW	Air Raid Warning
HW	Head Warden	HE	High Explosive
KENTROL	County Civil Defence Control		

The colours indicate the state of preparation:

Yellow	Be Prepared	White	All Clear
Red	Sirens sounded, Man the posts	Purple	Highest state of Alert

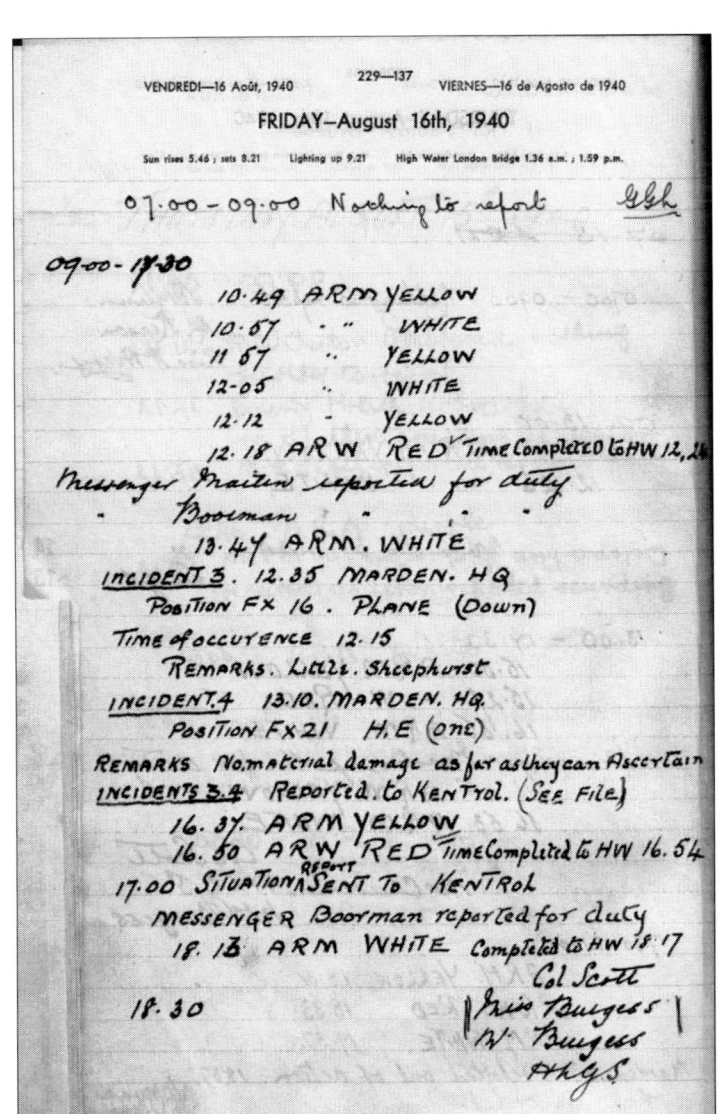

'Incident 5' relates to a collision in combat over Marden. Later research confirmed this involved Hurricane I registration number R4193 and a Dornier 17Z of 7/KG76.[9]

Flight Lieutenant (Pilot) Henry Ferris, Service No 40099 of 111 Squadron RAF was killed, aged 22.

Reproduced courtesy of Winnie Crapp

Reproduced courtesy of Winnie Crapp

This page also records an 'Incident 5'; An enemy aircraft crashed and burned following combat over Marden and Staplehurst.

Later research confirms that the crash followed an attack by Squadron Leader Pemberton of 15 Squadron RAF upon Messerschmitt Me109E4, registration number 2755 of 8/JG3.[10]

Obergefreiter Basell was killed.

The air combat battles which took place on 18 August 1940 are now recognised to have been amongst the largest aerial engagements during the war, becoming known as 'The Hardest Day'.

For much of 1940, after the fall of France and the evacuation of the remnants of the British Expeditionary Force from the beaches of Dunkirk, the invasion of Britain seemed a very real possibility. The question of how Britain could best be defended exercised the minds of the Home Defence Executive under General Sir Edmund Ironside and then General Brooke, Commander in Chief, Home Forces. To date, the war had been very different from the earlier conflict where troops had been bogged down in trenches for years. The fall of France was characterised by fast and very mobile German offensive action using a great number of armoured vehicles.

It was decided to divide England into several areas through 'Stop Lines'; which were a mixture of man-made obstacles and islands allied to the natural landscape. Under the scheme, the lines were built in a few weeks during July and August, planned by the Royal Engineers but mostly undertaken by civil contractors. Rivers and canals, railway embankments and cuttings were supplemented with ditches and a variety of anti-tank obstacles, frequently made from reinforced concrete.[11]

The Stop Lines were designed significantly to slow down and impede an invading force. Maidstone was part of the defence around the General Headquarters Line, which was designed to protect London and the industrial areas of the Midlands. The town already had an army barracks, so it was chosen as a 'fortress town' to further delay a German advance. A ring of defences was set up on the outer perimeter of Maidstone which encompassed Penenden Heath and also the outer parts of Thurnham. There was an inner defence ring which included Maidstone's High Street, Mill Street, Palace Avenue and Gabriel's Hill.

The latter was intended to be the final stand area in which the enemy would be fought by the Local Defence Volunteers (later called the Home Guard), until the last man standing.

Thurnham Hill was deemed to be a route which could be used by an invading force from the Medway estuary close by, and so concrete blocks intended to impede the progress of tanks were installed. The blocks were frequently known as 'dragon's teeth'; if a tank attempted to climb over them: the vulnerable parts of the vehicle would either be exposed or the tracks would slip down between the upper points.[12] Nearly all of the concrete blocks were supplemented with further barriers either side, which may have included substantial wooden poles and masses of barbed wire. These photographs show the concrete anti tank obstacles in 2011, still sitting at one of the bends on Thurnham Hill. After the war, they were moved to one side to allow traffic to pass.

Both reproduced courtesy of James Kersey

As part of the Civil Defence, a separate committee to that of each parish council was required to deal with emergency planning matters. The records for Thurnham have not survived, but a sub-committee of Bearsted parish council was set up after a request from Maidstone Rural District Council in late 1940. A preliminary meeting was held at the Memorial Hall on 14 January 1941 and representatives were in attendance from all the organisations involved in Civil Defence: the ARP Wardens; Sector Wardens; Special Constables; the Auxiliary Fire Service and the Home Guard.[13]

The committee's main task was to address National Emergency Regulations which needed to be put into force. Soon it was tackling the implementation of all sorts of civil defence matters including emergencies caused through enemy action, the evacuee scheme, billeting and their accommodation, the organisation of Air Raid Precautions, and of course, government circulars. First of all, though, the local population had to be advised that this committee had been formed. This poster shown below was for a meeting which introduced the committee: [14]

BEARSTED PARISH COUNCIL

WHAT DO I DO TO BEAT THE NAZI FIRE BOMBS?

A MEETING

will be held

IN BEARSTED CHURCH

Sunday, 26th January, 1941

at 4.15 p.m.

(AFTER EVENING SERVICE)

when the question of making local arrangements to deal with an emergency caused through enemy action will be explained.

Reproduced courtesy of Bearsted Parish Council
and Kent History and Library Centre

The ARP Wardens compiled Household Registers. They contained information on how many people were resident in each dwelling, where each person slept, where they sheltered, whether any resident was physically disabled or elderly and the names of the next of kin. This information was considered essential, saving vital time and unnecessary effort whilst dealing with the destruction wrought by bombing raids and their aftermath. The Wardens were frequently the first local contact point for people who were either homeless or whose homes were damaged due to enemy action.

The ARP casualty service came under the Ministry of Health. Doctors were assigned to sectors and First Aid Parties went directly to incidents. A local Medical Office of Health controlled emergency mortuaries, food-decontamination and gas cleansing.[15]

The committee oversaw salvage drives and the subsequent collection of material from the local centres, and offers to hold fund-raising efforts such as flag days. They also passed details of air raid casualties and war-related injuries on to the district council and were sometimes notified that damage caused to local roads had been filled in and made good.[16] The committee implemented local orders; a typical example was that concerning the clearance of lofts. In 1942, the National Fire Service directed, through an order obtained in November, that any loft, attic or space between ceiling and roof not furnished for human habitation was to be cleared and kept clear of all articles in an attempt to minimise damage from incendiary bombs. On a lighter note, they also dealt with letters received from officers in charge of armed services which were billeted nearby, including the Tudor House and Barty House, which requested permission to play football matches on the Green! [17]

Other matters came within the parish council's remit. The immediate requirements for people who had suffered bombing included emergency shelter, food, clothes and money - and in the longer term, permanent accommodation.

There was frequent correspondence between the committee and the Civil Defence offices over matters such as the installation of an automatic siren for the village and the adequate provision of a water supply.

In an exchange of letters about the latter, it was requested that the Rural District Council provide three brick built tanks holding not less than 5,000 gallons of water at the recommended sites of the Green, Roseacre, and the Royston estate on the Ashford Road. The reply from the district council indicated that they considered the request to be unwarranted! [18]

In April 1942, the fear of invasion remained potent. Maidstone Rural District Council made a further request of the parish councils; they asked that a local organisation, which became known as a Triumvirate be formed within each area. It was to comprise a civilian representative, a police representative and a local military commander.[19] In most small local areas it was expected that if invasion occurred, the civilian representative would assume powers of action as the capacity of a local leader. He would then contact the Home Guard Commander and the police. The aim of the local leader was, in the face of hostile enemy action, to try to maintain normal, everyday life for as long as possible. After appointment, the local leader then asked for volunteers who would oversee areas of civil responsibility should the need arise. These areas included: Water and Sanitation, Shelter for Casualties, Billeting, Registration of births and deaths, Aged and Infirm persons, Pregnant Women, Infectious Diseases, Paraffin and fuel, Food Supply, Labouring and Building, Maintenance Work and Damage Repair.[20]

> **PARISH OF BEARSTED**
>
> # A PUBLIC MEETING
>
> will be held at the
>
> **MEMORIAL HALL,**
> on Thursday, 30th July, 1942, at 8 p.m., when instructions and advice on invasion emergencies will be given.
>
> It is hoped that one member from each household will be present.
>
> STANLEY JOHNSON,
> for the Triumvirate.

Reproduced courtesy of Bearsted Parish Council
and Kent History and Library Centre

It is likely that in Bearsted and Thurnham, most of the people who volunteered would have viewed the tasks as an extension of their everyday jobs. An example would be the local nurses and midwives who already dealt with infectious diseases, looking after the pregnant, aged and infirm, who had rather more work added to their duties.

Mr Clayson was the first Chairman, but after a short while he stood down and Stanley Johnson was appointed both civilian representative and local leader. He therefore held a meeting at the Memorial Hall about this and the proposed work of the triumvirate and on the left is shown the poster advertising it.[21]

The parish councils were required to secure a supply of Emergency Food Rations for the local population. Bearsted parish council complied with this order. On 24 March 1943, it was advised by Mr Swain, the local Food Controller, that the Emergency Rations stored for the parish would suffice for eight days at a cost of ten shillings per person. Despite this provision, barely eight months later, the parish council learned that part of the ration had been destroyed by rats! The damaged stock was withdrawn by the Rural District Council and a fresh supply secured.[22]

Mr Moss, the butcher, succeeded Mr Swain on 17 March 1944. He then arranged for some of the food stock which was held at an un-named location in Madginford to be transferred and amalgamated with that already in the cellar of his shop. A further supply was also placed in the store at the rear of the adjacent grocery premises owned by H J Brook at Chestnut Place.[23]

Fortunately, the threat of invasion diminished as the war progressed and the emergency supplies were never used. After four years of hard, but varied work, both the Triumvirate and the committee were eventually disbanded in 1945. The Civil Defence was also finally stood down and their work ceased on 2 May 1945.

They Also Served

In the Kent Messenger, 18 May 1945, a tribute was paid to the work of the Civil Defence:

FAREWELL TO THE CIVIL DEFENCE
'Their Deeds Will Live In History's Most Glorious Pages'

Civil Defence personnel, would, in the main, be freed at the end of June, declared Alderman E S Oak-Rhind (Whitstable) moving the Civil Defence report at Wednesday's meeting of Kent County Council. Following that, so far as administration was concerned, there would be a great deal of clearing up to do, said the alderman, who is Chairman of one of the county's two Civil Defence committees. It was always hard to say goodbye, but especially so the men and women of Civil Defence. If it had not been for their work, the war could have been lost, for in any war, the biggest factor was the civil population.

A BATTLEGROUND

'It was the men and women of Civil Defence who had protected and given confidence to the civil population, and so, in turn, to the fighting men, who were able to know that families and homes were being looked after in a battleground just as fierce, just as dangerous, as any battleground in the world. These were the men and women we trained,' he said, 'and who set out so long ago and to face, practically, the unknown, under an instrument which was never intended for war - the instrument of local government. It speaks volumes for the greatness of local government, whether it was the county council, borough council, urban or rural, that this county of ours has carried through without calling for help from outside and never once let the people down. That in itself is a great record. If ever men and women played their part in the name of God and humanity, it has been these workers among your people of Kent.'

FAREWELL PARADE

Alderman Oak-Rhind mentioned that on Sunday, June 3rd, there would be a farewell parade in Maidstone of representatives of every authority in the county. He said that the Civil Defence committee had received nothing but help, consideration and sympathy from all, and concluded; 'Five and half years ago you placed your faith in the men and women we had organised through the county of Kent to fight this fight. Your faith and your trust was not for one moment misplaced. Their deed will live in the history of Kent among her most glorious pages. Their work, their help will never be forgotten.'

Reproduced courtesy of Kent Messenger newspaper group

Mr and Mrs Stanley Johnson

Mr and Mrs Stanley Johnson were living at Bearsted House before the outbreak of the Second World War. Mr Johnson had many business interests but prominent amongst these was a company based on the Isle of Sheppey. When war was declared, they immediately offered their home as accommodation for the headquarters for local wartime organisations. These included the Civil Defence, the ARP Wardens (Mr Johnson was both Deputy and Head Warden for a time), and the Home Guard. This photograph is undated but gives a good impression of Bearsted House before the Second World War:

Reproduced courtesy of Robin Rogers

Bearsted House was also a distribution point for gas masks and the point to which all the evacuees from Plumstead School arrived on 3 September 1939 before being billeted. Mrs Dorothy Whitehead of The Mount was the Assistant Billeting Officer for Bearsted at the time of their arrival. She was succeeded by Mr Abery of Yeoman Nurseries. It was estimated that by early 1940, over eighty two percent of the evacuees were still in the village. This number stands in contrast to the national figure of twenty five percent of evacuees that had remained at their billets.[24]

This photograph shows some of the evacuees arriving at Bearsted:

Reproduced courtesy of Jessie Page

Mr Johnson thoroughly supported the National Savings campaigns during the war known as Warship Weeks. He was committed to supporting all the armed forces and also worked with Lord Cornwallis, to introduce a Spitfire Fund. In August 1940, there was a fortunate juxtaposition of unexpected events! Lord Cornwallis had just received a donation from Mr Johnson for £5,000 with an accompanying note suggesting that the money be used to purchase a new Spitfire, when he unexpectedly entertained Squadron Leader Stanford Tuck who had bailed out from an aircraft during aerial combat on to his estate. Stanford Tuck thought the idea an excellent one. An appeal was made to the people of Kent, and the Kent County Spitfire Fund was born.[25]

By the winter of 1940, £29,370 had been collected - sufficient to buy three Spitfires. Lord Beaverbrook was in charge of aircraft production and wrote to Lord Cornwallis to express his admiration at the unselfish endeavour and generous hearted patriotism of the people of Kent.[26] Eventually, enough money was donated from the towns and villages of Kent to form and equip an entire Squadron. It was known as No 131 (County of Kent) Fighter squadron and formed on 30 June 1941. It was equipped with Mark I Spitfires and the squadron leader was J M Thompson, DFC. Many of the aircraft bore the names of Kentish towns. Operations continued throughout the war and the squadron later used the Spitfire 11A.[27]

In November 1944 the squadron was stood down and prepared for service overseas in India. Squadron Leader COJ Pegge, DFC, took command and Mark VIII Spitfires were introduced before it was announced that the aircraft would be used to re-equip the Indian Air Force and the squadron would be disbanded. The squadron was formally disbanded on 31 December 1945 'owing to the contraction of the RAF to peace time strength'.[28]

Red Cross

Amongst the most prominent of organisations during the war was the Red Cross. Bearsted House became the home for the Kent 226 and and Junior Red Cross, Kent 524 detachments. Training courses were held there; the facilities extended to a small hospital ward and Mr Johnson even bought a small ambulance for the area. Katharine Severne recalled that her mother, Janet Kemball, was the Commandant. Katharine frequently helped in their work by acting as the casualty for the training exercise!

This photograph was taken in the garden of Bearsted House, in 1944:

Reproduced courtesy of Jenni Hudson

<u>Back row includes</u>: Connie King; Eileen Blandford; Margery Foster

<u>Second row includes</u>: Joyce Clark; Billie Hilton, Assistant Commandant; Muriel Moss, Assistant Commandant; Mrs Bloggs, Commandant; Mrs Janet Kemball; Peggy Sanders

<u>Front row includes</u>: Sister Beeton Pull; Mrs Hollands; Mrs Wilkinson; Elsie Attwood; Sybil Mercer; Mildred Sierakowski; Mrs Winnie Jessel

<u>Seated at front</u>: Mrs Stanley Johnson and Katharine Kemball

This photograph is not dated, but shows the ambulance and includes Assistant Red Cross Commandant, Muriel Moss, on the left hand side:

Reproduced courtesy of Susan Imgrund

They Also Served

The local branch of the Red Cross made up parcels for prisoners of war to which residents had contributed. A parcel cost ten shillings to send and contained food and other comforts such as books. There were collection points in the village including the public houses, shops, the Men's Institute, the Women's Institute hall, Bearsted House and Jack Fludd's house. Jack was the churchwarden of St Mary's. The scheme was run by Mrs Stanley Johnson and Lilian MacKenzie Smith.

In addition to other duties, during the war, branches of the Red Cross helped to distribute over fifty million articles of aid including garments, blankets and quilts made and produced under a variety of schemes including one called 'Bundles for Britain'. The aid was arranged by many different overseas organisations but amongst the best known are the British War Relief Society, The Daughters of the Empire and the Canadian Red Cross Society. Quilts and blankets were particularly given as gifts to families made homeless by bombing and orphaned, injured and evacuee children.

Amongst services run by the Red Cross in Bearsted was a crèche facility. The photograph appeared in the South Eastern Gazette, 28 July 1942, under the title: 'Minding the Kiddies whilst Mothers do their shopping'. The report continued 'In the garden room at Snowfield, Bearsted (home of Mrs Litchfield Speer), Red Cross, Kent 524 detachment, Girls Cadet Corps, are doing a valuable war-time job looking after babies while their mothers are shopping.' The crèche was provided on three days per week for babies and children under school age and opened from 2pm to 5pm. On Tuesdays and Thursdays it was run by the Fellowship of Marriage and on Saturdays by the Youth Service Group. Both organisations were part of Holy Cross church.

Reproduced courtesy of Kent Messenger newspaper group

Back Row (Helpers include):
Eileen Blandford; Billie Hilton; Margery Green; Betty Weaver; Doris Bentley; Margery Mercer; Audrey Marsh

Seated Helpers in middle:
Betty Vane and Marion Smith

Children include:
Susan Lee; Roger Smith (on lap); Gerald Hunt; Peter Hunt (on rocking horse); Doreen Vane; Kenneth Smith; Roy and Leslie Datson.

They Also Served

Royal Observer Corps

Men in Bearsted and Thurnham who were not serving in the armed forces, frequently volunteered to join the Bearsted branch of the Observer Corps of Special Constables.

In 1924 the government decided that an organised system was essential for the rapid collection and distribution of information on the movements of hostile and friendly aircraft. The first Observer Corps Groups to be formed were Maidstone and Horsham in 1925. On 1 January 1929, control was handed over to the Air Ministry and the Observer Corps headquarters was established at RAF station Uxbridge. As the political situation deteriorated, and the threat of war increased, new observer Corps Groups continued to be formed. They were mobilised on 24 August 1939. The Corps proved invaluable during the Battle of Britain and Lord Dowding commented: [29]

> It is important to note that, at this time the Observer Corps constituted the whole means of tracking enemy raids once they had crossed the coastline, their work throughout was quite invaluable, without it, air raid warning systems could not have been operated and inland interceptions would rarely have been made.

On 9 April 1941 King George VI granted the Observer Corps the title 'Royal' in recognition of the dedicated service rendered.[30]

The Bearsted branch was known as Romeo 2: The Royal Observer Corps No 19 Group. During the war the Chief Observer was Robert Skinner, the headmaster of Bearsted School. The Leading Observer was Edward Taylor who received this certificate:

Reproduced courtesy of Bryan McCarthy

They Also Served

The Corps had several lookout posts including one on Bearsted golf course where there were also two concrete emplacements for anti-aircraft guns on the 8th and 9th fairways.[31] Another lookout post was later established on Mr Bradley's farmland, which is now part of The Landway. This photograph shows the members by the lookout post on the golf course:

Reproduced courtesy of Bryan McCarthy

This undated photograph is a rather more formal group:

Reproduced courtesy of Evelyn Pearce

Back row (left to right):
F W Waight, L Monckton; W A Abel; F Harnett; C W Simmons

Middle row (left to right) includes:
W B Barnes, F W Grout; W J Moss; R E MacOnegal; A N Dearing; A Walker

Front row (left to right):
A V Pearson; J Baldwin; E C Taylor; R Skinner; C W Peach; F Naylor; G Hunt

In 1945 the Corps was stood down but re-formed in January 1947 as the Cold War began. Romeo 2 was finally disbanded after a farewell dinner on 1 April 1968.

The Women's Land Army

The Women's Land Army had been originally created during the First World War to replace the men who worked in agriculture and on the land but who were serving in the armed forces. The scheme was restarted by the government in June 1939 under the leadership of Lady Denman and the direction of Ministry of Agriculture and Fisheries. The workforce was usually known as the 'Land Girls' and wore a distinctive uniform which included green ties, jumpers, corduroy trousers and brown hats.

A typical recruitment poster and the Women's Land Army badge:

Both reproduced courtesy of Malcolm Kersey

The average wage was 32 shillings a week, before deductions for accommodation. No one grew rich as a Land Girl and there was no such thing as a forty-eight hour week! Seasonal tasks on farms were often lengthy and when Double Summer Time was introduced, girls frequently worked until eleven at night.

A Women's Land Army hostel was built and opened at Friningham. Details of Land Girls who were resident there in 1945 can be found in Appendix 1.

By July 1941, there were over 1,000 Land Girls in Kent. A rally was held in Maidstone Zoo Park and during the afternoon, Lord Cornwallis presented badges to nine girls for courage shown whilst working in dangerous conditions. Three years later, it was estimated there were over 80,000 Land Girls in Britain, making the slogan, 'Food: A Munition of War' a reality.[32]

In December 2007, the government finally recognised their contribution to the war with a special commemorative badge. The design included a wheat sheaf surrounding a circle of pine branches and pine cones to indicate the work of both the Land Army and the Timber Corps. Over 30,000 were instantly awarded.

Reproduced courtesy of Malcolm Kersey

Bearsted Rifle Club and Range

During the war, Bearsted Rifle Club became a vital part of the local defences that were in place should invasion become imminent; it provided a practise venue for the Local Defence Volunteers, later known as the Home Guard.

Many local families also quietly, but regularly practised at the range. The close proximity of Bearsted and Thurnham to RAF station Detling, a railway line, Maidstone barracks and even the naval base at Chatham, all meant that if there was a German invasion, there was a distinct possibility that the villages would be involved in some sort of hostile action.

Robert Skinner, the headmaster of Bearsted School was also Chief Observer of the Bearsted branch of the Observer Corps. He was determined to be thoroughly prepared for enemy action and as part of his duties at the school he introduced many of his older pupils to shooting. In November 1941, it was noted in the school log book that every Tuesday there were practise shooting sessions at the Rifle Range.

Many of the boys from the school that went on to Maidstone Grammar School then joined the Combined Cadet Force. They were able to develop their shooting skills first acquired at Bearsted by using the range at the grammar school.

Bill Woolven, a member of the club for many years, recalled that members of the Air Training Corps who wanted to join the RAF had to learn to shoot. Bearsted was the only available rifle club nearby, so the club trained many members of the Corps.[33]

Women's Institute

Members of the Women's Institute fully played their part in the logistics surrounding the evacuation of the British Expeditionary Force from the beaches in Dunkirk. During the Battle of France, the troops had become trapped by the German invasion force. A quarter of a million British men, plus French, Polish, Belgian and Dutch troops were all rescued from the beaches in that extraordinary feat called Operation Dynamo which took place during 26 May to 4 June 1940.

Over 200,000 of the troops passed through Dover on 324 trains and another 82 trains ran from Ramsgate. The trains were called the 'Dynamo Specials' and passed through Kent onto Redhill, Guildford and Reading, in order to bypass London. From Reading, the special trains then went out all over the country.[34]

Feeding the rescued troops aboard the trains was a major challenge. Each trainload carried around 550 men which had to be fed during stops at stations estimated to last a maximum of eight minutes. Probably the best known arrangements in Kent were those at Headcorn, Paddock Wood, and Tonbridge. These stations had four tracks and wide platforms. This enabled Ambulance trains to carry straight on along the through lines while the other trains pulled into platforms in order for food and drink to be given to the troops.[35]

At Headcorn railway station a large barn was turned into a kitchen. Ladies from wide areas around the stations offered to help; including local branches of the Women's Institute, the Women's Voluntary Service and members of countless other local church and charitable groups. Shifts were arranged; groups of forty to fifty ladies worked for eight-hour stretches over nine days cutting up over 22,000 loaves of bread. Nineteen stoves constantly brewed tea. It was later estimated than in just under a day, 15,000 sandwiches, rolls, sausages and pies were supplied.[36]

Local canning factories supplied tins for the tea. As the stop drew to an end, the troops were told to throw the tins back onto the platform. The tins were then collected and washed in time for the next train. Through the efforts of the voluntary groups and countless helpers, over 145,000 troops were able to have their first decent meal in days.[37] Flora Crapp (née Burgess) recalled that like many ladies from Bearsted and Thurnham, she lent a hand making, and cutting up, sandwiches. She little realised at the time that among the rescued troops was Melvin, her future husband.

In 1939, the national Women's Institute formed a Produce Guild with the assistance of the Ministry of Agriculture. This was linked to the Dig For Victory campaign but it was the threat of waste that led to greater efforts because of the summer's abundant crop of fruit. The Produce Guild worked with local branches of the Women's Institute to set up fruit-preservation centres. In addition to jam-making, fruit was also canned using machines which had been sent from the United States. The machines could either be bought or hired weekly. The fruit was boiled in sugar syrup and once filled, was sealed in the cans before being cooled in a water bath. Labels were later pasted on the tins.[38] During 1940, one of these centres was set up by members of the Bearsted Women's Institute who were initially advised on the technical aspects of canning and preserving by staff from the Foster Clark factory.

The scheme was based in a room at Thurnham vicarage, under the direction of Mrs Derrick. Despite this excellent work, the Vicarage was soon requisitioned by the Air Ministry as accommodation for personnel from RAF station Detling. Mr Scutt and his family were moved to a property called St Hilda's situated by Lord Romney's Hill and The Fruit Preservation Centre was relocated to the Mission Hut in Ware Street.[39] The undated photograph on the next page shows the Mission Hut on the left hand side of Ware Street, today the site is now part of Sandy Mount:

Reproduced courtesy of Michael Perring

As the parish magazine recorded, the centre operated at the Mission Hut on Tuesdays, Thursdays and Saturdays during the fruit picking season. The Women's Institute gave £5 to use the premises and agreed to meet the cost of all the gas used. An initial £60 was required for the necessary sugar and the money was lent by residents in units of £1. Anyone with home-grown fruit, or fruit such as blackberries or damsons gathered from hedgerows, could bring it along to sell to the centre for preservation between 10 and 11.30am. Strawberries, blackcurrants and raspberries could only be made into jam rather than being canned. Official logbooks were issued by the Ministry of Food and accounts were settled weekly. Such was the success of the scheme that the centre opened a shop. Prices were governed by the Ministry. Among many remarkable statistics for the Women's Institute during this time is that in one six day period, over 800lb of jam was produced! [40]

This was not the only local endeavour organised by the Women's Institute though; by October 1940, the Women's Institute hall was turned into a canteen and a rest room for the troops, which included Canadian forces stationed in and around Bearsted and Thurnham. An appeal in the parish magazine soon yielded board and other games, books, and magazines for recreation. Keith Holtum recalled that, as a teenager his piano and accordion playing skills were in regular demand for 'sing-song' evenings too.

The appeal had also yielded sufficient catering equipment and cooking pots to start the provision of hot meals at the hall. Volunteer cooks reported to Mrs Daniell and men were recruited as stewards led by Lance Monckton. The canteen staff were led by Mrs Freddie Grout and a hundred volunteer helpers included Mrs Colgate, Mrs Swift, Mrs Pollard and Mrs Croucher. In 1943 it was estimated that 76,696 meals had been served: 211 a day. The canteen eventually closed on 22 November 1945 and the remaining funds donated to charity.[41]

There were other informal groups helping servicemen in the villages which were loosely linked to the Women's Institute. For example, a small band of women in Bearsted arranged a 'mending service' for the troops. They were led by Mrs Bracher of Gore Cottage. Ladies gathered at her home between 10am and 5pm to mend and refurbish articles of service uniform. The vicar also asked in the parish magazine if people could open their houses for a day or two a week on a rota basis to act as hosts for servicemen that needed simple comforts such as a hot bath or a chair by a fireside in a domestic setting.

Servicemen stationed in and around Bearsted and Thurnham appreciated that there was somewhere that could provide companionship and comfort in an environment similar to their home. The warm welcome led to some kind comments by Rev E Bennitt, Chaplain to the Forces when he attended the Women's Institute Canteen Committee Annual General Meeting in 1942. He recalled that he had been told that he was very lucky to visit the best canteen in Kent. Countless servicemen had told him how much they had appreciated the wonderful atmosphere of the Bearsted canteen!

Scouts and Guides

After the war began, it is not at all clear whether meetings of the Girl Guides or of the Scouts in Bearsted took place on any sort of regular basis as written records are sparse. Although the nature of this conflict was markedly different to the Great War, the national Scout Association encouraged all members to render service to the community, in a manner similar to the previous conflict.

Amongst other remarkable achievements by Association members during the war, following the evacuation of Dunkirk, in the early hours of the morning, one Scout helped to erect over four hundred tents for the troops' emergency accommodation.[42] Although Guides and Scouts in Bearsted and Thurnham could not lay claim to this achievement, their activities were still equally useful. During the conflict, they too tried to follow the adult example of a 'Business As Usual' approach to everyday life, trying to keep to normal work and leisure patterns wherever and whenever possible.

However, now more than ever, all of their activities had a definite purpose: this included making bandages out of old sheets, re-rolling bandages, acting as 'casualties' in Civil Defence exercises, learning to extinguish incendiary bombs and detect poison gas. They undertook shopping for people who could not stand in queues as they were on shifts in factories involved in the war effort, filling sandbags, and painting kerb stones white so they might be seen in the blackout.[43]

Scouts over the age of fourteen could receive a National Services Badge. There were over 180 approved activities and these included participating in the harvest and fruit picking, acting as messengers for Air Raid Precautions wardens and the Home Guard. As messengers they even cycled through streets during air raids: with only a tin hat for protection, enormous courage must have been required. By the end of the war, 60,000 Scouts had earned the badge.[44]

As part of the usual regular local events, the Beating of the Parish Bounds still took place and the Scouts and Guides both attended it in their uniforms. This photograph is undated but was taken during one such ceremony. The Scouts are on the left hand side:

Reproduced courtesy of Jessie Page

Alan Croucher joined the Scouts in 1943, so recruitment continued despite the conflict: he had been encouraged to join by his older brother, Bernard. Alan also recalled that all of the Troop was encouraged to participate in such wartime activities as the waste paper collection which was part of the Ministry of Supply salvage scheme. There were some short camps held locally. Like everything else, though, in the community life of Bearsted and Thurnham, the section meetings of both the Girl Guides and Scouts would have been disrupted by air raids.

They Also Served

As Alan recalled, a number of outdoor services were held on the Green at Bearsted during the war. Not many photographs survive but the following were taken during a wartime parade and outdoor service held in 1942. The parade included members of the armed forces, Holy Cross church choir, 1st Bearsted Girl Guides, Air Raid Precautions wardens, Red Cross, Kent 226 detachment, and Junior Red Cross, Kent 524 detachment and members of the RAF who travelled down from RAF station Detling to attend the service:

All reproduced courtesy of Jenni Hudson

Accommodation, Rest and Relaxation

During the war, many large properties in Bearsted and Thurnham were requisitioned for armed forces accommodation. The vicarage of St Mary's, together with an adjacent building which had once been used as a parish room, were also taken over by the Air Ministry as it was close to RAF station Detling, only around two miles away. There were billets arranged at some of the larger, but private, houses in the two villages; Friningham Manor, Thornham Friars and Cobham Manor were used by personnel from RAF station Detling, soldiers from Wiltshire were stationed in the house at Common Wood, whilst troops from New Zealand were billeted at Bearsted Cottage. A hostel for the Women's Land Army was built at Friningham Manor. At Bearsted Cottage, soldiers painted a large V for Victory sign and the Morse Code equivalent on the front of the property. Further troops from Australia and New Zealand were camped in fields around Spot Lane and on the golf course which bordered Ware Street and Thurnham Lane.

At the former vicarage, a bar for RAF officers was located in a ground floor room. Some redecoration of the rooms was undertaken, largely in shades of yellow, green and brown. It is thought that during this time, the bar area was decorated by an air force regiment with a series of wall paintings undertaken in aircraft paint. This photograph of the former vicarage was taken in the early years of the twentieth century:

Reproduced courtesy of Evelyn Fridd and Margaret Plowright

After the war, in 1946, the house was sold to Mr and Mrs White who undertook a thorough renovation. Later owners, Mr and Mrs Ashdown, uncovered the wall paintings once more in 1998. These photographs show details from two of them:

Reproduced courtesy of Downs Mail

Accommodation, Rest and Relaxation

In addition to the main property at the vicarage, the RAF constructed further buildings in the grounds which were used for accommodation and storage. There were at least five huts, which seem to have been quite substantial and included iron pot-bellied stoves, although the quality of the concrete bases used for them varied! There was a separate ablutions block which included wash basins and toilets but was also used as a laundry. Another hut was used as a canteen; it was attached to the vicarage with a connecting section. In addition to the huts, there was a water tower, several storage buildings, and two air raid shelters, one of which was on the front lawn of the vicarage. The former parish room, constructed around 1890, had been converted into a dwelling and now became accommodation for some WAAFs. This photograph shows the building around 1940:

During 1940 to 1941, these delightful photographs were taken of a group of the girls enjoying some relaxation time there and also in the grounds of the vicarage:

Only one of the photographs, taken in the summer, gives any details of their names:

All reproduced courtesy of John Allison

<u>Left to right</u>: Mitch, Iris, Niggy (slightly behind with arm raised), Joan, Sadie and Peggy

255

Accommodation, Rest and Relaxation

Thurnham Keep became a convalescence home for wounded aircrew, as well as accommodation and a mess for officers at RAF station Detling. The building dates from 1910 and it is believed that the flints dressing the walls may have come from the nearby ruins of Thurnham Castle. The fittings in the house were of a superb quality and included wooden panelling and marble. This recent photograph shows the outside of the house:

The cellars of the house were used to store important and highly confidential Air Ministry documents. An escape route also had to be devised for use in the event of the house being bombed so that personnel and documents could be safely removed. A short tunnel was excavated which led from the cellars into woodland in the North Downs behind the house. Fortunately, use of the tunnel was never required and it has now been blocked off at the far end. The photograph shows part of the tunnel today:

Both reproduced courtesy of Roger Vidler

Accommodation, Rest and Relaxation

Leisure pursuits for members of the armed forces stationed nearby largely involved participating in activities and social events in Bearsted and Thurnham. Events were held at many different venues in the villages including the function room at the Tudor House, the White Horse, the Memorial Hall and the Women's Institute Hall on a Wednesday night. George Cannon recalled that the Tudor House was designated as a casualty clearing station under Civil Defence for a time, and that the Women's Institute Hall held dances and concerts organised by the Entertainments National Service Association. Further afield in Maidstone, the attractions included five cinemas showing the latest films and the Royal Star Hotel which held regular dances for the RAF in the ballroom. Personnel in uniform were charged a lower admittance fee, or occasionally, there was no charge.

The Royal Oak, run by Edward Weaver and his family, was frequented by the soldiers from New Zealand. It was known that they were quite generous with their rations, which seemed to be ample in comparison to British allowances. Corned beef sandwiches were nearly always available at the pub, so it was assumed that some of the large tins used by military catering supplies had found their way there! This undated photograph shows part of the Royal Oak building and the main entrance:

Reproduced courtesy of Terry Clarke

The White Horse became part of the circuit of public houses visited by airmen from Detling including sergeants from Thurnham Court, and their officers based at Thornham Friars and Cobham Manor.

Roger Vidler was able to discover from older residents that the armed forces from the area were attracted to the regular dance nights held at the White Horse. Among those to attend were Canadian troops stationed at Vinters Park. The dances were held in a function room which had been added to the public house in Victorian times. Sometimes, over a hundred people would cram in to the confined space, waltzing, fox-trotting and jitter-bugging the night away to the sounds of an army band.

The dances were very popular but the armed forces were not known for their dancing skills; the events were referred to as 'football matches'. The events were hugely attractive to the young people of the village, but it is debatable whether the presence of some mothers acting as chaperones was regarded in a similar light! The dances continued throughout the war and were never once stopped by an air raid.

The landlady, Mrs Benjamin Brook, who was known to everyone as 'Auntie Ben', kept a special panel in one of the bars for the airmen to sign their names. In subsequent redecorations, she refused to have the panel painted over. This undated photograph of the White Horse gives some indication of the appearance of the pub. The building on the right hand side of the photograph was a stable block:

Reproduced courtesy of Roger Vidler

The Black Horse at Thurnham was one of the nearest public houses for the men stationed at Detling. This undated photograph of the Black Horse gives an indication of the appearance of the pub:

Reproduced courtesy of Martin Elms

RAF Station Detling

Reproduced courtesy of James Kersey

The site of Detling aerodrome is on top of the North Downs. The entrance was two miles from Detling. It is actually located in the parish of Thurnham, approximately one mile north east of St Mary's church.

The decision to set up the aerodrome almost certainly originated in the government realisation that before 1914, Britain's position as an island meant that it was best strategically defended from the sea. However, technology progressed and after the Wright brothers' first powered flight in 1903, the science of flight came to be better understood. As aircraft and lengthy flights in them were rapidly developed, it was realised that air defence was also necessary. By 1914, and so barely a decade after the first powered flight, an Air Battalion of the Royal Engineers, the RFC and RNAS, had been formed.

Although there is no record of the criteria for any of the sites chosen to establish air defence, Winston Churchill clearly regarded Zeppelins as an aerial menace. The need to repel enemy aircraft attacks had been identified and defence for strategic areas such as the Port of London established. Aircraft could be held in stations, but they would only operate when the Zeppelins crossed the coast. Curiously, there is little information about the decision over the naming of the sites. The station which had became known as Detling by 1916, was called 'Maidstone' in early official documents, but both of these names are inaccurate and do not reflect that the site is actually located in Thurnham! [1]

It was eventually decided that the Detling station would form part of the aerial defence for the Royal Navy port and base at Chatham and would be controlled by the RNAS. The level hilltop area to the south and east of Binbury Manor was opened as an air defence landing ground with aviators from the RNAS. Aircraft were accommodated in tents and canvas structures known as Bessonneau hangars before permanent buildings were constructed.[2] Some of the airmen were accommodated in local houses; Mr Cornford recalled that the airmen billeted with his parents in Detling included a Mr Gott and then a Captain G F Leaver and his wife. Mr Gott had a petrol-lighter made from a brass bullet case which was particularly fascinating to a small boy! The influx of personnel led to an increase in trade for the local public houses and the post offices as letters were sent and received between loved ones.[3]

The first planes at the aerodrome arrived in a convoy of Leyland lorries; each contained in a large, rectangular wooden box.[4] Manoeuvres and flying exercises began around 1915. The local residents were told that the aeroplanes would practice dropping bombs and that the shock waves from exploding bombs might cause damage to buildings. It was left to the householders to decide whether or not to protect their property! In the event, there were no explosions or damage to houses, but practice bombs were dropped by part of the Strategic Bombing Wing.[5]

RAF Station Detling

The cost of setting up and equipping the station was estimated to be £2,000. Nonetheless in April 1915 it was determined that Detling was not suitable for its intended role and that the aircraft were needed elsewhere.[6] The RNAS reverted the station to 'Care and Maintenance'. However, when 50 Squadron of the RFC was founded on 15 May 1916 to serve a home defence role, A Flight was allocated to Detling.

The RFC took over control of Detling station on 3 April 1917,[7] and. B Flight of 50 Squadron arrived in August. Following Zeppelin raids in October, in which properties near to the aerodrome were damaged, it was decided that greater defence measures were needed. After discussions with Home Forces Admiralty, it was agreed that the RNAS would assist the Home Defence Wing. The RFC and RNAS were later merged to form the RAF on 1 April 1918.[8]

The airfield was enlarged to ninety five acres. The canvas hangars were also replaced with more permanent constructions.[9] The RFC presence was enhanced in February 1918 by 143 Squadron which used Sopwith Camel aircraft against German bombers with some success. These aircraft were later replaced for a short time by Scout Experimental 5 fighters but their poor performance led to a reversion to Sopwith Camels.[10] This photograph is undated but gives an impression of the Scout Experimental 5:

This photograph, taken in 1918, shows a Sopwith Camel:

Both reproduced courtesy of Malcolm Kersey

There is little information about the operation and running of the station during the First World War, but Sydney Burdett, an RFC air mechanic with a mobile workshop for 143 Squadron, later recorded that he was posted to Detling during February 1918. He recalled that as the aerodrome was on high land, on a clear day, the pilots could see from the aerodrome down the Medway estuary and over to Sheerness.[11] It is known that his squadron had some success in averting some German air raids under Major Frederick Sowrey during May 1918.

As the war ended, many aerodromes were closed down. 143 Squadron was disbanded in October 1919 and Detling fairly soon reverted to a peacetime routine. As Sydney recalled, duties for the personnel at the aerodrome included the whitewashing of stones around the airfield perimeter and around the camp roads. White lines were painted where the planes stood and riggers shone up the flying wires on the aircraft with emery cloth.[12]

Although the defence of London, which included Kent, continued after the end of the First World War, the site was largely abandoned by the RAF. Some of the facilities were used by private pilots and gliding clubs but much of the area reverted to farmland.

In February 1930, the aerodrome was used as the venue for the first flight of a glider called Columbus built by Kent Gliding Club. A few months later this success was overshadowed by a tragic accident on 20 July when Mary Grace, (the grand-daughter of Dr W G Grace, the cricketer), and Lieutenant S E Spencer were killed.[13] This detailed report appeared in the Kent Messenger, 26 July 1930:

PLANE CRASHES AT DETLING

FIRE FIGHTING OUTFIT IN LOCKED SHED

Miss Mary Gladys Grace, the well-known airwoman, daughter of Rear-Admiral H E Grace, and grand-daughter of the great cricketer, W G Grace, was killed when a Moth aeroplane crashed at Detling on Sunday afternoon. Her companion, Lieutenant, S E H Spencer of the Royal Navy, was also a victim.

After taking leave of relatives from Gillingham, the ill-fated couple took off from Detling at 4.15 in Lieutenant Spencer's plane. They circled once, looped the loop, and were making a second loop when the machine fell from a height of about 200 feet. The wreckage burst into flames before onlookers, who rushed to the scene, could extricate the occupants. It appears that on the aerodrome is a shed containing a complete fire-fighting apparatus, but it is left locked and the key is in the charge of a man who lives a mile away!

"MAD TO TRY AND DO IT"

The crash was vividly described to a Kent Messenger representative by Mr G Foster, who lives near the aerodrome. "We were watching the plane from a window," he said, "when my little girl said to me, 'He's going to loop the loop, Dad.' I said, "Never. He's mad to try to do it at that height." Just after I had said it, down he came. There is no doubt that the crash occurred because he tried to loop the loop too low. I went to get a jacket and ran across the field, but I was only half-way across when the flames shot up. When I reached the spot, the flames were blazing so fiercely that we could do nothing. It's the only crash we have had at Detling since the war. I have never seen anything blaze up so quickly," added Mrs Foster.

A VIST TO GILLINGHAM

Miss Grace and Lieutenant Spencer, who has owned the plane, a two seater Moth, for nine months, left Hamble aerodrome, Hampshire, on Sunday morning, and flew to Kent to visit Paymaster Commander R E Worthington, Miss Grace's brother in law, at The Bungalow, Gillingham Green, Gillingham. They landed at Detling, spent the day at Gillingham and motored back to the aerodrome in the afternoon with Commander Worthington, his wife, sister and little daughter, who were eye-witnesses of the tragedy. Lieutenant Spencer was 27, Miss Grace, 26.

The Maidstone ambulance was summoned by telephone and raced to the scene. Chief Officer Dunk, with Driver Skinner and Private McKeough, arriving just as the bodies had been dragged from the smouldering wreckage. Miss Grace was a skilled pilot, and was a member of the Hampshire Airplane Club. She had a narrow escape last March, when her plane crashed from a height of about 2,000 feet. She escaped on that occasion with severe injuries.

THE LOCKED SHED

Considerable comment has been made locally of the fact that a telephone and fire-fighting apparatus are kept in a shed on the aerodrome, but were not available, as the key is in charge of a man who lives a mile away, and who was away for the day on Sunday. It is not suggested that anything in this case could have saved Miss Grace and Lieutenant Spencer, but circumstances can be imagined in which the speed with which such apparatus could be obtained might make all the difference between a life and a death.

> The nearest public telephone, if it is necessary to summon an ambulance, is a mile away, at Detling. The shed, which belongs to the RAF, which controls the aerodrome, now used as an emergency landing ground, contains among other things, fire extinguishers, asbestos sheeting and gloves and hooked poles for dragging people from blazing wreckage.
>
> It is true that private planes have no right use the ground at all, but while they do so, authorised or not, it is held that someone on the spot should possess a key to the shed. It is understood that a key to this shed may in future be kept in a glass case at the aerodrome.
>
> **Theory Advanced at Inquest**
>
> The inquest was conducted on Wednesday at The Cock, Detling, by Mr H W Peach, Deputy Coroner. Mr John Brown was foreman of the jury. Paymaster Commander R E Worthington described the events leading up to the tragedy. "The aeroplane was flying low, perhaps about two hundred feet," he said, "when it had gone some way past us, it turned to the right and looped. Immediately after recovering from the loop, it looped again. This time it did not recover and disappeared in a dive over a slight rise at the aerodrome. I ran towards it, and as I reached the top of the rise, I saw it burning fiercely." He added that when the plane started the second loop, it must have been lower than at the time of the first.
>
> A THEORY
>
> The Coroner: Can you help us with any theory as to the cause of the accident? We distinctly recollect one of them saying that the altitude gauge was not working correctly. "They were both very full of confidence," he added, "and I am quite sure from previous experience that they would not have looped if they had realised how low they were". Witness added that his mother had often been up with Lieutenant Spencer when he looped the loop.
>
> LAD'S PLUCKY ATTEMPT
>
> Arthur Philip Leigh, Tottenham Park, London, who was camping at the aerodrome at the time, said that when the machine had completed the first loop, it was about 50 feet from the ground. The engine was shut off. There was a gusty wind. "It just lost its grip on things and fell flat," He said, "I ran over as hard as I could. As soon as I got there, the petrol tank split and petrol poured over both the bodies and ignited. The wings and fuselage flared up. I tried to get them out, but my calico shirt and shorts burned a bit and I had to jump back." He said that the man was breathing, but unconscious after the crash.
>
> Victor George Love, 12 The Highlands, Detling, a labourer, gave similar evidence. Joseph Cornelius Dunk, Chief Officer of the Maidstone St John Ambulance Brigade, said both victims had fractured skulls and severe bodily injuries. The man had also a severe injury on the front of the skull. From the head injuries alone, he believed both were unconscious as soon as they touched the ground. Sergeant Groombridge gave evidence as to the disposal of the bodies. A verdict of 'Accidental Death' was returned.
>
> After the inquest, the coffins, draped with the Union Jack, were taken by Mr J T Pickard, undertaker, and funeral director, Lower Stone Street, Maidstone to Paddington. That of Lieutenant Spencer was conveyed by train to Taunton by his parents, while that of Miss Grace will be buried at Gosport where her parents live.

Reproduced courtesy of Kent Messenger newspaper group

There was a happier event in June the following year as the first aircraft-towed glider to carry passengers, successfully completed a maiden flight at Detling. It was named The Barbara Cartland, after the author, who had contributed to the financing of the aircraft built by British Aircraft Limited, Maidstone. Barbara attended the maiden flight, splashed champagne on the glider and made a speech to the spectators.[14]

As events in Europe moved towards the likelihood of another war, it was decided to re-open the aerodrome, upgrade and improve the facilities, although the runway would remain as grass. It was officially re-opened on 14 September 1938 and was part of No.6 (Auxiliary) Group, Bomber Command. An Auxiliary Air Force squadron, No.500 (County of Kent) Squadron moved from RAF station Manston to Detling in that same month.[15] There were technical and administrative buildings built close to Binbury Manor and perimeter defences. Aircraft were dispersed south of the Sittingbourne Road and the facility became formally known as RAF station Detling.[16]

RAF Station Detling

In May 1939, the RAF held an Empire Air Day, and as the Kent Messenger newspaper reported, the station would be open to the public for the first time. The squadron also staged a flypast over Maidstone whilst personnel marched past the mayor through the town. These events were impressive, and generated a lot of public interest. The Kent Messenger reported: [17]

> ...with the appearance of the RAF band, who led the way, the crowds flocked into the roadway, swarming round cars and blocking all traffic...the mayor, voiced the opinion of all who had seen the parade when he congratulated the Squadron on their very smart turn out... 'I should like to say how very proud the people of Maidstone are to have the 500th for their adopted Squadron'

Reproduced courtesy of Kent Messenger newspaper group

A poster advertising the Empire Air Day:

Reproduced courtesy of James Kersey

With the arrival of a 'home' squadron, RAF station Detling clearly became part of the local and public consciousness. The expansion of the aerodrome also had wider effects as local business benefitted from the commercial opportunities from provisioning arrangements, and job vacancies arose for civilian waiters and officers' personal valets. Also on the site there was also a Navy, Army and Air Force Institutes (usually known as the NAAFI) recreational facility and a Church Army hut.[18]

During the Second World War, the main entrance and the guardroom to RAF station Detling were located on the south perimeter road of the airfield by a junction with the A249. This is now a slip road off the A249 towards Yelsted leading to Binbury Lane (also known as Bimbury Lane).

The area enclosed by the airfield perimeter extended to Stockbury, Binbury Manor and Castle, part of Scragged Oak Road and continued onto the other side of the A249 where the dispersal areas were located, up to Cold Blow Farm. In nearby Binbury Lane, there were seven terraced houses which formed the married quarters.

RAF Station Detling

Detling station was part of Coastal Command under 16 Group. David King had joined the RAF and was posted to Detling as a clerk working in the Operations Room until 1942. He recalled that the main roles of Coastal Command in the early stages of the war were to undertake naval reconnaissance, to provide convoy protection, to attack enemy submarines and shipping. During operations, there was a duty squadron and an Operations Officer allocated specific aircrew. Every plane was equipped with a Codebook and a Syko cypher machine used for ground to air instruction. Reports were sent from the aircrew via Wireless Dispatch to Detling. The Operations Room included Intelligence sections and map officers together with a huge coastal chart of the British Isles. There was also a teleprinter room with a direct link to the naval headquarters at Chatham, a Wireless Operations section with telegraphy and a telephone exchange.

By 1940, there were several additional units based at Detling and these included some Fleet Air Arm squadrons. Ronald Hay, a pilot officer with 801 Squadron of the Fleet Air Arm, was posted to Detling in the spring. He recalled that many members of his squadron lived in tents as there was no space in the personnel huts or in the mess. Despite the accommodation arrangements, the food overseen by a lieutenant in the Fleet Air Arm, was excellent and RAF officers were frequent visitors. Everyone thought that the excellent standard of catering could not last and sure enough, questions were asked. A subsequent Board of Enquiry investigated the possible mismanagement of funds and it was found that victualling had been arranged from Fortnum and Mason! [19]

In May, a detachment of the Coast Artillery Co-operation Flight based at Eastchurch, was formed at Detling. In line with the assigned role of Coastal Command, the range of duties included co-operation with the gunnery defences in the Thames, Medway and Dover. Avro Anson and Bristol Blenheim aircraft were held in readiness to provide, at short notice, cover and support for the defences. Operations from Detling included spotting and reconnaissance for the guns at Dover but also sorties to the Cape Gris Nez and Calais Harbour area, and offensives against German E-boats.

David recalled that Operation Dynamo was probably the height of activity undertaken at the station. In order to achieve air support, personnel worked round the clock; when were not working in Operations, they would be at the bomb dump loading the carts with 250lb bombs ready to be towed out to the aircraft. Vice Admiral Charles Evans remembered that the Fleet Air Arm undertook sorties using Blackburn Skua aircraft from Detling. There were never more than four Skuas on patrol; frequently encountering at least eighteen Messerschmitts. Tactics deployed included trying to 'bait' the German aircraft in order to distract and outmanoeuvre them. The main duties performed by the Anson aircraft were undertaking anti-submarine work off Dunkirk whilst Blenheim fighter aircraft provided escorts for the 'Little Ships'. Every hour of daylight was used for sorties, extending to an hour before dawn and an hour after dusk. It was estimated that each sortie took four hours. This level of operation continued until the sixth day, by which time roughly half the aircraft available had been lost. As part of the evacuation, an entire wing of Lysanders were flown back from France but only four aircraft were received, all the rest had been shot down.[20]

This undated photograph shows an Avro Anson in mid-flight:

Reproduced courtesy of James Kersey

The Women's Auxiliary Air Force (usually known as WAAF) were also present at Detling. Initially, there were just three girls from 19th Company (County of Kent) WAAF, operating the telephone exchange, two of whom were Ann Tebbutt and Pamela Thorpe. The uniform comprised just arm-bands, but eventually further items of uniform were supplied and this came to include a raincoat and beret. After mobilisation, at least twenty five WAAFs were posted to the airfield and some were billeted at Binbury Cottages. Ann later recorded that this accommodation offered some challenges. Two girls occupied each tiny and very draughty room and limited heating was achieved with coal fires. The mess had to be located in the end cottage. The winter of 1939 was severe with frequent snowfalls; with great difficulty, Ann's father managed to drive up to the cottages and hand over an eiderdown and hot water bottle. The water tower at the station then froze solid but undaunted, Ann regularly filled a kettle with snow in order to obtain sufficient water to heat up and fill the bottle. Eventually even the Air Ministry noticed the conditions and every WAAF was issued with an airman's overcoat. However, so short were the supplies that the coats were only issued on the strict promise that if the recipient moved from Detling it was to be returned! May Winter, a WAAF who served as a cook, could recall other girls were accommodated in Maidstone, Stockbury, Thurnham and Yelsted.[21]

The activities of the station had a considerable impact upon the local community. Of paramount importance, was the security around the airfield, but this did not always sit comfortably with the agricultural activities of the surrounding farming community. William Buck, usually known as Billy, recalled that his family owned and farmed a large area of land which was occupied by the RAF. Farming activities stood side by side with the roar of engines from the airplanes. Billy remembered that in order to enter the site, his family were issued Air Ministry passes. The barriers made things feel quite different as there was always a chance of being stopped by the RAF Police because pitchforks, hay knives and other farm equipment were being moved around the farm. However, after a period of time, the Buck family became familiar faces to a number of the guards.

Wider security issues were highlighted by entries in the Operations Record Book which detail some incidents. On one occasion, complaints were received from a neighbouring landowner that game birds were being poached on local land. On 8 April 1940, a civilian, who had been recently been employed at the station was convicted of theft after an attempt to steal RAF property. He was sentenced to fourteen days hard labour. However, it was not always the case that the armed forces were entirely innocent in these matters; on 9 September 1940, airmen were instructed to stop removing building materials from Binbury Manor! [22]

In May 1940, an Anson aircraft crashed at the airfield as it returned from a patrol. It undershot on landing and hit trees before crashing into an adjacent field where it caught fire and a large explosion killed the navigator.

The bravery shown on that night by Daphne Pearson from the WAAF resulted in her becoming the first woman to receive a gallantry award in the Second World War. It was converted to a George Cross in 1941. Her actions earned a mention the House of Commons by Sir Winston Churchill.[23]

This photograph shows Daphne after receiving her George Cross.

Reproduced courtesy of
Marion and Peter Hebblethwaite

Some of the details of the incident were included in her obituary which appeared in the Daily Telegraph, 26 July 2000:

> DAPHNE PEARSON, who has died aged 89, was the first woman to be awarded the George Cross, after rescuing a pilot from his burning aircraft. In 1940 she was a 29-year-old medical corporal working as an attendant in the sick quarters of the RAF base at Detling in Kent. At around 1am on May 31 she was sleeping fitfully when she heard the noise of a plane in distress. One engine was cutting out and it seemed to be heading directly towards the base. She quickly dressed, put on gumboots and a tin hat and dashed outside in time to see the plane crash through the trees and slam into the ground. "A guard told me to stop but I said 'No'," she later recalled. "I ran on, opening the gate for an ambulance to get through."
>
> There was a dull glow where the plane had come to rest. She scrambled over a fence, tumbled down an incline, was stung by nettles in the ditch and finally reached the field with the wreckage. As she neared the aircraft, others appeared on the scene and started dragging the pilot clear. Running towards them, she yelled: "Leave him to me - go and get the fence down for the ambulance." On her own, she began to drag the pilot further away from the blaze, but he was groaning in pain and she stopped to give first aid. Unclipping his harness, she found that his neck was injured and she feared a broken back. The pilot then mumbled that there was a full load of bombs on board, so she pulled him further away, reaching the other side of a ridge just before the petrol tanks blew up. Daphne Pearson at once threw herself on top of the pilot to protect him from blast and splinters, placing her helmet over his head. As they lay there, a 120lb bomb went off, and she held his head to prevent any further dislocation.
>
> A soldier then crawled forward and leant her a handkerchief so that she could clean him up (there was a lot of blood around his mouth and a tooth protruding from his upper jaw) and she was about to examine his ankle when the plane went up in another huge explosion. The air around them seemed to collapse and the breath was sucked out of them. They were showered with splinters and debris, and other helpers were blown flat as before a hurricane-force wind. Fearing that other bombs would go off, Daphne Pearson ran to the fence to help the medical officer over with the stretcher. Shortly after the pilot had been removed by ambulance, there was yet another, even fiercer explosion. Daphne Pearson was undaunted and went back to the wreckage to look for the fourth member of the crew, the wireless operator; but he was dead. Afterwards, she returned to the base to help the doctor, and was on duty as usual at 8 am that day.

Reproduced courtesy of Daily Telegraph newspaper

Daphne was commissioned and then promoted to Section Officer, serving throughout the rest of the war with Bomber Command. The artist, Dame Laura Knight, RA, was asked by the Ministry of Public Relations to paint Daphne. The resulting portrait is shown here. A plan to depict her with a rifle was changed in favour of a respirator as Laura had been advised that 'WAAFs were not to carry arms'.[24]

On 27 July, there was another crash landing at Detling. Sergeant Norman Barron from 236 Squadron recalled that his aircraft, Blenheim 1F, registration number L1119 (ND-C), was running short on fuel at the end of one patrol. He lost one engine and then the other failed, so he came in low at 600 feet, but was too fast and ploughed through a nearby orchard! Fortunately he and Sergeant Lowe who was also onboard were unhurt. The aircraft was subsequently repaired and back in operation fairly soon afterwards.[25]

Reproduced courtesy and © Imperial War Museums (LD 626)

Transport for the station had a major impact on the local communities; the road network was continually affected by operations. David King recalled that the aircraft were dispersed either side of the main road running next to the airfield.[26] Traffic lights were installed to stop all vehicles when the aircraft were taxiing to use the runway. A new system was also devised whereby all traffic travelling to the station used a route going up Detling Hill while vehicles travelling away from it had to go down Castle Hill, Thurnham.

In November 1940; only passenger cars and light vans were able to use the road from The Cock Horse public house in Detling village to The Black Horse public house in the village of Thurnham.

There were further restrictions imposed upon the community when explosives and munitions were delivered. George Fletcher certainly recalled that on one occasion, bombs were unloaded from a railway box car at Bearsted Station, over to a waiting lorry by bouncing them on their noses.[27] The lorry then transported the munitions up Thurnham Lane to the airfield by a route which took it through residential areas in Bearsted and Thurnham, past the local schools and a row of shops. Military operations made an impact on the community in November 1941, as the headmaster of Bearsted School, Robert Skinner remarked in the school log book that there had been constant manoeuvres taking place with vehicles moving up and down the roads through the villages which had interrupted lessons as they created a 'perfect bedlam of sound'.[28]

In addition to the movement of aircraft and motor vehicles, members of the armed forces had to be conveyed from accommodation in the nearby villages to the station. Arrangements were made with Maidstone and District Motor Services Limited to provide a special bus service which was also used by support personnel.[29] The number of people at the station gave rise to sporting fixtures with local teams in a variety of activities and leisure pursuits. From the operational records, it is evident that a wide variety of sports were played with regular events involving local teams. These included football, cricket and rifle-shooting.[30] The close proximity of Bearsted Golf Course also led the secretary of the club to offer Honorary Membership to the RAF Officers and their families from September 1940. A Boy Scouts Rover Crew comprising personnel from the station was also set up by Corporal Slydel and held various meetings. In addition, all ranks enjoyed exclusive use of Maidstone Swimming Baths, one evening a week.[31]

Probably the most influential events of the Second World War, that affected not just RAF station Detling, but all the surrounding villages and the county town of Maidstone, were the air raids which occurred. The first took place on 13 August 1940, when Stuka aircraft from Luftlotte 2 of the Luftwaffe mounted an attack. William Smith, a wireless operator and airgunner based at the station, later recalled that he came out of a workshop and was shocked to spot a formation of nine Stuka aircraft overhead as they emerged from clouds, unopposed with no ground resistance. The aircraft bombed the Operations Room and hangars then strafed aircraft. There was extensive damage to the living accommodation and administrative buildings, hangers were burned, more than twenty aircraft loaded with bombs were destroyed but the airfield suffered only light damage. The Station Commander, Group Captain Davis, was killed when the Operations Room received a direct hit; he had been trying to contact the Observer Corps. There was also at least one civilian casualty; Jesse Hunt, who lived at Friningham Cottages in Thurnham and had been working at the station. Two station doctors and Dr Bernard from Detling were quickly on the scene but sixty seven people died and a further ninety four were injured.[32] Some of the casualties were taken to the Tudor House, which acted as a temporary clearing station overseen by Officer Wallace Beale.[33] Most of the casualties were subsequently buried in Maidstone Cemetery.[34]

The attack, in clear daylight, took everyone by surprise. The sound of the raid carried straight over the hills from Detling and could be heard for many miles. However, it did not take long before the station was at work once more. After the All Clear sounded, within ten minutes or so and with more than a touch of British spirit, the cookhouse managed to produce a large bucket of hot tea; the achievement raised everyone's morale! The next day the base was largely operational once more; there was a direct line to the Observer Corps and David could recall that the Operations Room was again tracking aircraft, albeit with a pile of concrete rubble in the middle of it. As the airfield runways were grass, a steam roller was fairly rapidly deployed to flatten out the worst of the craters. The Operations Room was moved to Detling Manor for a while whilst the building was properly repaired, but by November 1940, it had moved back to the airfield.[35]

Several members of the armed services at Detling were decorated for their bravery and actions during and after the air raids. This included another member of the WAAF, Josephine Robins, who was awarded the Military Medal.[36] The citation said that her shelter had received a direct hit during the raid, filling it with dust and fumes but she immediately rendered first aid to the wounded, displaying courage in extreme danger. Josephine also had her portrait painted by Dame Laura Knight and later recalled having to travel to the artist's studio in Malvern for sittings. The portrait can be seen here.

Another major raid took place on 31 August 1940: Messerschmitt 109 and 110 aircraft strafed the field with canon and machine-gun fire. There was considerable damage as the fuel stores were ignited. As the main electricity cable was cut, no communications with the station were possible for fifteen hours. Fortunately, only a few casualties were sustained. A few days later, the Luftwaffe returned and peppered the airfield with more than a hundred High Explosive bombs which caused further damage.[37]

Reproduced courtesy and © Imperial War Museums (LD 1467)

The aftermath of the raids was felt by all the community; personnel now had to be billeted in the surrounding area because most of the accommodation had been destroyed. Everyone in 500 Squadron who had a home within ten miles was advised to live there and report for duty. Cooking was undertaken from a field kitchen using a crude, but effective, paraffin-fuelled blow lamp and air pump, located in a wooden shack used by the Motor Transport section. The senior officers and their mess now moved to Thurnham Keep, the junior officers moved to Thornham Friars and the WAAF quarters were at Friningham Manor before moving Thurnham Vicarage.[38] Further personnel were stationed around the villages of Bearsted and Thurnham in the large houses; Cobham Manor, Friningham Manor, Thurnham Court were all requisitioned for armed forces accommodation. Pilots were also billeted in the nearby village of Detling; new crew members were arriving every fortnight due to the losses incurred during operations. The aircraft dispersal areas were moved to Beaux Aires wood, fields adjacent to Binbury Lane, and the woodland areas around Binbury meadow.

The airfield was re-built early in 1941 and remained fully operational until the end of 1944. It was later assessed that that although Detling took a while to fully recover from the air raids in 1940, it still played an active part in the Battle of Britain. It is now thought that Detling acted as a distraction for the Luftwaffe's attention, ultimately relieving pressure from Fighter Command.[39]

Undoubtedly, 1940 marked a high point of operations at the station. 500 Squadron subsequently left due to Coastal Command operations changing from protecting the English Channel, to focus on the Battle of the Atlantic.[40] From 1941 through to 1944, many squadrons and personnel spent a few months at RAF station Detling, and then moved on to other airfields. This included 80 Squadron (Air Sea Rescue); 118 Squadron; 453 Royal Australian Air Force Squadron; 405 Repair and Salvage Unit; Photographic Reconnaissance Units; personnel from the Royal New Zealand Air Force, the Royal Canadian Air Force and the 8th United States Army Air Force. For a short time, 328 (Polish) Squadron and 165 (Ceylon) Squadron were also at Detling.[41] Aircraft at the station also included Spitfires, Lysanders and Mustangs.

An extensive list of operations is beyond the scope of this book, but as the war continued, there were many incidents. Some of these were tragic and involved casualties, some involved heroism and courage of the highest order. Not all the aircraft successfully returned and crews frequently encountered problems taking off and landing as the airfield was frequently fog-bound. On 13 February 1944, a B17 crash landed at Detling but the crew survived. The station was involved in many operations including, those for D Day over the Normandy coast, and after Hitler began the V1 offensive, pilots and aircraft from Detling were regularly deployed with instructions to shoot the rockets down.

After the war, the aerodrome continued to be used but the level of activity was reduced on 1 January 1945 to a 'Care and Maintenance' basis once more. On 1 October 1945, the station was taken over by 60 Group 1136 Wing RAF Regiment. For a time, the base was occupied by the Air Disarmament School and 2814, 2878 and 2749 squadrons which tackled bomb disposal. 75 Signals Wing was also resident for a time before the wing was replaced by Southern Signals Area Headquarters.[42] Fairly rapidly, there was further decommissioning and this included property associated with the airfield. Evelyn Fridd and Margaret Plowright recalled that in 1946, their father, Walter White, purchased the former Thurnham Vicarage. The temporary buildings and accommodation used by personnel still stood in the grounds of the property. At first, the concrete huts were rented to local families as there was a housing shortage after the war. Mr White was a builder and used many of the buildings for storage of materials and supplies before eventual conversion to accommodation. An air raid shelter survives, and continues to be used as a store.

The station was handed over to Reserve Command in November 1947. Units from the RAF Home Command Gliding School, including No 141 Gliding School and apprentices from the gliding section of the Royal Aircraft Establishment were also stationed there. Glider operations at the aerodrome were highly dependent on the wind direction. All aircraft landed and took off into the wind so the winches for the gliders had to be repositioned daily according to the wind direction and velocity, using the width of the airfield as appropriate. In 1955 an Army Observation Post was stationed at Detling after returning from Korea. The Kent Gliding Club also used some of the facilities before moving to a permanent home in Challock. By 1956, military operations had finished but the buildings still had a part to play. After the Hungarian Revolution, refugees that fled to Britain were accommodated there. The refugees did not stay for long but frequently used the buses travelling to and from Detling Hill.[43]

During 1959, the aerodrome was derequisitioned. Parts of the station were sold off to local farmers and the land reverted to agricultural use. Some of the land was purchased as a site for the County Showground. The airfield water tower was demolished in 1960. After this, much of the remaining site became a light industrial estate, providing premises for agricultural, motor and civil engineering companies.[44]

In 1989, it was realised that many of the pipe mines which had been laid during the Second World War around the airfields in the south east of Britain, including Detling, were still in place. If a German invasion had taken place, the mines would have been detonated, rendering the airfields unusable. The mines had been constructed from cast iron water pipes filled with explosive and rammed into the ground at a shallow angle. With the passage of time, the explosive had deteriorated and was now very unstable. During the summer there was an echo of times past for local residents as the Royal Engineers efficiently removed the mines but a section of the A249 was closed for two days to ensure public safety.

A memorial to everyone who served at Detling from 1915-1945, was unveiled in Detling village on 6 September 1998 in a special service, with a flypast by a Hawker Hurricane from the Battle of Britain Memorial Flight. The memorial stone bears an inscription to commemorate the units and squadrons of the RFC, RAF, RNAS, Fleet Air Arm, Army, and Civilian personnel. The occasion was a formal opportunity for local people officially to thank everyone who served in some way at the airfield.

Today, there is little evidence of recent, but turbulent, national history at Binbury, Thurnham and Detling. However, an Air Traffic Control beacon remains, together with several pillboxes and a hangar which all survive in the now quiet fields.

James Kersey

Memories of the Second World War

As the historian Katherine Knight has written, the trouble with history is that we think we know what happened; it is like reading the last page of a detective story before the beginning.[1] But for people living through the Second World War there was no guarantee of a happy ending. When people were in the position of not knowing how things would turn out, hoping for the best was the wisest option.

Here then, are some experiences and impressions of local people and children. They include several children growing up in wartime, a young woman called to serve her country, a district nurse and midwife working in the community, a family living by RAF station Detling, information on how a small local business was affected, and the overall impact and impressions upon a family whose older members had already experienced tremendous personal suffering in the earlier conflict. Overall, they capture not only the details of everyday life but the emotional truth of a past only known by that of an eye-witness.[2]

Beryl Doig

In 1939, Beryl Doig (née Potton) was approaching her fifth birthday. Beryl's mother, Daisy, was married to Leonard Potton, and until 1936 had lived at Station House, Bearsted. They frequently visited Daisy's parents, Richard and Lucy Baker, at Bell Farm House in Ware Street and Beryl was born there. Richard Baker ran a busy wood yard on the premises. During the early part of the war, Beryl and her mother returned to live at Bell Farm while her father was away. Here are some of her recollections of life during this time:

Bell Farm in the Spring

Reproduced courtesy of Beryl Doig

> Bell Farm House stood fairly close to the railway line and bridge in Ware Street, but had land all around it. There was a long front garden with lawns, flower beds, hundreds of daffodils and tulips in spring time, old apple and cobnut trees, a huge overhanging 'snowball' bush and others, all ideal for hide-and-seek games.
>
> I loved being with my grandparents in their happy home, surrounded by unconditional love and security. The Baker family was a large one and because my mother had numerous brothers and sisters, it was a busy house with people coming and going all the time. There were cousins to play games with and many activities taking place. My grandmother, sleeves rolled up, seemed to make endless pastries and pies in the big kitchen. The cooking aromas were mouth watering, and I spent many hours watching her work. Granddad kept a huge kitchen garden, and up in the small orchard were damson and cherry trees, so home-grown vegetables and fruits were always available.

The wood yard was a fascinating place. Although we were never permitted to stand too close, it was interesting to see how the timber was cut, planed and shaped into fencing and to watch how the sparks flew. Even today the aroma from a log fire reminds me of the smell of fresh pared shavings.

The day war was declared, 3 September 1939, we all sat around the radio waiting for the statement from the Prime Minister. Then my mother decided we should walk to Weavering Street to visit her sister, Grace. It was not a great distance, but I clearly remember the anxiety in my mother's face as we quickened our pace. Grace was actually sitting behind a big wardrobe which she had manoeuvred away from the wall! We laughed at the sight, but she was already petrified hearing the wail of the siren. My mother pacified her and I felt all would be well.

Soon after, we were issued with our gas masks. Mine was in dark grey rubber, not the pink Mickey Mouse version issued to tiny tots. It smelled strongly of rubber and felt very enclosed, making breathing unpleasant. Fortunately it was never actually needed, although we had to practise and always had them with us in case of a gas attack. They were carried in a square box with a long cord to go over the shoulder.

As Bell Farm House had a large cellar, it was decided to whitewash it again and prepare the space as a shelter by adding a cot and some narrow beds. A living area was also devised. So, with the onset of the Battle of Britain in 1940, my memories are of being down in the cellar with granddad and baby cousin Joan, and adults coming and going up and down the steep stairs bringing food and drinks. The skies over Bearsted became part of the battle, but we felt protected down there while the noise above droned on for hours.

One dark evening, an unexploded bomb landed on the railway line to the left of the house, so the police insisted we evacuate immediately. Several other bombs were dropped over the community that night. I remember sitting on the knee of a policeman in the front of a police car, directing the driver to Hockers Lane where my uncle, Jack Baker, and family lived. My mother and her sisters, Hilda and Mabs with baby Joan, sat in the back. My grandparents travelled in another car. We were all gathered there until it was safe to return.

My cousin, Thelma Baker (Jack's daughter), had a close friend who was a pilot. I thought the pilots came from Biggin Hill, but it is much more likely to have been from Detling aerodrome. These lovely young men were welcomed at Bell Farm, and when not flying or on call, my grandmother would feed them, and they would spend time with us. They dressed me up in their flying jackets and huge boots and I thought they were magnificent and such fun. Sadly, they died in combat one by one; Thelma mourned their loss and so did our family.

My father worked for the railway, which was a reserved occupation, so we never knew when or where we would see him. Later we learned he had worked in a secret underground communications centre, non-stop over many weeks, organising the rail transport for the troops. He was particularly involved in the 'Dynamo Specials', arranging the return of evacuated troops from Dunkirk. On another occasion, a German plane was shot down and went through the roof of one of the village stations, possibly Headcorn. For several weeks my mother and I joined him there while he organised repairs to get the station up and running again. I was even permitted to look inside the cockpit before it was removed and saw the remains of a chocolate bar. Later, he became Station Master at London Bridge and was remembered for his smart braided uniform and top hat. His photograph, with others, was posted up, thanking them on behalf of the troops for their war efforts.

For a short time, I was signed on at a small local private school in Fauchons Lane run by Mrs Jackson. After a while I was able to walk there alone, up through the back garden of Bell Farm, the orchard, the wood yard, and across the fields to Fauchons Lane. There was a felled tree in the field which creaked and groaned in the wind - I always felt it was alive and used to race past it as quickly as my feet would carry me. But in spite of wartime, for me they were happy days. Bell Farm House was the centre of my early world. Life changed radically when we eventually returned to our Orpington home at the end of 1940.

Marjorie Wicks

These memories from Marjorie Wicks (née Avery) give an excellent picture of life at the school and in the local area during the war:

During the war, I attended school in the village of Bearsted. It only had three classrooms. In each was a tall black, coke burning stove. This was fine for the children sitting in the front of the class, but the ceiling and windows were high, and the back of the room was cold. There was an ink well in each desk, and when it was very cold the ink used to freeze. Each child was allowed a small bottle of milk a day, the cost being one halfpenny. I enjoyed it in the summer, but it was warmed by the stove in the winter, which was horrid.

We walked to school. I lived about three miles away and we always went, whatever the weather. Sometimes we skipped, if skipping was in, or maybe played hopscotch, or two-ball. When marbles were the rage we were often late. School started at 9am and finished at 4pm.

There was not sufficient room at the school to cook or eat school dinners. It had no kitchen or staff room. The cloakrooms had hand basins with only cold water, which we used for drinking, washing, mixing paint, and whatever water was needed for. The toilets were in the school yard. But we did have school dinners, and how good they were. They were cooked by the ladies of the Women's Institute. The Women's Institute Hall was a few yards away from the school. Their stew and jam tart and custard, were out of this world. It always impressed me to think that the president of the Women's Institute had cooked my dinner.

One of the dinner ladies used to rush around the village on her bike, making sure that we all attended Sunday school. This wasn't easy as the venue often changed due to air raids. On one of her trips a chicken ran in front of her bike. I am glad to say she wasn't hurt but we all enjoyed chicken casserole the next day.

At the beginning of the war many evacuees from London came to our village. The school was much too small to house them and us all together, so a plan was devised. We all had to have a timetable. This was written on the blackboard. Those capable copied it, plus an extra one for the children that couldn't manage it. Woe betide the children that lost their timetables, they lost house points!

It worked out that on some days we only attended for half a day. On another day our class would meet at the 'mission room'. This was just a large wooden hut in a field. It stood a little higher than the main village street. It was fitted out with desks, the idea being that we achieved some written work, but the windows were low and there was so much to see. The milk lady came by with her churns and ladles, which she swished in the milk to make sure the cream was well distributed for the housewife waiting with her jug. The baker's boy would ride by, with the bread piled in a basket on the front of his bike. None of it was wrapped, but if it rained hard he had a mackintosh cover to put over it. Sometimes we could see a horse being led to the forge so that the blacksmith could make a shoe. One day an army convoy came one way, as the farmer drove his cows the other way. Only the really dedicated finished their work that day. Once a week our class went to the oast house. This was a round building with a rough brick wall. No desks here, just a circle of chairs. There we would learn our spellings or maybe have a general knowledge quiz. We would spend another half day in the Chapel rooms. This was a dreary place, with no outlook, no reason to daydream, and only the noise of the steam train to disturb us.

There were certain places that we had to pass, where it was imperative that we held our breath until well by. Any house where the occupant had tuberculosis was a great fear, and we didn't dare breathe any air nearby. The same applied to another very large house for unmarried mothers! My favourite half day was taken, when we went to the King George V Memorial Hall. It was large, bright, and the newest building that we used, with shiny red oilcloth curtains and a polished floor. Here we had singing, play reading or Physical Training. The girls wore navy blue knickers with a vest or blouse; the boys just took off their shirts, as they all wore short trousers, winter and summer, until they left school when they were fourteen.

We never minded walking to school as there were many routes that we could take, with lots to see and do. In the spring and summer we looked for wild flowers. Each week our teacher would list six for us and we gained a house point for each one we found. We nibbled the new leaves of the 'Bread and Cheese' tree (hawthorn), we sucked the nectar from the dead-nettle flower, and chewed the stem of the fresh tall grass. In the autumn conkers kept us busy for hours. We collected chestnuts, hazelnuts, cobnuts and walnuts. We would roast the chestnuts in the ashes of our open fire and enjoy them while we listened to the wireless in the evening.

In the winter we couldn't wait for the village pond to freeze over. It wasn't very big, but large enough to make a grand slide and deep enough to fill your wellingtons when the ice gave way.

We also passed the village laundry, which had an air raid siren on its roof. We would rush by and hope that it would not go off; the noise at close quarters was more frightening than the raid.

Doris Britcher

Doris Britcher (neé Bentley) moved from Liverpool to Bearsted in October 1935. These are some of her memories about her life in the village during the war:

I was about twelve years old when war broke out. My teacher at Bearsted School was Miss Horsman. She lived with her mother in a house near Yeoman shops and we all knew that her father was German. I remember that before the war, she was always keen to hurry her class home at the end of the day as she liked to listen to the German programme broadcast on the wireless at 4pm, two to three times a week. She was an excellent teacher, kind but firm to her class and had no favourites. However, as the international situation worsened, there were suspicions in the village that her loyalty was elsewhere. We all knew that she had a German boyfriend who was a member of the Nazi party.

A few months before war was declared, she selected the ten best writers in the class to write some letters to a German boys school. The idea was that there would then be a correspondence between the schools. Miss Horsman gave us some ideas to put in our letters: I clearly recall that I thought it was rather strange when she said that the information that she would like to see included was that Bearsted was just over a mile away from an airfield at Detling, the school had a railway line running along one side of the boundary, the cathedral city of Canterbury was only twenty or so miles away and could be easily reached by train, the nearest town was Maidstone which was just over two miles away and regularly had soldiers stationed there. However, all of this information had to be mixed with descriptions of some of the children's other activities such as Guides and the King's Messengers (this was a church group in the village that supported the work of missionaries such as Grace Dibble).

I eventually received a reply from a boy called Willi Wintermere. Parts of the letter seemed strange though. He included the information that he went to a Youth Group which was similar to the Boy Scouts but was called the "German Youth Movement". After war was declared, I was rather worried about the letter so I destroyed it. I do sometimes wonder what happened to Willi Wintermere. Miss Horsman stayed on at the school but I think that Robert Skinner, the headmaster, was well aware where her sympathies lay and she eventually left. I am not entirely sure if she was interned.

Until the summer of 1939, everything seemed to be quite normal to nearly everyone in the village. However, once war was declared, the school did not properly re-open until October 1939 as the evacuees from Plumstead School arrived. Extra classrooms had to be used in the village including the Clock Room of the Men's Institute, the Methodist Chapel, the Women's Institute and the Mission Room in Ware Street. Half-days of school were arranged but although the majority of the Plumstead children were on good terms with us, there was very little joint teaching with the London school. The headmaster of the Plumstead School lived in Yeoman Way with his family.

For many children like Doris living in Bearsted and Thurnham, everyday life and school began to change in other ways. In May 1940, the Archbishop of Canterbury, Cosmo Lang, visited the school which had just celebrated its centenary. He gave the school a present of a motto board: [3]

Courtesy, Fidelity & Courage to endure

Reproduced courtesy of Roseacre school

Perhaps these words were to inspire the morale of the school as shortly after this, the British Army began to be evacuated from Dunkirk. Robert Skinner, the headmaster, noted in the school log book: [4]

> 31 May 1940
> This has been a ghastly week…. The British Expeditionary Force seemed trapped in Flanders and everyone expected the whole half million to be cut to pieces. The children have been on edge all week and very difficult to deal with...

Other signs of the hostilities were visible: the school windows had fine-gauge wire netting placed over them to prevent splinters from bomb bursts in the locality injuring the children. The windows at the Memorial Hall were painted with a special varnish for the same reason and buckets of sand readied. Until the air raid shelter was completed at the school, both children and staff would dive for shelter under whatever protection was available. More often than not, it was a desk but children who lived in very close proximity to the school were allowed to go home if the air-raid siren sounded. The construction of the shelter may have taken a while because it included a decontamination unit for gas attacks.

This photograph shows Bearsted School in 1943; note that the foundation stone above the middle window on the left hand side of the school, which mentions Bearsted, Thurnham and Detling has been carefully obscured.

Robert Skinner arranged for every child to be taught initial, and then advanced, first aid. Perhaps his reasoning was that in the event of a bomb falling on the school or nearby, the children who were unhurt might be able to assist some of the wounded until help arrived.

Robert was highly aware of the momentous international events which were taking place, hence this entry from the school log book: [5]

> 19 June 1940
> The news seems rather depressing, on account of the complete collapse of the French Army. This country is now left alone with a great part of the world against it - a position not entirely new to us or in our history.

All reproduced courtesy of Roseacre school

Memories of the Second World War

Early in August, there was a heavy air raid and Doris has very clear memories of this event:

> I remember the day that Detling airfield was bombed very clearly indeed. On 13 August 1940, we had decided to have a family picnic on the Green that day. We played lots of games and had spread a blanket on the grass.
>
> We had just started to eat our sandwiches when a terrific roaring sound approached from the direction of the church (it certainly didn't sound like Spitfire or Lancaster airplanes) came over the Green and straight over our heads just as the air raid siren sounded. It was unusual for an attack to take place on a cloudy day as we had heard that the German pilots preferred to see the ground that they intended to bomb. Somehow the planes had avoided the radar system: the air was black with them. We later estimated that there had been around forty planes. We were terrified and threw everything into the baby's pram whilst we tried to think where we could shelter as there did not seem to be anyone else around.
>
> Almost miraculously, Mrs Pellet appeared at the front door of her house, which was near the Men's Institute, and frantically beckoned us to come in. We stayed at her house for hours whilst the raid took place. The sound of the raid carried straight over the hills from Detling and we could hear it so clearly. During the raid, I tried so hard not to think of where my father was and not to worry, but it was quite impossible. He was based at Detling and working as a clerk for a construction company. Finally, I saw him approaching on a bicycle passing by the pond on the Green. He had managed to escape the bombing but was deeply shocked. A neighbour, Mrs Munn, had advised him of the whereabouts of his family.
>
> At the same time I was on the Green, Roy Barham and some of his friends were at his house, Sweetbriars, in Yeoman Lane. Roy later said that they had been out in his garden when they saw the airplanes. As they passed overhead, they made a banking turn and they realised that the undercarriages of the airplanes were not those of the Allied forces. They quickly went to the air raid shelter in the garden but before they reached it, saw Allen Carr, the landlord from the Kentish Yeoman, and Frank Page, who worked at Yeoman garage, heading up Yeoman Lane in the direction of the airfield. They were driving the garage breakdown truck (which was the local vehicle for the Auxiliary Fire Service) wearing tin hats and determined looks on their faces. Both of us could remember wondering what their reactions were when they reached the airfield: it seemed such a short time before an ominous thick black column of smoke could be seen on the horizon.
>
> We later found out that the information the Germans possessed on British airfields was not complete and that Detling airfield had been mistaken for West Malling. Vera Croucher's uncle drove a steam roller for Maidstone Corporation and helped to re-construct the grass runways on the airfield before they were bombed again.
>
> Mr Skinner was always very careful about children whose relatives were killed or posted as "Missing" in the war. On one occasion, I remember that he sent Betty Gibbens on an errand and used the time to tell the children that a boat had been sunk and it looked as if her father had been lost with the rest of the crew. Several local families had a near miss one night, when unexploded bombs had lodged on a nearby railway embankment, near Bell Farm House and a little further up the line, close to the Hodges family who were living at Rosemount Dairy farm in Ware Street. Robert Skinner's look of sheer relief when Jean walked into school the next day said so much about the way he cared for all of his pupils.
>
> Robert Skinner looked after us extremely well during the war years. It could not have been easy for him having to cope with the extra children that had been evacuated from Plumstead, but he was determined that we would be fully prepared for every eventuality. I think that my generation certainly owes an immense debt to Robert Skinner, and to the older generations in Bearsted and Thurnham that had already lived through the First World War. Although they now had another war to cope with, the outstanding care and examples of courage that they displayed every day helped the younger people to meet the difficulties and shortages which occurred on a regular basis.

Miriam Stevens

Miriam Stevens (née Gardener) was nine years old when her parents moved to Bearsted from Wye during September 1939, immediately after the outbreak of war. These are some of her memories of wartime:

As a family, we were fortunate in that neither my father nor my brother were 'called up'. My father was over forty and my brother was then twelve, so neither was liable for conscription into the armed forces. My father went to work for Shorts Brothers of Rochester to help the company build airplanes.

My father had become a fundamentalist Christian during the First World War and my mother, although rather sceptic, went along with him to his various churches. This meant that he considered his family had no such need of things such as air raid shelters. While everyone else was frantically digging enormous holes in their gardens to accommodate air raid shelters, my father was certain 'that God would look after us'. During night time raids we all used to gather in a bedroom.

Bearsted School was less than three miles from home so I walked every day and that included a journey home for lunch, or 'dinner', as we called it in those days, and another journey back again to school until 3.30pm. Although there were few pavements all the way from the school up Roseacre Lane and down Yeoman Lane as far as The Yeoman public house, there was little danger from traffic. Only people with essential needs such as doctors had a petrol ration. The few people in Bearsted that owned cars before the war had to put them away in a garage 'for the duration'.

My family included four children and as soon as food rationing started my mother had quite a problem keeping us all well fed on the meagre amounts allowed. In 1940 the rations for a week for one person included 4 oz bacon, 12 oz sugar and 4 oz butter/margarine. Meat was rationed by price at the rate of one shilling and ten pence a week. Spam was a wartime alternative to fresh meat as was snoek (this was a name used to disguise that it was actually whale meat). The government persuaded women to 'help the war effort' by doing essential war work or caring for evacuees. As my mother already had four children she decided two evacuees would not be a hardship and the extra rations would help make the food go further.

We had quite a large garden containing a Worcester Pearmain apple tree, so when the government encouraged everyone to 'dig for victory' she decided to live up to the name she had married into and become a gardener in her own right! Throughout the war, and for the rest of her life, my mother's main interests were in the garden. She produced all our vegetables and some of the fruit to feed us all during the war. This made a tremendous addition to the meagre rations. We took it for granted that we should eat fresh food every day but at that time there was nothing much in the way of imported food due to the German U-boats menacing the shipping convoys.

It was sometime before we had a 'points' system for some things like jams and preserves, tinned fruit, biscuits and dried fruit. There were limited supplies of sweets and chocolates which were also available on a separate 'points' system. Later in the war, eggs could be bought in powder form. In my family, each child had their own pot of jam which was named and there was trouble if anyone else used it!

One lovely summer day in 1940 my mother took several of us into Mote Park for a picnic. I saw what appeared at first to be a flock of lapwings dipping and swerving, glinting in the sunshine further over towards Maidstone. It soon became clear that they were not lapwings at all, but airplanes fighting for supremacy of the sky. Every now and again one would slide down towards the earth with flames and smoke billowing out behind. Then we would look up with bated breath for one of the others to perform what we called a 'victory roll' across the sky - another German plane had been destroyed. We cheered them on as the boys showed off their knowledge of Spitfires and Hurricanes. We did not comprehend at the time that what we were observing was The Battle of Britain: an important part of the hostilities.

Memories of the Second World War

These three photographs are rarities: they were taken in 1940. Robin Brooks has confirmed that the first two show the airplane trails formed in very high altitude in the sky over Bearsted and Thurnham, during the dogfights which took place in the Battle of Britain. The first shows the sky above Datson's Bakery in The Street and the second shows the sky above Ware Street:

Reproduced courtesy of Lesley Reynolds

Reproduced courtesy of Thomas Gilbert

This photograph shows members of the Litchfield-Speer family at the front door of Snowfield watching a dogfight high in the air above the house during 1940.

Reproduced courtesy of Mark Litchfield

Memories of the Second World War

Rowland Fairbrass

Rowland Fairbrass's family lived in Spot Lane and his father worked for Roseacre Laundry. These are some his recollections about being a boy growing up during the war:

> Just before the Second World War, the laundry took delivery of a beautiful, brand-new Commer van. My father was very proud of the vehicle as it had big mudguards, lovely swooping mouldings and calligraphy across the sides of it. However, the local police thought it might be used if the village was invaded and so took it away to be destroyed. He was not impressed!
>
> When the raid began on Detling airfield in August 1940, I was walking down Spot Lane. The only place to hide was by the huge ragstone wall of Greystones House: I seemed to spend a long time sheltering there before running home. Later on, public air raid shelters were built in the middle of the road in Cavendish Way. I think this was to enable people travelling along the Ashford Road to have some shelter available if an air raid began during their journey.
>
> When I think about it, the air-raid provisions at Bearsted School were remarkable! When the flying bombs began to arrive later on in the war, the headmaster, Mr Skinner, set up a system for doodlebug watching: two chairs were placed on the top of the air-raid shelters to sit upon. Children that Mr Skinner regarded as 'responsible' kept watch and if they spotted one, a whistle was blown. At this signal, the entire school piled into the air-raid shelters until the all-clear siren. I believe the school record for evacuation was less than three minutes! The main air-raid siren for the village was on the top of Roseacre laundry.
>
> We were all encouraged to make things at school: the girls usually knitted or sewed and we boys tried to make models of things like tanks and airplanes. I remember that Derek Finnis made a really marvellous model of a Lancaster airplane. It won first prize in three categories for model aircraft at the Horticultural Show in 1942 held at the Men's Institute. At the end of the show the model was auctioned, reaching over £3. The monies were passed to the Red Cross.

This photograph shows Derek (on the left) and Keith Vane looking at the model. It was taken by the corner of the school air raid shelter:

Reproduced courtesy of Roseacre school

> During the war, our family took in one of the boys that had been evacuated to Bearsted. There were particular problems over his meals as all he wanted to eat was crisps and lemonade. It did not take us long to realise that these items comprised a regular diet for the lad. Previously there had been no other option for him than to wait for endless hours outside public houses whilst his father drank inside. He found the relative peace and quiet of Bearsted and Thurnham difficult to cope

with too. Things were so very different in Bearsted that he only stayed for a short while before returning to Plumstead.

I took an active part in the government salvage schemes. In addition to collecting paper and metal, such was the enthusiasm of the children at Bearsted School that 147lbs of rose hips and 212lbs of horse chestnuts were also collected!

We also took part in the Dig For Victory campaign on a plot of land at the school that had been donated by Mrs Litchfield-Speer known as The Spinney. Gardening duties included regular weeding sessions. The first potatoes grown amounted to half a bushel. They were put up for auction at the Red Cross sale and raised 18 shillings.

By 1944, the war seemed to have gone on for a long time. A big army encampment had been established in Mote Park. Some American soldiers were stationed there and we children visited them, asking "Got any gum, chum?" They were normally very generous. American chocolate tasted different, but was still very satisfying to eat. The soldiers took us for rides on pontoons across Mote Park lake.

They seemed a happy bunch with a good sense of humour and enjoyed joking with us. One day we went to visit them and there was nothing there - the camp and all the men had vanished. It was only very much later that I realised that this was the start of things changing: the men had embarked on the D-Day landings.

John Naylor

In September 1939 I was 6½ years old and remember standing by the wireless and clearly remember hearing Mr Chamberlain say "and as a result we are at war" and wondering what would happen. It was not long after that when I had my tonsils and adenoids removed, as one did in those days, and my parents began to think it likely the Germans would soon be invading.

In 1940, my father had an aunt and uncle in Cornwall and so it was decided that mother and I should evacuate there as it would be safer. Uncle Willy had a house on three floors which presumably was not fully furnished, so father loaded one of his lorries with some furniture and our personal belongings, and we set forth on the long and uncomfortable journey. After a day's rest, father returned with his cousin who had also left his wife behind.

I remember Uncle Willy spent a lot of time in the loft making camouflage nets. I also cherish the memory of going round to Jelberts' ice cream shop where the 'poor wan looking boy' from Kent was given a dollop of clotted cream on top of his ice to build him up! Whilst we were in Newlyn, several boat loads of Belgians arrived with little more than the clothes they stood up in. Local people opened up some old cottages down by the harbour and an appeal was made for bedding, clothes and cooking utensils.

After about a month, it didn't look as if the Germans were coming after all. Father and my uncle, Malcolm Marshall, had become fed up with looking after themselves and so we were collected and brought back to Bearsted. With hindsight, we were probably more at risk from radon gas in Uncle Willy's granite house than from the Germans!

Like many people during the war we kept rabbits and chicken and in the winter months I can remember father bringing a bucket of bran into the kitchen to be mixed with hot water off the kitchen range. Mother went to glove making lessons in the Women's Institute and some of the rabbits ended up on the back of my hands as gloves. In September we collected acorns and took them to school for collection as pig feed.

In the early part of the war, our family had a corn and coal business. One day father was upstairs in the warehouse with Arthur Wickens milling some feedstuffs for cattle or sheep. There was a clattering noise coming from inside the machine which sounded as if there was a stone going round. Arthur said 'turn it off governor and I'll get it out'. He stood on an upturned bushel measure and reached inside and pulled out something. It wasn't a stone but an unexploded cannon shell! When they looked up a hole in the roof could be seen where it had come in. The army came to collect it and said that had it gone off both men would probably have been killed.

One morning in 1940 an army convoy stopped in the village street and everyone was asked to provide facilities for the soldiers and I can remember this enormous Maori officer washing in the kitchen sink. We often wondered what happened to him and the others. At one point we also had members of the armed forces from New Zealand stationed nearby and it was with difficulty that they were persuaded not to erect rugby posts on the Green: it would not have been popular in an area known for cricket!

They got up to other activities too as one morning we awoke to find the 'Hovis' sign on Datson's bakery next door had almost been tied into a knot, the result of too much alcohol the night before!

This detail from an undated photograph shows the bakery on the left hand side: the golden letters advertising Hovis bread can just be seen.

Reproduced courtesy of Tony and Sheila Foster

Father was too old for the army and so was enrolled into the Observer Corps. I can remember having to test him on the recognition of aeroplane silhouettes. He fitted his business in with sessions at the observer post on a little hill just outside the village where the Observers had a good view to the south and east looking for approaching German aircraft. With the aid of some unsophisticated instruments the details of their height, direction and identification were passed on by telephone to the headquarters at Bromley.

Like most youngsters, I regularly watched the dogfights which took place overhead between Allied and German aircraft during the Battle of Britain. It seemed amazing that the sky could suddenly fill with chaotic noise and speed; I later found out that during combat, the airplanes could travel at over 500mph relative speed! Collecting souvenirs became quite a thing and living in part of 'Hellfire Corner' it was quite easy to pick up various shaped pieces of shrapnel, ammunition clips, fragments of aircraft and parachutes. In fact, the most desirable were pieces of bloodstained parachutes. I wonder if the shrapnel mark in the concrete outside the back door is still there.

On one occasion we went up to the golf course and found the ground covered with the silver and black strips (the name escapes me) which the Germans dropped to confuse our radar. One day I was looking out of my grandmother's bedroom window as the German Stuka aircraft dive-bombed Detling aerodrome. Apart from the service personnel there were a number of village people killed that day.

I was at primary school, which was a French speaking convent until 1944, and we often spent time in the shelters. One morning we arrived to find our wooden hut had been hit by an incendiary bomb during the night and we had to move into the main building. I can still remember the smell inside that burnt out building. By the time I reached Maidstone Grammar School, the time spent in the shelters was much reduced.

In June 1944 towards the end of the war came the doodlebugs. Two memories come to mind here - the worry at night when the engine stopped on the wretched things, had it passed over or was it heading down towards us? The other more exciting thing was watching the Czech or Polish pilots flying alongside and then tipping up one wing so that it turned down towards the ground, instead of carrying on towards London. Somewhere one had landed but didn't explode and it was loaded onto a trailer and brought round so that people could see exactly what it was that Hitler had been sending over.

I suppose compared with people in the towns we did not do too badly for food, although it seemed to be topic of constant conversation. We had rabbits and chickens, Uncle Malcolm had pigs on the farm and we had friends in Maidstone who kept a grocery shop. Father saw to it that they didn't run out of coal and we usually gained some extra bacon or butter. Mother would probably have said that the worst thing was grappling with the clothing coupons for school uniforms.

All these years later, memories begin inevitable to fade and become blurred for many people, but I still have my National Registration Identity Card, issued shortly after my sixteenth birthday. The number is DKLH 263-3.

Bill Drake

At the outbreak of war, Stanley and May Drake, together with their children, Cyril (usually called Bill) and June, were living at The Poplars in Roseacre Lane. Bill's father was a carpenter working for Cruttenden's builders in Maidstone and Bill was attending Maidstone Grammar School, having gained a scholarship. Here are some of Bill's memories of wartime:

> None of my immediate family had served on a battle front or been injured during the Great War but there were constant reminders of its impact; disabled or unemployed ex-servicemen regularly called at our house to try to sell goods, or stood on street corners in Maidstone trying to earn a meagre living by selling matches and bootlaces. Throughout my childhood, Remembrance Day was a day of real meaning to all of us.
>
> As the countdown to war began, Bearsted received a visit from an Army searchlight unit complete with the not-very effective aircraft sound locator and one Sunday evening during 1938 I observed a German Zeppelin flying over Bearsted. Our summer holiday in 1939 saw most of my class from the Grammar School engaged either working in the school vegetable garden, or like me, at work in Astley House which was then the Royal Air Force Drill Hall in Hastings Road, Maidstone. We sorted piles of boots and other uniform items for later issue. We received payment for this work which was very welcome!
>
> I do not recall when the evacuees arrived. We acquired a little girl, Audrey, who was roughly the same age as my sister and like most of the Bearsted evacuees, came from Plumstead. Our immediate neighbours, the Goodenough family, looked after a Mrs Morley and her daughter Barbara but I seem to recall that they were not official evacuees. After this, we all continued to wait to hear if we were to go to war. Family preparations included digging and constructing an air raid shelter at the top of our garden. Dad and I, with the help of Arthur Maxted, a good friend, dug the deep hole to accommodate it. Arthur told us that he had an old saw pit in his garden at Crismill which he planned to use. Dad then began to construct concrete inner walls for the shelter but in the end it was never completed nor used during any air raid. Dad also constructed wooden blackout frames and I helped to attach fabric mesh anti-splinter sheets to several windows; these had a water activated adhesive backing and required some patience. Nevertheless, we felt we were prepared for the expected air raids.
>
> On the radio announcement of the start of the war by Neville Chamberlain, our elderly neighbours and their two lodgers put on their gas masks and sheltered in their cellar. Of course the anticipated air raids did not take place until 1940 and until then the war seemed to be a 'phoney war' to those not directly involved. However because so many of the basic commodities for life were imported by sea, rationing became essential.
>
> Dad joined the Bearsted Home Guard. From his comments it certainly bore close resemblance to Dad's Army but he was a keen member of the Rifle Club, so was able to use his skills to good effect. He became a Corporal but never sewed his stripes or marksman's badge on to his uniform!
>
> When our school term started, we found that our school building was being shared with pupils evacuated from Dulwich. This gave us all just half of our normal time at school, the rest of our schooling required completing vast amounts of work and reading at home. For me and many others this simply did not work and once the Battle of Britain began in earnest we were far more interested in watching events unfold around us, cycling off to bomb and crash sites.
>
> I used my Dad's Dollond and Aitchison telescope to watch the air battles taking place all around us and on one occasion saw a RAF Hurricane attack an Anson heading for Detling. The Anson rear gunner returned fire, and the Hurricane turned away while the Anson continued toward Detling. Subsequent research has shown that the Anson crashed and burned on landing at Detling on 12 July 1940 and there were no survivors. The records show no evidence of a friendly-fire incident so it seems clear that the crew was unable to radio to Detling and I was the only witness.

With many other local people, I visited the deeply buried remains of a Messerschmitt 109 which had crashed in Thurnham. The site was covered with aircraft parts and ammunition and in common with many of my contemporaries, retrieved a small souvenir - I returned home with a damping strut. When I dismantled the strut I found that every single component was stamped with a German eagle.

On another occasion a Hurricane Mk1 P3201 crashed in Bearsted and this photograph below shows my friend Keith Holtum with parts retrieved from the crash site.

Reproduced courtesy of Bill Drake

Although Bearsted was clearly located on a key route from France to London many of the seemingly large numbers of bombs that fell nearby were largely random events having no clear target, and most likely the result of them being jettisoned. The Methodist Chapel in Ware Street sustained some damage in a raid during 1943 and the Holtum family, who lived in Roseacre Lane also had the side wall of their house blown out.

The later V1 or "doodlebug" events were either faulty equipment or the result of our defences by fighter aircraft or anti-aircraft fire. Nonetheless many houses were damaged. During the earlier night raids we used to sit uncomfortably in the pantry under the stairs, but later on we did not bother. I was not present when a V1 exploded in the orchard opposite (this is now the site of Roseacre School). This did break windows but otherwise there no obvious structural damage to our house. After D-Day, I stood on the platform at Victoria Station waiting for a train to Bearsted and watched as a V1 flew across, cut out its engine, crash and explode nearby.

By mid-1940, my disinterest in school and enthusiasm for flying directed my thoughts to joining the RAF, but at 15 it was not possible. My uncle suggested an apprenticeship. There was a Naval Air Apprentice training programme and I applied to take the Entrance Exam conducted as a Civil Service Scheme. In October 1940 I was on my way to the Grammar School to arrange the exam and cycled as usual through Mote Park. As I reached the gatehouse at the Maidstone end I heard a whistling sound and rapidly recognised it as the noise of falling bombs despite never hearing this before. I looked up and recognised the source as a Dornier bomber. My instant response was to ride over the bank to my right and throw myself down until the explosions ended. I then continued to school passing the house in Hastings Road where the first of four small bombs had fallen. Had I been just a few minutes earlier I would have been passing when the bomb fell. There was nobody to be seen in the road and it never even occurred to me to seek, or call for help.

Although the daylight raids continued throughout the war, by September 1940 it became too costly for Germany due to heavy losses and thereafter the Luftwaffe concentrated on night bombing. Shortly after this, I witnessed the first massed bombing of London when a seemingly vast fleet of heavy bombers could be seen flying just beyond the North Downs seemingly unscathed by the bursts of heavy anti-aircraft fire. Later we could see the smoke from the bombing.

I subsequently passed the examination and was accepted as an Air Apprentice on 4 March 1941, signing up for twelve years service from the age of 18. Prior to that I had to attend a Medical Exam at Alhambra House in London and my Father took me there. It was only my second visit to London, and we saw some of the severe bomb damage en route.

As Regular Service Recruits our training was lengthy and not completed until December 1943 followed by further experience in the field at Naval Air Stations. During this period D-Day took place and as I was stationed at Worthy Down near Winchester saw the massing of troops and equipment and the invasion fleet in the Solent. During leave from naval training I used regularly to visit the Royal Observer Corps Post in the field opposite the junction of Hog Hill and Sandy Lane where our butcher boy, Percy Leadbetter was one of the Observers. These visits enabled me not only to see them in action but to look through the Aircraft Identification books which included many new or unusual aircraft many still on the Secret List. Our training course was still in its infancy and we did not have working aircraft on which to train and in fact the first contact was while on leave when I joined my Grammar school Air Training Corps unit for a visit to West Malling and was lucky enough to grab a flight in an RAF Airspeed Oxford. A visiting Naval Fairey Fulmar was unserviceable - something that became a regular feature of service life.

Finally in 1944 I was posted to a new Squadron forming in South Africa. News from home and letters from friends which I received showed that many of my school friends and teachers from Maidstone Grammar had joined one of the services; they included Percy and Denis Matthews whose parents ran Roseacre Stores on the Ashford Road. Percy joined the RAF and flew Lancaster bombers. He was shot down but reappeared after being spirited back to England by the underground movement. Denis joined the Navy as an Air Apprentice and told me that he had followed my example. Geoff Small, also from Maidstone Grammar, but my senior by a year or so had joined as a Petty Officer Radio / Radar Mechanic and was serving in my squadron.

This photograph was taken standing next to my father during my 'eve of embarkation leave':

Our squadron embarked for the first time on *HMS Ameer* in Durban, and sailed to Columbo arriving on VE Day 8 May 1945. Our orders were to defeat the Japanese and we were part of the large British fleet now gathered in South East Asia. Our first operation was against the Nicobar Islands in Operation Collie and the second against Puket Island in Operation Livery. In the latter we were operating from *HMS Empress* when the fleet was attacked by air and a suicide bomber was shot down by the gunners of *HMS Ameer*. The Gunnery Officer *of HMS Ameer* was Lieutenant Blamire Brown of Bearsted who lived with his parents in Tower Lane! A very large force was then sent directly toward Singapore in Operation Zipper but our ship was returned to Trincomalee with a defect, and suddenly after the two atomic bombs were dropped on Hiroshima and Nagasaki our war ended.

This photograph shows some of the VJ Day celebrations in Trincomalee:

Both reproduced courtesy of Bill Drake

At the end of the war I was in Ceylon, and it was clear, from the letters and newspapers that were sent me, that the austerity of life in England was very hard indeed on all, especially housewives who continued to scrimp and save to find the goods they needed. Mum seemed in despair, and even such things as knicker elastic and hairpins were unobtainable. It became possible to send some of these commodities home, and I did so together with at least one box of tea. Returning home I bought some souvenir goods for the family and a rather nice silver mounted sapphire pendant for June. Probably the most welcome were a few bananas, brought on board as we passed Gibraltar.

After I returned home in 1945 Bearsted had arranged a celebration event for returning service men and women but somehow I was overlooked! My hope of actually becoming a pilot never matured after the war ceased but I continued my Naval Career until 1971. I later joined the Ministry of Defence and managed advanced Research and Development Programmes as a Chartered Engineer.

Kathleen Smith

Kathleen Smith (née Marshall) was almost thirteen years old and living with her family in Yeoman Lane at the outbreak of war. Some of her relatives were local farmers. These are some of her memories of wartime:

I was doing something very ordinary - picking beans in the garden - when a neighbour came out and told me war had been declared. It seemed as if my heart went straight into my boots as although I had no real idea of what war might involve, I immediately thought of fighting and people being killed.

There had been prior indications that war might happen though. My family's house had a long garden which almost bordered onto to the Memorial Hall. Just before the declaration, my sister and I were at the top of the garden one evening when we noticed activity going on in the hall. We decided to investigate and found a group of ladies making boxes for gas masks. We were asked to help and happily lent a hand; anything to get out of homework!

I attended a school in Maidstone and there seemed to be a lot of confusion over when term would start. The summer holidays were usually quite long, about nine weeks. The school announced that under the circumstances, the holiday would be curtailed to seven weeks but then it was extended to eleven weeks. Perhaps the delay was due to bomb shelters being built at the premises. Later, half-time schooling was introduced but academic life seemed to carry on as normal other than during air raids. When the siren sounded, everyone went straight down the air raid shelters which seemed to be a long underground concrete corridor.

Rations were a fair system of ensuring a food supply but the allocation seemed to be limited. Many people undertook 'small actions' to help food go further, such as completely scraping the butter wrapping clean in order to have 'something' to put on scones. It was not a good day when my sister became distracted and tipped an entire packet of tea into the teapot instead of the tea caddy and added hot water to it! Like other local families, we kept chickens and grew fruit and vegetables which helped to boost our diet.

The air raid in August 1940 on Detling aerodrome was a terrible event. Some people in Bearsted thought that the German aircraft had used the glasshouses at Yeoman nurseries as a landmark before moving onto the aerodrome. The smoke from the destruction was clearly visible from our house. Later on that day, my uncle, Malcolm Marshall, who owned Beaux Aires farm near to the aerodrome, arrived and asked to borrow a hosepipe. Many of his outbuildings were burning as his farm had also been bombed.

Other incidents that I can recall include a whole cluster of incendiary bombs falling in our garden one night. Our family spent many hours trying to extinguish them by piling sand and earth on top and, then trying to beat out flames with spades. Unsurprisingly, my school homework was not completed that night but my teacher, Miss Maggs, was not impressed! Several high explosive bombs fell near to our house; one landed, unexploded, into a soft earth bank opposite, but another which fell in Yeoman Lane blew out the windows. At the time, my father was crouching by the back door, thinking the whole building was going to collapse. He was hit on the head and shoulder by a piece of one of the windows and was badly shaken.

Shortly after this incident we woke up one morning to find an enormous piece of tarmac on our front lawn. A further bomb had fallen on Yeoman Lane and a fragment of the road surface had flown up and landed in our garden; if it had hit anyone they would have been killed. Fortunately, the only injuries that night were sustained by a cyclist who ran into the crater. The lane had to be closed for a time in order to repair it.

The arrival of the V1 flying bombs known as 'doodlebugs' marked the start of a new offensive and a fresh challenge. On one occasion, I was crossing the Green with some friends when a doodlebug came over being pursued by a Spitfire. As we watched, the pilot somehow managed to damage it. We realised it was going to explode and the blast promptly blew us flat onto the grass. The remains of a doodlebug went on public display for a time outside Woolworths in Week Street, Maidstone. It was probably not complete, but it seemed to be a substantial weapon!

I am now not now sure whether there was further war damage to property, overall, in Bearsted and Thurnham but this may have been because there were fewer houses in the villages than today. A bungalow on the Ashford Road close to Otham Lane was also destroyed due to enemy action. This may have been caused by a doodlebug which fell in the vicinity of the Tudor House in 1944. The blast also damaged Mote House and the main window of Holy Cross church. All buses were diverted from Ashford Road down Yeoman Lane whilst repairs were undertaken. The buses were double deckers, so the vehicles had to carefully negotiate the route!

After I left school, I became a bank clerk in Maidstone but I also did voluntary work with the Red Cross. My duties included changing bandages and dressings and helping to nurse some wounded soldiers who were patients at Preston Hall after D Day. I was also one of three nurses chosen to meet Queen Elizabeth (later the Queen Mother) during the war. By this time I had completed all my Red Cross training. It was a proud moment to parade on Buckingham Palace lawn along with Millie Baker and Daphne Wood to be duly inspected.

When VE Day arrived, I was working as usual in the bank, but later that day, I cycled around with my friends to see what was going on. We ventured up to County Hall in Maidstone; the area was packed with people celebrating and dancing. Like most of my experiences during the war, the day was an odd mixture of the unknown tinged by fright and exhilaration; longed-for peace had arrived but what did the future hold in store?

Joan Harden

During the Second World War, many women went out to work; some of them for the first time. Women filled gaps in the workforce that were left by men who were serving in the armed forces. In December 1941, the Government called up unmarried women between 20 and 30 years of age to serve in the auxiliary forces: Auxiliary Territorial Services, Women's Royal Naval Service, Women's Army Auxiliary Corps and the Women's Auxiliary Air Force. Women were employed as mechanics, radio operators or ambulance drivers.

The late Joan Harden (née Margetts) joined the Auxiliary Territorial Service. She began her service career in 1942 working on anti-aircraft and searchlight batteries and ended the war as a corporal. Joan recalled that when the radar showed enemy aircraft approaching, her team was immediately deployed. At first, the Auxiliary Territorial Service girls acted primarily as height and range-finders. German bombers would be located and then the exact position was plotted so that the guns would be on target. These calculations were done by machine and passed onto the team in control of the guns. At the order, 'on target, fire', the guns opened up with a deafening roar and the ground shook beneath their feet.

At the end of 1940, the pressing shortage of numbers forced the authorities to give women a wider role in the armed forces. By August 1941, the first anti-aircraft battery to include both men and women was deployed in Richmond Park. They became the first women to take a combatant role in an army anywhere in the world.

Joan was sent to France after the country was liberated in 1944 and became part of the team manning the anti-aircraft gun defences along the channel coast. She assisted in the controlled use of barrage balloons. The discipline was strict: they were not allowed out of their quarters at night and a strict curfew was enforced. Despite the privations, the dangers and the routine fourteen mile marches that were part of her training, Joan thoroughly enjoyed every minute of her time in the forces. It was not all hard work and the social side of army life was great fun.

Memories of the Second World War

Marion Beeton Pull

Marion Beeton Pull was well known to many local people; from 1929 to 1960 she was the District Nurse and Midwife for the Nursing Association which covered Bearsted, Thurnham, Hollingbourne, Detling and Hucking. In 1944, she qualified as a Queen's Nurse, and so was entitled to be addressed as Sister. During the Second World War, Nurse Pull (as she is called here) lodged with the Misses Twort, two sisters who ran a bakery and tea shop in the Yeoman area on Ashford Road.

After Nurse Pull retired, she wrote down some of her memories of her nursing experiences.[6] Some of these are reproduced here providing an insight into the life of a professional person in wartime. They have been slightly edited and one or two names added which were omitted in the original.

> I can so clearly remember when war was declared: I was up at Hollingbourne delivering a mother of her 10lb infant whilst a midwife was also in labour at the other end of the village with her second. I was backwards and forwards as the cases were four miles apart, when the other nurse said, 'Where is your gas mask? War is declared, a raid is on and you are floating about?' I didn't care and was too tired to bother. I went on to deliver the midwife of a 9lb son.
>
> We only had one car between two nurses covering the area at this time. This arrangement was quite absurd as we both had the same ground to cover. So I bought my own second hand Morris motorcar. I was delighted with the independence and when rations permitted, could take my landladies out for a time. We used to pack up some food and a flask of tea and we enjoyed it in a bit of the quiet countryside, and didn't mind the dog fights overhead when sitting in a field. I would also undertake some of my ante natal visits in the evening during the summer and I was so glad to get away from the Ashford Road and its traffic which often included the heavy rumble of military vehicles.
>
> At the outbreak of the war, I thought about volunteering for foreign service, but before the letter was posted, we had a letter from headquarters telling District Nurses that they had to remain at their posts as civilians would need nursing too. I joined the Red Cross and became Superintendent of the Youth Detachment; both Junior and Senior divisions. Mr Stanley Johnson handed over his billiard room for a first aid station and his gardener's cottage was turned into a decontamination centre. Tin hats were not provided, so he bought some. I lived and almost slept in mine, yet as soon as I got to a patient, I took it off and put on my white nursing cap. I always felt happier working; there was no time to think of self when a woman patient was in labour - and fright always seemed to hurry these babies on!
>
> One day I asked one of my landladies if she would like a ride up to the local aerodrome at Detling but coming back, the guard had changed, and as my landlady had no pass, it was a long time before he let her go and she was getting nervous, having left her identity card at home.
>
> The next day, I was sitting by a window when I heard the drone of a plane, and looking up, said 'I'm sure that's a Junkers. It's the enemy - look there are hundreds of them, I bet they are going to bomb the aerodrome.' I tore upstairs and grabbed the phone to ring the aerodrome, but instead, stood transfixed as I gazed in horror watching hordes of planes sweeping in low. They divided into four and then came lower still as they dive bombed the aerodrome. It was a bad raid and we never knew how many casualties. A patient's son was beheaded as he tried to run to a haycot in a nearby field. It was all over so swiftly, before we really had time to realise what was happening. I looked at my watch and found out it was the exact time that we would have been there had I gone the next day. The man who signed my card was killed.
>
> The raid upset a patient, who was a young girl, expecting her first baby and I was called up there the next day to the very isolated cottage but it was a false alarm through fright. So I stayed for a while and went up in the afternoon the next day, arriving just as the air siren went. When I got to the cottage, there was no one in sight. The guns and bombs were very noisy. I had my tin hat on my head and looked wildly around when I heard a voice 'Nurse, quick, come in here' and found they were all in a dug out in the ground. Their spaniel dog was tied up and howling with fright, so I let it loose. Shrapnel came pinging down, riddled a row of napkins with holes and then a piece hit me on the head, knocking my helmet on my nose. I fell into the dugout, saying 'I've been hit' and put my hand to my nose, expecting to find blood but it was quite okay. We sat there for three hours whilst they pounded us. When the All Clear came, I went home with shaking legs to listen to my landladies talking about the raid; the shop was flooded with customers wanting tea, which helped.

A few days later, the patient really did want me but the labour took a long time. During the process, she shouted down to Grandpa, 'Please don't keep banging the doors, bits of ceiling keep falling on the bed'. He shouted back, 'That ain't me a-banging of them doors; it's that ole Jerry a-dropping of his bombs'. She replied from the bed 'Coo...I wish I could drop this bomb'. I called the doctor as she had been in labour for so long, but he said that all was well and went back. I delivered her of a 9lb baby boy in the night and went home happy but exhausted. It's a funny thing that the births were usually much quicker in air raids!

A lull in raids for a while meant that folk did get a bit of sleep but not for long, as one day in September, over 156 aircraft were involved in a raid, I believe. On that day, I had just finished my duties, as I thought, when the telephone rang and our doctor asked me to go to a patient expecting her first baby. She was staying at a local hotel and her own doctor and nurse had been appointed but could not get through because of the heavy raid. The baby was going to be a very well-connected grandchild, and even though I had several of my own patients due, I went. As I got the car out and set off at 9pm the siren went again. My driving was also impeded by the hooded car headlights which were compulsory due to blackout regulations; the hoods were really covers over the headlights and showed just a very thin slit of illumination whilst driving. Sometimes the dangers in the blackout seemed to be as great as the raids; how difficult it was to drive with hooded lights, but it had to be managed.

There were many comic songs about the difficulties of the blackout, and even postcards and posters were produced. This is one example:

Reproduced courtesy of Malcolm Kersey

I crawled along the main road, becoming very frightened as a lot of noise and a strange shape came towards me. It was a barrage balloon which had broken loose; it banged into the car and suddenly, I momentarily lost control of the vehicle, ending up in a ditch as a terrific explosion took place. I later learned that it was a landmine. I was, frankly, terrified. There was not a soul about and the sky was alive with searchlights. Somehow, I got the car out of the ditch, reached the hotel and hammered on the door. I kicked the door, which was locked, the bell was not working either and still no-one appeared. It was nerve-wracking, standing there all alone and with the enemy above. In desperation, I took my tin hat off, and holding it with two hands, clouted the door with the hardest blow. A man opened it an inch and said 'Who's there? We've been warned about spies'. When I said I was the midwife, he almost hauled me in, shutting the door instantly.

He showed me to the patient's room where I met an agitated mother-in-law hovering around a delightful blond young girl. She was very sweet and quite nervous but did not need me yet. They begged me to stay and rest and by morning she was in real labour. The doctor arrived just before lunch and whilst we washed our hands at a table rigged up for our equipment, I looked out of the window saying, 'Look Sir, what is that?' He replied, 'Well surely you have seen a parachute before Nurse?' Another raid was on, and then dozens of white 'mushrooms' appeared plus a lot of noise. We stood fascinated, and I said, 'Look, that's a Messerschmitt coming down but he said, 'No, it's a Heinkel', then a separate voice said 'No, it's one of ours, and what's going on?' To our amazement, the patient was out of bed watching - we had forgotten her! Her baby nearly arrived on the floor and we bundled her back on to the bed as a fine baby boy of 8lbs arrived along with the All Clear siren. I attended the patient until her own staff arrived and when I had tea with her later on, she gave me a beautiful pair of seal skin gloves which I wore for years.

Later on that week, I was called to a rather more distant village for a third baby. As usual, the siren had gone and it was at night-time. Her husband was in Burma and no one was with the patient in the middle of a very noisy raid. The two little boys in the next room woke up and cried with fright, trying to open the door to come in. The patient said 'The baby won't be long, I know' - when a shattering explosion happened and the lights went out. The patient broke her waters at the same time, gushing all over the floor. I slipped on the oil cloth and knocked over the oil stove. It was a terrifying moment as I beat the flames out with the mat; the patient groaned, the children were crying and bombs and guns were all going off! We thought our last hour might have come, so I groped round to the next room and brought the two little boys in, taking them over to their mother to hold. I thought that if we were all killed, then it would be together. Then there was a shriek from the mother as she said 'It's coming, nurse'. Of course, she meant the baby, but I thought she meant another bomb and so said, 'Never mind, let them all come' her reply was 'Well, I don't want twins'. I felt round the mother and the baby arrived into complete darkness. By the time she realised the baby was another boy, I had fished around for matches and found a candle. The two little boys were so astonished at their baby brother that I let them hold him, while I attended to their mother.

We had now been at war some time and no matter how grim things seemed to be, I always seemed to be cheered by Mr Churchill's quiet courage and stirring speeches. When I went to bed, I used to tune my radio very quietly, so no-one could hear it, put my stethoscope in my ears, and tie it to the loudspeaker and listen to Moscow and all sorts of places late at night. Once, when the siren went, which was not far from us, at the local laundry in Roseacre Lane, the noise was much amplified in my ears with the stethoscope!

One evening, I turned the set off and then heard a frightful banging at the door. I found a very agitated woman who said that here had been an accident involving a man, a gun carriage and a New Zealand soldier in the blackout. The soldier, wearing a tin hat with leaves which looked rather like an oak tree, was helping a bleeding man through the door. We helped him to my room and sat him down. He was plastered in blood and holding his chest with pain. He had been driving home and in the dim light drove into the back of the gun carriage; the gun stuck out at the back and had hit him in the chest and gashed his temple. He was a farmer from the next village, so I rang the doctor who told me to send him to hospital. I was glad about this as the air raid was getting noisy. I dressed his wound, cleaned him up before phoning his wife and an ambulance took him off to hospital. He made a full recovery but had a quite a scar on his temple.

There was no respite to the enemy action, and the raids were getting worse when I received some official advice which sent that no nurse was to proceed in gunfire. I paid no attention but, though I might have lost compensation for disobeying official orders, I did it all the same. I also taught patients what to do in an emergency - perhaps if the road was blocked and I couldn't get through. I remember so well a girl three miles away, sent for me but when I arrived, the baby was already in the world. I said 'Why didn't you send before?' She said 'Oh it was such a bad raid that we didn't want you killed, so we waited, but the baby didn't...' the patients were so often far more brave than me.

But despite all this; the raids, the shortages, rationing and a sense of constant danger and not really being able to plan for tomorrow - one was still able to *hope,* and somehow during the war life went on. There were times when trying to conquer one's fears and worries about bombings and other dangers took a back seat. I loved lecturing the members of the Red Cross and we did have some great fun; many of the girls married and became mothers, our common experiences setting up friendships for life.

In the Line of Fire: Life near to RAF Station Detling

These memories recalled by Gertrude Johnson (née Penney), are particularly valuable as they are an eye-witness account of life in Binbury, which was very close to RAF station Detling. Gertrude is usually known as Trudy. There are very few first-hand accounts of the air raids and wartime conditions of this area due to the high level of security and disruption for local residents before, during, and after the war.

When I was young, my family lived at Maple Bar Gate, in one of the most northern parts of Thurnham parish. Our bungalow was situated at the top of Thurnham Hill, opposite some meadows known as the Race Course. Originally, it was planned to build around fifty to a hundred houses in this area. However, what property had been built was then demolished around 1939, presumably to make room for the enlarged airfield at Detling. The airfield station had been originally opened and used in the First World War but was closed around 1919. In 1938 it was re-opened and became part of Coastal Command.

When the Second World War broke out, an Auxiliary Squadron moved into the airfield and brought with them some Avro Anson aircraft. The flying duties were said to involve reconnaissance operations, but everyone who lived nearby was aware of security and seldom spoke directly about the activities at the airfield.

My mother, Frances Penney, opened a cafe in which I helped. It was a very rough time as we had many air raids and had to be escorted to the shelters. Unhappily the German planes soon discovered where our shelters were and tried to machine-gun us as we ran for cover. So we had to take to the woods along Castle Hill until it was safe to emerge. As a precaution against spying we were given a new password every day.

On 30 May 1940, an Anson aircraft crash-landed on the airfield at night. It soon became known what had happened: the aircraft had developed problems and tried to return. Near the airfield, an engine burst into flames as it came into land, still loaded with bombs.

Many of the local people were very impressed with the bravery shown by Corporal Daphne Pearson, who ran over from her accommodation and rescued several of the aircrew from the vicinity of the burning fuselage. As she moved the pilot away from the wreckage, she became aware that the bombs were still on the aircraft. Daphne managed to protect the pilot from the subsequent devastating explosion.

For her bravery, Daphne was awarded the Empire Gallantry Medal which she was later able to exchange for a George Cross. She was the first woman to receive a gallantry award in the Second World War.

On 13 August, 1940, we were subjected to a massive raid by Stuka planes in which many servicemen and women were killed. During the raid, the German pilots used their machine guns. The Anson airplanes, which were dispersed round the airfield, were laden with two bombs each on board. They were sitting targets: as the planes were set on fire, tremendous explosions took place. All the hangers were burned too. Afterwards, there were so many people that had been killed that we witnessed the dead being taken away on lorries. Some casualties were taken to local clearing centres such as the Red Cross centre at Bearsted House and also, I believe, the Tudor House. The Commander of the Station, Group Captain Davis, was killed. Many people were badly injured and the devastation caused by the raid was immense.

Whilst the raid was going on, my mother, myself and a baker who was delivering supplies to us, took refuge under our big table. Our house caught the blast; the roof and ceilings, doors and windows were blown in upon us. The table was two hundred years old and very sturdy: it saved our lives as it all came crashing in. Luck was with us, and we managed to escape without much injury apart from a few cuts.

One of our jobs at this time was to supply the Anson crews with flasks of coffee, rolls, chocolates and fruit before they set out on bombing missions. After we lost our house we went to live with relatives for a few weeks in the Weald of Kent but it was not long before we were back in our 'homeland', as we moved into a house on the Friningham Manor Estate. The air raid shelter and cookhouse for the airmen were in our garden.

There were two more raids on the airfield on 31 August and 1 September 1940. Messerschmitt airplanes caused enormous damage and dropped high explosive bombs but there were far fewer casualties. When the time came for my son to be born, the air raids were so intense that the nurse from Bearsted, Marion Beeton Pull, had to sleep in our house for two nights. I had to spend long periods on the floor under the bed for some shelter.

A radar station was built at the top of Cold Blow Hill and a Land Army Hostel was built and opened at Friningham where there was once a fox farm. In 1942, the Duke of Kent visited Detling. This was shortly before his plane crashed in Scotland while he was on a flight to inspect the British forces in Iceland.

Business as Usual?

The war, food regulations and rationing affected many local businesses and Datson's bakery in The Street was no exception. In addition to making and supplying bread, there was a small cake and confectionery department at the bakery. The sweets were kept in large glass jars on a high shelf running around two sides of the shop. John Hardy remembered that although sweets could be bought there, after 26 July 1942, a ration book also had to be presented - and all to obtain just two ounces of peppermints a week!

Lesley Reynolds (née Datson) and her brother, Roy, recalled that their parents, Laurence and Ethel, had a very difficult time during the war. In addition to the rationing of sugar, in July 1940 the government introduced a ban on the making and selling of iced cakes. So the trade in decorated celebration cakes, for which the bakery had won many awards, almost immediately ceased. However, British ingenuity gave rise to the idea of cake covers, particularly used at weddings. Many people who married during the war used these and may recall that the cake cover was made from cardboard decorated to look like a real cake. It was slipped over the real, and much smaller, undecorated cake whilst on display at the reception. When it was time to cut the cake, it would be carried into another room and the real cake would be sliced into small portions to be distributed.

Laurence and Ethel's concerns were not helped by both of their children contracting scarlet fever. Lesley and Roy were nursed at an isolation hospital at Pembury but their parents could only pay one visit a week due to petrol rationing. Even then, visitors had to keep their distance during visits because of the risk of infection.

This undated photograph shows Lesley and Roy with their mother during the Second World War. Note the camouflage markings on the roof behind Mrs Datson:

Reproduced courtesy of Lesley Reynolds

Area Bread officers were appointed by the Ministry of Food and they knew the capacity of the bakeries in their localities. It was their job to make sure there was no interruption or reduction in supply as bread was regarded as an essential food. Even after the bombing raids on Coventry during 1940, bread was still delivered to the areas worst affected in the city because other bakeries that were nearby worked twenty four shifts when required.[7]

Despite business concerns, there were lighter moments during the war and there was one incident which amused many local people. Harry Smith was assisting Laurence in the bakery. Bread making was begun every evening by putting flour and water and yeast into a mixer. The temperature of the mixture was assessed using a thermometer before the yeast was added. If it was too hot or too cold, the yeast would not start to work and the bread would not rise. Harry put the thermometer into the mixture but then forgot to remove it. He switched on the machine and promptly smashed the thermometer. Harry and Laurence were concerned about the situation as there were very strict regulations controlling the waste of food; in March 1940 the penalties included imprisonment with a tariff from three months to two years. The threat of prosecution was a potent one for many businesses. So they decided to bury the dough in a piece of ground adjacent to the Royal Oak public house. Lesley distinctly remembered both men struggling with a huge armful of dough mixture. Next morning a small crater had appeared in the ground. For a few moments, Laurence thought a bomb had dropped but was baffled by the lack of damage to other nearby buildings. Then he realised that the depression was the result of the yeast continuing to work until it was spent. The dough had then sunk and left a crater. The area of ground became known as the Bearsted Volcano!

In 1942, as shipping losses began to mount due to the success of German U-boat action in the Atlantic, the government became concerned about the increasing shortages of imported white flour. The London Wholesale and Multiple Bakers joined with regional organisations to form The Federation of Bakers, to assist in organising the wartime production and distribution of bread.

The 'National Wheatmeal Loaf' or 'National Wheatmeal Bread' was introduced on 11 March 1942 and used whole wheat flour. It used most of the grain and was very different from white, refined flour.[8] All bakeries now had to produce 'National Bread' but it met a mixed reaction from the public as the texture of the bread was dry, brown and very heavy. National Flour was also available for domestic consumption and baking; cakes made from it were close textured and pastry had to be carefully prepared if it was not to be heavy and indigestible.[9]

These are details from two wartime advertisements promoting 'National Wheatmeal Bread' and the careful use of bread to assist the war effort:

Both reproduced courtesy of Malcolm Kersey

Lesley recalled that there was a sense of almost overwhelming joy and happiness in Bearsted and Thurnham on V E Day which accompanied the celebrations. The bells of Holy Cross church were rung for a long time. Her mother, Ethel, in her excitement, broke a pane of glass in a window that overlooked the pavement by trying to put her head out! Many flags were hung out in the village. Lesley was very pleased to see the Union flag proudly being displayed. Intriguingly, there was also an American flag and even a flag bearing a hammer and sickle appeared from somewhere!

Memories of the Second World War

A Family During War Time

The Palmer family came to Bearsted when their home in London was bombed in 1940. There were six children: Rose, Mary, Joan, Ann, Edward and Joyce. Their parents had met shortly after the First World War, whilst hop-picking in Caring Lane, so the family knew the area very well. They lived in Manor Rise before moving to Shirley Way in 1942.

Mr Palmer had been severely injured in the First World War. His injuries had left him physically quite weak and regarded as completely disabled; at the age of eighteen and a half. Four years before the Second World War started, Mr Palmer had been advised by a doctor that he was still so physically frail that if he continued to work, he would not see his fortieth birthday. He therefore spent a great deal of his time looking after the family whilst his wife went out to work.

When war was declared, Ann and Joan were evacuated with their school to Somerset. Many of their classmates swiftly returned to London. Instead, Ann and Joan joined their family in Bearsted and for a short time attended Bearsted School before leaving in 1943.

Normal life during the war was difficult. Food rationing was a challenge with a large family to feed, but they were all continually amazed at the way Mrs Palmer managed to produce meals for them. They were registered as customers of the Yeoman branch of the Co-operative store. Mary always regarded dried egg as tasting unpleasant but Spam was completely unpalatable, despite her mother's best efforts to disguise it in batter!!

One of Joan's first jobs was working in a dress shop, or 'gown shop' as it was known, in Week Street. She recalled that there was a cellar under the shop and it was rumoured that a river ran below the premise. The shop had very little stock due to the ration restrictions and the introduction of clothing coupons. Clothes from wholesale stockists could only be obtained through coupons, redeemed from customers. As there was very little in the shop to sell, it was difficult to produce these and prove to wholesalers that there was a demand.

One day, Joan and another colleague decided to see if there was anything in the cellar that they could bring into use for stock, as the shop was looking very bare. They found a chest of drawers in a corner but it could not be easily opened due to the damp atmosphere. Eventually, they prised the drawers open and discovered many items, including taffeta bridesmaids dresses, which had been put away, seemingly 'for the duration'. They made up a window display with some of the clothes. Their pride in their resourcefulness was short-lived however, as a passer-by was heard referring to the shop as selling stock which appeared to be 'what came out before the ark'!

If clothing was difficult to obtain, new shoes were almost impossible to find at times, even if enough points were accumulated. Joan and Mary decided to wear clogs for while and thereby spare extra wear and tear on their shoes. They were rather surprised to find that the clogs had wooden soles and were studded with hobnails. It did not take them long to discover that it was difficult to walk any distance wearing them as they were just too uncomfortable. Also, if the wood splintered or was rough, there was a good chance of a ladder or hole appearing in a very precious pair of stockings.

During the war, their brother Edward became eligible to be called up for service in either the armed forces or other war work. Freddie Grout, who owned Yeoman Garage, offered to employ him in his machine shop. The garage's usual business of supplying petrol was limited due to restrictions and rationing, so Freddie took on different contracts which assisted the war effort and employed local people. The garage employees finished aircraft parts. It was known locally that Freddie Grout regarded it as his patriotic duty to employ people on this sort of work. The majority of the contracts involved assembling parts for planes which were delivered in packs in a rough state. They were then prepared, drilled and tapped, machined and assembled.

Despite all the restrictions imposed through rationing, Joan recalled that one of the very worst aspects about the war was the bombing of the towns and cities. The very act of bombing, that people could inflict such horrific damage on each other, was a major shock.

Mary remembered that after the first night of bombing in England when the London docks were attacked by the Luftwaffe, the blaze was clearly visible from Wrotham Hill as she travelled there on a bus. The journey came to an abrupt end when they reached the High Street at New Cross. Mary remembered the bus coming to a halt by some two-storey shops as the air raid siren sounded. She was advised to head for a shelter of some sort as it would not be long before the German airplanes would be overhead. All the passengers took shelter at one end of a nearby school building. The raid continued for many hours. When Mary emerged after the all clear signal sounded, she found the scene was reminiscent of Dante's Inferno. The two storey shops were all destroyed. The air was permeated with a smell which was a mixture of cordite, smoke and gas. Nothing was clearly visible as dust hung in the air like fog. The smell of gas came from a broken mains pipe in the wrecked road and small fires, which had not been wholly extinguished, lingered in areas that were blocked with shattered fragments of buildings. She was extremely lucky; the opposite end of the school in which she had sheltered had also been bombed and partially destroyed.

Mary could also vividly remember the bombing of Mill Street in Maidstone which took place 31 October 1941. At this time, Mary was working in Stonham chemists in Bank Street, Maidstone. Fairly early one morning, she caught a bus from Bearsted and was on the way into work when her bus passed a bus stop in the Sittingbourne Road. It was crowded with airmen who were waiting there for transport to Detling. As they went past, Mary noticed that all the men were looking up, watching as a stick of bombs fell from a German plane. The airmen suddenly dropped onto the ground as they realised what was going to happen and tried to take cover. The bus stopped and Mary went no further. Once again, she was immensely lucky; fourteen people died and the back of the chemists premises was destroyed in the subsequent bomb blast in Mill Street.

This photograph shows Mill Street after the bombing and gives an indication of the level of destruction:

Reproduced courtesy of Kent Messenger newspaper group

After an interminable six years of war, the great news of Victory in Europe announced on 8 May 1945 was welcomed with joy. But, of course, hostilities continued in other places in the world; Victory in Japan was not announced until 15 August after atomic bombs had been dropped on Hiroshima and Nagasaki.

And so it was that for some people, that despite this good news, when still faced with continuing struggles of everyday life, bereavement, loss of housing and possessions, it took rather a long time for it to sink in that that there was going to be no more bombing and destruction. However, for the majority of the population, it was enough that the war was over. For the first time in six years, people could now dare to think that there would be a tomorrow, a future was possible, and to enjoy the luxury of making plans.

Peace Regained and Welcome Home

Winifred Harris recalled that on V E Day, some of her family went into Maidstone town centre and stayed until the evening. A very large crowd of people were in the High Street near the town hall, all dancing and talking, even cheering: no more Careless Talk Costs Lives! What was particularly startling was the lack of blackout restrictions - all the street lamps were on and seemed amazingly bright. There was also a big fireworks display held in Mote Park and later there were victory parades by various sections of the armed forces.

A (slightly edited) transcript of the front page, Kent Messenger, 11 May 1945:

THANK GOD FOR VICTORY

GREAT SCENES OF REJOICING IN KENT
AS CROWDS CELEBRATE ON V E DAY

Never in its history has Kent witnessed such memorable scenes as it did on Tuesday, the long-awaited V E Day. Nature opened the day with a thunderous Victory salute, then the dark clouds swept away and the morning was kissed by the sun. The crowds were also early. They came out in their thousands and they were full of rejoicing. It seemed as if almost everyone sported a red, white and blue rosette.

Red, white and blue! It was astonishing where it all came from. Girls had blouses and skirts, made from Union Jacks. Men wore red, white and blue tam o'shanters. Even cats and dogs had 'necklaces' of red, white and blue, while horses had loin cloths made from Union Jacks. Kent streets have never blazed with so much colour before. Flags, streamers, bunting, coats of arms and golden crests adorned every street. Men and women queued up on Monday for any bunting they could get. Some people were offering as much as £5 for a Union Jack. Nearly all the kiddies waved their flags, and perambulators were decorated.

There appeared to be a little reserve at first. After years of war it was difficult to give way to one's feelings. But as the day proceeded they captured the Victory spirit. Hands were linked, girls kissed Servicemen - and Servicemen even kissed policeman - and the fun began. But before that the church bells pealed joyfully and thousands went to church to render their thanks.

Hardest worked people were the publicans and their assistants. The taverns were packed and it was difficult to get served. They had extensions to midnight in most places, but 'Sold Out' notices were being displayed long before that. Free drinks for men in uniform was the order of the day in a number of 'pubs'. Many publicans of long experience report record takings.

The kiddies were not forgotten. Street teas were held by the score, people giving up their rations to provide the food. The streets became even denser with people in the evening. Bonfires and beacons lit the county, and effigies of the Nazi gangsters met a popular fate. The people were happy and excited but orderly. There was restraint in their joy.

It was as though they were always conscious of the fact that there are battles still to be won.

Reproduced courtesy of Kent Messenger newspaper group

People in Bearsted and Thurnham also organised celebrations. Houses were decorated: the outside of Bearsted Cottage in particular bore an enormous 'V for Victory' and there were street parties. The residents of Sutton Street held one of these and almost certainly followed the pattern of many other street parties; tables were covered with sheets to serve as tablecloths and from nowhere appeared all sorts of good things for the children and adults to eat. The ample supply of sandwiches, cakes, jellies and blancmange must have only been possible through each family making a contribution from their carefully stored small supply of 'luxury' items. Few would have guessed six years previously how groceries viewed as everyday and mundane would have become precious.

Everyone that lived in Sutton Street remembered the street party that was held to celebrate the end of the war and decided they rather liked it! As a result, street parties were held in Sutton Street for several years afterwards. This photograph shows one such party. Few photographs of the local celebrations were taken: film and developing chemicals were virtually impossible to obtain, so this slightly later party provides a good impression of a typical event.

Reproduced courtesy of Rosemary Pearce

People living in Shirley Way also organised activities which included a massive bonfire built on open land which is now the site of the roundabout in the road, hopefully nowhere near the public air raid shelter! Rowland Fairbrass's uncle, who was in the army, was home on leave at the time so the celebrations were assisted by the generous donation and then detonation of some army thunder flashes!

This photograph was taken in Shirley Way in front of an unlit bonfire. From the left hand side, the photograph includes Len Mercer, Bill Fairbrass, Herbert Coales, Ron Fairbrass (Rowland's uncle), Jimmy Hadley, Mr Benger, James Strettle, and Mr Rayner-Sharp. The front row includes Mr Passmore and John Coales in RAF uniform, as he was home on leave at the time.

Reproduced courtesy of Edith Coales

Peace Regained and Welcome Home

The following two photographs were also taken at the celebrations in Shirley Way. Included in this photograph are Grace Baker, Mollie Carr, Pat Liverton, Peter Trott, John Munn, Nurse Beeton Pull and Jean Harvey:

Reproduced courtesy of Allen Carr

This photograph includes Nurse Beeton Pull in the centre of the back row, Raymond 'Bubbles' Feakins and Trevor Osborne:

Reproduced courtesy of Tony and Sheila Foster

Doris Britcher and Joyce Bourne (née Palmer) recalled that Mr Grout also arranged a marvellous sports day to celebrate the ending of the war. Cavendish Way was used as the sports ground and a starting pistol was unearthed so that the events could be started correctly. Hilda, Muriel and Rita, sisters to Doris, all participated. Hilda was a gifted athlete and won so many of the races that Mr Grout asked her to stand down from some of the events in order to give the other children a chance! The prizes were books of savings stamps.

Peace Regained and Welcome Home

As so many people from Bearsted and Thurnham had served in the armed forces, the parish councils decided to work together and established a joint committee to consider ideas for an official Welcome Home celebration. It was agreed that souvenir scrolls would be presented and a dinner or concert held, if funds allowed. Recipients would be any man or woman who served in the forces between 1939 and 1945, having joined up before Victory over Japan Day, and included all the Merchant Services.[1]

In order to establish a list of those who should be invited, the committee members checked a card index held at the Bearsted branch of the British Legion, the Services Voting Register, subscriptions lists for the parish magazine and records held by the Red Cross. It was found that far more people than they had originally envisaged were eligible, so it was thought that around £500 needed to be raised to cover costs. It is not clear whether this amount was actually raised, but it was also quickly agreed that if there were any surplus funds, they would be passed onto the British Legion.[2] Collection tins were distributed and posters, such as that shown here were printed: [3]

BEARSTED & THURNHAM FORCES WELCOME HOME FUND

President : Mr. W. H. WHITEHEAD.
Hon. Treasurer: Mr. A. BARKER, Little Snowfield, Bearsted
Committee : Mrs. Markwick, Miss Sage, Rev. W. H. Yeandle, Messrs. L. R. S. Monckton. R. Skinner, E. A. Abery, W. B. Barnes, H. Humphrey, F. W. Grout, R. L. Lord, J. Flood, A. S. Perrin, Hon. Sec.

£500 WANTED

to welcome the men and women of the two parishes (over 300 in number) who have served in H.M. Forces.

Your help is invited.

Contributions, small or large, will be gratefully received by any of the above.

Reproduced courtesy of Kent History and Library Centre

Peace Regained and Welcome Home

In order to accommodate the number of people expected to attend, it was arranged to hold two separate concerts which would take place during September 1946 and October 1947.

Here is a card and letter of invitation: [4]

Subscribers to the
Bearsted & Thurnham Forces Welcome Home
Fund
request the pleasure of the company of
_____
at a
Smoking Concert
to be held at the
Women's Institute, on Saturday, 28 SEP. 1946,
at 7 p.m.

R.S.V.P   PLEASE PRESENT THIS CARD AT THE DOOR.

BEARSTED & THURNHAM FORCES WELCOME HOME FUND.

Hon. Sec. A. S. Perrin,
"Wendings,"
Roseacre Lane,
BEARSTED

Dear

The people of Bearsted and Thurnham, who have subscribed to the above Fund, extend a most hearty welcome to you to attend the first of a series of Smoking Concerts, arranged for Saturday, 28 SEP. 1946 at the Women's Institute. As admission will be by card only, you are requested to present the enclosed official invitation card upon arrival.

This informal gathering is being held to welcome you back amongst your friends and to mark their appreciation of your past services. A most attractive programme of entertainment by Miss Colleen Clifford and her party of Radio and Television Artists has been arranged; there will be a buffet supper with both beer and soft drinks, in fact the whole evening is being organised in that spirit of happy informality which they feel would be your wish.

Please come along if you possibly can, and in order to help the ladies who have kindly undertaken the very difficult job of catering, will you please complete and post the enclosed postcard to reach me by September 15th, at the latest. You will appreciate how essential it is that the number attending should be known in good time.

Yours truly,

A S Perrin

Hon. Secretary,
Bearsted and Thurnham Forces Welcome Home Fund.

2nd September, 1946.

Reproduced courtesy of Kent History and Library Centre

This is one of the commemorative certificates presented at the concerts:

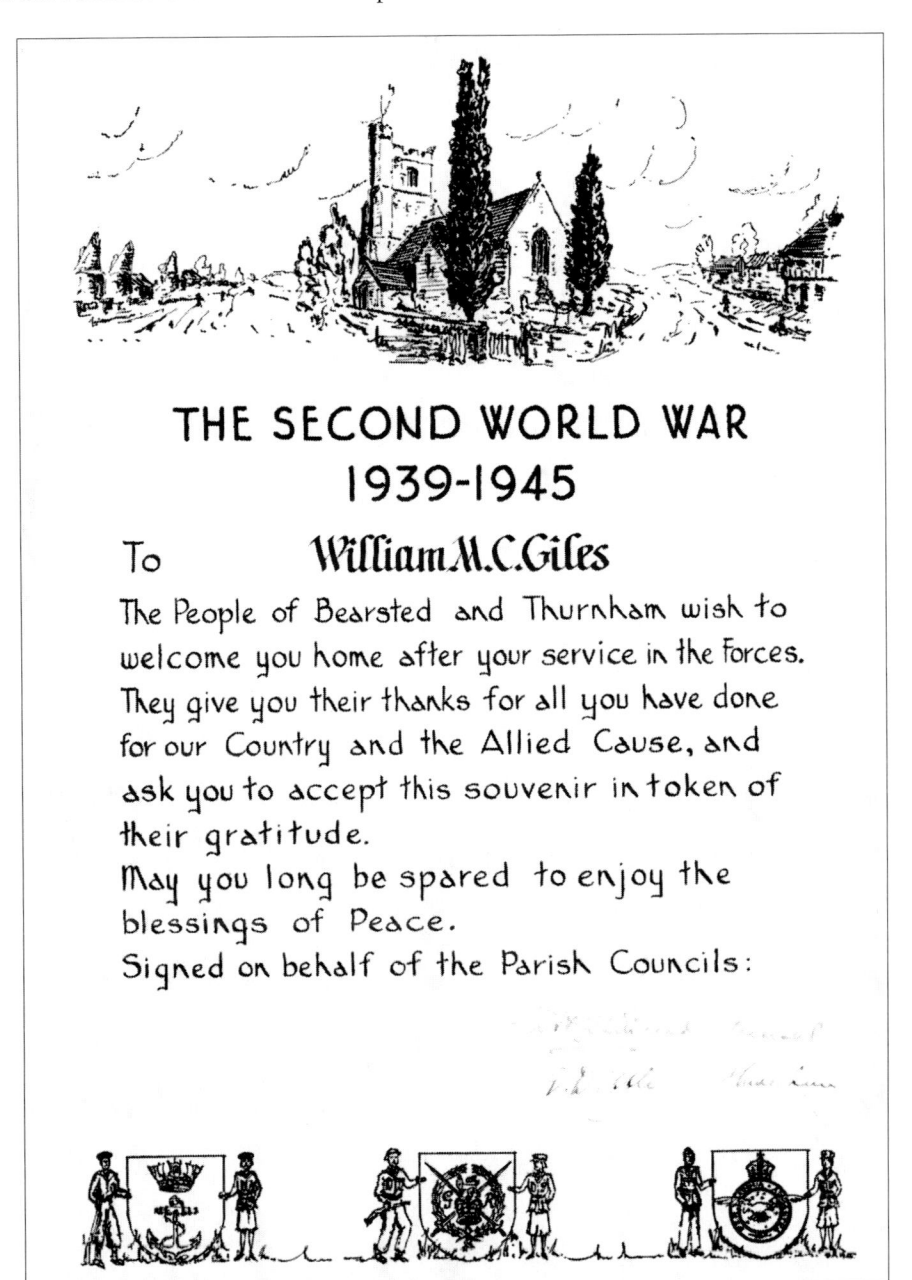

THE SECOND WORLD WAR
1939-1945

To William M.C. Giles

The People of Bearsted and Thurnham wish to welcome you home after your service in the Forces. They give you their thanks for all you have done for our Country and the Allied Cause, and ask you to accept this souvenir in token of their gratitude.

May you long be spared to enjoy the blessings of Peace.

Signed on behalf of the Parish Councils:

Reproduced courtesy of Norah Giles

The concerts were well received, but Harold Yeandle, the vicar of Bearsted, was aware that more was needed as people required space and time to adjust to everyday life once the hostilities were over. He decided that a list of what Bearsted and Thurnham could offer to returning servicemen and former Prisoners of War for leisure and recreation was required. With the assistance of the Parochial Church Council, he then compiled a small booklet called *Life in Bearsted: Towards Community*.[5] All members of the armed forces were given a copy upon their return to Bearsted. Of course, many of these clubs and societies took a considerable time to restart their activities; some struggled to hold meetings and some did not recommence at all. However, a start towards normal life was made by the majority of the organisations and the residents of the two villages as Britain began the first steps towards a post-war recovery, reconstructing and rebuilding the economy in peacetime.

War memorials and records in Bearsted and Thurnham

The effects of the two World Wars were so apparent that they could never be ignored. The daily problems of war and its immediate aftermath at home were as nothing compared to the dislocating pain of bereavement. Families in Bearsted and Thurnham felt that recent events, and sacrifices made, needed to be commemorated in some way.

First World War

During and after the First World War, many communities and villages compiled lists of everyone who served the country in some way during the hostilities; the Chairman of Bearsted Parish Council asked for names of all serving members in the community to be noted so that a Roll of Honour might be kept. A Roll of Service was also compiled for Thurnham, but it is not clear who either decided to do this or undertook the work. It was written in red and black ink with white highlighting, in flowing calligraphy, mounted on cardboard with a wooden frame, and hung for many years in St Mary's church. Nearly a hundred years have elapsed since it was first displayed Almost inevitably, parts of the record have now deteriorated through the ingress of damp and the work of silverfish, rendering much of it sadly illegible particularly for names in the latter part of the alphabet. This is a detail from the Thurnham Roll of Service:

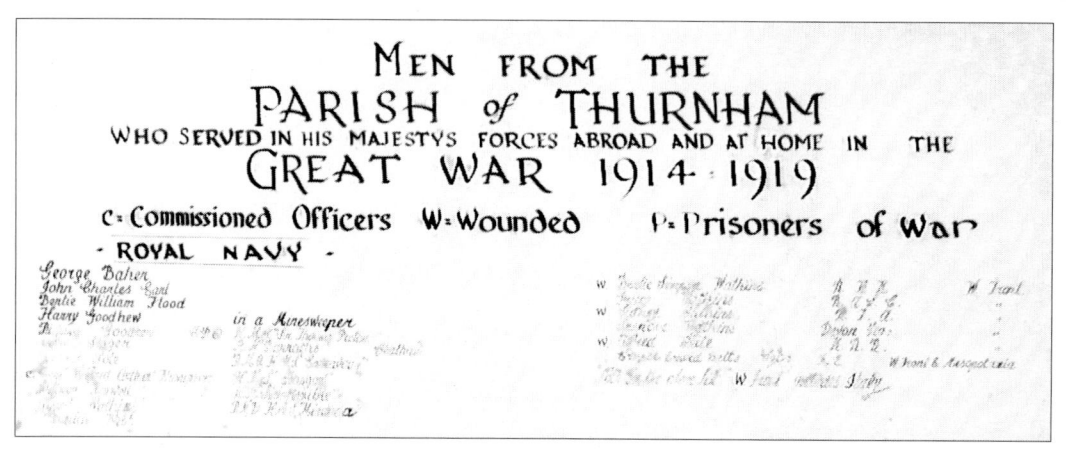

Reproduced courtesy of St Mary's church

The Rev Frederick Blamire Brown, vicar of Bearsted, had a more elaborate and, as it has turned out, rather more durable scheme. In 1919 he began to compile details of all the people in Bearsted who gave wartime service; those who rendered, as he said 'Dutifulness and Endurance'. The details were put into a booklet published in 1920 and three hundred copies were printed. This is a detail from the booklet:

And yet all of these initiatives, excellent as they were, did not seem sufficient. Early in 1916, Frederick was conscious that Bearsted had already sustained eleven casualties and so decided to begin discussions about a possible war memorial.[1] Mr W D Caroë, a well-respected church architect, was approached for some designs and following the receipt of several ideas, which included a wayside shrine for location on the Green and a crucifix, local opinion was sought. The ideas met a rather wary response. There was some overall support but at least one parishioner was of the very firm opinion that there was a danger that it could become a tomb to the living: his son was due to be deployed and he felt that he could not bear to pass something everyday which might eventually include his son's name upon it.

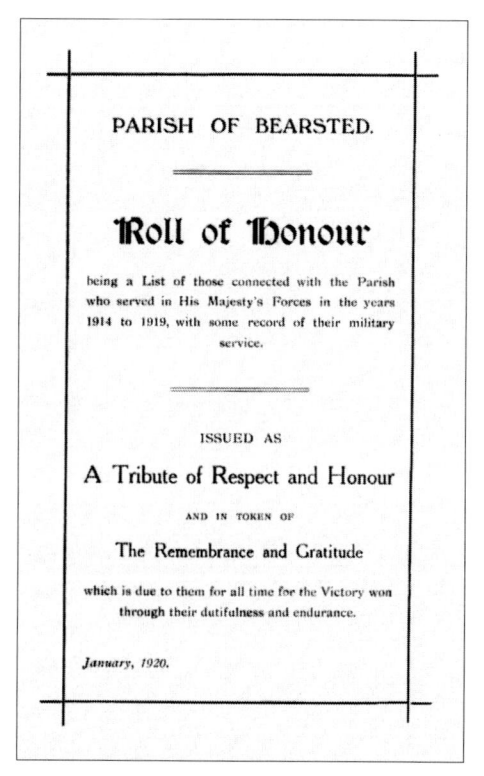

Reproduced courtesy of Evelyn Pearce

Perhaps the idea of a memorial was a little premature, but Mr Caroë was asked for a further design and by the time this was delivered in 1917, support had certainly grown in Bearsted. The new design included a plain cross on an octagonal base and the suggested materials were brick and stone.[2]

After the armistice, a war memorial committee for Bearsted was formed under the Chairmanship of General Whitacre Allen. He was assisted by Mr Jones and Mr Tasker, together with Mr Harman, Mr Watts and Mr Charles Wilkinson. Although the concept of a plain cross was well-regarded, other ideas for memorials which were considered included raising money for disabled soldiers, supporting needy and bereaved relatives in some manner, a stained glass window in the church, a war shrine on the Green, a memorial tablet and a new chalice for the church.[3]

Frederick Blamire Brown, General Whitacre-Allen and the committee, considered all of these in ideas turn, but what seemed to prevail was the idea of simple stone cross with the names of all the fallen from Bearsted would be engraved upon it. This in itself was a radical departure from previous traditions and perhaps, marked a change in democracy and society - previously the names on memorials had largely been confined to people of influence and wealth in local communities. An area by Holy Cross church was felt to be a suitable site and which could be accessible by all. The location would be a closed area of the graveyard which was felt was more appropriate, rather than the previously suggested west wall. As this area had been closed to all burials in 1880, special permission had to be granted by the Diocese.[4]

This photograph is believed to show an experimental model which was almost certainly made to provide to give an indication of the dimensions and appearance of the real memorial. Although dated 1919, there are no further details about this image, including the identity of the man standing next to the model, but it would be good to think that it was Mr Caroë, looking at his design:

Reproduced courtesy of Holy Cross church and Kent History and Library Centre

Construction was undertaken by Messrs Corben and Son of Maidstone and the stone masons were led by Mr W H Kirk, Mr A Grayland, Mr H Palmer, Mr W Bowyer and Mr H Holloway. The cost was covered by the funds raised; around £270. The memorial was unveiled and dedicated 31 October 1919.[5] John Blamire Brown recalled that following a discussion with his father, one of the toy lead soldiers from the vicarage nursery was incorporated in the foundations as a tribute from the children of the village.

A partial transcript of the very full report from the Kent Messenger, 1 November 1919:

Memorial Cross Dedicated

Full of exquisite beauty and great solemnity was the service at the Church of the Holy Cross, Bearsted, on Thursday afternoon in commemoration of the villagers who have fallen in the war, and for the dedication of the memorial cross erected in the churchyard.

The business premises in the village were closed during the service; the flag of St George flew from the church tower at half mast, whilst a half muffled peal was rung on the bells. The chantry was reserved for relatives of the fallen, and the nave was reserved for some 60 men and women who had seen service with the colours. Not only was the church crowded, but many were unable to obtain admission...

The Vicar conducted the service...At the close of the prayers the Last Post was sounded as the congregation stood in silence. From the chancel steps, the Bishop delivered an eloquent address...The choir and clergy, with the processional crosses and banners, and followed by the congregation, then proceeded to the churchyard, where the cross had been erected.

Mr W H Whitehead, Chairman of the Parish Council, then presented to the Bishop the petition requesting him to dedicate the memorial, which he did, committing it to the care of the Vicar and Churchwardens. The hymns 'When I Survey the Wondrous Cross', 'The Cross, The Cross,' and the Te Deum were sung during the dedication, and the Reveille sounded.

At the close of the service the flag was hoisted to the top of the mast and a peal was rung on the bells.

The cross, which stands 24 feet high, has a base of five tiers and is worked in Clipsham stone. The inscription reads: 'In thankful remembrance of the Cross of Christ and of the men of Bearsted, who laid down their lives.'

The names of the 25 men who fell are inscribed in panels...

Reproduced courtesy of Kent Messenger newspaper group

The war memorial in Bearsted churchyard formed a focal point for the local commemoration of Armistice Day and later, Remembrance Sunday. This photograph is undated but gives a good overall impression of the church as a backdrop to the quiet dignity of the memorial:

Reproduced courtesy of Robin Rogers

St Mary's church has several memorials to the First World War: in addition to the Roll of Service there is an engraved brass plaque and a stained glass window shown below. The latter two were both dedicated on 5 June 1920. A partial transcript of a report of the dedication report from the Kent Messenger appears on the next page:

THIS WINDOW IS DEDICATED TO THE GLORY OF GOD AND IN MEMORY OF
THE MEN OF THURNHAM PARISH,
WHO FELL IN THE GREAT WAR 1914 - 1918.

	PERCY BAXTER,	
GEORGE HENRY PENFOLD,	STANLEY CROFT,	ROBERT RICHARD ROSE,
GEORGE VERNON HOLMES,	THOMAS SLENDER,	GEORGE HENRY COOPER,
GEORGE JAMES CLARKE,	ALFRED COTTERELL,	ERNEST ALBERT WHITE,
ANDREW DAVID CATHCART	CHARLIE CROUCHER,	FRANK WHITE,
JOHN WILLIAM SAGE,	HORACE CHAPMAN,	EDGAR SWIFT,
LEOPOLD GRAHAME STERN,	LESLIE WATKINS,	THOMAS SIMPSON.

Reproduced courtesy of Michael Perring and Roger Vidler

THURNHAM'S WAR MEMORIAL

Stained Glass Window Dedicated

On Monday evening, Thurnham Church was crowded on occasion of the dedication of a handsome stained glass memorial window in honour of the nineteen Thurnham heroes who made the grand sacrifice in the Great War. The service, which was characterised by much impressiveness, commenced with the processional choir being followed up the aisle by the Rev F J Blamire Brown (Bearsted), S R Wigan (vicar) and the Bishop of Dover. Colonel A Wood Martyn unveiled the window, which was dedicated by the Bishop, who read the names of the men.

After the singing of 'For all the saints, who from their labours rest', the Bishop preached from the text 'Greater love hath no man than this: that a man lay down his life for his friends'. He reminded those who had lost loved ones that with their natural sorrow must come a feeling of reverent pride at the thought that it was through their hopes, and brothers, and others like them, in all parts of the country that our land today was safe by God's mercy. It was fitting that those who had bravely given of their lives should never be forgotten, and the memorial window would through generations be the beautiful reminder of what the brave lads of Thurnham did in the Great War. The concluding hymn was 'O God, our help in ages past', and the National Anthem was also sung. Mr Gardner presided at the organ and at the conclusion, impressively played the Dead March.

The memorial window, which is on the south side of the church, is a beautiful representation of St Michael and St George - executed by Messrs Heaton, Butler and Rayne, of Garrick Street, London. Below the window, upon a brass tablet, are the names of the men, engraved by Mr R C Godden, of Maidstone.

Reproduced courtesy of Kent Messenger newspaper group

Second World War

After the Second World War, Thurnham parish council arranged for a simple, but elegant, wooden memorial plaque to be placed in St Mary's church, recording the names of those who died in the war. A Roll of Honour and Service, similar to that produced for the First World War was also framed and hung in the porch of the church. This photograph shows the wooden plaque:

TO THE MEMORY OF THE MEN
OF THURNHAM PARISH WHO
DIED IN THE WAR 1939-1945

CHARLES H.D. FROST
WALTER COOKSON   JOHN A. GILBERT
ROBERT G. GUEST   THOMAS HARRISON
JESSE G. HUNT   FREDERICK LOCKYER
JOHN C. MACIVER   REGINALD PENNEY
THOMAS R. SCOTT   WARDEN A. WICKS

Reproduced courtesy of Michael Perring and Roger Vidler

War memorials and records in Bearsted and Thurnham

In 1946, Rev Harold Yeandle received several suggestions from parishioners about the possibility of turning the Milgate Chantry at Holy Cross church into a war memorial chapel. But, Mr Yeandle was aware that this was not going to be a straightforward matter as the chantry was regarded as private property and he would have to approach the owners. He therefore wrote to Captain and Mrs Bence at Milgate House, about the matter. Captain Bence carefully considered the matter before regretfully refusing the idea.[6]

However, it was decided to go ahead with another idea; a war memorial committee was formed under the Chairmanship of Harold Yeandle. The committee comprised the two churchwardens from Holy Cross, representatives from the parish council, the Methodist church, the British Legion, the Women's Institute, and the Men's Institute.[7]

After the first meeting of the committee in November 1946, a list of names was drawn up for inclusion on the memorial and this was then advertised in the parish magazine for amendments and alterations. There was one amendment: Pamela Lawrence's parents requested that her maiden name of Thorpe be added. The committee decided that the names of two civilian war dead would also be included because the nature of the conflict had been one of total war.[8]

In keeping with the existing details of the memorial, all the names would be rendered in lettering which matched that already used, and to also avoid unnecessary distinctions, the details of rank and service would be omitted. After consultation with several companies, Messrs Witcombe and Son of Maidstone were engaged to undertake the work.[9]

Witcombe and Son had soon assessed the existing memorial and advised that the idea of using part of the existing memorial was feasible but problematic. Due to the various sizes and design of the steps, it would not be possible to keep to strict alphabetical order but names would be fitted in wherever possible. Nevertheless, the company had every confidence that an harmonious whole would be achieved. The cost was estimated to be around £33 and was met by a grant from proceeds of Bearsted Fayre.[10]

Reproduced courtesy of Malcolm Kersey

After the alterations, the memorial was unveiled and re-dedicated in a service held in Bearsted churchyard on 17 June 1947. The following special prayer was used:

> In the Faith of Jesus Christ, we re-dedicate this Cross to the Glory of God and in memory of those who gave their lives in the Two World Wars for Freedom, in the Name of the Father, and of the Son, and of the Holy Ghost. *Amen*

Reproduced courtesy of Jenni Hudson

The inscription was unveiled by Mr Thomas R Lee, late Company Quarter Master Sergeant of the 2nd Battalion, Royal Warwickshire Regiment, who had been held as a prisoner of war in Germany from 1940 to 1945. As he undertook the unveiling, Thomas said these words:

> ...on behalf of those who served in the war, I unveil the memorial in tribute to those who will not return. We remember the sacrifice with gratitude and we hold their memory in honour. May their souls rest in peace and may we preserve the freedom for which they died...

Reproduced courtesy of Holy Cross church

Wreaths were laid by Mr A H Holtum and Mr E A Abery on behalf of the Bearsted and Thurnham branch of the British Legion. Mr Skinner and Mr Gregg also laid wreaths on behalf of Bearsted School parents and the Old Scholars Association.[11]

This is the front of service booklet:

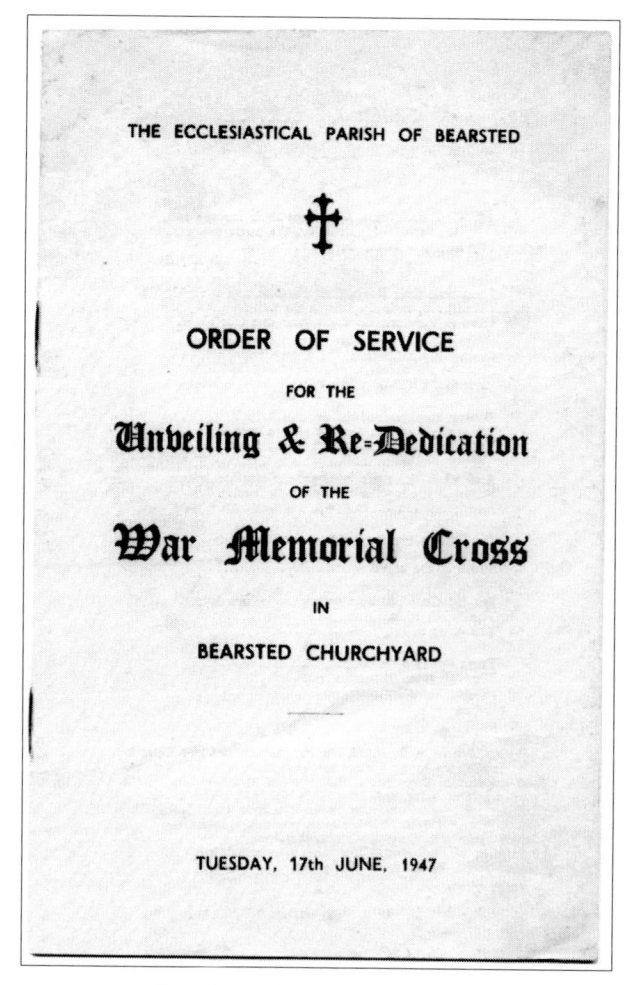

THE ECCLESIASTICAL PARISH OF BEARSTED

✝

ORDER OF SERVICE

FOR THE

Unveiling & Re-Dedication

OF THE

War Memorial Cross

IN

BEARSTED CHURCHYARD

TUESDAY, 17th JUNE, 1947

Reproduced courtesy of Jenni Hudson

Holy Cross church also has a memorial stained glass window that is dedicated to the memory of William Hugh Parkin and the crew of *HMS Glorious*. The window replaced one of Victorian design that had been badly damaged by bomb blasts during the war. The church authorities took the opportunity that the installation of the new window provided to make a number of changes to the building. On either side of the east window, and on the north and south sides of the sanctuary, were six paintings of saints. Below these were panels of coloured tiling. Permission was given for all the decoration to be removed. It was hoped that by simplifying the setting, the window could be given greater prominence. The pictures of the saints were carefully reframed and hung elsewhere in the church. The new window was commissioned by the Whitehead family and designed by Mr Francis H Spear, ARCA, FRSA, of Stanmore, Middlesex. He was an artist in stained glass who made his own materials in his studio. The theme of the new window was the Lord in Glory.

In this photograph can be seen the finished window. The centre light shows Christ seated on the Throne of Glory, with the earth as His footstool. In the tracery above are the emblems of Christ's passion. The left and right hand lights contain images of the patron saints of the armed forces. On the left is Saint George, wearing armour and holding a palm branch; emblematic of martyrdom. Below him is Saint Nicholas, the patron saint of sailors. He is holding a representation of *HMS Glorious*.

Reproduced courtesy of Roger Vidler

In the right hand light is St Michael, 'Captain of the Hosts of the Lord', holding a flaming sword outstretched. He became, by common consent, the patron saint of the RAF. Above him is Saint Stephen. He is emblematic of Civil Defence workers and all others, not in the three main armed services, but who lost their lives in the war. At the foot of the left hand light are the arms and crest of the Parkin family. Slightly above them is the crest of *HMS Glorious*; a Tudor rose, from which emerges rays of gold and silver.

At the foot of the right hand light are the arms of the See of Canterbury and the County of Kent. The original inscription was slightly amended. It was planned that it would read:

> May the Lord in Glory mercifully receive William Hugh Parkin and those aboard *HMS Glorious* who perished with him, and the men and women from Bearsted, who died that we may live.

However, it was realised that because there had only been one female casualty, Pamela Lawrence, that this would read awkwardly, so it was amended to read: [12]

> May the Lord in Glory mercifully receive William Hugh Parkin and those aboard *HMS Glorious* who perished with him, and all others from Bearsted and elsewhere, who died that we may live.

Both reproduced courtesy of Holy Cross church

This photograph shows the detail of Saint Nicholas:

Reproduced courtesy of Roger Vidler

On 18 January 1948, on his thirteenth birthday, William Parkin unveiled the window that was dedicated to his father and the 1,200 other members of the crew that had also died. The service was conducted by the Vicar of Bearsted and the dedication was made by the Bishop of Dover, the Right Rev A C W Rose. The Bishop also preached on the Communion of Saints.

Robert Skinner, Headmaster of Bearsted School, recorded the names of the five Old Scholars who were killed in the war on a memorial sundial. It was erected at the front of the school and on 27 July 1949 dedicated by the Bishop of Dover. Although Mr Skinner had hoped to obtain a printed copy of an order of service, there was not time. Instead there was a duplicated typed sheet in which he advised that that he hoped to prepare a printed leaflet about the memorial in due course.[13]

A transcript of the service sheet:

> A prayer for the school
>
> A prayer of thanks for the school founders and benefactors
>
> A prayer of General Thanksgiving
>
> Psalm 23 (sung by the school)
>
> The Dedication of the Sundial by the Rt Rev, the Bishop of Dover
>
> A prayer for the fallen
>
> The Lord's Prayer
>
> Hymn 128 from The Children's Hymn Book: *Land of our Birth*
> (words by Rudyard Kipling, tune: *Psalmodia Evangelica* 1790)
>
> The National Anthem (verses 1-3)

Reproduced courtesy of Edith Coales

This photograph accompanied a report in the Kent Messenger newspaper about the service:

Reproduced courtesy of Kent Messenger newspaper group

The children marked Armistice Day later that year by laying a wreath at the sundial and thereby began a tradition at the school for every Remembrance Day. When the school relocated to new premises at The Landway in 1972, the sundial was also moved and was placed in the central courtyard of the school. Although the memorial was subsequently moved and is now set in a beautiful garden, a Remembrance Service continues to be held in recognition of the sacrifice made by the Old Scholars.[14]

Appendix 1

Further entries for both World Wars

First World War

BAIRD, William Dodds Haldane
10 Warrender Park Crescent, Edinburgh
Single
Parents Mr and Mrs William Baird of Edinburgh
112th Squadron, Royal Air Force
Lieutenant
Air Force Cross
Killed over Bimbury 22 November 1918, aged 23
Buried in grave J101, Edinburgh (Morningside) Cemetery, Scotland

After the Armistice had been signed, William Baird was one further casualty who lost his life in the skies above Thurnham in 1918. Although not strictly a casualty of war, nonetheless he was still a serving officer. A transcript of a report which appeared 30 November 1918, of the Coroner's inquest:

A YOUNG AIRMAN KILLED

Fatal Descent Near Thurnham

Lieut. W D H Baird, a young airman from Throwley, was killed on Friday while returning to his station.

Belonging to Edinburgh, Lieut. Baird, who was about 23 years of age, was well known in sporting circles in the North, especially as a boxer and a Rugby Footballer. He was an experienced flyer and had rendered excellent service in France. On Friday morning, November 22nd, he came over to Detling, in a single-seater and on leaving, climbed about 3,000 feet, when he proceeded to loop. Accordingly to a fellow officer, who witnessed the ascent, while on top of the loop the machine 'flicked round to the right', its left wing dropped and it commenced to sideslip, tail first, with deceased on his back. It continued to spin until about 3,000 feet, when it appeared to right itself, but only temporarily. Deceased, had by now probably lost consciousness, and the machine crashed down. It was found in fragments at Bimbury Farm, Thurnham, in the occupation of Mr Murray. Deceased, minus his flying helmet, which he had apparently snatched off to relive the pressure of blood, was in a forward posture, quite dead, from a double fracture of the skull, his forehead being smashed right in.

The body was removed to the Maidstone Barracks, where on Monday afternoon an inquest was held by the Borough Coroner, Mr W H Day, without a jury. Lieut. J Bursey, RAF, who had flown with deceased in France on a similar machine, gave evidence as an eye-witness of the accident, explaining that it was due to the speed of the machine while at the top of the loop - the speed might have been either too fast or too slow. In that case that particular type of machine had a tendency to the flick to the right. In the end he thought deceased lost consciousness through the rush of blood to the head, owing to his having been too long in an upside-down position. Deceased on arrival at Detling had said the engine ran beautifully. He was in good health, and quite sober, on starting to return, having had nothing but teetotal drinks at the mess.

Captain Bent, of the Maidstone Depot, who was called to the scene of the accident, and found the body entangled in the wreckage, described the injuries, and said that in addition to the fractures of the skull, which were the cause of death, there were fractures of one arm and thigh and of both legs above the ankle.

A verdict of Accidental Death was recorded. The body was afterwards removed to Edinburgh for burial

Reproduced courtesy of Kent Messenger newspaper group

Appendix 1

The following marriage entries are found in the registers of St Mary's parish church. They have been included because at least one of the parties was stationed in the area at the time of marriage.

First World War

WHITWORTH, Smith Herbert
aged 30, Sergeant in the Camp of the Royal Sussex Regiment, Thurnham

and

MACKENZIE, Helen
aged 27, of Bexhill
were married 7 August 1915

TOON, Reginald
aged 30, 13th Battalion, Royal Sussex Regiment at Thurnham Camp

and

REEVES, Doris Marion
aged 25, of Ponteland, Northumberland
were married 9 September 1915

Reginald was a Lance Corporal   Service Number 2802
Killed in Action 30 June 1916
Buried in grave III S2   St Vaast Post Military Cemetery, Richebourg-L'avoue, Pas de Calais, France

Second World War

LUDLEN, Edward
aged 26, Royal Air Force, RAF station Detling

and

MORGAN, Mary
aged 25, RAF station Detling
were married 6 December 1941, service conducted by Philip Edwards, Chaplain, RAF

WHITEHEAD, Thomas Wylie
aged 33, Royal Air Force, RAF station Detling

and

VALENTINE, Edna
aged 34, Women's Auxiliary Air Force, RAF station Detling
were married 19 January 1942, service conducted by Philip Edwards, Chaplain, RAF

REDSULL, George William
aged 28, soldier at RAF station Detling

and

ADES, Glades
aged 23, Women's Auxiliary Air Force, RAF station Detling
were married 4 February 1942

Appendix 1

WARRINGTON, Arthur Reginald
aged 21, Royal Air Force, RAF station Detling

and

HAMPTON, Iris Mary
aged 18, Women's Auxiliary Air Force, RAF station Detling
were married 8 April 1942

COWIE, Gordon Stephen
aged 25, Royal Air Force, RAF station Detling

and

BARRETT, Margaret Mary
aged 21, Women's Auxiliary Air Force, RAF station Detling
were married 3 July 1942

KEMP, Mervyn Maurice
aged 24, Airman, Royal Air Force, RAF station Detling

and

SMITH, Joan Maud
aged 24, Munitions worker of 54 Langley Street, Luton, Bedfordshire
were married 15 March 1943, service conducted by Richard M Taylor, Chaplain, RAF station Detling

WALLER, John Reginald
aged 28. Airman, Royal Air Force, RAF station Detling

and

KERRISON, Freda
aged 19, a domestic of 718a Maidstone Road, Wigmore, Gillingham, Kent
were married 8 June 1943, service conducted by Richard M Taylor, Chaplain, RAF station Detling

HARRISON, Arthur
aged 28, Flight Lieutenant, Royal Air Force, RAF station Detling

and

INCHLEY, Ella Joan
aged 26, on domestic duties of 67 Sally Park Road, Sally Park, Birmingham
were married 26 February 1944, service conducted by Chaplain, Royal Air Force Volunteer Reserve

HEATH, Victor Charles,
aged 23, Leading Aircraftman, Royal Air Force, RAF station Hawkinge

and

BUNSTEAD, Jacqueline Mary
aged 20, Aircraft Woman, Women's Auxiliary Air Force, RAF station Detling
were married 9 December 1944, service conducted by T S Haward, Chaplain, RAF

Appendix 1

Other Personnel

The following names were included in the 1945 electoral register for Maidstone as eligible to vote and resident in Thurnham. They have been included here as all of them were serving their country.

Womens Land Army Hostel, Friningham Lodge

CALLARD, Amy	**CLARKE**, Kathleen
EXWORTHY, Ella D	**GOOSSENS**, Fernande
GORDON, Una	**HARRISON**, May
HUGHES, Pamela	**JOHNSON**, Dorothy A
KILLIAN, Kathleen E	**LARCOMBE**, Alma R
MERRICKS, Phyllis	**O'CONNOR**, Constance
PANTREY, Kathleen	**SIM**, Margaret
TAYLOR, Fanny E	**WHITING**, Emily L

NAAFI

The organisation called the Navy, Army and Air Force Institutes, is probably better known by the initials NAAFI. It was created by the government in 1921 to run recreational establishments such as canteens for the armed forces and to sell goods to serving personnel through shops and stores. In 1945 these people were registered as living at the following NAAFI local outlets:

NAAFI staff at RAF station Detling

CLARK, Bertie	**COLE**, James J
COLLINS, Margery M	**DIVALL**, Lena
FISHER, Winifred	**GOLDSMITH**, Rosemary H
GRAVES, Rosina	**KING**, Ella
WINTER, May	

NAAFI staff at Friningham Manor

BELTON, Joan	**HAZELDEN**, Elsie

NAAFI staff at Thurnham Vicarage

CARR, Monica

NAAFI staff at the Tudor House, Ashford Road

BARRY-BARTELLE, James

Appendix 2
Battle of Britain casualties

There were at least two incidents in Thurnham during the Battle of Britain. The first occurred on 8 September 1940; a Hurricane aircraft, registration number P3201, was shot down in enemy action over the Isle of Sheppey during an attack by Luftwaffe aircraft. Sub-lieutenant J C Carpenter of 46 Squadron bailed out but was killed. His body was found by wardens in the vicinity of Green Pastures, Thurnham. He was based at Stapleford Tawney, Essex.[1]

On 15 September 1940, a Messerschmitt Bf109E, of 2/JG53, attacked by Pilot Officer McPhail of 603 Squadron RAF, crashed and burned at about 12.30pm in Gore Wood at Aldington Court Farm. Oberleutnant Rudolf Schmidt, aged 23, bailed out but his parachute failed to open and he fell on the (then) thirteenth green of Bearsted golf course, just north of Chapel Lane. The Revd Arthur Scutt, vicar of St Mary's, noted the same day: [2]

> Much fighting over Thurnham during the Morning Service at 11am.

Reproduced courtesy of St Mary's church

Miss Elsie Attwood remembered that no-one dared to leave the church because of the aerial battles taking place overhead. The Register of Services shows that eleven, rather than the usual five or six people, stayed to receive communion.

The air fights during the Battle of Britain were amongst the most important battles of the war. In September 1940, the air conflict had reached a critical stage and it was later acknowledged that this offensive was the turning point of the whole war.[3] Although few realised it, Britain had begun to benefit from some cumulative effects: despite suffering heavy bombing, the production rate for the aircraft factories was actually double that of Germany, so aircraft could be replaced at a reasonable rate. Britain also had the advantage of conducting air fights over home territory; any British pilot who bailed out of a damaged aircraft over England without serious injury stood a good chance of rejoining the battle. German pilots or air crew members who bailed out were captured as prisoners of war, so there was a steady reduction in their numbers.

This photograph shows the airplane trails formed during combat over Bearsted and was taken in the early evening of 15 September:

Reproduced courtesy of Bill Drake

Appendix 2

Two of the fighter aircraft used by the Luftwaffe had serious limitations in aggressive combat. The Messerschmitt Bf109E had a combat radius of 125 miles. Although the aircraft could escort bombers to London, there was no spare fuel for extensive combat. The Messerschmitt Bf110 was designed as a heavy fighter and carried five machine guns and two cannon, but it did not possess the rapid manoeuvrability that was needed in combat.[4]

On 15 September, 25 Dornier bombers escorted by 120 Messerschmitt Bf109s assembled in the morning and flew over Thurnham towards London. The aim was to provoke the remaining RAF fighter aircraft into action so they could be destroyed.

In the afternoon, a larger force of 475 aircraft with a ratio of 4:1 fighters to bombers, flew across Kent to London and were attacked by larger numbers of RAF fighters. The German High Command believed that the British Fighter Command was so weakened that it could be finally defeated over London.

At the end of the fighting it was estimated that 188 enemy aircraft were destroyed, 54 enemy aircraft were probably destroyed and 78 enemy aircraft damaged. The air campaign faltered as the Luftwaffe crews began to suffer 'Kanalkrankheit': combat stress. Hitler hesitated for three days and then decided to postpone the invasion of Britain. 15 September 1940 later became known as Battle of Britain Day.[5]

Oberleutnant Schmidt was buried on 18 September 1940 in St Mary's churchyard.[6] In compliance with a faculty for the exhumation of German air crew from Kent churchyards, issued by Canterbury Diocese, he was disinterred on 29 October 1961.[7] His body was taken to the German War Cemetery at Cannock Chase, Staffordshire. Thence it was presumably repatriated to Germany as no records of burial at the cemetery can be found.[8]

Michael Perring

Appendix 3
Sources used for
Pamela and George: two lives interrupted by war

The following are some of the many contacts John Franklin made during the research behind the story of Pamela and George. He remains indebted to all of these organisations and individuals for their assistance:

The Aircraft Restoration Company (Propshop Limited)
Building 425, Duxford Airfield, Cambridge CB22 4QR

Air Force Association of Canada   email:aldworth@airforce.ca
Box 2460, Stn D, Ottawa, Ontario, Canada K1P 5W6

Air Historical Branch (RAF)
Ministry of Defence, Room G1, Building 266, RAF Bentley Priory, Stanmore, Middlesex HA7 3HH

The Blenheim Society   http://www.blenheimsociety.org.uk

Mr Robin J Brooks, author *Kent Airfields in the Second World War*

Canadian High Commission
1 Grosvenor Square, London W1K 4AB

Commonwealth War Graves Commission
Enquiries Section, 2 Marlow Road, Maidenhead, Berkshire SL6 7DX

Mr Peter Connon, aviation author and historian

Dumfries & Galloway Aviation Museum
Heathhall Industrial Estate, Heathhall, Dumfries DG1 3PH

Errol Martyn, aviation author based in New Zealand

Friends of War Memorials
4 Lower Belgrave Street, London SW1W 0LA

Rev J Corbyn and the staff in the parish office of Holy Cross church
The Vicarage, Church Lane, Bearsted, Maidstone, Kent ME14 4EF

Kent County Council, Kent History and Library Centre   email: archives@kent.gov.uk
James Whatman Way, Maidstone, Kent ME14 1LQ

Kent County Council; Registrar, Birth Deaths & Marriages
The Register Office, The Archbishop's Palace, Mill Street, Maidstone, Kent ME15 6YE

Kent on Sunday, KOS Media Limited   email: editorial@kosmedia.co.uk
Apple Barn, Hythe Road, Smeeth, Ashford, Kent TN25 6SR

National Archives of Canada, Personnel Records Unit   http://www.archives.ca
Researcher Services Division, Ottawa, Canada K1A 0N3

RAF DPA SAR Section
Room 220, Trenchard Hall, RAF Cranwell, Sleaford, Lincolnshire NG34 8HB

Royal British Legion
Kent County HQ, Royal British Legion Village, Aylesford, Kent ME20 7NY

RCAF Memorial Museum   email: curator@airforcemuseum.ca
P O Box 1000, Station Forces Astra, Ontario, Canada K0K 3W0

Surrey History Centre
Surrey County Council, 30 Goldsworth Road, Woking, Surrey GU21 6ND

Woking News and Mail
Review House, 9 Poole Road, Woking, Surrey GU21 1DY

Veterans UK   http://www.veterans-uk.info/index.htm

Veteran Affairs VAC Canada Remembers   http://www.vac.acc.gc.ca

Women's Auxiliary Air Forces Association
Mrs Florence Mahoney - Hon Secretary, 91 Marina Drive, New Malden, Surrey KT3 6NG

Appendix 4
The Commonwealth War Graves Commission

The work of the Commonwealth War Graves Commission is familiar to many but it may not be widely known that it took some time for the Commission to be established.

In the first two years of the First World War, when a soldier was killed in action on the Western Front, he was often buried in a hastily dug grave. Sometimes the grave was a shell hole. If losses to each unit were heavy, or shelling had continued so that men could not be spared to form burial parties, there were no burials. Soldiers who died of wounds in a Casualty Clearing Station behind the front line or in one of the military hospitals which were set up on the French Coast, were buried in a nearby cemetery, but it was rare for family members to attend. In the absence of a funeral or a grave, many grieving families could only hold memorial services at their local church.

The decision that the bodies of casualties from the armed forces would not be sent home for burial had been made in 1915. Until then, repatriation had been allowed if the family could afford it. In April, Marshal Joffre banned French casualties being returned to their families. There were several reasons for this, but, above all, the authorities were trying to establish equality between the rich and the poor serving their country.

The other members of the Allied Forces followed France's lead but for slightly different reasons: by now, the nature of the fighting, which involved repeated advances and retreats over the same land, frequently made it impossible to retrieve the bodies which had often been hastily interred in nearby shell holes. Given that, at times, the fiercest fighting saw the virtual extinction of entire companies, the home churchyards for brigades particularly formed from specific areas or businesses, sometimes known as 'Pals', would have soon been filled. It was thought that the scale of repatriation and witnessing the mass burials of such brigades would sap the morale of the nation. The decision was an unpopular one; bereaved families were left without graves to visit and a focus for their grief.

The organisation was originally established as the Imperial War Graves Commission by a royal charter in 1917. The principles for were drawn up by the founder, Sir Fabian Ware, who had been concerned that the final resting places of casualties would be lost forever. Early in the First World War, he had set up a unit to record and care for all the graves which had been located. By 1915 the unit's work was recognised by the War Office. Eventually, the unit became part of the British army known as the Graves Registration Commission.[1]

After the war had ended and land obtained for cemeteries and memorials in Europe, the huge task of recording the details of the dead began. By 1918, some 587,000 graves had been identified and a further 559,000 casualties were registered as having no known grave. The Commission was advised on the design of cemeteries and memorials by the architects Sir Edwin Lutyens, Sir Herbert Baker and Sir Reginald Blomfield. Advice concerning landscaping and planting schemes was also sought from eminent gardeners such as Getrude Jekyll.[2]

Three experimental cemeteries were built. Forceville in France was agreed to be the most successful: it was a walled cemetery with uniform headstones in a garden setting and included a Cross of Sacrifice and a Stone of Remembrance. Rudyard Kipling, who had lost his son in the war, suggested the wording for the Stone, 'Their Name Liveth For Evermore' taken from a Biblical text. He also advised on other memorial inscriptions; the best known is that for unidentified soldiers 'A Soldier of the Great War, known unto God'. After some adjustments were made, Forceville and the inscriptions became the templates for all the Commission's cemeteries.[3]

In 1920 Kipling visited a Commission cemetery at Rouen in France. He later commented on being particularly struck by: [4]

> ...the extraordinary beauty of the cemetery and the great care that the attendants had taken of it, and the almost heartbroken thankfulness of the relatives of the dead who were there...

Appendix 4

The work of the Commission continued through every subsequent conflict and has spread throughout the world. Today, it is charged with a duty is to mark and maintain graves of the members of the armed forces from the Commonwealth who were killed in active service. The graves are in dedicated cemeteries but there are also some Commission graves in churchyards, particularly of men who had returned home and later died of their wounds.[5]

The principles of the Commission include that each casualty should be permanently commemorated individually by name on a headstone or memorial. The headstone is of a uniform size with no distinction made on account of military or civil rank, race or creed. The rounded top is to deflect rain. The lettering and details have been specially designed to be easily read by a visitor standing in front of the grave or looking across the rows of headstones.[6]

The Commission also constructs memorials to those who have no known grave. It holds extensive records and registers of casualties from conflicts. There is also a record of civilian war dead from the Second World War. It assists many families with their queries concerning 'lost' family members and has a superb and very informative website.

This photograph shows part of a leaflet which was included in the information that was sent to the bereaved families during the Second World War. It gives an indication of the typical shape and size of headstone design that was used during both wars, although the individual designs varied:

Reproduced courtesy of Louie Smith

Throughout these processes, the Commission endeavoured to keep the families fully advised. Many of the permanent cemeteries have undergone substantial landscaping to provide a setting that is appropriate to the nature of the individual site. Those who have visited the cemeteries frequently express favourable comments upon the dignified tranquillity which can be experienced.

Notes to the text

First World War: 1914 to 1919

1   Holy Cross Parish Magazine July 1917 KHLC reference P18/28/15

2-5   i   http://www.historylearningsite.co.uk/womens_land_army.htm

       ii   p.37 *If War Should Come; defence preparations of the south coast 1935-1939*
Philip MacDougall, Spellmount, 2011

6   Holy Cross Parish Magazine February 1915 KHLC reference P18/28/14

7-15   i   pp.51-52, 87, 137, 281-296, 327, 440, 452 *First Blitz*, Neil Hanson, Corgi 2008

          Neil Hanson also writes (p.452) '...the First Blitz on London during the Great War led to the air defence system, which served so effectively in the Battle of Britain during the Second World War. The ring of fighter bases, the air defence zones, the listening stations, barrage balloon screens, mobile and static anti-aircraft batteries... the communications net and the Operations Room with its giant map table manned by staff plotting the movements of attacking and defending aircraft with the aid of counters and wooden rakes was already in place in 1918. The single exception was the addition of radar...'

       ii   *Disaster to a Fleet of Zeppelins*, Kent Messenger report, 27 October 1917

       iii   p.7 *Maidstone Peace Souvenir*, Maidstone Borough Council and South Eastern Gazette 1919
KHLC reference WKR/BZ/Z31

       iv   p.81 Entry for Maidstone, *East Kent Gazetteer in the Great War*, Hazel Basford and K H McKintosh
East Kent Branch of the Western Front Association 2008

16   i   The batch of aircraft that included this plane was built by the furniture company Waring and Gillow of Hammersmith, London

       ii   I am indebted to David Barnes for this information and research into the history of the Royal Flying Corps, Royal Naval Air Service and Royal Air Force

       iii   p.189 *Aces Falling: war above the trenches 1918*, Peter Hart, Phoenix 2008

17   Holy Cross Parish Magazine February 1916 KHLC reference P18/28/15

18   http://www.historylearningsite.co.uk/rationing_and_world_war_one.htm

19   p.108 *Breadcrumbs and Banana Skins; The Birth of Thrift*, Jacqueline Percival, History Press 2010

20-22   i   *op.cit.* http://www.historylearningsite.co.uk/rationing_and_world_war_one.htm

       ii   pp.12-15 *Rationing in the Second World War Spuds, Spam and eating for Victory,* Katherine Knight
Tempus 2007

       iii   *op.cit.* pp.36-37 *If War Should Come; defence preparations of the south coast 1935-1939*

       iv   Admittance to the workhouse remained as a very real threat to poor families and lasted until the abolition of the institution in 1930. Many families found themselves under increased economic pressures; the main breadwinner was absent and earning low wages in the armed forces, or unable to resume employment through injuries received. Many bereaved families went straight into the workhouse.

23   *op.cit.* http://www.historylearningsite.co.uk/rationing_and_world_war_one.htm

24   *op.cit.* pp.12-15 *Rationing in the Second World War Spuds, Spam and eating for Victory*

25   pp.104-105 *Kent's Care For The Wounded - a record of the work of the Voluntary Aid Detachments*
Paul Creswick, G. Stanley Pond & P H Ashton, Hodder & Stoughton, 1915

Memories of the First World War

1-2   i   p.81 *Detling: a village in Kent*, C E Cornford, Lincoln 1980

       ii   *Blown to Eternity! The Princess Irene Story*, John Hendy, Ferry Publication 2001

3   i   Album 2/13 Box E31, Royal Engineers Library, Brompton Barracks, Chatham

       ii   Bearsted School Log Book 1908-1921 KHLC reference C/ES/18/1/14
Thurnham School Log Book 1906-1933 KHLC reference C/ES/369/1/3

4-5   i   *op.cit. Maidstone Peace Souvenir*

       ii   *op.cit.* p.80 *Detling: a village in Kent*

       iii   Correspondence about the early operations of the aerodrome at Detling
Construction and Equipment Committee NA reference AIR1/146/548/15/51

Notes to the Text

6	i		p.16 *Echoes from the Sky*, Richard N Scarth, Hythe Civic Society 1999
	ii		NA reference AIR1/121/15/40/105
	iii		*op.cit.* p.42 *East Kent Gazetteer in the Great War*
7-10			*op.cit.* p.16 *Echoes from the Sky*
11			pp.57-61 *No Return Tickets*, L Grace Dibble, Stockwell Books 1989
12			pp.25, 29 *The Home Front: civilian life in World War One*, Peter Cooksley

Armistice, Peace and Aftermath

1-4   pp.328, 354, 362, 378-380 *Eleventh month, Eleventh day, Eleventh hour: World War 1 and its violent climax* Joseph E Persico, Random House 2004

5   *op.cit.* Thurnham School Log Book 1906-1933 and Bearsted School Log Book 1908-1921
Curiously, the start of the war had also been marked at Bearsted School by an outbreak of mumps!

6-7   pp.73-78 *The Great Silence 1918-1920: living in the shadow of the Great War,* Juliet Nicolson John Murray 2009

8-9   i   http://www.aftermathww1.com/peaceday2.asp

       ii   Bearsted School had an extended holiday in August 1919 'in accordance with the expressed desire of HM The King as a Peace Holiday'.
op.cit. Bearsted School Log Book 1908-1921

10   i   *op.cit.* p.263 *The Great Silence 1918-1920: living in the shadow of the Great War*

      ii   p.375 *The Unknown Soldier*, Neil Hanson, Doubleday 2005

11   *ibid.* p.266

12-13   *op.cit. Maidstone Peace Souvenir*

14-16   *op.cit.* pp.267-268 *passim. The Unknown Soldier*

It has now become a tradition at royal weddings that the bride's bouquet is subsequently placed on the tomb of the Unknown Soldier. The first bride to do this was Lady Elizabeth Bowes-Lyon after her marriage to the Duke of York in 1923. It is believed that it was a tribute to her late brother the Honourable Fergus Bowes-Lyon, a Captain in the Black Watch who had been killed at Loos on 27 September 1915. However, Princess Mary, the daughter of George V had paid an earlier tribute in 1922, stopping her carriage at the Cenotaph on the return from her wedding to Viscount Lascelles in order to lay her bouquet at the memorial.

17-19   For the majority of this information, and the origins of the Poppy Appeal, I am indebted to an article written by David Randall, Independent On Sunday newspaper, 12 November 2006.

See also the websites for the Royal British Legion (http://www.britishlegion.org.uk) and the Commonwealth War Graves Commission (http://www.cwgc.org.uk).

20   A report about Samuel Green's design was featured in 10 November 2006 edition of the Kent Messenger: Samuel's widow, Lilly, aged 93, was still selling poppies for the appeal!

21   *op.cit.* Royal British Legion website

Second World War: 1939 to 1945

1   pp.115-116 *A School at Bearsted*, Kathryn Kersey, 2003

2   *ibid.* p.205

3   pp.326-329 *Black Diamonds: the rise and fall of an English dynasty*, Catherine Bailey, Penguin 2008

4   *op.cit.* p.121 *A School at Bearsted*

5   Holy Cross Parish Magazine August 1945 KHLC reference P18/28/20

6-14   i   *op.cit.* pp.22-24, 105-107 *Rationing in the Second World War Spuds, Spam and eating for Victory*

       ii   Emergency Planning Committee and Circulars, Bearsted Parish Council 1939-1945
KHLC reference PC252/C/1/4

15   Entries in School Log Book 1933-1959, Bearsted Church of England School
Roseacre School, The Landway

16   Information about Pig Clubs during the war from http://www.britishpigs.org.uk/history5.htm

17-18   i   http://www.uboat.net/allies/commanders/2234.html

       ii   Obituary New York Times, 11 July 1994

Notes to the Text

They Also Served

1-8		pp.1-8 *Put That Light Out! Britain's Civil Defence Services At War 1939-1945*, Mike Brown Sutton Publishing Limited 1999
9		No.410 *Aircraft Casualties* in Kent 1939-1940, Kent Aviation Historical Research Group 1990
10		No.466 *Aircraft Casualties* in Kent 1939-1940, Kent Aviation Historical Research Group 1990
11	i	NA reference WO 199/1800
	ii	pp.90-91 *The Battlefields That Nearly Were*, Michael Foot, Tempus 2006
12	i	pp.96-99 *Penenden Heath's Story*, Robin Ambrose 2010
	ii	It is now widely believed that the Stop Lines, although fairly rudimentary, may well have prevented a wide scale German invasion of Britain but at a cost: many parts of the country around the GHQ Line would have been laid waste, an area which would have undoubtedly included Bearsted, Thurnham and Maidstone.
13-22	i	Emergency Planning Committee and Circulars, Bearsted Parish Council 1939-1945 KHLC reference PC252/C/1/4
	ii	p.391 *Wartime Britain*, Juliet Gardiner, Headline Book Publishing 2005
	iii	*op.cit.* pp.55-58 *Put That Light Out! Britain's Civil Defence Services At War 1939-1945*
23-24		*Bearsted Parish Council: a miscellany of its history*, R A F Cooks 1977 KHLC reference XK Bearsted
25-29	i	Correspondence with Robin J Brooks
	ii	http://www.kentspitfire.co.uk/history/kent/
30		Information from http://www.rocassoc.org.uk/
31		p.31 *One Hundred Years of Golf at Bearsted 1895-1995*, Clive Horton, Bearsted Golf Club 1995
32	i	p.97 *Kent at War*, Bob Ogley, Froglets Publications and the Kent Messenger Newspaper Group 1994
	ii	*op.cit.* pp.92-94 *Rationing in the Second World War Spuds, Spam and eating for Victory*
33		pp.155-162 *Bearsted and Thurnham at Play*, Kathryn Kersey and Ian Lambert, Kathryn Kersey 2008
34-37		*Special Report: Remembering the Little Ships*, 27 May 2010 http://www.railnews.co.uk/news/2010/05/27-special-report-rememberig-the-little.html (*sic*)
38-41	i	Personal recollections of Jessie Page, Vera Banner and Ella Cardwell
	ii	pp.155-157 *A History of the Women's Institute*, Jane Robinson, Virago 2011
	iii	Parish magazine for Bearsted and Thurnham 1940 KHLC reference P18/28/19
42-44		pp.66, 137, 141, 164 *The Children's War*, Juliet Gardiner, Portrait, Piatkus Books Limited 2005

RAF Station Detling

1	i	p.16 *Strategy without slide-rule: British Air Strategy, 1914-1939*, Barry D Powers, Taylor & Francis, 1976
	ii	Notes from Headquarters Home Command, Officers Course, RAF station Detling 1954
2		Operational Records NA reference AIR1/146/548/15/51
3-5	i	*op.cit.* Maidstone Peace Souvenir
	ii	*op.cit.* pp.61-63, *Detling; a village in Kent*
	iii	Correspondence about the aerodrome at Detling, Construction and Equipment Committee NA reference AIR1/146/548/15/51
6		Operational Records NA references AIR1/146/548/15/58 and AIR1/146/548/15/45
7	i	p.73 *Stockbury: A stroll through the past*, Stockbury History Group 2001
	ii	*op.cit.* p.42 *East Kent Gazetteer in the Great War*
	iii	*op.cit.* pp.61, 77 *Detling; a village in Kent*
8		p.27 *Coastal Command 1939-1945*, Ian Carter, Ian Allan Publishing Ltd 2004
9-10	i	K D 14,13 *Kent's Defence Heritage - Gazetteer*, A Saunders, V Smith, Kent County Council 1998
	ii	*op.cit.* p.42 *East Kent Gazetteer in the Great War*
11-12		Memoirs of Sydney Burdett IWM reference PP/MCR/73

Notes to the Text

13-14	i	pp.45-47, 51 *Detling Airfield; a history 1915-1959*, Anthony J Moor, Amberley Publishing 2011
	ii	pp.258-263 *When Colombus Ruled The Skies*, David Collyer, Volume 2, Bygone Kent
15		p.19 *Kent's Own, The History of 500 (County of Kent) Squadron, Royal Auxiliary Air Force* Robin Brooks, Meresborough Books 1982
16		pp.75-76 *Stockbury: A Stroll through the Past*
17		'Great RAF Show for Kent', Report in Kent Messenger newspaper, 13 May 1939
18	i	Operational Records NA reference AIR28/192-198
	ii	In 1945, Emily and Frederick Read were resident at the Church Army hut 1945 Electoral Register for Thurnham, Maidstone Parliamentary Division
19		Oral history recording, Ronald Hay IWM reference ID 13856
20	i	Operational Records 1939 NA reference AIR28/192-198
	ii	Oral History recording Charles Evans IWM reference ID1087
21	i	*op.cit.* p.51 *Detling Airfield; a history 1915-1959*
	ii	*op.cit.* p.29 *Kent's Own: The History of 500 (County of Kent) Squadron*
	iii	Oral history recording, May Winter IWM reference ID 15800
22		Operational Records NA reference AIR28/192
23-24	i	Daphne Pearson, and other George Cross awards http://en.ww2awards.com/award/2#
	ii	http://airpictorial.wordpress.com/2013/07/19/artist-dame-laura-knight/
25		Oral history recording, Norman Barron IWM reference ID 12611
26		Interview with David King, 6 September 2010
27		Oral history recording George Fletcher IWM reference ID158192
28		*op.cit.* Entry for 14 November 1941 in School Log Book 1933-1959, Bearsted Church of England School
29-31		Operational Records NA references AIR28/193 and AIR28/198
32	i	*op.cit.* pp.75-76 *Stockbury: A Stroll through the Past*
	ii	Oral history recording Squadron Leader William Smith IWM reference ID 10472
	iii	Undated report interviewing Josephine Robins, Kent Messenger
33	i	pp.150-156 *Villagers Memories of Wartime Detling,* Joan Brown, Volume 10, Bygone Kent
	ii	Interview with Michael Perring, 21 June 2011
34		*Air Raid Victims Buried*, Kent Messenger newspaper, 24 August 1940
35-36	i	Interview with John Allison, 20 June 2011
	ii	*op.cit.* Undated report interviewing Josephine Robins
	iii	*op.cit.* Interview with David King
37-38	i	Interview with Dorothy Hope; Jean Hope, 4 March 2010
	ii	*op.cit.* pp.75-76 *Stockbury: A Stroll through the Past*
	iii	Oral history recording, Josephine Fairclough (née Robins) IWM reference ID15818
39		*op.cit.* Interview with David King
40		p.46 *The Cinderella Service: Coastal Command 1939-1945*, Andrew Hendrie, Pen & Sword Aviation, 2006
41		A full list of Squadrons and Units based at Detling can be found in *Detling Airfield; a history 1915-1959*
42-43	i	Southern Signals Area HQ, Operational Record Book and Appendices for Detling 1946 to 1947 NA references AIR28/883 and AIR29/1934-1936
	ii	*op.cit.* Interview with David King
44		Kent Messenger, 26 February 1961

Memories of the Second World War

1-2	*op.cit.* p.10 *Rationing in the Second World War Spuds, Spam and eating for Victory*
3-5	*op.cit.* Entries in School Log Book 1933-1959, Bearsted Church of England School
6	Typewritten autobiographical notes by Marion Beeton Pull KHLC reference U3590 Z11/1

Notes to the Text

7-9   *op.cit.* p.45 *Rationing in the Second World War Spuds, Spam and eating for Victory*

Peace Regained and Welcome Home

1-4   Minutes of Welcome Home Fund 1945-1947, Bearsted and Thurnham parish councils KHLC reference P18/29/9

5   *Life in Bearsted: Towards Community*, Harold Yeandle KHLC reference U1401 Z14

War memorials and records in Bearsted and Thurnham

1-5   i   Details from Bearsted War Memorial 1915-1919 KHLC reference P18/6/45

      ii   *op.cit.* p.27 *If War Should Come; defence preparations of the south coast 1935-1939*

6   Correspondence concerning conversion of Milgate Chantry to a war memorial chapel 1946 KHLC reference P18/6/48

7-12   i   Minutes War Memorial Committee 1946-1947 KHLC reference P18/6/49

      ii   Correspondence concerning memorial window *HMS Glorious* 1946 to 1947 KHLC reference P18/6/19

13-14   *op.cit.* p.123 *A School at Bearsted*

Appendix 2 Battle of Britain casualties

1   i   p.55 *Aircraft Casualties in Kent, Part 1: 1939 to 1940*, G G Baxter, K A Owen and P Baldock, Meresborough Books 1990

    ii   Entry for 8 September 1940
        Battle of Britain Historical Society website (http://www.battleofbritain1940.net/0038.html)

2   i   *op.cit.* p.60 *Aircraft Casualties in Kent*

    ii   p.41 *Battle of Britain Day*, Dr Alfred Price, Greenhill Books 2000

    iii   Undated conversation with Ron Gamage about Oberleutnant Schmidt

    iv   Private correspondence between Mr E H Clark and Michael Perring concerning burials of German war dead, dated 10 February 2005

3   Entries for 15 September 1940 Battle of Britain Historical Society website (http://www.battleofbritain1940.net/0041.html and http://www.battleofbritain1940.net/0042.html)

4-5   i   *op.cit.* Entries for 15 September 1940 Battle of Britain Historical Society website

     ii   p.326 *The Most Dangerous Enemy*, Stephen Bungay, Aurum Press 2001

6   *op.cit.* Private correspondence

7   Faculty concerning burial of German war dead, 5 October 1961 KHLC reference P369/6/7

8   Private correspondence between Mr S Lumas, Commonwealth War Grave Commission and Michael Perring, dated 3 January 2006

Appendix 4 The Commonwealth War Graves Commission

1-6   i   Information from the Commonwealth War Graves Commission website http://www.cwgc.org/

     ii   pp.20-21, 26, 32 *Remembered; The History of the Commonwealth War Graves Commission*
        Julie Summers, Merrell 2007

Select Bibliography

Note: this is not an extensive list of books consulted during the research for this book but it is intended as a guide for anyone interested in undertaking further reading or study.

First World War

A Kingdom United - popular responses to the outbreak of the First World War in Britain and Ireland
Catriona Pennell
Oxford University Press 2012

All Quiet on the Home Front - an oral history of life in Britain during the First World War
Richard Van Emden and Steve Humphries
Headline 2003

The British Army of August 1914
Ray Westlake
Spellmount Limited 2005

Catastrophe - Europe goes to war 1914
Sir Max Hastings
William Collins 2013

Defeat at Gallipoli
Nigel Steel and Peter Hart
Papermac 1995

Detling: a village in Kent
C E Cornford
C E Cornford 1980

East Kent Gazetteer in the Great War
Hazel Basford and K H McKintosh
East Kent Branch of the Western Front Association 2008

Echoes from the Sky
Richard N Scarth
Hythe Civic Society 1999

Eleventh month, Eleventh day, Eleventh hour: World War 1 and its violent climax
Joseph E Persico
Random House 2004

First Blitz
Neil Hanson
Corgi 2008

Forgotten Voices of the Great War
Max Arthur
Ebury Press 2002

The Great Silence: 1918-1920 Living in the Shadow of the Great War
Juliet Nicolson
John Murray 2009

No Return Tickets
L Grace Dibble
Stockwell Books 1989

Penenden Heath's Story
Robin Ambrose
Robin Ambrose 2010

Select Bibliography

Remembered. The History of the Commonwealth War Graves Commission
Juliet Summers
Merrell 2007

Tommy: the British Soldier in the First World War
Richard Holmes
Harper Collins 2003

The Unknown Soldier
Neil Hanson
Doubleday 2005

Second World War

Aircraft Casualties in Kent 1939-1940
G G Baxter and P Baldock
Meresborough Books 1990

The Battlefields That Nearly Were: Defended England 1940
William Foot
Tempus 2006

The Battle of Britain
James Holland
Corgi 2011

The Blitz
Juliet Gardiner
Harper Press 2010

The Children's War
Juliet Gardiner
Portrait, Piatkus Books Limited 2005

Detling Airfield: a history 1915-1959
Anthony J Moor
Amberley Publishing 2011

If War Should Come; defence preparations of the south coast 1935-1939
Philip MacDougall
Spellmount, 2011

Kent and the Battle of Britain
Robin J Brooks
Countryside Books 2009

Kent Airfields in the Second World War
Robin J Brooks
Countryside Books 1998

Kent's Own: the history of 500 (County of Kent) Squadron, Royal Auxiliary Air Force
Robin J Brooks
Meresborough Books 1982

Millions Like Us - women's lives during the Second World War
Virginia Nicholson
Penguin 2012

Put That Light Out! Britain's Civil Defence Services at War 1939-1945
Mike Brown
Sutton Publishing 1999

The Royal Air Force - a history
Michael Armitage
Brockhampton 1993

Select Bibliography

Stockbury: A Stroll Through The Past
Stockbury History Group (undated)

They Fought In The Fields: The Women's Land Army - the story of a Forgotten Victory
Nicola Tyrer
Sinclair Stevens 1996

Wartime Britain 1939-1945
Juliet Gardiner
Headline 2004
Demobilised 14 September 1919

Internet Sites for both World Wars

There are many sites on the internet giving a great deal of information about both First and Second World Wars. Some of those quoted in the notes are no longer active, but more information appears on the internet almost every day, so this is only a limited selection of sites, correct at the time of going to press. Internet sites are certainly worth exploring, particularly the Commonwealth War Graves site and others giving details of individual regiments and medals awarded.

Battle of Britain Historical Society
  http://www.battleofbritain1940.net

Commonwealth War Graves Commission
  http://www.cwgc.org

Find a Soldier's Will: (casualties whilst serving in British armed forces 1850-1986)
  https://www.gov.uk/probate-search

George Cross and Albert Medals:
  http://www.marionhebblethwaite.co.uk/gcindex.htm

The Great War 1914-1918
  http://www.greatwar.co.uk

The Long, Long Trail - The British Army in the Great War of 1914-1918
  http://www.1914-1918.net

The Royal British Legion
  http://www.britishlegion.org.uk

Sound mirrors
  http://www.doramusic.com/soundmirrors.htm

Useful information about the Home Front during World War Two
  http://www.wartimegardening.co.uk

War Memorials Archive
  http://www.ukniwm.org.uk/

War Memorials Trust
  http://www.warmemorials.org

World War One aircraft
  http://www.theaerodrome.com

World War One army organisation
  http://www.warpath.orbat.com

World War One Centenary: Continuations and Beginnings
  http://ww1centenary.oucs.ox.ac.uk